MAZZAROTH

FRANCES ROLLESTON

COSIMOCLASSICS

NEW YORK

Mazzaroth
Cover Copyright © 2007 by Cosimo, Inc.

Mazzaroth was originally published in 1862.

For information, address:
P.O. Box 416, Old Chelsea Station
New York, NY 10011

or visit our website at:
www.cosimobooks.com

Ordering Information:
Cosimo publications are available at online bookstores. They may
also be purchased for educational, business or promotional use:
- *Bulk orders:* special discounts are available on bulk orders for reading
groups, organizations, businesses, and others. For details contact
Cosimo Special Sales at the address above or at info@cosimobooks.com.
- *Custom-label orders:* we can prepare selected books with your cover or
logo of choice. For more information, please contact Cosimo
at info@cosimobooks.com.

Cover Design by www.popshopstudio.com

ISBN: 978-1-60520-139-9

These names, and the ideas conveyed by the figures,
are traced in the mythology of the nations' and it will be shown,
from the confused and incongruous use there made of them,
that the fables were invented from the constellations,
and not the constellations from the fables.... In this work such reasons
will be brought forward, and adequate cause assigned, in the revelation made
to Adam and recorded by the subsequent prophets...

—from the Preface

A WORD ABOUT PRINT QUALITY...

Some pages in this edition may be difficult to read due to the aged original text. It is possible that there are blurred pages, or other issues beyond our control.

As this title is such a significant and exceptional work, we believe it is best to reproduce this book in spite of the condition of the original edition.

Thank you for choosing Cosimo Classics.

CONTENTS

CONTENTS OF THE FIRST PART

CONTENTS OF THE SECOND PART

CONTENTS OF THE THIRD PART

CONTENTS OF THE FOURTH PART

CONTENTS OF THE FIFTH PART

MAZZAROTH

PART I

MAZZAROTH;[1]

OR,

THE CONSTELLATIONS.

" Canst thou bring forth Mazzaroth in his season ?"—Job xxxviii. 32.

FIRST PART.

PREFACE.

MOST persons have been taught the names and figures of the signs of the zodiac. Many have been repelled by the explanations usually given of these and the other constellations; others have considered them not only useless, but burthensome to the astronomer; and it has been proposed to substitute a kind of survey of the heavens, where lines and angles should take the place of the traditional figures. Should this alteration be adopted, the message these figures were intended to transmit will not be less impressive when the types in which it was conveyed are no longer made sub-servient to the purposes of practical astronomy; especially as through being thus used the forms of the emblems are already disguised and modernized, and new figures, the most incongruous and absurd, have been intruded among them, while the names of the stars are becoming continually more corrupted.

The object of this work is to show, by the combined testimony of tradition and of ancient writers, and from the meaning of the yet extant ancient names of stars and emblems, that they were invented to transmit the earliest and most important know-ledge possessed by the first fathers of mankind. Such records were supposed to exist in the hieroglyphics of Egypt, but among them have only been discovered the names and dates, the conquests and the praises of sovereigns. It is intended in this work to prove that far higher and more important records, those of the only true wisdom of

---

[1] Mazzaroth, though sometimes in modern lexicons differently interpreted, is here used as meaning the constellations. In Job xxxviii. 32, it stands in the text of the English Bible untranslated: in the margin it is rendered "the twelve signs." Mazzaroth is a feminine or neuter plural noun, applied to separate chambers or divisions, such as the constellations. Mazaloth, a word with which it is sometimes identified, means a way through which any thing goes, as the sun through the zodiac, and the moon through the lunar mansions, or Manzil al Kamar, the Arabic appellation of the lunar zodiac, still used in the East. It occurs in the sacred Scriptures only in 2 Kings xxiii. 5, probably in the same sense.

man, are contained in the emblems of the constellations. The agreement of the figures will be shown, with the types used by "the holy prophets who have been since the world began," in their predictions of Him, first promised to Adam as the seed of the woman and the conqueror of the serpent; also that in the names the very words in which their prophecies were delivered are frequently to be recognized; and that the primitive roots (by which the Assyrian and Babylonish records are now interpreted) exist alike in the names of the stars and in the dialects used by the prophets. These names, and the ideas conveyed by the figures, are traced in the mythology of the nations; and it will be shown, from the confused and incongruous use there made of them, that the fables were invented from the constellations, and not the constellations from the fables.[1] It has been attemped by means of these coincidences[2] to derive the origin of all religions from the constellations; but no reasons have been given why the constellations should be thus figured and thus named. In this work such reasons will be brought forward, and adequate cause assigned, in the revelation made to Adam and recorded by the subsequent prophets, for the invention of these names and figures; their origin being sought in the religion given by God, and in their perversion being found the origin of the false religions set up by man.

NOTE ON "CONSTELLATIONS."

The ancients divided the heavens by forty-eight constellations, imaginary and arbitrary divisions, sometimes, but not always, comprising remarkable stars. Among the twelve signs, Aries, Taurus, Gemini, Scorpio, and Virgo, have bright stars, leading the eye to fix on them as constellations, but the others have not; and would not be naturally distinguished as such. It is therefore evident that the distinction of the starry heavens into constellations, like the division of the earth into districts, is the work of man's imagination for his own purposes. In this case the purpose was to declare the glory of God. Orion, the Great Bear, Cassiopea, Lyra, the Southern Cross, and perhaps some others, have bright stars pointing them out, but the records of ancient astronomy only determine what minor stars are reckoned as belonging to them; for instance the serpentine emblems are so mingled with the others as to be complained of as causing confusion by those who did not see in them an intentional type of the works of the enemy as intricately interwoven with the destinies of man.

---

[1] The evidences by which these statements are supported will be found in the Second Part.

[2] Lupuis, L'Origine des Cultes.

QUESTIONS

TO WHICH IT IS GENERALLY BELIEVED THAT THERE IS NO CERTAIN

ANSWER TO BE GIVEN, TRADITION OR CONJECTURE BEING

ALL THAT IS EVER ALLEGED.

Questions.	Traditional Answers.	Answers given by this Explanation.
Who was the inventor of astronomy ?	Seth or Thoth, or Hermes ; Enoch or Edris, Oannes or Noah.	Seth, the son of Adam, with Adam and Enoch.[1]
When was it invented ?	Very early.	In the first age of mankind.[1]
Where ?	In the East : some say Chaldea ; some, Egypt or India.	In their first habitations, in or near the land of Eden, said to have been between Chaldea and India.[1]
When, where, and by whom were the yet extant names and emblems invented ?	Unknown, as to the signs ; Necepsos, king of Egypt (B.C. 900), is said to have introduced the decans into Egypt.	At the same time, by the same persons, and in the same locality.[1]
What is the meaning of those names and those emblems ?	Unknown, but the subject of various conjectures.	They express the promises and prophecies revealed to Adam, Seth, and Enoch.[2]
Why chosen ?	Wholly unknown.	Because they conveyed that meaning, and to keep that early revelation in mind.[2]
Why were the thirty-six decans or constellations allotted three to each sign, and why so figured and so allotted ?	Unknown.	The decans, as far as ascertained from Oriental traditions, accord with the signs in which they are found, and for this reason were so formed and allotted.[2]

Jewish, Persian, and Arabian ancient writers preserve the tradition, that "the family of Seth," Adam, Seth, and Enoch, "invented astronomy," the Egyptians attributing it to Seth or Thoth, said to be the same as Hermes Trismegistus, the thrice-great.

Plutarch mentions Seth, "to whom the third day of the five of the epact was dedicated," as worshipped in Egypt. He was said to be the third son of Set and Netpthè, the father and mother of the gods, whose names are given by Bunsen as Seb and Nutpè.

Bunsen says that Thoth or Hermes was called the scribe of truth, the twice-great; and that they held Set to be the name of the god of the Asiatic people. In the "Book of the Dead," it is said, "Tet, which is Set," thus confirming the identification of Seth and Thoth.

[1] Part II. p. 5, &c.   [2] Part II. pp. 60, 61.

OBJECTIONS

SOMETIMES URGED AS TO THE ORIGIN AND MEANING OF THE NAMES AND FIGURES OF THE ANCIENT CONSTELLATIONS.

OBJECTION I.

That the signs typify the seasons, and their accompanying events, such as we now see them.

ANSWER I.

If they did so in Italy in the time of Macrobius (A.D. 400), who first gave this explanation, they could not have done so in the East, where he allows they were invented, and in the ancient times to which he himself refers them, as does all ancient tradition.[1]

II.

That they were invented by the Egyptians to show the seasons of their climate;

II.

The Egyptians have no where said so, neither can the analogy be carried out. The inundation of the Nile must have been there; and if it took place under Aquarius, as has been conjectured, it must have been more than 12,000 years before the time when the monuments of Egypt show the signs depicted on them, and when geology assures us man did not exist on the earth.[2]

III.

Or by the Egyptians, to express their mythology;

III.

That mythology has sufficient resemblance with the signs to have been borrowed from them, but not to have originated them. Isis may be traced, perhaps Horus, but not Osiris; and Apis is not like any other name of the bull of the zodiac, neither had he, like Apis, an eagle connected with his figure.[3]

IV.

By the Greeks, to express the twelve labours of Hercules;

IV.

The order of the twelve signs is invariable. Authorities differ as to that of the twelve labours, which yet sufficiently allude to the signs to show that they were derived from the zodiac.[4]

V.

By Chiron, for the events of the Argonautic expedition.

V.

The signs are known to have been borne on the banners of the tribes of Israel long before the time of the Argonauts.[5]

VI.

According to Olaus Rudbeck the Swede, they typify the seasons of Scandinavia.

VI.

The merits of this explanation may be judged by that of the twins, as showing when infants may be bathed in the rivers. It however proves that the Scandinavian tribes preserved the twelve signs.

VII.

That the names have no meaning.

VII.

Aben Ezra records the meaning of some of them as they were understood by the ancient Jews. Every name has a clear meaning, to be found in Hebrew, and generally in Arabic, applicable to the emblem in which it occurs.[6]

---

[1] Part I. p. 18.   [2] Part I. ch. 1.   [3] Part II., on Egypt.
[4] Part II. p. 88.   [5] Part II. p. 37, &c.   [6] Part II., Tables of the Signs, pp. 9—25.

OBJECTION VIII.

That in Arabic the names sometimes have strange and incongruous meanings.

ANSWER VIII.

If a forced and modern usage of the root be taken, this may be so; as, for instance, in placing a company of virgins in the throat of the dog, where the epithet clear, pure, from the root Adar, glorious, is applied to the emblem of the coming of the promised seed, as it has also been applied to a clear, pure virgin. By referring to the *ancient* Arabic, particularly the two-lettered roots, these absurdities are got rid of, and the Arabic will corroborate the Hebrew.[1]

NOTE ON ANSWER I.—In those ancient times the solstices and equinoxes did not occur in the signs to which Macrobius would refer them. The sun did not then begin to recede under the Crab, nor to ascend under the Goat. By the precession of the equinoxes, the solstices, earlier in Leo and Aquarius, had in his time passed into Cancer and Capricorn, as they have now into Gemini and Sagittarius. Those who in later times have tried to explain the signs by the seasons of modern Europe have these and yet greater difficulties to encounter.

ON ANSWER II.—Some writers have fancied an allusion to the inundation in Aquarius : a small stream issuing from an urn in the hand of a human figure, and received in the mouth of a fish, does not, however, seem to suit it.[2] Arago, acknowledged to be as deficient in languages as he was accomplished in astronomy, has ventured, in his popular lectures, on explanations of the emblems of the signs with very forced applications to the climate of Egypt; doing this from what he supposes may be the derivation of their Coptic names, or those of the Egyptian months to which he would adapt them. That on this point he is no authority may be seen from his assertion that "the Hebrew verb *fafa* signifies obtenebrescere;" that the letter F does not exist in the Hebrew Alphabet is but a trifling objection, for the sound does, and would be written *phapha;* but not one word with that root in it has any connexion with the idea of darkness, while the numerous words in which it appears have all some relation to splendour, light, beauty; the Greek derivatives having that meaning, as *phaino,* will at once occur to the Greek scholar. The Egyptian Pa-pa according to Bunsen means to bear, to bring forth; if it was an Egyptian name of any sign, it would probably be of Virgo; he says the Egyptian harvest begins in February, where he would place Leo, and sowing in November, where he would place Taurus. Aquarius he gives to "the second month of summer," and says, "during this month or *thereabouts* the sources of the Nile give forth their full complement of water." According to the place of the sun in the signs about the time of the Christian era, and for 2000 years before it, the harvest of Egypt could not take place under Virgo, nor the inundation under Aquarius.

ON ANSWER V.—This conjecture, though adopted by Sir I. Newton, is also confuted by Sir W. Jones and others, who have found the signs used in Oriental astronomy long before the Argonautic expedition.[3]

ON ANSWER VII.—On the meanings early attributed to the signs the very ancient science of astrology is founded.

The evidence by which these answers and those on p. 3 are supported, will be found in the Second Part, especially in the pages referred to.

---

[1] Part II., Tables, pp. 9—25; p. 16, Virgo.   [2] Part II. p. 22.   [3] Part II. pp. 6—8.

WHAT ARE THE REAL MEANINGS OF THE EMBLEMS OF THE SIGNS?

One of the greatest of uninspired teachers, the Socrates of Plato, is said to have always appealed to the common sense of his hearers. There is an appeal to the common sense of mankind as to the meanings of the emblems of ancient astronomy, which it was apparently intended they should make. The aid of history, languages, and traditions may have been required to ascertain what these meanings were; but when pointed out, any one acquainted with the Holy Scriptures can judge of their suitability to express the prophecies there recorded, as given to the first parents of mankind. The seed of the woman shall [Gen. 3. 15.] bruise the serpent's head, the serpent shall bruise his heel. There is a tradition that at the creation of man the sun at the summer solstice was among the stars called the sign of the Virgin. In that place was figured, long before the Christian era, in the Egyptian zodiac, the figure of a woman with an ear of corn in her hand, and below another female figure holding an infant. Here, then, is recognized the seed, the offspring of the woman. In the next sign, the scales at once convey the idea of purchase. He comes to buy, to redeem. There is [Deut. 32. 6.] then the figure of a man grasping a serpent as in conflict, his [2 Pet. 2. 1.] foot on the head of a scorpion, whose reverted sting appears to [Ps. 91. 13.] have wounded his heel. Here the seed, the offspring of the woman, is bruising the enemy's head, after having received the predicted bruise in the heel. The first prophecy is thus fully figured out: the first part of it is as fully accomplished; the heel of the virgin's Son was bruised when nailed upon the cross.

Virgo. (margin)
Libra. (margin)
Scorpio. (margin)

In the next sign an arrow is coming forth from the bow. [Deut. 49. 10.] Can any one fail to see here expressed, that He shall come, [Exod. 4. 13.] speedily, surely? Then a kid or goat, sinking down as the [Lev. 16.] sacrifice appointed to be slain for sin. Then the promised seed, [Ezek. 47.] the man, is arising, and pouring out water as to purify, sustain [Hab. 1. 19.] life. Two fishes, joined together by a band, come next: water [Gen. 1. 20.] is their element, abundantly multiplying is their characteristic. To the Christian there is but to name the Church of Christ, and [Isa. 44. 3.] the fitness of the emblem will at once be recognized. The [John 3.] primitive institution of sacrifice was equally of a kid or a lamb. [Exod. 12. 5.] The lamb, or young ram, is next, as it had been slain, but [Rev. 5. 6.] now living, on high. The bull, also a sacrificial animal, but [Exod. 29. 10.] living, and in an attitude of victory. He who died in the kid [Heb. 9. 13.] is now alive again, and to Him all power is given. The twins, [Matt. 28. 18.] [Zech. 6. 13.] the closest visible image of two natures in one person, are next; and the Scriptural believer will not fail to recognize their import. The crab holds fast what it has once grasped. [John 10. 28.]

Sagittarius. (margin)
Capricornus. (margin)
Aquarius. (margin)
Pisces. (margin)
Aries. (margin)
Taurus. (margin)
Gemini. (margin)
Cancer. (margin)

Leo.

The lion rends apart whatever he seizes, as at the last awful day the Judge will separate good from evil. | Gen. 49. 10.
Matt. 25. 32.

"Take and read," as the voice cried to the saint of old.[1] "Search the Scriptures," as the Lord Himself has enjoined, even if never searched before; and see if these simple and expressive emblems are not faithful interpreters of the prophecies there contained. The coincidences cannot be overlooked; they are too complete to be unintentional: the common sense of mankind at once recognizes the marks of design. To that universal faculty the appeal is made: are there not here those marks, and in the correspondence with Scripture the proof of what was that design? Was it not indeed in another, yet consistent, record to show forth the glory of God? | John 5. 39.

This appeal to the ordinary faculties of the human mind, to its powers of comparison and judgment, may well hope for the verdict that the signs[2] were intended to symbolize prophecy, as recorded in the Holy Scriptures. A connecting link is the signification of the ancient names in the original[3] language of mankind, as transmitted in the Hebrew of the Holy Scriptures and the most ancient Arabic: but to appreciate this additional evidence there must be either a knowledge of the languages, or a due estimate of the force of testimony. Those acquainted with the original Scriptures will testify to the occurrence of the root[4] of the name in those writings, as shown by the references given in the subsequent Tables.

---

[1] Augustin, Confess.

[2] The zodiac in its present forms and order, as beginning with Aries, is transmitted by Hipparchus and Ptolemy, who lived about the time of the Christian era, as "of unquestioned authority, unknown origin, and unsearchable antiquity." The explanation here given follows the course of prophecy, and the order of the stars arising in the evening, with the sun in Aries.

[3] Part II. p. 76.

[4] "The root" may be explained by English examples; as, "The idea of a *family* of words is *familiar* to the reader," "*Familiarity* with the search will *familiarize* the result."

THE LATIN NAMES OF THE TWELVE SIGNS

ACCOUNTED FOR BY THEIR SEMITIC ROOTS.

	Texts where the word or its root is used in this sense in the Hebrew Bible.	Hebrew roots.
ARIES, the Ram or Lamb, *coming forth.* _goeth._	Job 34. 8.	ארח
Ars, *lamb,* Gr. Luke x. 3.		
TAURUS, the Bull (Deut. xxxiii. 17), coming to rule { *chief* (Chald. form), coming, Isa. lvii. 9 . . { *rule*	Gen. 40. 2. / Isa. 32. 1.	שר
GEMINI, the Twins, *united* . . . *fellow*	Zech. 13. 7.	עם
CANCER, the Crab, *gained, encircled* . { *gotten* { *the possession*	Gen. 4. 1. / Gen. 26. 14.	קן
LEO, the Lion, *leaping forth,* as a flame of fire . . *flame*	Exod. 3. 2.	לבה
VIRGO, the Woman bearing the seed, *the branch* { *young ones* *offspring* { *grow*	Job 39. 30. / Isa. 11. 1.	פרח
LIBRA, the Balance or Scales, *librating,* moving up and down, as the *heart*	Gen. 18. 5.	לב
SCORPIO, the Scorpion, which cleaves in *conflict* . . *battle*	Deut. 20. 2.	קרב
SAGITTARIUS, the Archer, which sends forth the *arrow* .	1 Sa. 20. 20.	חץ
CAPRICORNUS, the Atoning Sacrifice, *sinking down* { *atonement* as slain . . . . . { *bowed*	Ex. 30. 10. / Judg. 5. 27.	כפר / כרע
AQUARIUS, the Water-bearer, water as rising in { *rising* the urn . . . . { *sending forth*	Ezek. 47. 5. / 1 Sa. 20. 20.	נאה / ירה
PISCES, the Fish, *multiplying* (Arab. sense) . . *spread*	Hab. 1. 8.	פש

All names have meanings, if not in the language into which
they are adopted, yet in some other from which they are
derived. The names applied by the Romans to their divinities
are considered to be derived from the Etruscan; it is therefore
probable that the names by which they called the Twelve
Signs also had the same origin. These names are here shown
to contain roots having the same meanings as those of the
Semitic names of the same figures. This derivation is confirmed by the recent Ninevite discoveries, from which it is
inferred that Etruria "had an intimate conne----n with
Assyria."

Names of ancient Italy, when referred to Semitic roots, will
also point to an Oriental origin, as, for instance,—

Etruria, abundant, very rich . . . *abundance*	Isa. 15. 7.	יתר
Latium, hidden . . . . . *covering*	Isa. 25. 7.	לט
Roma, great, high . . . . *high*	Deut. 12. 2.	רם
Alba, great of heart, Job. xi. 12; Heb. also *white* .	Gen. 49. 12.	לבן
Oscan, dwelling, dwellers . . . *dwelt*	Gen. 16. 12.	שפן
Italia, Arab. long; the Chaldee gives the sense *to cover*	Neh. 3. 15.	טלל
Sabine is also from another root, *dwell* . .	Gen. 20. 15.	ישב
Samnite, fertile . . . . *fruitful*	Isa. 5. 1.	שמן

Etruscan words, of which the meaning is known:—

Lucumo, prince, king, 2 Sam. xxiv. 23 . . *king*	Gen. 14. 1.	מלך
Aesar, God; chief, ruler, Gen. xii. 15 . *prince*	Isa. 9. 6.	שר
Tinia, Supreme God, *for ever continuing* . .	Ps. 72. 17.	ינן
Capra, a goat, the sacrifice of *atonement* . .	Lev. 16. 18.	כפר

THE TWELVE SIGNS OF THE ZODIAC,

AS CONNECTED WITH THE PRIMITIVE PROPHECIES.

THE antiquity and wide diffusion of these emblems, and the mystic veneration in which they were ever held, are traced in the accompanying pages: it is also shown that the notion of the signs having any reference to the seasons is of comparatively late origin, and could not at any time have been sustained consistently with the times and climates of their well-known previous existence.[1]

It was not till the diffusion of the light of Christianity had cast into shade these dim foreshowings of its great events, that the vague awe with which these emblems were formerly regarded gave place to indifference and neglect, or was only preserved in the reveries of astrology. This reverence,[2] in some cases leading even to idolatry, indicated a tradition that their message was divine. They each represented an action, still to be traced in the fables connected with them,[3] a type, of which the true antitype is to be found in the great subject of the ancient prophecies contained in the Hebrew Scriptures.[4] The primitive year began in the sign Virgo, the stars of which were seen most strikingly in the evening sky when the sun was in Aries, the splendid star still by us called Spica, the ear of corn, in the woman's hand, marking the leading idea, the Promised Seed. Thus was represented the subject of the first promise, the foundation of the hopes of fallen man. In the next sign, Libra, we have His work, which was to be to buy, to redeem, figured in the balance weighing the price against the purchase. Then in Scorpio follows the indication of what that price was to be; the conflict, in which the seed of the woman receives the wound in his heel, while his other foot is on the head of the enemy, here figured by the scorpion, a venomous reptile, who can sting even while his head is bruised.

Next we find the Archer, with his arrow in the act of going out from the bow, expressing that the promised Deliverer should be sent forth.

Then Capricornus, the goat, the victim or sacrifice sinking down as wounded, showing that the promised Deliverer must be slain as a sacrifice. In Aquarius we see the rising up and pouring forth of water, as to cleanse and fertilize, showing that the sacrifice was to bring purification and benediction by means of the risen Messiah.

In Pisces two fishes are bound together by a band, which is continued to and held by the fore-feet of Aries, figuring the leading idea of union. The fishes, a well-known emblem of the Church among the early Christians, represent the redeemed and purified multitudes of the Church before and after the first coming, in union with each other and with their Redeemer.

---

[1] Part I. ch. 1; Part II. p. 5, &c.   [2] Part II., on Egypt and Assyria.
[3] Part II. p. 81, &c.   [4] Part II. p. 60, also the Tables from pp. 9 to 25.

The subsequent sign, the Lamb or ram of sacrifice, here not dying, but as it had been slain, is now reigning triumphant, with one foot on the head of the enemy, bound also by a band, which that foot holds.

We then see Taurus, the bull, showing forth the dominion of Him who had been a sacrifice for sin, now reigning over all.

In Gemini, the twins, whether human or of the sacrificial goat or sheep, the leading idea of combining, entwining, is equally conveyed, expressing the union of the divine and human nature in the promised seed.

Cancer, the crab or beetle, holding fast its prey or its nest, well conveys the image of tenacious possession by Him who has assured us, as to His purchased flock, that no man can pluck them out of His hand.

Leo, the majestic lion, rending the prey, represents irresistible strength, and final separation between good and evil. His foot is over the head of the prostrate serpent, closing the series as we are told by the Apostle that the dispensation must be closed: " For He shall reign till He has put all things under His feet." [1]

Here, then, we have represented in action twelve leading ideas, twelve principal truths of Divine revelation,—

1. The seed of the woman shall come.

2. There shall be a price paid by Him for a purchased possession.

3. The price shall be a conflict with the serpent-foe, and a wound in the conqueror's heel.

4. He shall be sent forth swiftly, surely, as an arrow from a bow.

5. He shall be slain as a sacrifice.

6. He shall rise again and pour out blessings on His people.

7. His people shall be multitudes, and held in union with each other and Himself.

8. He who was slain, whose heel was bruised, shall rule, and shall tread His enemy under foot.

9. He shall come in power, triumphant, and have dominion.

10. He shall be the Son of GOD and the son of man, the victim and the ruler.

11. He shall hold fast His purchased possession, the reward of His work.

12. He shall finally put all enemies under His feet, coming with ten thousand of His saints to execute judgment upon all, separating the evil from the good.

These leading ideas are to be traced in the yet extant names of the signs as pre-served in the Hebrew and Arabic appellations. Eight of these agree: of the other four, two are in Arabic different names of the same object, the other two contain the leading idea here attributed to the sign.

Two of the Syriac names from Ulugh Beigh differ from the Hebrew, as being other names of the same thing. Where the Hebrew and Arabic agree, there can be little doubt but that they preserve the name originally given: as where the words differ they still express the same idea, it seems that the emblems were invented, and universally known to the children of Noah, before the dispersion from Babel. [2]

From ancient authorities we find that in the Aramæan and Coptic or early Egyptian names the same ideas are presented. They are also found in the Sanscrit, &c. [3]

The ancient Rabbins said that the astronomy of the Jews was in the Babylonish

---

[1] Part II., Tables, pp. 9—25.   [2] Ibid.   [3] Part II. p. 26.

captivity corrupted by the astrology of the Chaldeans; but as the Chaldean dialect differs so little from the Hebrew, the names would not be materially altered. Slight Chaldee changes may be traced in one or two of the names of stars; but in the names of the twelve signs they do not occur, even where the interchangeable letters are found.

The existence of primitive roots in Arabic words, common to the Hebrew and other Semitic dialects, (however the usage of these words may have been varied and extended,) is evident to Hebraists, though sometimes disputed by the scholar whose Oriental acquirements have not included the Hebrew. Such may be compared to the traveller in the desert, who, delighted with the fruit and shade of the palm-tree, thinks not of the source of strength and nourishment below, the deep and steadfast root hidden in the sand that has gathered around it in the lapse of ages. The root is obvious in these antique appellations of visible objects, as in the proper names of persons and places contained in the Scriptures, and, though less obviously, may be traced even in those of other nations. Proper names, however corrupted in the spelling, generally retain something of the sound of the root whence they were formed: words used in expressing the varying actions and feelings of common life are much more subject to be perverted from their original meanings. The appellations of visible objects, if less *fixed* than proper names, are less liable to variation than those; accordingly we find these twelve names to have corresponding Arabic ones, even if in some places other, but synonymous, names are now used in Arabic astronomy.

The mythological fables attached to these emblems, and the titles under which they were worshipped, contribute to throw light on these meanings.[1] All are connected with an offspring of the Deity; all say with the Evangelical Prophet, " Unto us a child is born, unto us a son is given: and the government shall be upon his shoulder." [2]

If indeed Seth and his family were the inventors of these emblems and the givers of these names, intending to express in them the prophecies known to the antediluvian Church, such might well be their figures and their meaning. If the intention was what it is here considered to be, it is consistently developed by comparison with the written records of Hebrew prophecy, as delivered to the patriarchal and Jewish Church, and preserved for the Christian by those faithful witnesses for the authority and integrity of Scripture, the yet unconverted Jews. As the Jews have kept the word of prophecy, the Arabs have preserved the names of the stars which so remarkably correspond with it, while the Greeks and Egpytians have transmitted the figures to which they belong.

These independent but concurring testimonies not only witness to the purpose of the long misunderstood emblems, but to the existence of a revelation anterior to their formation; for if their purport be prophetic, He who seeth the end from the beginning had already given to man that knowledge of future events which He alone can impart.

It is not doubted that about eighteen centuries ago there arose a remarkable person claiming to have no father but Him in heaven, who was put to death at the time of the slaying of the paschal lamb at Jerusalem. His death, the time and manner of it, were not in his own power. If predicted by the prophets, prefigured in these ancient

---

[1] Part II. p. 81, &c.   [2] Isa. ix. 6.

emblems, and indicated in their primitive names,—that death, its manner and its time, must have been revealed by Him who by the mouth of Isaiah appeals to prophecy as the proof of His power and His Godhead, saying to the idols of the heathen, "Show the things that are to come hereafter, that we may know that ye are gods."[1] By prophecy and its fulfilment God speaks to man, at once displaying His foreknowledge and His sovereignty. So He spake to our first parents in Eden; and the echo of that voice was in the ears of the fathers of mankind, when these emblems were framed in memorial of the revelation.

NOTES.

In the sacred year, as ordained by Moses, beginning when the sun was in Aries, the signs would appear in the evening sky in the progression commencing with Virgo. In this succession coming events were to be accomplished. In the earlier ages, when the year naturally began from the anniversary of the creation,[2] at the junction of Leo and Virgo, Aries, the first sign of the patriarchal zodiac, arose in the evening twilight, beginning at once the day and the year, the day with its evening, the year with its decline. As the night drew on, the Lamb as it had been slain, but arising in power, was followed by the other signs proclaiming His glory, His kingdom, and His final victory.

Always and everywhere the series of the signs has begun with Aries, whether in Latium, in Egypt, in Arabia, India, or China. Some ancient nations began their year with this sign, but others, as the Chinese, from Aquarius, where the winter solstice took place about the time of the dispersion at Babel; even these, however, began the zodiac with Aries.

Before the time of Moses the year of the Hebrews had begun, as the civil year of the Jews still begins, with the entrance of the sun into Virgo; it seems probable that originally the woman, as now figured in the Egyptian zodiac of Dendera, held the ear of corn in one hand, the palm-branch in the other; while as Albumazer records in the ancient spheres,[3] a woman, as the first Decan of Virgo, was figured nursing an infant. The Arabians figured Virgo herself holding the infant, but these may have been the Christian Arabs, as it is said the ancient Arabs admitted no figures, human or animal, but represented Virgo by a branch.

It is not known how the ancient Hebrews figured the signs, except by the blessing of Jacob and that of Moses;[4] but from these records it is evident that animal and even human forms were on the banners of Israel,—the Man that of Reuben, the Lion borne by Judah, the Bull by Joseph, the Eagle or the Basilisk by Dan. Balaam also evidently had the Lion of Judah before his eyes. Moses, speaking after the giving of the second commandment, dwells on the Lion of Judah and the Bull of Joseph without disapprobation. It was, therefore, the worshipping of these "likenesses" that was forbidden. The Jews in after times, warned by the idolatry of their forefathers, are said to have abstained from making any "likenesses" whatsoever; and the early Arabs are said to have followed their example. In the temple of Solomon, besides the consecrated cherubic images, there were pomegranates[5] and flowers of lilies and palm-trees, but no animal likenesses, except the cherubic lions and oxen. There is here a proof that not the making the likeness, but the worshipping it was the sin. Israel had been punished for desiring the golden calf to go before them, but Solomon was unblamed for forming the twelve oxen that upheld the molten sea.[6]

---

[1] Isa. xli. 23.   [2] Part II. p. 15.
[3] Albumazer, who lived at the court of the Caliphs of Grenada early in the ninth century, in his description of the signs and their Decans, to which the annexed tables refer, concludes by saying that they had come down to his time unaltered; that they were known all over the world, and had been the objects of long speculation, and that "many had attributed to them a divine and even a prophetic virtue." Unfortunately he perverts this "prophetic virtue" to the purposes of astrology. Part II. p. 16.
[4] Part II. pp. 38—47.
[5] The Hebrew name of this fruit, Rimmon, may mean exaltation; that of the lily, joyfulness, rejoicing.
[6] 1 Kings vii. 2 Chron. iii. 16; iv. 5.

MAZZAROTH.

CHAPTER I.

THE power and majesty of the Creator have ever been admired in the starry heavens; and still, as in the days of the inspired poet, in that firmament which showeth the works of His hands are the traces of His infinite wisdom sought out of all those who have pleasure therein; but His glory has long ceased to be deciphered, where it was once clearly read, in those long misunderstood records of remote antiquity, the names and figures of the ancient constellations,[1] as attributed to them beyond the memory of man, beyond the range of history. The first vague yet sublime impression with which all behold the splendid luminaries of the midnight sky is weakened, if not destroyed, when taught to associate with them the debasing legends of heathen mythology, or the trifling allusions[2] to the seasons of the revolving year and the habits of the beasts that perish. How has the poetry of heaven been lowered into the most miserable, the dullest prose! How has that ignorance, which was bliss, been regretted, when exchanged for that wisdom of the world, which it may be a relief to find utter foolishness!

Most incongruous are such associations with the great honour which has of late been put on astronomy, by an argument now urged from its recent discoveries. That science is now appealed to in proof of the unity of God. By the universe of worlds obeying one law is indicated that all were originated by one mind, the work of one Creator: that law which brought the apple to the ground is found to rule the remotest stars, which, if scarcely discernible, are still ascertained to influence each other in obedience to the force of gravitation.

Geology, showing that the earth was once a molten mass, on which nothing that now lives on it could have existed, proves that there must be a Creator. Astronomy not only manifests the existence, but the unity, the omnipotence,

---

[1] These constellations are imaginary divisions of those stars which are seen in the north temperate zone.

[2] After the refutation of these supposed allusions, by the great astronomer Montucla, it might be superfluous to expose their absurdity, but that they are still met with in popular lectures and elementary books for education.

the omnipresence of that Creator. If this mind-exalting study can be freed from desecrating incumbrances, over which many of its most gifted students have lamented, they will surely rejoice in its rescue.

If a high, pure, and spiritualizing purpose can be shown to have suggested the invention of the names and symbols of ancient astronomy, will it not gladden all who love to contemplate the glory of God as made known in His magnificent creation?

If we may connect with every constellation, and each remarkable star, some divine truth, some prophetic annunciation, how adequately grand becomes the contemplation, how congenial the interpretation![1]

If there we find recorded some hope, some promise given to the first parents of mankind, to support them under the loss of innocence and of Eden, will not that memorial be equally precious even now, shining like the stars that bear it, with undiminished lustre, on us their remote descendants? So read, the "poetry of heaven" will become its Scripture, and its line once more go out to the ends of the earth, declaring the glory of God to every nation.

Now that the hieroglyphics of Egypt are interpreted, and the characters of Babylon and Assyria deciphered, should those far more ancient and more widely diffused, the primitive hieroglyphics of the whole human race, be neglected? Those, the great enigma of ages, transmitting far more important intelligence, shall they not seem worthy of investigation? The Egyptian, belonging to a peculiar people, in a most peculiar climate, numerous and complex as they are, yield up their meaning lost for so many centuries. Those of the constellations, few and simple, formed from familiar objects and conveying ideas intelligible to all, should they be left hopelessly obscured in the darkness that has gathered around them?

The sculptures of Assyria in their stern grandeur have great analogy with the leading symbols of astronomy, but have corrupted in imitating them. Still it may be seen whence they originated.[2] Those Egyptian hieroglyphics hitherto explained inform us only of the names and conquests of a race of half-forgotten monarchs. The Assyrian inscriptions seem mostly of the same nature. Both, however, corroborate historical allusions in the Holy Scriptures, thus warning unbelievers to respect what they cannot fathom, and encouraging believers to trust what they cannot as yet explain.

A far higher purpose is latent in the names and emblems of ancient astronomy: from them we may learn the all-important fact that God has spoken, that He gave to the earliest of mankind a revelation, equally important to the latest, even of those very truths afterwards written for the admonition of those "on whom the ends of the world" should come. Then, as now, the heaven-

---

[1] Part II. p. 4.   [2] Part II. p. 51, &c.

guided spirit in man sought to trace the glory of the Creator in His works: then, as now, the best aid was found in His revelation. That there was a revelation is shown by the prophetic import of these names and emblems, even that revelation recorded in the book with which they correspond.

Without the history of the fall of man we should not know by what types it had pleased God to foreshow his restoration. The seed of the woman in the ear of corn, the enemy in the serpent, might have been in vain set forth in the constellations, as unintelligible from their beginning as they became in the lapse of ages, and even now are when not viewed by the light of revelation. Without the figures of the sphere, " the record in heaven," that revelation had wanted the witness of its being coeval with the calamity whose remedy it declared.

There are few who have not heard of the Twelve Signs of the Zodiac; but what they are is not always distinctly understood. It is sometimes imagined that the forms of a ram, bull, or lion may be traced among the stars: but none such can be recognized. Those stars said to belong to the Ram might as well be supposed to belong to the Bull or the Lion. Only one of the constellations has a definite figure: the Northern Crown is circular, resembling a diadem. In all the others the names have no affinity with the natural position of the stars: they are what the inventors of astronomy thought fit to annex. They will be seen to convey prophecy,[1] as regularly, as systematically arranged, as the stars to which they are applied are apparently irregularly scattered over the dome of heaven. There must doubtless be Divine wisdom in this apparent confusion, but as yet the science of man has failed to trace it.

Abundant evidence exists that the explanation of these emblems by prophecy is no new system, not a theory spun from raw materials, but a thread of gold, unravelled from an ancient and neglected but superb tissue, originating with the early patriarchs, in which, as in the embroidery of old, were inwoven the records they desired to transmit.[2]

These signs were known among all nations and in all ages. From the almost antediluvian chronologies of China, India, and Egypt, to the traditions of the recently discovered islands of the South Sea, traces of them are discerned, most clearly among the most ancient and earliest civilized nations. In the remains of Assyria they are recognized; in those of Egypt they are perfectly preserved; in those of Etruria and Mexico they are traceable.

This wide diffusion indicates a common origin, both of the race of man and of the symbols of astronomy. The love of symbols has been considered as natural to man; the creation amid which he is placed, as symbolical.[3] Of this

---

[1] Part II. p. 4.   [2] Part II. p. 32, &c.   [3] Part II. p. 54.

universal tendency the inventors of astronomy seem to have availed themselves, rendering it subservient to man's spiritual education, by familiarizing to his mind the lofty truths of Divine revelation.

The signs were in use before the corresponding prophecies were written, unless, as has been supposed by many authorities ancient and modern, the art of writing were invented by those to whom the origin of astronomy is attributed.[1] Even then the two records were coeval. If Adam caused to be transmitted to his descendants, either by writing or by memory, the words of the first promise, the ideas of it were repeated in the emblems of the constellations. That promise announced that the seed of the woman was to come to bruise the serpent's head, and to be Himself bruised in the heel. He has come, He has received the predicted bruise. The fulfilled part of the prediction is delineated in action in several of the starry emblems, as in Virgo, in Ophiuchus, in Capricornus: the unfulfilled in Leo, in Hercules, and in Aries. As the reflection in the water doubles the evidence that the sun has risen, so the early existence of these emblems corroborates that of the recorded revelation.

The most determined sceptic does not deny that a person claiming to be born of a woman without a human father, did come, and, dying on the cross, did both literally and figuratively receive the predicted wound in the heel. Nor can he deny, when looking on the ancient monuments of Egypt, that before his birth and crucifixion, the woman in the zodiac held the seed, the ear of corn, and that the serpent was under the foot of the lion. Let him examine the sphere as now figured, supposed to have come to us from the ancient Chaldeans,[2] and there he will see the prophecy even more strikingly portrayed, as in the figure of Ophiuchus conflicting with the serpent. How can that sceptic account for the existence of these emblems? How can they be explained but by the previous revelation with which they correspond? If future events are foretold with a decision and particularity beyond human sagacity, that Infinite Spirit who governs while He foresees, the Sovereign of the universe, has spoken. The father of mankind heard, repeated the message, and his descendants all and everywhere have transmitted the echo of that sound. He alone who is the First and will be the Last sees the end from the beginning: He alone enables man to describe it.

The earliest positive evidence of the primeval existence of the signs is in the Chinese annals,[3] where it is said that the Emperor Yao, 2317 years before the Christian era, divided the twelve signs of the zodiac by the twenty-eight mansions of the moon:[4] but it is not said that he invented them. The Chinese national emblem of the dragon appears to be the dragon of the sphere,

---

[1] Part II. p. 109.   [2] Part II. p. 5, &c.   [3] Part II. p. 5.   [4] Part II. p. 24.

rhich was at that time the polar constellation, the brightest star in the ragon's head having been the pole-star in the antediluvian ages.

The Signs are next alluded to by the patriarch Jacob, who in his dying bless-ıg was held by the ancient Hebrews to have spoken of them as the appointed ognizances of his twelve sons, and as such they were borne on the standards f Israel in the wilderness.[1]

The Egyptians, on whose early monuments the signs are found, acknow-ıdged that they derived their astronomy from the Chaldeans. The ʰhaldeans attributed their science to Oannes, supposed to be Noah. The ₁rabs and Brahmins, among whom astronomy was early cultivated, seem ɔ have derived it from Abraham, through Ishmael and the children of ₍eturah. The Greeks supposed their imperfect knowledge of the subject ₁me through the Egyptians and the Chaldeans. The Romans are thought ɔ have received through the Etrurians the names of the signs still in se among European nations.[2] The Etrurians are considered to have derived ₁em, with their other arts and sciences, from Assyria. The early Greek oet Hesiod is said to have made use of Assyrian records. He mentions some f the constellations by the names they now bear.

Pythagoras taught in Greece what he learnt in Phœnicia; but what he ₁ight know of the signs has not reached us. Other Greek philosophers, it is ₑrtain, were acquainted with them, as Cleostratus, who wrote on Aries and agittarius. A later Greek poet, Aratus, described the constellations such as ₑ now have them, and by equivalent names. He gave neither history nor ɔnjecture as to their date, their meaning, nor their origin. They were to him, ₑ to us, of immemorial antiquity. Cicero, in translating from Aratus, says, "The signs are measured out, that in so many descriptions Divine wisdom ₁ight appear:" but he does not say in what manner. No attempt is made by ny of these writers to explain the figures, or to assign any inventor to them. 'he fables annexed to them must have been known to Cicero, but he seems ɔ have held them unworthy of notice. None of these earlier writers llude to any tradition concerning the meanings of the names and emblems f the constellations, nor as to where, when, or by whom they were riginated.

Soon after the time of Cicero these fables were collected by Hyginus, who haracterizes them as little to be depended on. Still through his whole detail ₁ay be traced the tradition of a Son of the Supreme Deity, sometimes as the onqueror of the serpent, sometimes as the suffering benefactor of the human ₁ce, dying by the serpent's venom. Often he is wholly divine and immortal, r is born of a human mother, dying on earth to live again in heaven; some-

---

[1] Part II. p. 38.   [2] Part I. p. 5.

C

times as a divinity, sometimes as a constellation. If the unenlightened heathen thus still acknowledged among the starry heavens some vestiges of ancient prophecy, shall Christians neglect to trace there the memorials of a revelation from the Divine Creator?

Nonnus afterwards sought to account for the signs by the twelve labours of Hercules.[1] No two authorities agreed as to what these twelve labours were, or in what order they were accomplished.[2] At all times and in all places the order of the signs is invariable: they could not therefore have been borrowed from the labours, though these might have been, and probably were, borrowed from them.

Before the Christian era, and for three centuries after it, no attempt was made to explain the meaning of these emblems: but as distance adds to indistinctness, antiquity stimulates imagination. The ancients on this point knew that they knew nothing; but Macrobius, in the fourth century, fancied in them a possible suitability to the seasons of his age and country. He either overlooked or was ignorant of the astronomical fact of the precession of the equinoxes, by which, if they suited Italy at that time, they could not have been adapted to those Eastern climates and remote ages to which he attributes their invention. He however says that not Leo alone, but all the signs have reference to the nature of the sun. Censorinus also asserted that all the constellations referred to the sun. The sun, as an appointed type of Him who was to come, the Light of the world, the Sun of righteousness, is indeed referred to in all the constellations; for even in the female figures, typifying the Church, there is in the hand a branch, His well-known emblem; and those of the serpent, the enemy, are under the foot of figures representing Him.

Though the signs are found nearly as we now have them on early Egyptian monuments, no Egyptian explanation of them has yet been discovered; but from the various minor emblems accompanying them, it should seem the Egyptians themselves attached to them some meaning. It has been thought that in Aquarius might be traced some allusion to the inundation of the Nile: but here again geology interposes. When the summer solstice, and consequently the inundation, would have taken place in that sign, man did not exist; after his creation, when these stars would be seen at night, at that season, could it be traced in a slender stream poured into the mouth of a fish? If a symbolical meaning be given to one of these figures, the rest should be taken as equally significant: if one be interpreted of the seasons, so should the others. If one be taken as seen at midnight, so should the remainder. But it will be found that when any one of the signs is made to coincide with any particular season, there is seldom a plausible explanation to be given of another, and never

---

[1] Nonnus lived about A.D. 400.   [2] Part II. p. 88.

f all of them. If the Nile overflowed under Aquarius, the harvest of Egypt ould not take place under Virgo, nor either equinox under Gemini, as has been ometimes supposed. Could these difficulties be overlooked, and the inundation e imagined to be figured where the Egyptians have not traced it, would it not emain to be told why events which every returning year brought in due succession should need to be typified among the stars of heaven? Has it been sual to institute memorials of what cannot be forgotten, or to take precautions gainst overlooking what is present to the senses?

Some record of the past, some admonition addressed to the future, has ever een the purpose of such aids to memory. Some such origin might therefore ave been looked for in these names and emblems, even if to it they had not orne internal testimony. Invariably connected with the most striking, the ost sublime appearances in the visible creation, seen in all climates, accompanying the wandering tribes of man in all their migrations, the only unhanging, the only fixed among the objects of his senses,—should we not expect ɔ find among the names and figures annexed to the stars some memorial of reat and universal importance to the whole human race? Guided by the ispired writer, should we not confidently look up to the starry heavens, ex. ecting to trace in the names and symbols universally and from all antiquity ssociated with them, some signification that shall verily be found to declare ie glory of God?

NOTE.

Like others of the sceptic school, Volney reports everywhere in antiquity the existence f the tradition of the expected conqueror of the serpent, a divine person, born of a roman, who was to come; and sees this tradition reflected in the constellations, but why ɔ should be there he does not say. He inclines to think the constellations referred to. he seasons, but as to what the serpent could have to do with those seasons, he offers no onjecture; the only point on which he is very decided is that the seed-bearing woman of he zodiac figured the harvest. That the harvests in different countries are at different imes he overlooks, and also that in the same country the lapse of ages would transfer he time of harvest from one sign to another. When the summer solstice was in Leo, or ven in Cancer, Egypt was under water in Virgo. The Nile, says Herodotus, rises for a undred days, and sinks for a hundred more. During those days there could be no arvest. It is only in modern times and more northerly climates that the time of harvest ɔ while the sun is among the stars of Virgo. In Egypt and Palestine, in the time of Ioses, the corn was in the ear at the time of the passover, at the vernal equinox, then ust entering Aries. There was then some other reason than that of the harvest for the gure of the woman bearing the ear of corn, even that it set forth the prophecy of the eed of the woman who should come to bruise the serpent's head.

Volney seems also to have traced some idea of analogy between the sun and the xpected conqueror of the serpent; but the sun is not the enemy of serpents, they are ɔstered by his rays. The true analogy he did not perceive; the sun comes, enlightens, lesses, goes away, but surely comes again. Thus the sun of this world daily teaches, aily prophesies of the Sun of righteousness, arising with healing on his wings, setting s it were for a while, but surely to return in the glory of morning to renew the face ɔf earth.

CHAPTER II.

In whatever obscurity the origin of the emblems of astronomy may appear to be enveloped, in the traditions of the nations where they are preserved, no such doubts hang over that of the science itself. It has always and everywhere been traced back to the earliest race of man. The Hebrews, Chaldeans, Persians, and Arabs imputed its invention to Adam, Seth, and Enoch; the earlier Greeks to their mythical and mysterious personage Prometheus. Soon after the usual date assigned to Noah's flood, astronomy is found in high cultivation in the commencing empire of China; and equally early records of observed eclipses were preserved at Babylon, proving considerable attainments in that science. Those modern writers who acknowledge the authority of the Hebrew Scriptures, if only as historical, generally refer its origination to the antediluvian patriarchs; and to Noah, its transmission to the ancient nations. Those who do not admit that authority, claim for astronomy, from its internal evidence, the antiquity of between five and six thousand years. There is no appearance of the science ever having existed separate from the emblems; and as they are in no way essential to it, their constant connexion with it can only be explained by their having been invented at the same time and by the same persons. Why did those inventors adopt these particular emblems, when others might equally have marked out the division of the sun's path by that of the moon?[1] It has been pointed out that with the phenomena of the circling year they cannot be consistently made to agree, nor with those of the climate of Egypt.[2] The mythology of the nations, though reflecting their shadow, will be found insufficient to account for their imagery. If these traditional names and figures can be shown to symbolize prophecy, as imparted in the earliest ages, sufficient reason appears for the selection of such images, at such a time, and by such persons as those primeval fathers of mankind, with whom the science has always been supposed to originate.

Sublime as is the study of those supremest visible works of the Divine Creator, the host of heaven, far more sublime is the contemplation of the unspeakably greater work of Redemption. That stupendous mystery, then first presented to the mind of man, might well predominate in the meditations of the newly fallen, the redeemed race. To the memorial of that invisible but

---

[1] Part II. p. 5, &c.   [2] Part I. p. 17.

ranscending miracle they appear to have consecrated the splendours of the tarry heavens. To the glory of Jehovah Sabaoth, the Lord of Hosts, of those nultitudes of multitudes, the countless myriads of far-spreading orbs of light, iave they dedicated the magnificent system of sacred hieroglyphics, arranged o His praise in connexion with " the stars of light."

A remarkable testimony that then and with these inventors astronomy riginated is extant and accessible. It is that of the learned Jew Josephus, vho, living at the time of the destruction of the Temple by Titus, refers for us authorities to ancient writers whose names alone remain to us. He ttributes the invention of the science to " the family of Seth the son of Idam," when, the life of man then extending to near a thousand years, they vere enabled to ascertain from actual observation the return of the heavenly odies to the same positions in cycles and periods, which in after ages it has equired the labour of successive generations to verify.

Adam, divinely led to give names to what he saw, must have had such for he sun and moon, and probably for the planets,[1] whose movements would ttract his notice. Those celestial splendours shone in the far-off and in-ccessible heaven, the abode or the path to the abode of his Creator and Redeemer, whence Divine instruction and yet more Divine mercy had de-cended upon him. Thither his eyes would reverently and most habitually urn : the starry world on high would be, if not the first, the most absorbing bject of his contemplation ; and astronomy would naturally be, as tradition leclares, the earliest study, the first science of mankind. Seth, the son of his onsolation and heir of his promises, the traditional father of astronomy, is aid to have commenced its arrangement with that of the twelve signs. To Jeth is also attributed the great period of the relative positions of sun and noon, the cycle of six hundred years, by modern computation found so won-lerfully exact. In this no use is made of the fixed stars beyond the zodiac.

Enoch, his descendant, with whom he was long cotemporary, is said by radition to have given names to the stars : the further development of pro-hecy that appears among the constellations annexed to the signs, above and elow them, may then be referred to him.[2] " The family of Seth " thus levised, carried on, and completed this great work, which remains to us an inchanged memorial of their piety, their intellect, and the revelation which hey were endeavouring to perpetuate.

To the conclusion that at such a time, and under such circumstances, astro-nomy must have been invented, many learned men, after long investigation, iave come at last. This result of their researches will be found to be con-irmed by the book of Genesis and the other records of the Mosaic dispensation ;

---

[1] Part II., Table of Sun, Moon, and Planets.   [2] Part II., Table, pp. 4. 34.

the high antiquity of which is acknowledged to be far anterior to that of any other writings, by all persons competent to the investigation, or capable of appreciating the proofs by which it is established.

These books, so confessedly ancient, and so abounding with internal marks of proceeding from the same Divine Power which formed the host of heaven, contain many astronomical allusions. Some of these are evident even in translations;[1] but many more are recognized by the ancient Jewish commentators, and are manifest to the careful student of the Hebrew Scriptures.

These allusions not only tend to corroborate the account of the antediluvian origin of astronomy, but appear to imply the co-existence of emblems and names with which those at present in use retain a remarkable agreement, and not only so, but indicate their meaning and design.

In the beginning of Genesis it is declared that "God made lights in the firmament of heaven, to divide between the day and the night, and to be for *signs*,[2] and for seasons,[3] and for days, and for years." It is not said that on the fourth day God *created* them, but that He made them appear as lights in the firmament, where previously vapours might have obscured their orbs. The word "signs" should lead us to ask, what do they signify? The primitive word Othath,[4] rendered *signs* in Gen. i. 14, and *mark* in Gen. iv. 15, is something that testifies, foreshows. Their prophetic import may thus be seen, as implied in their name from the beginning. These *signs* in the firmament of heaven may then be expected to teach, to instruct, to foreshow. If these emblems, the signs of the zodiac and other constellations, are calculated to set forth important truths fitted to rule the hopes of man as well as the computation of his earthly time, this declaration seems to authorize the conclusion, that the patriarchs, desiring to act according to the mind and will of God, so devoted them to show forth His glory. If the inventors of astronomy were indeed acquainted with truths of the utmost importance to the whole human race, might they not wisely desire to connect the remembrance of them with those memorials, those signs, by which they measured the path of the sun in the heavens, thus with the observations of earthly time associating the revealed glories of eternity beyond? They, whose accurate knowledge of the movements of the celestial orbs still astonishes posterity, might well desire to annex

---

[1] Job. ix. 9; and xxxviii. 31, 32.

[2] Jer. x. 2: "Be ye not dismayed at the *signs* of heaven, for the heathen are dismayed at them," unduly venerating, being influenced by them. There appears here an allusion to the idolatrous use of them. The same word is rendered *token*, as applied to the rainbow (Gen. ix. 12); and by it Korah and his company are said to be a *sign* unto the children of Israel. Again, it is said of the lights of heaven, that they were to *rule* the day and the night.

[3] The original word means "periods," having no reference to summer, winter, &c.

[4] Like our word "oath," evidently derived from it.

the message of everlasting mercy with which they had been entrusted, to the only visible works of creation that at all times and in all places present the same aspect of unalterable splendour. Adam, to whom the first revelation was made; Seth, in whose time it was begun to proclaim[1] the name of the Lord; and Enoch, walking with God, who prophesied of His final victory, might well be led to express the promises and predictions they had received in the very figures, and even words, constantly recurring in the written records of the subsequent revelations to patriarch and prophet, from the dying Jacob, who spake of the Lion of Judah, to him who saw the Lamb, the light thereof, in the holy city of the Apocalypse.

From the beginning of Genesis to the end of the Revelation, as through the whole sphere of the starry heavens, the enemy is represented in the serpent, the Messiah in the seed, the lion, and the lamb. Everywhere He goes forth triumphant; yet everywhere He is seen, the Bruised, the Pierced, the Lamb as it had been slain.[2]

If the words of that first revelation, as recorded in Scripture, do not convey the full disclosure of the work of redemption as indicated in these emblems, yet it is not said that such further light was withheld. The rite of sacrifice, showing forth the Lord's death till His first coming, was with them, and the faith of Abel, which applied it. To Enoch had been foreshown the coming of the Lord to judgment. If they were uncertain of the time of "the sufferings of Christ," as we are of "the glory that should follow," still they knew, for they have prefigured, that He should come, should suffer, and should reign.

It might be expected from such an origin, from inventors so circumstanced, that the promised Redeemer, His actions, His enemy, and His people, would be the subject of every emblem annexed to the constellations visible in the north temperate zone, the primitive habitation of mankind. It would seem improbable that any reference less high, less holy, should be mingled with those of such surpassing interest.

Should the tradition of the Divine yet woman-born Conqueror of the serpent, crushing His foe, but suffering from its venom, be met with among all nations, it is only what might have been anticipated among the descendants of one common father. From the Grecian Hercules, half human and half divine, subduing the hydra and dying from its poison; from the Indian incarnation of the Divinity, the virgin-born Krishna, slaying a serpent and wounded by it in the heel, to the serpent-worship of Mexico, and that of the woman-born and unfathered deity Mexitli, this image is everywhere present, pointing to one origin of the tradition and of the race.

---

[1] The word is so rendered in Exod. xxxiv. 5, 6.
[2] Gen. iii. 15; xlix. 10. Isa. xxxii. 1; liii. 4. Rev. v. 6; xix. 16.

Though by some it has been suggested[1] that these mythological tales were derived from the constellations, yet it has not by them been even conjectured why the constellations should have been so designated as to give rise to these stories. If, however, they were so named to record the revelation made to the first fathers of mankind, their connexion with the mythologies of the nations is explained.

The only evidence as to their origin, as found in the still existing records of ancient tradition, attributes it to "the family of Seth." As no conflicting evidence exists, may it not be received as conclusive? May we not confidently speak of Adam, to whom the promise of the Redeemer was made, Seth, who calculated so precisely the movements of the great luminaries of day and night in the zodiac, and Enoch,[2] said to have named the stars after "the Righteous upon the earth," the incarnate Saviour, as the authors and originators of the emblems of astronomy?

---

[1] Dupuis and the writers of his school have done much to establish the facts that confute their inferences. Dupuis himself has collected ancient authorities abundantly proving that in all nations the tradition had always prevailed, of a Divine person, born of a woman, suffering in the conflict with a serpent, but triumphing over him at last. This tradition he finds reflected in the emblems of the ancient constellations. He seems to take it for granted, that because the stars themselves existed before the tradition, that therefore the emblems annexed to them also preceded it. Who, then, annexed those ideas to the stars, which certainly do not suggest them? When and why did such an annexation occur to the mind of man? These questions he does not anticipate, and assuredly he does not answer. He calls his attack on revelation "L'Origine des Cultes," "The Origin of Religions," which he would find in the constellations. The defence shows that the first religion was the origin of the emblems of the constellations.

It should be borne in mind that these constellations are not natural groups of stars, but arbitrary connexions of various stars by means of imaginary figures, sometimes so interwoven with each other as to be inseparable by the unaccustomed eye. This is particularly observable in the figures of the serpent, of which Sir J. Herschell complains, that "the heavens are scribbled over with interminable snakes." Even so are intertwined the wiles of the enemy with the course and history of redemption.

[2] Part II. p. 34.

MAZZAROTH

PART II

MAZZAROTH;

OR,

THE CONSTELLATIONS.

"Canst thou bring forth Mazzaroth in his season?"—Job xxxiii. 32.

SECOND PART.

EXPLANATION OF THE TABLES.

THE apparent places and movements of the sun, moon, and planets have always been described by their relation to the fixed stars. From time immemorial these fixed stars have been distinguished into constellations, called by the names of various earthly objects. Few of these constellations appear to the eye as distinct groups, and still fewer have any similitude in form to the things after which they are named. Twelve of these, through which the sun, moon, and planets appear to move, have every where and always been named after the same, or nearly the same, objects. These names have varied according to the dialects of the nations, but are to, be traced to the same ideas. Those transmitted by the Hebrews* may be taken as the most ancient. From these the Arabic and Syriac little differ. The Coptic† have been thought to preserve the ancient Egyptian; the Greek ‡, to have been translated from the Egyptian; the Latin §, to have been derived from the Etruscans. The arts and sciences of Etruria being supposed to have come from Assyria, will account for Semitic roots being found in the Latin names.

The other thirty-six constellations, called decans, apparently of equal antiquity, comprise the rest of the stars known to the north temperate zone. These have varied more in their names and figures: but Semitic roots appear in the names; and the figures, like those of the signs, will be found used as types by the Hebrew prophets.

The previously unknown stars of the southern hemisphere have been observed since the passage to India by the Cape. Tradition had said that the south polar constellation was in the shape of a cross||. So it had been seen in the early ages, and so it was called by those who again beheld it. By the precession of the equinoxes it had

---

* See Hyde, Relig. Vet. Pers.; Gaffarelli, Curios. Liter., &c.
† Montucla, Astro. Ancien.; Ulugh Beigh, &c.
‡ Plato in Cratylus.   § Modern writers on Etruria, Humboldt (Cosmos).
|| Buxt. Rab. Lex.; Com. on Deut.; Aben Ezra, &c.

B

disappeared from sight in the north temperate zone about the time of the Christian era*; but the memory of it survived among the nations. Subsequently an English astronomer, cotemporary with Newton, but not consulting him, applied to stars, whose relation to the ancient constellations was not recognized, names and figures utterly incongruous with those already existing. With these modern interpolations this examination of the ancient astronomical records has no connexion.

The annexed tables are intended to show that the meanings attributed to the ancient names of the signs, constellations, and stars, are really to be found in them, the proof being sought in the use of those words or their roots in the Hebrew Scriptures, and other Oriental dialects.

The Hebraist will find the roots in the margin of the right-hand column, and in the texts referred to, with occasional allowance for differences in the divisions of the English version. The English reader will find the meanings here assigned to the names in the corresponding texts to which references are given.

In the left-hand column some of the Scripture prophecies are pointed out with which the names and emblems, as here explained, correspond†. The prophecies frequently containing the very words transmitted as the names, an asterisk indicates where they do so.

The tables are also intended to show the marks of design in the arrangement and correspondence of the names and figures, and the adaptation of the decans to the signs, as developing the leading ideas of those signs which they accompany. Those ideas are here shown to be expressed in various prophecies of the Holy Scriptures.

By Plato we are informed that Solon made an investigation, apparently on scientific and theological subjects, into the power of names, and found that the Egyptians, from whom the Greeks derived them, had transferred them from " barbarian " dialects into their own language. According to ancient authorities, the Egyptians had learnt their astronomy from the Chaldeans. The meaning of the names of astronomy transmitted by the Greeks should therefore be sought in the dialect of those from whom the Egyptians received the science. In the Chaldee contained in the Hebrew Scriptures it may be seen that every Chaldee word is explicable by the cognate Hebrew root, to which, therefore, those names are here referred. The early Arabic is thus equally intelligible. The refinements of modern Arabic have scarcely at all affected the names of ancient astronomy. Its descriptive epithets used as synonymes, and its melodious profusion of inserted vowels, ornament and may a little obscure the original idea, but do not alter the sense.

The writers of the Scriptural annunciations of the prophecies had the same divine truths communicated to them as had been revealed to Adam, Abel, Seth, and Enoch. They have delivered them, speaking as they were moved by the Holy Spirit. Those who invented the emblems seem to have desired to perpetuate symbolically the unwritten revelation, made to that earliest race. The agreement of the results of the two modes of transmission, the written and the emblematic, will here be seen. In some instances it may appear intentional, in others incidental to the unity of the subject. That subject, the great theme of prophecy in all ages, was in both the seed of the woman who should bruise the serpent's head, the Lamb of God, slain from the foundation of the world, and returning in glory to triumph and to reign.

The prophecies were given of God: the words in which the prophets expressed them

---

* Cosmos.

† The names in use in Arab astronomy may have belonged to the primitive language, as it is said that Al was originally the Hebrew article. (See Moses Stuart's Grammar.)

were of the Holy Spirit. The names and emblems of astronomy, intended to convey those divine truths, were of man, the efforts of human intellect to aid in extending and perpetuating the knowledge of those prophecies at first orally communicated.

The names are here explained on the supposition that the first language was given by the Creator to the first man, conveying ideas to the mind by sounds, as impressions of form and colour are conveyed by sight. In all languages these sounds are traceable, conveying the same ideas. In the dialects of the most ancient and earliest civilized nations they are the most recognizable: in those of the most barbarous the most obscured. This primitive language appears to have been spoken by Noah, from the names given by him to his sons. In the confusion of the lip at Babel, pronunciation, not words or roots, were altered. This may be inferred from the presence of Hebrew roots in the dialects of all nations.

The simple and consistent explanations obtained in this manner often widely differ from those derived in other ways. Plato* long ago observed that all things possess some quality which is the proper reason of their appellations, and that those names which express things as they exist are the true names. The qualities from whence the things figured in the constellations were named made them suitable types of higher objects in which these qualities, though in a subordinate degree, were also to be found. So the innocence of the lamb suited with the holiness of the Saviour; so the force of the lion, His all-subduing power. But these, though increasing the beauty of the type, do not express the leading ideas as contained in the original names. Taleh, the lamb, is the sent forth, as the lamb from its mother, as He who is our passover from God. Shur, the bull, from his strength; Thaumim, the twins, from their unitedness; Sartan, the crab or beetle, from its fast holding; Arieh, the lion, from rending the prey; Bethulah, the offspring, as daughter or branch; Mozanaim, the scales, encompassing as in weighing; Akrab, the scorpion, wounding him that cometh; Kesith, the archer sending forth the arrow; Gedi, the cut off, the slain victim; Deli, the pouring forth of water; Dagin, the fish, as multitudes: these are all names that meet Plato's requirement.

---

* In Cratylus.

Note.—The names with Al prefixed in use in Arabic astronomy are now used merely as proper names, their meaning being lost. They may be held to belong to the primitive language. Al is supposed by Stuart, &c., to have been the original Hebrew article.

Asterisks in the first column mark where the word existing as the name occurs in the Hebrew prophecy where the figure is used.

The Hebrew characters are here given without points, for the sake of clearness, as in the titles, &c., of pointed Hebrew Bibles. Two-lettered roots have been used as often as might be, partly because Rawlinson and Layard, and some Egyptologers explain their languages chiefly by them, and partly because some lexicographers prefer them where admissible. Three-lettered roots, made by vau inserted, add the idea of duration; by he postfixed, add the idea of existence; doubling the last radical adds that of intensity. In Arabic two-lettered roots become three-lettered by teshdid, in Hebrew two-lettered roots remain, probably belonging to the primitive language, which many now believe to have been only a less copious Hebrew.

Prophecies of the Messiah,

HIS PEOPLE AND HIS ENEMY,
CORRESPONDING WITH THE THIRTY-SIX DECANS OR CONSTELLATIONS ACCOMPANYING THE SIGNS.

Signs.		Predictions of fulfilment.
ARIES, The lamb as it had been slain. Rev. 5. 6.	Cassiopeia, the Church set free, raised, enthroned. 1 Sam. ii. 8. Isa. lx.; lxii.	Rev. 21. 9. Rev. 19. 7, 8.
	Cetus, the serpent bound. Isa. xxvii. 1.	Rev. 20. 2.
	Perseus, the Deliverer, breaking the bonds of the afflicted Church. Mic. ii. 13.	Isa. 54. 11.
TAURUS, The bull, once a sacrifice, now ruling.	Orion, the coming of Him mighty to save. Isa. lxiii. 1.	Rev. 19.
	Eridanus, the river; converted nations under the type of water.	Ezek. 47.
	Auriga, the Good Shepherd and his redeemed flock. John x. 11, 14.	Isa. 40. 11. Ezek. 34. 23.
GEMINI, The Messiah uniting the Divine and human nature.	Lepus, the enemy under his feet. Ps. viii. 6.	1 Cor. 15. 27.
	Sirius, He that cometh, as the Prince. Isa. ix. 6.	Dan. 9. 25.
	Procyon, He that cometh, as the Redeemer.	Isa. 59. 20.
CANCER, The possession, the reward of his sufferings.	Ursa Minor, the lesser sheepfold, the Church before the first coming of Christ.	Jer. 23. 3.
	Ursa Major, the greater sheepfold, the Church after the first coming of Christ.	Ezek. 36. 37.
	Argo, the company of travellers to the heavenly Canaan.	John 10. 16.
LEO. The Lion of Judah punishing the enemy.	Hydra, the serpent, the enemy. Rev. xx. 2.	Isa. 27. 1.
	Crater, the cup of the wrath of God resting upon him.	Ps. 75. 8.
	Corvus, the bird of prey feeding on his flesh.	Rev. 19. 17.
VIRGO, The woman with the branch.	Coma, the desired, the infant held by the woman; the seed.	Isa. 9. 6.
	The Centaur, the King Messiah offering himself as a sacrifice. John x. 18.	Matt. 20. 28.
	Bootes, the coming of the Branch as the guardian of the flock.	John 10. 14.
LIBRA, The scales of redeeming.	The Cross, the finishing of the work of redemption. John xix. 30.	Dan. 9. 24. Dan. 9. 26.
	The Victim, of the sacrifice.	Gen. 22. 8.
	The Crown, of his glory. Ps. viii. 5; cxxxii. 18.	Rev. 19. 12.
SCORPIO, The conflict of the Messiah.	The Serpent, the enemy with which he contends. Heb. v. 7.	Gen. 3. 15.
	Ophiuchus, the Desired, holding the serpent, his foot on the head of the Scorpion.	Hag. 2. 7.
	Hercules, he who bruises, his foot over the head of the Dragon. Ps. xci. 13.	Gen. 3. 15.
SAGITTARIUS, The sending forth of the Gospel.	Lyra, the eagle holding the harp; the triumph. Mark xiii. 26.	Matt. 16. 27. Rev. 19. 15.
	Ara, the altar of the completed sacrifice. Ps. xliii. 4.	Heb. 13. 10.
	Draco, the enemy who is to be trodden under foot.	Ps. 91. 13.
CAPRICORNUS, The slaying of the victim.	Sagitta, the arrow of slaying. Ps. xxxviii. 2.	Isa. 53.
	Aquila, the falling eagle; his dying.	
	Delphinus, the pouring out of his soul unto death.	
AQUARIUS, The pouring forth of spiritual blessings.	The Southern Fish, the Church drinking in the water of life.	John 4. 14.
	Pegasus, the winged horse, going to return again. Zech. vi. 7. Rev. xix. 11.	John 14. 3.
	Cygnus, the swan, the bird of passage who goes and comes again.	Acts 1. 11.
PISCES, The multitudes of the redeemed.	The Band, uniting the Church before and after the first coming of the Lord.	John 10. 16.
	Cepheus, the branch, crowned King. Rev. xiv. 14.	Jer. 23. 5.
	Andromeda, the Church released by the Deliverer, who breaks the bonds of death.	Isa. 61. 1. Rev. 20. 5.

AUTHORITIES FOR THE ANTIQUITY OF THE SIGNS OF THE ZODIAC, THEIR NAMES AND FORMS.

			Texts where the word or its root is used in this sense in the Hebrew Bible.	*Hebrew roots.*
Greek, Zodiakos, { a way having *steps* *. { having.		*gone, paces* *having*	2 Sa. 6. 14. Job 30. 16.	צער אחז
— Zodion, a sign, or *step* of the way.		*march* {	Hab. 3. 12. Ps. 68. 7.	צער
Hebrew, Mazzaloth, the zodiac. 2 Kings xxiii. 5.		*flowing*	Jer. 18. 14.	מזל
Arabic, Mazaloth, the zodiac. Arab, sense, descending.				
Sanscrit, Sodi, as Zodiac, way; Mandalam, as Mazaloth, *z* changed for *d*.				

If the correspondence between the meanings of the names of the antediluvian patriarchs with those of the signs be intentional, it affords the earliest evidence of the antiquity of those figures. Surely such a coincidence in such unbroken series cannot be esteemed the work of chance. The co-existence of the signs is to be inferred from the widely diffused ancient tradition that astronomy was invented by the first fathers of mankind, from the date assigned to it by modern astronomers, and from the allowed fact that the science was never known to exist unaccompanied by these figures. The evidence next in antiquity is that of the Chinese records†. Modern algebraists confirm these, while they dispute those of India. From those records‡ we learn that a winter solstice has been observed in 18° Aquarius 2342 B.C.; also, that a remarkable conjunction of the four planets, Saturn, Jupiter, Venus, and Mercury, with the moon in Pisces, when the sun was in 20° Aquarius, was observed in China. This conjunction is said by modern astronomers to have taken place 2012 B.C. These records were brought to Europe by the learned Jesuit missionaries who visited China in the seventeenth century. The Chinese emperor Yao is there said to have divided the twelve signs by the twenty-eight Mansions of the Moon, but is not said to have invented any of them. An eclipse is there correctly recorded as early as the time of Abraham.

Chaldean astronomical observations for 1900 years back were found, reaching to much the same time as those of the Chinese, at Babylon, when taken by Alexander§. To the Chaldeans ancient writers attribute the division of the zodiac, as well as the introduction of astronomy into Egypt. That line of the family of Noah of which Abraham came would be Chaldean. That "the traditions of the Chaldean astronomy seem the fragments of a mighty system fallen into ruin," has been observed by Sir W. Drummond.

Astronomy is found highly cultivated in Egypt in the very earliest time of its history. Ptolemy records, on the faith of Thebaic astronomers, the heliacal rising of Sirius on the fourth day after the summer solstice, 2250 B.C. Nouet, a French astronomer, infers that the Egyptian astronomy must have arisen 5400 B.C. This date accords with the assertion of Josephus, that astronomy originated with the family of Seth, and with the traditions of the ancient Persians and Arabs, attributing its invention to Adam, Seth, and Enoch. In the notes to Gill's Commentary on Genesis will be found the names of ancient writers, Jewish, Persian, and Arabic, by whom these traditions have been transmitted.

Hamilton, in his Ægyptiaca, remarks the rudeness and imperfection of the mechanical instru-

---

* Those who derive zodiac from Zao, to live, as composed of living creatures, instead of from the primitive root Zoad, way, going on by steps, not only overlook the balance in Libra, but the vase for Aquarius, and the bow for Sagittarius, of the Eastern nations.

† Nicholl's Outlines of Astronomy.

‡ Martini, Hist. Sini.

§ Sextus Empiricus, &c. See Montucla.

ments of the Egyptians. He asks, How was this compatible with their knowledge of the sublimer sciences? It may be suggested in reply, that they would derive their knowledge of astronomy from Noah, of the line of Seth, while the workers in metals, the mechanicians, the children of Cain, had perished in the deluge. Josephus not only transmits the tradition of his Hebrew ancestors, but also refers for corroboration to eight ancient writers of other nations whose works are totally lost, as well as to others of whom some fragments remain. These all, he says, asserted that they of the first world lived a thousand years; also, that "God gave the antediluvians such long life, that they might perfect those things which they had invented in astronomy." As the great year or period of 600 years. This period has been examined and verified by the celebrated French mathematician Cassini, who gives it as his opinion that nothing but the observation of a life of that duration could have sufficed to its discovery. From Noah the Egyptians and the Chinese would derive their early scientific knowledge, as would those others of his descendants who are found to possess it. Montucla, another well-known mathematician and astronomer, attributes the origin of astronomy to the antediluvians. Cassini thus commences his History of Astronomy: "It is impossible to doubt that astronomy was invented from the beginning of the world: history, profane as well as sacred, testifies to this truth." He refers to Philo for the assertion that "Terah, the father of Abraham, who lived more than a hundred years with Noah, had much studied astronomy, and taught it to Abraham," who is said by Josephus to have taught it to the Egyptians. That people, however, had probably from their ancestor Noah the same knowledge of it which Sir Wm. Jones considers all the early nations possessed. Abraham may have added the superior science which all antiquity attributes to the Chaldeans. Bailly and others have asserted that astronomy must have been invented when the summer solstice was in the first degree of Virgo, and that the solar and lunar zodiacs were of a similar antiquity. This would have been about 4000 years before the Christian era. They suppose this science to have originated with an ancient and highly civilized people, who lived at that time in about lat. 40°, and that they were swept away by some sudden destruction, leaving, however, traces of their knowledge behind them. This people may have been the antediluvians, and their destruction the flood. Bailly attributes the invention of both zodiacs to Hermes. Hermes is said by Manetho to be antediluvian.

Equally ancient authority may be derived from the book of Job, in which is found Mazzaroth, the constellations (the twelve signs according to the margin of the English Bible), with names of stars still to be traced among those now in use. Jobab, in Gen. x. 29, third in descent from Eber, is by some supposed to be Job, living before the time of Abraham, who was the sixth from their common ancestor. If so, the call of Abraham being about 1980 B.C., the time of Job would not be later than 2000 B.C., approaching to that of the Chinese and Babylonish records. The book of Job speaks of Ash, the assembled, still to be traced in Ursa Major; Chima, the accumulated, mentioned by Aben Ezra; and Chesil, the bound, at the foot of Orion. The voice from heaven superadded Mazzaroth, the separated, set apart, divided, as the signs in the circle of the zodiac, the constellations in the starry heavens.

The English Version, Septuagint, and Vulgate thus render these words:—

JOB ix. 9.					JOB xxxviii. 31, 32.			
Heb.	*E. V.*	*Sept.*	*Vulg.*		*Heb.*	*E. V.*	*Sept.*	*Vulg.*
Ash,	Arcturus,	Pleiades,	Arcturus.		Chima,	Pleiades,	Pleiades,	Pleiades.
Chima,	Pleiades,	Arcturus,	Hyades.		Chesil,	Orion,	Orion,	Arcturus.
Chesil,	Orion,	Hesperus,	Orion.		Ash,	Arcturus,	Hesperus,	Vesperus.
					Mazzaroth,	Mazzaroth,	Mazzaroth,	Lucifer.

Hadri Teman, the chambers of the south, chap. ix., seems equivalent to Mazzaroth, chap. xxxviii. The ancient translations, as if by tradition, refer all these names to stars, but seem quite uncertain as to what stars they mean. The English version follows sometimes the one, sometimes the other, sometimes neither.

If, as some have thought, the book of Job was brought by Moses from the land of Midian, it must have been Job's own relation of his trials, either left by him in writing, or orally transmitted as other ancient poems have been. As it contains prophecies of the coming Redeemer, it must have been composed under the influence of the Holy Spirit. Moses is supposed to have prefixed the two first chapters and added the last. The difference in the style of those three chapters from the rest, and its likeness to that of the narrative parts of the Pentateuch, has been pointed out. The highly poetical style of the intermediate part of the book of Job does not resemble that of the sublime and imaginative song of Moses. The difference may be perceived even in translations, much more in the originals.

Whatever age is assigned to the book, it will be seen that these names are mentioned as of familiar objects, great works of God, which He alone can bring forth in their season. They were from of old, ancient even when spoken of in this most ancient record.

Sir W. Drummond writes in 1824: "The fact is certain, that at some remote period there were mathematicians and astronomers who knew that the sun is in the centre of our system, and that the earth, itself a planet, revolves round it," &c. He refers to his Essay on the Science of the Egyptians and Chaldeans for his authorities. He also says: "Origen tells us that it was asserted in the book of Enoch, that in the time of that patriarch the constellations were already named and divided." Origen is thought to allude to a book of Enoch, not that now known as such.

El Macinus, Abulfaragius, and other Arabic writers call Enoch Edris, or the glorious, saying he was skilled in astronomy and other sciences, and that he was the same with Hermes Trismegistus. The Jews (as in the Targum of Jonathan) call him the great scribe, and say that he was the first who composed books of astronomy. So Eupolemus, who says he was the first inventor of astrology, and not the Egyptians.

Ricciolus thought the ancient Arab names of stars and constellations were antediluvian.

Albumazer refers for the ancient Persian sphere to the two Hermes and Ascalius. Hermes, meaning great, Ascalius, the skilful, are probably only epithets: and on the Arab authority, Enoch may be meant by "the first Hermes" to whom ancient writers so often attribute the origin of human science.

Albumazer, describing Virgo, says that the Persians, Chaldeans, and Egyptians all agree as to the figure of the young woman (puella, maiden) holding an infant, and also refers for it to "two of the name of Hermes."

Manetho is referred to as saying the first Hermes was antediluvian. A work called Pimander is attributed to Hermes Trismegistus, in which the zodiac is called a tabernacle. (Ps. xix.) If Pi is taken as the Egyptian article, Mander may mean by its primitive root, devoted, consecrated: a *religious* work.

It is said by Achilles Tatius, that the Egyptian and Chaldean signs were the same as every where else, but differently named.

Dupuis, tracing all mythologies to the constellations, says, "All astronomers agree that the origin of astronomy is not to be found in history."

Bailly says, "The Persians in their books assert, that in remote periods four stars were so placed as to form the four colures." They are considered to be Al Debaran in Taurus, Regulus in Leo, Antares in Scorpio, and Fom al Haut in the Southern Fish, in Aquarius. Humboldt adds, "These four, called royal stars, are celebrated throughout Asia." This position of the colures could only be in antediluvian times.

In a modern astronomical work, "The Orbs of Heaven," it is said, "Allusions to the constellations of the zodiac in the old Hebrew Scriptures, and in the works of all ancient writers, sufficiently attest their extreme antiquity. From these allusions may be corroborated many of their forms as delineated on Egyptian, Assyrian, and Indian monuments. The most ancient are those of the Hebrew Scriptures."

"When Virgil says, The white bull with golden horns opens the year, this not being true in his day, must be the record of an ancient tradition that once it did so, as it had done 4000 years before his time."

"Callysthenes, the Greek philosopher who accompanied Alexander in his Eastern conquests, sent to Aristotle a series of observations made at Babylon nineteen centuries before that time." This date remounts to the time of Noah, whether according to the Jewish or modern chronology.

Thales and Pythagoras were both acquainted with the Saros or sacred period of the Chaldees. Both were instructed by the Chaldeans. Ptolemy afterwards used the calculations of the Chaldeans. Saros is root, foundation, in Job xxviii. 9.

Mrs. Somerville says, "La Place disputes the antiquity of the Indian lunar tables," but adds, "Every circumstance concurs in showing that astronomy was cultivated in the highest ages of antiquity."

Sir W. Drummond, in his Essay on the Zodiacs of Esne and Dendera, says of these zodiacs, "It seems generally agreed that they represent the heavens at the commencement of a Sothaic period (1460 years), which might be 2782 B.C." These temples are now known to have been built about the Christian era; but the zodiacs, like our own, might have been of much earlier date. That now in use is as we have it from Ptolemy. The Sothaic period would thus commence during the antediluvian study of astronomy attributed to the family of Seth, from whom it might take its name.

In the planisphere of Dendera, a headless figure, apparently a horse, is placed over Aquarius, marking the place of the ascending node. The winter solstice was in that sign before and after the time usually assigned to the deluge. A figure of Osiris, or the sun, standing on the figure of Capricorn, would seem intended to show that the precession of the equinoxes had removed the solstice thither.

In these, as in other ancient monuments, Egyptian and Oriental, the order of the signs is that which Ptolemy (A.D. 150) transmits from Hipparchus (130 B.C.) as of unquestioned authority, unknown origin, and unsearchable antiquity. As such it has descended to us. Aries has always and every where been the first of the signs: no natural cause can be alleged why it should have been so. Not till about the time of the Christian era did equinox or solstice take place in that sign.

The Sabian Arabs began their year from Aries. The Chinese, and other ancient nations who began their year from Aquarius, still reckoned Aries the first of the signs: there, too, the Lunar Zodiacs always commenced.

Astronomy never having been known to exist without the signs, testimonies to the antiquity of the science include that of these emblems. Still some more direct evidence may be adduced.

Montucla refers to Malalas as saying that "Seth himself divided the sky into constellations."

The Chinese emperor Yao, B.C. 2317, divided the twelve signs by the twenty-eight mansions of the moon.

It is said by Dupuis that the Persian magi made much use of the signs.

Jewish writers are agreed that the tribes of Israel carried the twelve signs on their standards in the wilderness; also, that Jacob in his farewell blessing speaks of them in connexion with those sons whose descendants so bore them.

It is well known that the ancient tribes of Arabia called themselves by the names of various constellations, probably after the example of their brethren of Israel. In course of time these were idolatrously worshipped. Mahomet abolished the idolatry; but some of the tribes still call themselves by those names.

As in the divinely ordained cherubic forms there was the face of a man, the Sethites would not scruple to include human figures in the constellations. When the prohibition in the second commandment was issued, it has been thought that the Jews discontinued them, substituting the palm-branch in Gemini, the ear of corn in Virgo, the bow and arrow in Sagittarius, the vase in Aquarius. It is well known that the ancient Arabs did so, assigning as a reason the command from Sinai. Among the Brahmans and other easterns who appear to have learnt from them, this scruple did not exist. If they were, as is supposed, the descendants of Abraham, by Keturah, it should seem not to have been known to the astronomy of that patriarch, who, deriving the science through Noah from the family of Seth, appears to have followed the original Sethite delineations, in the form of the man typifying the human nature of the Messiah, and the woman typifying His Church. The Christian Arabs in later times are said to have used the figure of the woman and the infant.

"It is certain that the Chaldeans knew the mean motions of the moon with great exactness. Ptolemy refers often to them by the name of Chaldeans, Aristotle by that of Babylonians." (Cosmos.)

Humboldt says, "The Greek zodiac was probably taken from the Dodecatamora of the Chaldeans," and also attributes to the Arabian astronomy a Chaldean origin.

It is supposed that Hipparchus and Ptolemy followed the Greek sphere. Clemens Alexandrinus quotes from an ancient author, that "Chiron delineated the scheme of heaven." This does not imply that he invented, but that he drew a plan or map of it. Sir Isaac Newton considers Chiron to have been a great astronomer. He places him about 937 B.C., but others much earlier. Cleostratus, a Greek philosopher, 536 B.C., wrote concerning the constellations, particularly Aries and Sagittarius; but what, is not known.

As the movements of the sun, moon, and planets have always been described by their position in the zodiac, the ancient observations of the Chinese and Chaldeans establish the coeval antiquity of the signs.

It may be asked on what authority the figures of the constellations are drawn as we now have them. The earliest enumerations of the stars speak of them as *this* in the head, *that* in the shoulder, body, arm, leg, or foot, thus determining their positions. Some of these stars are reckoned twice over, as El Nath, once in the horn of Taurus, again in the heel of Auriga, thus determining their connexion. They are thus distinguished by Hipparchus, B.C. 150, and again by Ulugh Beigh, A.D. 1420.

F. Bailly says, "The origin of astronomy ascends beyond the period of authentic history;" Smythe, that "there can be little doubt that astronomy was nearly coeval with the world." (Celest. Cyc.)

Aries.

THE RAM, OR LAMB, COMING FORTH.

Prophecies corresponding in word or type with the figures and the names.		Texts where the word or its root is used in this sense in the Hebrew Bible.	Hebrew roots.
Gen. 22. 8. Exod. 4. 13.	Hebrew name, Taleh, { *the lamb.* *sent forth.* cast*	Isa. 40. 11.	} טל
Isa. 16. 1.	Arabic, Al Hamal, *the sheep, gentle, merciful.*	Gen. 19. 16.	חמל
Gen. 4. 4.	Syriac, Amroo, *the lamb.* Syr. N.T. John i. 29.	Ezr. 6. 9.	אמר
Exod. 4. 13. Rev. 5. 6.	Coptic, Tametouris Ammon, *reign of Ammon.*		
Gen. 22. 13. Hos. 6. 3.	Greek, Krios, *the ram.* Sept. *lamb,* Gen. xxii. 13.	Deu. 32. 14. Isa. 16. 1.	כר
Isa. 61. 1. Mic. 5. 2.	Latin, Aries, *the ram.* Coming forth, Gen. xxii. 13, Vulg. *goeth*	Job 34. 8.	ארח
Isa. 27. 1.	*Names in the Sign.*		
Rev. 20. 2.	Heb., Mesartim, *the bound, or binding.*	Gen. 49. 11.	אסד
Ps. 22. 16.	Arab., β Al Sheratan, *the bruised, wounded.* *cut*	Lev. 12. 28.	שרט
Dan. 9. 26.	— α El Nath, or El Natik, *wounded, slain.* *cut*	Lev. 8. 20.	נתח
Is. 53. 7; 6. 1. Num. 24. 7.	Heb., Shalisha, the triangle over the head of { Aries, *exalted, chief.* *captains*	Ps. 30. 1. 1 Kgs. 9. 22.	שלש
Isa. 52. 13.	Arab., α Ras al Thalitha, *head of the triangle.* *head*	Gen. 49. 26.	ראש
Ps. 118. 22.	Gr., Deltoton, triangle, *high* (Arab., *lifted up*). *drew up*	Exod. 2. 16.	דלה

First Decan.
CASSIOPEIA, The throned Woman.

Ps. 45. 9. 1 Sam. 2. 8.	Heb., Cassiopeia, *the enthroned, the beautiful.* { *throne* *beauty*	1 Sam. 2. 8. Ps. 45. 11.	כסא יפה
	— α Shedar, *the freed.* *liberty*	Isa. 61. 1.	דר
Isa. 60. 21.	— Caph, *the branch,* in the hand.	Job 15. 23.	כף
	Chald. and Arab., Dat al Cursa, *the set, enthroned.*	Dan. 5. 20.	כרסא
	Arab., Ruchba, *the enthroned, or seated.*	Jer. 22. 4.	רכב

Second Decan.
CETUS, The Sea-monster, Leviathan, the bound Serpent.

		Ps. 104. 25. Isa. 27. 1.	חיות לויתן
*Isa. 27. 1.	Heb., α Menkar, *the bound or chained enemy.* { *chain* *enemy*	Dan. 5. 7. Ps. 139. 20.	מנך ער
	— Mira, *the changeable star in the neck, the rebel.*	Hos. 13. 16.	מרה
Rev. 20. 2.	— β Diphda, *overthrown.* *thrust down*	Job 32. 13.	נדף

Third Decan.
PERSEUS, an armed man holding a head with serpents.

Ps. 2. 9; 72. 4.	Heb., Perseus, *the breaker.*	Mic. 2. 13.	פרץ
*Mic. 2. 13.	— Athik, *who breaks.*	Judg. 16. 9.	נתק
	— α Mirfak, *who assists.* *leaning on*	Cant. 8. 5.	רפק
	Arab., γ Al Genib, *who carries away.*	Job 21. 18.	גנב
	Pers., Bershaush, as Perseus.		

In the Head, carried by Perseus.

Gen. 3. 15. Isa. 27. 1.	Heb., Medusa, *the trodden under foot.*	Job 39. 15.	דשה
Ps. 68. 21.	— Rosh Satan, *the head of the enemy.* *head*	Ps. 74. 14.	ראש
	— Al Oneh, *the subdued, weakened.*	Ps. 102. 23.	ענה
Rom. 16. 20.	Arab., Al Ghoul, *the evil spirit.* *wicked*	Job 18. 21.	עיל

The changeable Star in the Head.

	Arab., β Al Gol, *coming and going, rolling round* { *rolled* (Heb., *head*).	Gen. 29. 10. Num. 1. 2.	ל לג לת

The Ram or Lamb is figured as the first sign wherever sheep are found. In some parts of India an animal like a small dog is substituted; in others, an antelope; in Mexico, a white rabbit, called "the emblem of suffering innocence." Aratus places the triangle over the head of Aries. Cetus, in Greek fable, was the *enemy* of Andromeda; Perseus, the *breaker* of her bonds.

TABLE I.

Taurus.

THE BULL, COMING TO RULE.

Prophecies corresponding with the figures and the names.		Texts where the word or its root is used in this sense in the Hebrew Bible.	Hebrew roots.
*Deu.33.17.	Hebrew name, Shur, *the Bull, coming* { *bullock*	Deut.33.17.	שור
Gen. 22.17.	Arabic, Al Thaur, *the same.* [*ruling.* { *step*	Job 31.7.	אשר
Nu. 24.8,19.	Syriac, *the same.* (*rule*	Isa. 32.1.	שר
Ps. 72.2, 8.	Coptic, Isis, *who saves mightily.* *salvation*	Hab. 3.13.	ישע
Mic. 5.2, [E.V.	— Apis, *who cometh.* *pass*	Ex. 12.23.	פסח
2 Sa. 23.3,4.	— Station of Horus, *coming.* *wayfaring*	2Sam.12.4.	ארח
	Greek, Tauros, *the Bull.* Sept. Deut. xxxiii. 17.		
	Latin, Taurus, *the same.* Vulg. *the same.*		

Names in the Sign.

	Heb., Chima, *the heap, accumulation* (Arab.). *Pleiades*	Job 9.9.	כימה
Gen. 49.10.	— Pleiades, *congregation of the judge, or ruler.* {	Lev. 4.13. / Job 31.11.	ערה / פלל
Ps. 22.22.	— Hyades, *the congregated.* *congregation*	Num. 16.3.	עדה
Ps. 89.5;} 107.32.}	— Palilicium, *belonging to the judge.* *judge*	Job 31.11.	פליל
Isa. 60.5, 6, 7.	Arab., Wasat, *centre, or foundation.*	Ps. 11.3.	שת
	— Al Thuraiya, *the abundance.*	Isa. 15.7.	יתר
	Lat., Vergiliæ, *the centre* (Arab. *vertex*) *turned on, rolled round.*	Gen. 29.10.	גל

Names of Stars in the Sign.

	Chald., α Al Debaran, *the leader, governor.* { *counsellor subduing*	Dan. 3.24. / Ps. 47.3.	דבר
Dan. 9.26.	Arab., β El Nath, *in the northern horn, as in Aries.*		
	— η Al Cyone, *in the Pleiades, the centre.* { *base foundation established*	1 Kg.7.29,30 / Ps. 104.5. / Ps. 89.38.	כון

First Decan.

ORION, a human figure walking.

Mic. 5.2, [E.V.	Heb., Orion, *coming forth as light.* {	Gen. 1.17. / Isa. 60.1.	אור
Hab. 2.3.} Heb.10.37}	Arab., Al Giauzâ, *the branch.* *stem*	Isa. 11.1.	נוע
Isa. 60.1.	— Al Gebor, *the mighty.*	Ps. 24.8.	בר
	— Al Mirzam, *the prince, the ruler.*	Ps. 2.2.	רון
	— Al Nagjed, *the prince.*	Dan. 9.26.	נגד
	— δ Al Nitak, *the wounded.* *cut*	Lev. 1.6.	נתח
	— α Betelguez, *coming,* Mal. iii. 2, *of the branch.* *stock*	Isa. 40.24.	נוע
	— β Rigol, *the foot, or who treadeth under foot.*	Job 39.15.	רגל
Ps. 91.13.	— Al Rai, *the bruising.* *bruise*	Dan. 2.40.	רע
	— γ Bellatrix, *hastily coming.* { *haste treadeth*	Ezra 4.23. / Job 9.8.	בהל / דרך
	— δ Mintaka, *dividing, the belt.* *cut*	Lev. 8.20.	נתח
	Chald., Heka, *coming.* *brought*	Ezra 6.5.	הך
	— Niphla, *the mighty.* *giants*	Gen. 6.4.	נפל
	Heb., Meissa, *coming forth.*	Mic. 1.3.	יצא
	— Nux, *the strong.*	Ps. 24.8.	עז
	— Thabit, *treading on* (Arab.). *kick*	1 Sam.2.29.	בעט
*Gen. 3.15.	— κ Saiph, *in the foot, bruised.*	Gen. 3.15.	שף
	— Chesil, *bound together,* the nebula. *Constellations.*	Isa. 13.10.	כסל
	Gr., Orion, anciently Oarion. Sept. Job xxxviii. 31.		
	Lat., Orion. Vulg. Job ix. 9.		

If the flatterers of Nimrod (like those of Napoleon I.) tried to devote the stars of Orion to his glory, still it will be seen that in the names in the constellation there is no trace of that of the man, while the wounded, the bruised, or the branch, could not apply to Nimrod. Of the Latin Auriga, which in Hebrew is the shepherd, it may be asked, Why should a charioteer carry a goat and be followed by kids? Their band or leash may have suggested reins.

TABLE II.

Prophecies corresponding with the figures and the names.	TAURUS (continued).		Texts where the word or its root is used in this sense in the Hebrew Bible.	Hebrew roots.
	Second Decan.			
Isa. 66. 12.	ERIDANUS, The River.			
Ezek. 47. 9.	Heb., Eridanus, *river of the judge or ruler.*	{ streams { judge	Isa. 33. 21. Gen. 15. 14.	יאר דן
*Gen. 49. 16.	— Cursa, *bent down.*	stoopeth	Isa. 46. 1.	קרס
Ps. 46. 4.	— α Achernar, *after part of the river.*	{ after { river	Gen. 33. 2. Gen. 2. 10.	אחר נהר
Rev. 22. 1.	— Phaet, *mouth (of the river).*		Exod. 4. 11.	פה
	— Theemin, *the water.*		Gen. 1. 6.	ים
	— Ozha, *the going forth.*		Gen. 2. 10.	יצא
Isa. 41. 18.	Arab., Zourak, *flowing.*	sprinkle	Lev. 1. 5.	זרק
	Third Decan.			
*Ps. 23. 1; 80. 1.	AURIGA, a human figure holding a goat.			
*Isa. 40. 11.	Heb., Auriga, *the shepherd.*		Isa. 40. 11.	רע
	Arab., Aiyuk, *wounded* in the foot.	lame	2 Sam. 4. 4.	נכה
Mic. 5. 4.	— El Nath, *wounded* in the heel, also reckoned in the horn of Taurus, as in Aries.	cut	Lev. 8. 20.	נתח
Ezek. 34. 23.	— Maaz, *flock of goats.*		Lev. 16. 10.	עז
	Chald., Menkalinon, *band or chain of the goats,*	{ chain	Dan. 5. 7.	מנך
John 10. 4, 11.	or ewes.	{ hinds	2 Sa. 22. 34.	איל
	Heb., Gedi, *the kid* (following Auriga).		Cant. 1. 8.	גדי
	— Alioth, *she-goat, or ewe.*		Ps. 78. 71.	עלת
	Lat., α Capella, *the goat, atonement.*		Lev. 16. 10.	כפר

AUTHORITIES FOR THE NAMES OF THE SIGNS.

Hebrew, Buxtorf's Rabbinical Lexicon, &c.
Arabic, Freytag's Arabic Lexicon, Ulugh Beigh, &c.
Syriac, Hyde's Syntagma and Comment. &c.
Coptic, Montucla, Hist. de Mathématiques, from Ulugh Beigh.
Greek, Aratus, Ptolemy, &c.
Latin, Cicero, Virgil, Ovid, &c.

FOR THE NAMES OF THE STARS.

Hyde de Vct. Pers. Rel. for Chaldee, Persian, and other names; also for Rosh Satan, Al Oneh, and Auriga, from Aben Ezra. Arabic names of stars are from Ulugh Beigh, and catalogues in various other astronomical works, in which, though the spelling is frequently corrupted, the primitive root is still evident. Greek names may be found in Hesiod and Homer, also in Aratus, who lived about 300 B.C. St. Paul is supposed to quote from his poem on Astronomy, Acts xvii. 28. Latin, in Cicero, Hyginus, Macrobius, and the poets. The book of Job contains the three most ancient names: Ash, Chima, and Chesil. Aben Ezra has said that Ash is the Great Bear, where the word is still found in Benet Naish. He has also said that Chima and Chesil were opposite constellations. The Pleiades and Orion are on opposite sides of the ecliptic and equator. The Septuagint and Vulgate, in Job ix. 9 and xxxviii. 32, seem to recognize Chima as the Pleiades, and Chesil as Orion. Chesil is still found at the foot of Orion, as in Adams's globes. As it occurs in Isaiah xiii. 10 in the plural, it cannot apply to the figure Orion, of which there is only one, but may well mean the Nebulæ, of which there are many. The Arabic name Wasat, *the centre,* transmitted by Ulugh Beigh as of the Pleiades, and Al Cyone, the ancient Greek name of their brightest star, both indicate primæval knowledge of the late announcement of modern science, that in this group is the centre round which circles the galaxy or astral system to which our sun belongs. (See Orbs of Heaven, &c.)

A.D. 1252, an astronomical congress was held at Toledo, under Alfonso, king of Castile, in which a Jewish rabbin, Isaac Hazen, took an important part. He is spoken of by Cornelius Agrippa as a great astronomer. About that time Rabbi Judas interpreted the treatise in which Avicenna had named the 1022 fixed stars, till then unknown to our western parts. Avicenna was an Arab physician at Bagdad, A.D. 1030.

On Adams's large globes names will be found which are omitted on the more recent. Many are there given in Arabic characters, from which those misspelt in modern catalogues may be corrected, as also from Ulugh Beigh.

Gemini.

THE TWINS, THE UNITED.

Prophecies corresponding with the figures and the names.		Texts where the word or its root is used in this sense in the Hebrew Bible.	Hebrew roots.
	Hebrew name, Thaumim, *the united.* twined	Ex. 26. 24.	תאם
Ps. 22. 20.	Arabic, Al Tauman, *the twins, or pair.*		
Zec. 6. 13;	Syriac, as the Hebrew.		
*13. 7.	Coptic, Pi Mahi, *the united. as in brotherhood*	Zech. 11. 14.	אחה
	— Clusus, or Claustrum Hori, *station of the coming.* *wayfaring men*	Jer. 9. 2, [E.V.	ארח
	Greek, Didumoi, *twins.* Sept. Cant. iv. 5.		
	Latin, Gemini, *twins.* Vulg. Gen. xxv. 24; *fellow.*	Zech. 13. 7.	עם

Names in the Sign.

Prophecies corresponding with the figures and the names.		Texts where the word or its root is used in this sense in the Hebrew Bible.	Hebrew roots.
Jer. 23. 5; 33. 15.	Heb., Propus, *the branch, spreading.* { bough spread	Isa. 10. 33. Hab. 1. 8.	פר פש
Gen. 3. 15.	— ε Mebsuta, *treading under foot.*	Isa. 14. 19.	בס
*Ps. 16. 8.	Arab., Wasat, *set.* appointed	Gen. 4. 25.	שת
Rev. 22. 20.	— Al Giauzâ, *the palm branch, stem.*	Isa. 11. 1.	גוע
	— γ Al Henah, in the foot, *hurt, afflicted.* sorrow	Gen. 35. 18.	אנה
Isa. 11. 1.	— Al Dirâ, *the seed (or branch).*	Gen. 3. 15.	זרע
Zech. 3. 8; 6. 12.	Gr. and Lat., α { Castor, *bearing an arrow, haste.*	Deut. 32. 35.	חש
	— { Apollo, *ruler, or judge.*	Job 31. 11.	
Mic. 5. 2.	— — β { Pollux, bearing a branch, *ruler, or judge.* {	Deut. 32. 31.	פלל
	— — { Hercules, bearing a branch or club, *coming to suffer.* { to suffer grief	Jer. 9. 1. Isa. 53. 3.	חל

First Decan.

(Called the HARE.)   THE ENEMY, or Serpent.

Prophecies corresponding with the figures and the names.		Texts where the word or its root is used in this sense in the Hebrew Bible.	Hebrew roots.
Isa. 27. 1.	Heb., Arnebo, *the enemy of him that cometh.* { enemies he that cometh	Ps. 139. 20. Ps. 118. 26.	ער בא
Ps. 110. 1.	— Nibal, *the mad.* fool	1 Sa. 25. 25.	נבל
	— Rakis, *the bound (Arab., with a chain).*	Ex. 28. 28.	רכס
Rev. 20.	— Sugia, *the deceiver.*	Job 12. 16.	שג
	Arab., Arnebeth, *the hare, enemy of what cometh.* pluck	Ps. 80. 12.	ארה
	Lat., Lepus, *the hare, treading under foot.*	Ps. 108. 13.	בס

Second Decan.

(Called the DOG, or Wolf.)   SIRIUS, The Prince.

Prophecies corresponding with the figures and the names.		Texts where the word or its root is used in this sense in the Hebrew Bible.	Hebrew roots.
		Gen. 49. 27.	זאב
*Isa. 9. 6.	Heb., α Sirius, *the prince.*	Isa. 9. 6.	שר
Isa. 32. 1.	— Aschere, *who shall come.* go	Prov. 4. 14.	אשר
Gen. 35. 18.	Arab., Al Shira Al Jemeniya, *the prince, or chief of the right hand.*	Jon. 4. 11.	ימן
Acts 5. 31.	Egyptian name, Seir, *the prince.* (E. V.)	Isa. 9. 6.	שר
Ps. 110. 1.	Heb., Abur, *the mighty.*	Gen. 49. 24.	} אבר
	Arab., Al Habor, *the mighty.*	Isa. 1. 24.	
Isa. 4. 2; 11. 10.	— ε Adhara, *the glorious.* (Al Adra, Aludra.)	Ex. 15. 6.	אדר
	— β Mirzam, *the prince or* ruler	Ps. 2. 2.	רזן
	— Muliphen, *the leader, the chief.* duke	Gen. 36. 15.	אלף
Isa. 55. 4.	— δ Wesen, *the bright, shining.* scarlet	Josh. 2. 18.	שן

Third Decan.

(Called the SECOND DOG.)   PROCYON, The Redeemer.

Prophecies corresponding with the figures and the names.		Texts where the word or its root is used in this sense in the Hebrew Bible.	Hebrew roots.
Isa. 49. 26; 59. 20.	Heb., α Procyon, *the Redeemer.* redeemed	Ps. 136. 24.	פרק
	Arab., Al Shira, Al Shemeliya, { *the prince, or chief of the left hand*	Dan. 12. 1. Jon. 4. 11.	שר שמל
Mic. 5. 2.	— Al Mirzam, *the prince or ruler.*	Ps. 2. 2.	רזן
	— Al Gomeyra, *who completes, perfects.*	Ps. 138. 8.	גמר
Isa. 53. 12.	— β Al Gomeisa, *the burdened, loaded, bearing for others.* {	Ps. 68. 19. Zech. 12. 3.	עמס

In the First Decan, according to the Persians, there was a serpent, also in the Egyptian zodiac, in the French Egypte. Zeeb, *the wolf,* in Arabic means *coming quickly;* in Heb., *this shall come.* In the Persian sphere, the Second Decan was figured as a wolf: one of the Twins had also the head of a wolf in some Oriental zodiacs. Some ancient forms of this sign are said by Hyde to have been two kids. (Dupuis, Richer.)

TABLE III.

Cancer.

THE CRAB OR SCARABÆUS, HOLDING THE POSSESSION.

Prophecies corresponding in word or type with the figures and the names.	Cancer.	Texts where the word or its root is used in this sense in the Hebrew Bible.	Hebrew roots.
*Gen. 49. 11. John 10. 28.	Hebrew name, Sartan, *who holds, or binds.*		
	Arabic, Al Sartan, *the same.* [*binding*	Gen. 49. 11.	אסר
	Syriac, Sartano, *the same.*		
	Coptic, Klaria, *the cattle-folds.* *folds*	Ps. 50. 9.	מכלא
Num. 24. 18.	Greek, Karkinos, *the crab,* } *holding, encircling*		
Eph. 1. 14.	Latin, { Cancer, *the crab,* } *the possession*	Gen. 26. 14.	קנה
	{ Cer, *encircling,* Arab. sense.		כר
	Names in the Sign.		
Isa. 60. 6.	Heb., Præsepe, the nebula, *a multitude, off-* { *young spring.*	Deut. 22. 6. Isa. 60. 6.	פרח שפע
	Heb. and Arab., α Acubene, *the sheltering. hiding-place*	Isa. 32. 2.	חבא
	— — Ma'alaph, *assembled thousands.*	Ps. 144. 13.	אלף
Isa. 40. 11.	Arab., Al Himarein, *the kids, or lambs.*	Ezra 6. 9.	אמר
	Gr., Nepa, *grasping.* *lifted up*	Deut. 27. 5.	נוף
	Lat., Asellus Boreas, and Asellus Australis. Vulg. *she-ass*	Gen. 49. 11.	אתן

First Decan.
URSA MINOR, (Called the LESSER BEAR.)
The Lesser Fold, or Flock.

Prophecies	First Decan	Texts	Hebrew roots
		Ps. 33. 20.	חכה
John 10. 4, 16.	Heb., β Kochab, *waiting him who cometh.* { *wait* { *come*	Gen. 49. 18. Ibid. 10.	קוה בא
	Arab., Al Pherkadain, *the calves,* { (Heb., *the redeemed* *young.* Deut. xxii. 6. { *assembly*)	Ps. 136. 24. Exod. 12. 3.	פרק עדר
	— Al Gedi, *the kid.* *kid*	Judg. 6. 19.	גדי
	— Al Ruccaba, *the pole-star, the turned, or ridden on.*		רכב
Ps. 23. 3.	— Al Kaid, *assembled,* as in Ursa Major.		
	Gr. and } α Cynosura, { *centre or* *base*	Ezr. 3. 3.	כן
	Lat., } { *of the constellations. Mazzaroth*	Job 38. 32.	נזר
	— Arcas, or Arctos, *travelling company.*	Gen. 37. 25.	ארחת

Second Decan.
URSA MAJOR, (called the GREAT BEAR.)
The Sheepfold and Sheep.

Prophecies	Second Decan	Texts	Hebrew roots
Isa. 60. 7. Mic. 2. 12.	Heb. name, Ash, *the assembled,* (Arcturus.) Job ix. 9. *assemble*	Joel 3. 11.	עש
	Arab., α Dubheh, *herd of animals.* Chald. *wealth.* Heb. *strength*	Deut. 33. 25.	דבא
	— El Acola, *the sheepfold.* Ps. xcv. 7; c. 3.	Ps. 78. 70.	מכלה
Zech. 9. 16.	— Benet Nash, *daughters of the assembly* Joel iii. 11. *daughters*	Cant. 1. 5.	בנת
Ps. 77. 20.	— Cab'd al Asad, *wealth or multitude* { *many* { *assembled*	Nah. 3. 15. Gen. 49. 6.	כבר סד
	— Annaish, *the assembled,* as Ash.	Joel 3. 11.	
Isa. 40. 11; 60. 7.	Heb., β Merach, *the flock* (Arab., *purchased*).	Jer. 10. 21.	רע
	— Megrez, *separated, as the flock in the fold. cut off*	Ps. 31. 22.	נרז
Jer. 23. 3.	— Phacad, or Phacda, *visited, guarded, numbered.*	Zech. 10. 3.	פקד
	— ε Mizar, *separate.*	Num. 6. 3.	מזר

The Scarabæus is thought to have been the original emblem in Cancer. Sartan, who holds, would well apply to the "sacred beetle" of the Egyptians, who holds its "progeny" fast even in death. The Scarabæus was placed here in the Persian sphere.

Some of the Arabs called Ursa Major El Naish, the bier, or funeral *assembly.* (Ideler, Hyde, Barnes, &c.) The Christian Arabs called it the funeral of Lazarus, with Mary and Martha walking after it. (Hyde, &c.)

TABLE IV.

Prophecies corresponding in word or type with the figures and the names.	CANCER (continued).		Texts where the word or its root is used in this sense in the Hebrew Bible.	Hebrew roots.
John 10. 16.	Heb., ε Alioth, *the she-goat, or ewe.*		Ps. 78. 71.	עלה
	— ι Talita, *the lamb.*		Isa. 40. 11.	טלה
	Arab., Al Cor, *the lamb.*		Deut. 32.14.	כר
	— El Kaphrah, *protected, covered* (Heb., *redeemed, ransomed*).		Ex. 30. 12.	כפר
Ezek.34.11, 12; 36. 37.	— Dubheh Lachar, *the latter herd, or flock.*	*latter*	Hag. 2. 9.	אחר
	— η Al Kaiad, *the assembled.*	*together*	Gen. 13. 6.	יחר
	Gr., Helikè, *company of travellers, walking,* (Iliad.)	*companies*	Job 6. 19.	הלך
	— Amaza, *coming, and going.*	*to and fro*	Gen. 8. 7.	יצא
	— Arctos, *travelling.*	*company*	Gen. 37. 25.	ארחת
John 10. 1.	— Calisto, *the sheepfold, set or appointed.*	{ *sheepfold* *appointed* }	Ps. 78. 70. Gen. 4. 25.	מכלא שת
	Lat., Ursa, *the bear, the strong.*	*mighty*	Job 6. 23.	ערץ

Third Decan.

ARGO, (called the SHIP.)

Ps. 68. 11.	Heb., Argo, *the company of travellers.*		Gen. 37. 25.	ארח
Ps. 2. 8.	— Sephina, *the multitude, nebula?*	*abundance*	Deut. 33.19.	שפע
	— Tureis, *the possession.*		Num. 24.18.	ירש
Isa. 49. 12;	— α Canopus, or { *the possession*		Gen. 26. 14.	קנה
*60. 6.	— Canobus, { *of him who cometh.*		Ps. 96. 13.	בא
	— Asmidiska, *the released who travel.*	{ *release* *run* }	Deut. 15. 9. Joel 2. 9.	שמט שק
Hag. 2. 7.	Arab., Soheil, *the desired.*	*asked*	1 Sam.1.27.	שאל
Isa. 4. 2.	— Subilon, *the branch.*		Zech. 4. 12.	שבל
Jer. 23. 5.	Gr. and Lat., Argo, *the company of travellers.*	{	Gen. 37. 25. Job 6. 19.	ארח

AUTHORITIES (continued).

Decan, *a part* or *piece*, Heb. and Arab. Dan. ii. 45. דיק.

Decans are divisions of a sign, each occupying about a third. This division is said to have been introduced into Egypt by King Necepsos, about 730 years B.C. The Decans are here arranged from a work by Albumazer, Flor. Astro., a Latin translation of which is in the Library of the British Museum. Albumazer speaks of them as in the Persian, Egyptian, and Indian spheres. The Persians, he says, understood, but the Indians perverted them with inventions. He describes them from both. Amidst considerable variations, analogies may be traced to the constellations as now figured. Of the Signs and other thirty-six constellations as received in his time, he says, all the names and figures had been transmitted unaltered.

Albumazer, or Abu Masher, lived about the year 800 (A.D.). He is known as a great Arab physician and astronomer. At that time astronomy was much studied by the Arabs: it had also been cultivated by the Gerbanites, a sect of Arab astronomers, some centuries before the Christian era. Lyell, in his Geology, says of them, "These were evidently great astronomers." Ricciolus, an astronomical writer A.D. 1598, says that it appears from Arab astronomy, that it was as old as Adam, and the names preserved by the Arabs antediluvian. Aben Ezra, a celebrated Jewish writer who lived in the thirteenth century, refers to Albumazer as a great authority. He records that Auriga was called the Shepherd by the ancient Hebrews.

Ulugh Beigh, a Tartar prince and astronomer who lived about the middle of the fifteenth century, is considered to have transmitted the ancient Arabian science. His catalogue of the stars was printed by Dr. Hyde, with Commentaries, about 1660. See Hyde's Syntagma, &c. It has been since reprinted in England.

None of the Arabic names in Ursa Major and Minor have any reference to a bear. Dub in Hebrew is a bear; Dubhè is strength in Hebrew and Chaldee.[*] The bear was probably so named from its strength. El Acola, Hebrew and Arabic, is explicitly sheepfold, as other names are sheep and flock. In the Persian sphere there are three damsels walking, as "the daughters of Ash," and the same figures in Ursa Minor and Argo. There is no trace of a ship in any of them.

---

[*] Buxtorf.

Leo.

THE LION, THE SEPARATING.

Prophecies corresponding with the figures and the names.		Texts where the word or its root is used in this sense in the Hebrew Bible.	Hebrew roots.
Gen. 3. 15.	Hebrew name, Arieh, *the lion rending.* pluck	Ps. 80. 12.	ארה
*Gen. 49. 9.	Arabic, Al Asad, *the lion, who rends, who wasteth.*	Ps. 91. 6.	שד
Num. 23. 24; 24. 9.			
Prov. 19. 12.	Syriac, Aryo, *the lion, who rends.*		
Hos. 13. 3. ⎱ Mat. 25. 32 ⎰	Coptic, Pi-Mentekeon, *the plucking asunder.*	Jer. 22. 24.	נתק
Prov. 20. 2.	Greek, Leon, *the lion.* Sept. Gen. xlix. 9.		
Ezek. 1. 10.	N. T. Rev. v. 5.		
Rev. 4. 7.	Latin, Leo, *the lion.* Arab. and Syr. *coming vehemently, leaping forth as a flame.*		
	Vulg. *the same.*	Exod. 3. 2.	לבה

Names in the Sign.

Ps. 91. 13.	Heb., α Regulus, *the treading under foot.*	Isa. 32. 20.	רגל
Ps. 50. 2.	— Zosma, *the shining forth.* sparkled	Ezek. 1. 7.	צץ
Matt. 24. 27.	— Sarcam, *the joining.* wrapped together	Job 40. 17.	שרג
	Arab., Minchir al Asad, *the punishing, tearing, of the lion,* (*piercing.*)	Job 30. 17.	נקר
Isa. 2. 11.	— γ Al Giebha, *the exaltation.*	Ezek. 17. 24.	נבה
Enoch in Jude, 14.	Heb., β Denebola, *the judge or Lord who cometh* ⎱ Lord ⎰ *quickly.* ⎱ hasty ⎰	Ps. 110. 1. Eccle. 7. 9.	דן בהל
	— Deneb, Aleced, *the judge cometh, who* ⎱ *judge* ⎰ *seizes.* ⎱ catch ⎰	Ps. 50. 4; 35. 8.	דן לכד
	— Arab. Al Defera, *the enemy put down.* thrust down	Job 32. 13.	דפה

First Decan.
HYDRA, The Serpent.

Rev. 20. 2, 3, 10.	Heb., Hydra, *he is the abhorred.*	Isa. 66. 24.	דראון
	Arab., α Al Phard, *the separated.*	Prov. 19. 4.	פרד
	— Al Drian, *the abhorred.*	Isa. 66. 24.	דראון
	— Minchir al Sugia, *piercing of the deceiver.* ⎱ ⎰	Job 30. 17; 12. 16.	נקר שג

Second Decan.
CRATER, The Cup.

Ps. 75. 8.			
Rev. 16. 19.	Heb. and Arab., Al Ches, *the cup.* Also reckoned in Hydra.	Ps. 75. 8. Isa. 51. 17.	כס

Third Decan.
CORVUS, The Crow, or Raven.

Ezek. 39. 17.	Heb., Chiba, *the accursed.*	Num. 23. 8.	קבה
	Arab., Al Gorab, *the raven.*	Lev. 11. 15.	ערב
Rev. 19. 17.	— Al Chibar, *the joining together.* coupled	Exod. 26. 3.	חבר
	— Minchir al Gorab, *piercing of the raven.*		

"The Lion of the tribe of Judah" (Rev. v. 5) is known to have been always borne on the standard of Judah, whether in the wilderness (Num. ii.), or in after-times. Bailly says the zodiac must have been first divided when the sun at the summer solstice was in 1° Virgo, where the Woman's head joins the Lion's tail. Necepsos and Petosiris, Egyptian astronomers about 700 B.C., taught that at the creation the sun rose in Leo, at the summer solstice, the moon in Cancer.

Dupuis says, "The ancient Persians called the starry serpent the Serpent of Eve." He refers to a book of Zoroaster, the Boundesh, which he calls their Genesis. The same star, Al Chibar, *the joined,* is reckoned both in the Raven and in Hydra; as El Nath in the horn of Taurus and in the heel of Auriga, Antares in the head of Scorpio and the heel of Ophiuchus, &c. By these junctions the places of the figures were preserved; also by naming one star as the head, as Ras al Awa in Ophiuchus, others the hand, as Caph in Cassiopeia, and Rigol, the foot, in Orion. Ulugh Beigh thus describes most of the constellations.

TABLE V.

Virgo.

THE WOMAN, BEARING THE BRANCH.

Prophecies corresponding with the figures and the names.		Texts where the word or its root is used in this sense in the Hebrew Bible.	Hebrew roots.
Isa. 11. 1.	Hebrew name, Bethulah, *a virgin*, Arab. *branch*.	Gen. 24. 16.	בתלה
Jer. 23. 5; 33. 15.	Arabic, Sunbula, *who bears*. carry	Isa. 46. 4.	סבל
Zech. 3. 8; 6. 12.	— Sunbul, *ear of corn*.	Job 24. 24.	שבל
	Syriac, Bethulto, as Bethulah.		
Ps. 80. 15.	Copt., Aspolia, *station of the desired, the branch*.	Zech. 4. 12.	שבל
	Greek, Parthenos, *the virgin*. Sept. Isa. vii. 14.		
Isa. 7. 14. Mic. 5. 3.	Latin, Virgo, *the virgin*, Virga, *branch*. Vulg. Isa. xi. 1.	Isa. 5. 24.	פרח
	Names in the Sign.		
*Isa. 4. 2.	Arab., *a* Al Zimach, *the branch or shoot*, the star now called Spica. {	Isa. 4. 2; 11. 1.	צמח
	— Subilah, *who carries*. Isa. xlvi. 4.		
	— Aziman, *two ears of corn*. {	Jer. 23. 5. Zech. 3. 8.	צמח
	— Al Azal, *the branch*.	Isa. 18. 5.	זל
	— Subilon, *the spike of corn*. ears	Isa. 17. 5.	שבל
	First Decan.		
Gen. 3. 15. Isa. 9. 6.	COMA, the Branch or Infant near or held by the Woman.		
	Names of the Woman.		
	Heb., Subilah, *who bears*.	Isa. 46. 4.	סבל
Isa. 7. 14.	Arab., Adarah, *a pure virgin, separated*. chambers	Job 9. 9.	חרר
	— Adrenosa, *the virgin who* carries	Gen. 46. 5.	נשא
	Gr. and Lat., Astrea, *the starry, the bright*.	Ezek. 8. 2.	זהר
	Names of the Infant.		
*Hag. 2. 7.	Heb., Coma, *the desired, longed for*.	Ps. 63. 1.	כמה
*Isa. 26. 8,9.	Arab., Al Awa, *the desired*.	Gen. 3. 6.	אוה
	— Al Zimon, *the desired*.	Ps. 42. 2.	צמא
	— Al Thaum, *the twin, or united*.	Exod. 26. 24.	תאם
Zech. 13. 7.	— Aleced, *the united*. darling	Ps. 22. 20.	יחד
	— β Zavijavah, *the glorious*, (Arab. form.) beautiful	Isa. 4. 2.	צאי
*Ps. 72. 8.	— ε Al Mureddin, *who shall come down, shall have dominion*. {	Ps. 72. 6. Ibid. 8.	ירד רדה
Isa. 4. 2.	— Hazamethon, *the branch*, (in Coma.) { branch	Ps. 80. 15.	בן
Zech. 9. 10.	Chald., Vindemiatrix, *the son, who cometh, or the branch*. { son come	Num. 24. 17.	דרד
	Gr., Prometheus, *the deliverer, who cometh*, { avenging came	Judg. 5. 2. Deut. 33. 2.	פרע אתא
	or the branch (Arab.) *who cometh*. bough	Lev. 23. 40.	פרי
	Second Decan.		
	CENTAURUS, a figure half human, half horse, holding a dart and an animal.		
	Names in the Figure.		
*Isa. 53. 3. Dan. 9. 26.	Heb., Beze, } *the despised*. Arab., Al Beze, }	Isa. 53. 3.	בנה
*Isa. 53. 10.	Heb., Asmeath, *the sin-offering*.	Lev. 5. 6.	אשם

Bethulah in Arabic is the sucker or branch of the palm (Castel), also a virgin. Beu in Hebrew branch, also son, as in Ps. lxxx. 15, 17.

In the Pythian procession, the Greeks spoke of breaking from the laurel "the atoning bough." The branch-bearing sibyl of the Æneid will here be traced.

The First Decan of Virgo, Albumazer says, was every where a woman with an infant. In the planisphere of Dendera, the woman, as the sign. carries the branch : below is a woman holding an infant. The palm-branches, John xii. 13, with which the multitudes greeted the entry of our Lord into Jerusalem, acknowledged him as the promised "Branch," Zech. iii. 8, &c.

Baion is the comer, from Bao, to come. Erigone (Georg. I.), who bears the coming One.

TABLE VI.

Prophecies corresponding with the figures and the names.	VIRGO (continued).	Texts where the word or its root is used in this sense in the Hebrew Bible.	Hebrew roots.
	α Toliman (in the foot), *the heretofore and hereafter.*	Deut. 32. 7. Ps. 10. 16.	עלם
Isa. 9. 6.	Gr., Chiron, *the pierced, who pierces.*	Ps. 22. 16.	כאר
	— Pholas, *the mediator.* prayed	Gen. 20. 7, 17.	פלל
Zech. 12. 10.	Lat., Rex. Centaurus, *the king, the centaur,* { king, smitten, who cometh	Isa. 32. 1. Isa. 53. 4. Job 34. 8.	מלך נכה ארח

Third Decan.

BOOTES, a human figure as walking, bearing a branch.

Names in the Figure.

*Ps. 96. 13.	Heb., Bootes, *the coming.* coming	Ps. 121. 8.	בא
Ps. 121. 3.	— α Arcturus, { *he cometh.* yoeth, *the guardian, keeper.* Ps. cxxi. 5. keeper	Job 34. 8. Cant. 1. 6.	ארח נטר
Hag. 2. 7.	— Mirach, *the coming forth, as an arrow.* shoot	Ps. 64. 7.	ירה
Isa. 40. 10.	— ε Mizar, or Izar, *guarding, the preserver.* preserver	Job 7. 20.	נצר
Ps. 91. 13.	— Muphride, *who separates.* separate	Gen. 13. 9.	פרד
	Arab., Aramech, *being sent forth, as a dart.* bowman	Jer. 4. 29.	רמח
	Heb., Merga, *who bruises.* break	Ps. 2. 9.	רע
*Zec. 12. 10.	— Nekkar, *the pierced.* Zech. xii. 10. pierced	Ps. 22. 16.	כאר
Gen. 3. 15.	Arab., Al Katurops, *the branch, treading* { rod	Isa. 11. 1.	חטר
Isa. 63. 1.	*under foot.* { stamped	Dan. 7. 7.	רפס
	Gr., Arctophylax, *the guardian of Arctos.* Acts v. 23. keeper		
	— α Arcturus, *the star so called.* Sept. Job ix. 9.		

Albumazer describes Virgo as "a sign of two parts and three forms." Apparently the woman and the branch are the two parts, the ears of corn the third form. He then says, "There arises in the First Decan, as the Persians, Chaldeans, and Egyptians, the two Hermes, and Ascalius teach, a young woman, whose Persian name translated into Arabic is Adrenedefa *, a pure and immaculate virgin, holding in the hand two ears of corn, sitting on a throne, nourishing an infant, in the act of feeding him, who has a Hebrew name (the boy, I say), by some nations named Ihesu, with the signification Ieza, which we in Greek call Christ." Ieza is evidently the Hebrew verb "yesha," to save.

The infant seems to have been figured in this place in the time of Shakespear, as in Titus Andronicus an arrow is to be shot up to "the good boy in Virgo's lap." Coma (the desired in the Oriental dialects, the head of hair in Greek and Latin) seems to occupy the place of the branch. From the Greek meaning of the word, the Alexandrian astronomer seems to have taken the idea of calling it the hair of Berenice. That princess had given her hair as a votive offering for the safety of her brother. It was lost; and Conon met the difficulty by the assurance that it shone in heaven in the constellation Coma.

Layard gives the figure of an Assyrian goddess who holds an infant in her arms, and reads her name Mylitt, or Mylitta, which would be "she who brings forth." Eratosthenes called Virgo Isis. Isis, with other Egyptian goddesses differently named, is often figured holding the infant deity Horus, he who cometh. From Gaffarelli it appears that "the ancient Arabs figured Virgo as a fruitful branch." The Christian Arabs placed an infant near Virgo, as Coma.

In the sacred books of the Chinese, it was said that "a virgin should bring forth a child in the West."

Among the Gauls, 100 B.C., an altar was found with this inscription, "To the virgin who is to bring forth."

The Taurians in the Crimea had human sacrifices to a virgin. Krishna, in India, Mexitli, in Mexico, had no human father.

All these nations had the zodiac, where they might find the woman and the branch; but that the woman was a virgin, the infant the seed of the woman, prophecy only could have told them. R. Ben Jochai on Gen. iii. speaks of Messiah as to be born of a virgin, probably from Isaiah vii.

The brightest star in the Centaur has been observed by Sir John Herschell to be growing rapidly brighter: it seems, therefore, one of the changeable stars. The name Toliman, annexed to it by Ulugh Beigh, the star of heretofore and hereafter, indicates an early observation of its changes.

Bootes has by all antiquity been called the guardian of the constellations called the Great and Little Bear. The name Arcturus has been given to the figure, as well as to its brightest star.

---

* Adrenedefa, Heb. a pure virgin, *offering.* Exod. xxxv. 29.

𝕷𝖎𝖇𝖗𝖆.

THE SCALES, THE REDEEMING.

Prophecies corresponding with the figures and the names.		Texts where the word or its root is used in this sense in the Hebrew Bible.	Hebrew roots.
*Isa. 40. 12.	Hebrew name of the sign, Mozanaim, *the scales, weighing.*	Isa. 40. 12.	אזן
Ps. 130. 8.	Arabic, Al Zubena, *purchase, redemption, gain.*	Dan. 2. 8.	זבן
Ex. 15. 16.	Syriac, Mazatho, *scales.*		
Deut. 32. 6.	Coptic, Lambadia, *station of propitiation.*	Prov. 18. 8.	להם
Isa. 60. 12.	Lam, Arab. *graciousness ;* badia, *branch.*	Ezek. 17. 6.	בד
Isa. 63. 9.	Greek, Zugos. Sept. Isa. xl. 12. N. T. Rev. vi. 5.		
Rev. 5. 9.	Latin, Libra, *weighing.* Vulg. Isa. xl. 12.		

Names in the Sign.

	Heb., Graffias, *swept away.*	Jud. 5. 21.	
Ps. 74. 2.	Arab., α Zuben al Genubi, *the purchase or price which is deficient.* *stolen*	Gen. 31. 39.	גנב
1 Cor. 6. 20.	— Zuben al Shemali, *the purchase which covers.*		
Acts 20. 28.	*raiment*	Deut. 10. 18.	שמל
	— Zubenelg, and Zubenesh, corruptions of the above.		
	— Al Gubi, *heaped up, high.*	Ps. 68. 15.	נב
Ephes. 1. 14.	— Zuben Akrabi, *redemption of the conflict.* *battle*	Ps. 55. 18.	קרב
Rev. 14. 4.	Syr., Zuben, *buying, gaining.*		

First Decan.
THE CROSS.

	The Mark of Boundary, or Limitation { *bound* { *mark*	Gen. 49. 26. / Ezek. 9. 4.	תאו
Dan. 9. 26.	Hebrew name, Adom, *cutting off,*	Isa. 38. 10.	רם
Num. 21. 8.	Given by Aben Ezra as the name of the South Polar Constellation, which ancient tradition said was in the form of a cross, as was the pole on which the brazen serpent was lifted up. Num. xxi. 8.		
John 12. 32.			

Second Decan.

THE VICTIM, the animal held by the Centaur.

Names of the Figure.

Isa. 53. 7.			
Ps. 118. 27.	Heb., Aseda, *to be slain.* *destroyed*	Ps. 137. 8.	שד
Zech. 12. 10.	Arab., Asedaton, *the same.*		
	Gr., Thera, *beast.* Sept. { Gen. viii. 19. { Gen. xlix. 27.		
	— Lycos, *wolf.*		
	Lat., Victima, Bestia, *the victim, the animal.* Vulg. Gen. viii. 17.		

Third Decan.

THE NORTHERN CROWN.

Names of the Figure.

*Ps. 21. 3 ;	Heb., Atarah, *a kingly crown.* { *crown* { *encompassing*	Cant. 3. 11. / Zech. 6. 11. / 1 Sa. 23. 26.	עטר
132. 18.			
Rev. 19. 12;	Arab., Al Iclil, *ornament, or jewel.*	Gen. 24. 53.	כלי
14. 14.	Gr., Stephanos. Sept., Zech. vi. 11. N. T. Rev. vi. 2.		
	Lat., Corona. Vulg., Zech. vi. 11. N. T. Rev. vi. 2.		

Name of the chief Star.

	Arab., α Al Phecca, *the shining.*	Ps. 50. 2.	יפע

The emblem of the Scales, or Balance, is found in all the Eastern zodiacs. In some it is said to have been held in the claws of the Scorpion; whence Chelæ, the claws, was sometimes substituted in the West for Libra. (Virg. Georg.)

In the Persian sphere, the First Decan was a man as in wrath, holding a balance in one hand, a lamb in the other. Thau, bound or limit, *finished,* is the name of the last letter of the Hebrew alphabet, originally in the form of a cross. Long before the Christian era, the cross was a most sacred emblem among the Egyptians. A few days before the sun entered Aries, the ancient Persians had the feast of the cross. At that time the Southern Cross was visible by night, probably about 10° above the horizon. They called Aries, the Lamb. (Dupuis, &c.)

TABLE VII.

Prophecies corresponding with the figures and the names.	Scorpio. THE SCORPION, THE CONFLICT.	Texts where the word or its root is used in this sense in the Hebrew Bible.	Hebrew roots.
Gen. 3. 15.	Hebrew name, Akrab, *the scorpion, or the conflict.* { *war*	Ps. 91. 13.	עקרב
		Ps. 144. 1.	קרב
*Ps. 91. 13.	Arabic, Al Akrab, *the same, wounding Him*	Gen. 49. 6.	עקר
Isa. 53.	Syriac, *the same.* [*that cometh.*	Gen. 49. 10.	בא
	Coptic, Isidis, *attack of the enemy.* *oppress*	Ps. 17. 9.	שד
	Greek, Scorpios. { Sept. and Vulg. } Ps. xci. 13. N.T. Rev. ix. 3. Latin, Scorpio. *cleaving in conflict.*		
	battle	Job 38. 23.	(ש)קרב
	Names in the Sign.		
	Heb., Lesath, *in the figure of the Scorpion, the perverse.*	Prov. 4. 24.	לות
	Arab., Al Kalb, *the cleaving as in conflict, the enemy. dog*	Ps. 22. 16.	כלב
Zech. 13. 6.	— a Antares, *the wounding.* (Arab. form.) (*cutting.*)	Jer. 36. 23.	תער
	First Decan. THE SERPENT, held by Ophiuchus.		
Gen. 3. 14.	Heb., Alyah, *the accursed.*	Judg. 17. 2.	אלה
	— a Unuk, *encompassing.*	Ps. 73. 6.	ענק
	Arab., Al Hay, *the reptile.* *living thing*	Gen. 8. 17.	חיה
	Second Decan. OPHIUCHUS, Or Serpentarius, a human figure grasping the serpent, treading on the scorpion.		
Ps. 91. 13.	Heb. and Arab., Afeichus, { *the serpent.* *viper*	Isa. 59. 5.	אפע
	{ *held.* *take*	Exod. 4. 4.	אחז
	Arab., β Cheleb, or Chelbalrai, *in the serpent, enfolding.*		
	Heb., Triophas, *treading under foot.* *stamped*	Dan. 7. 7.	רפס
	— Saigh, *in the foot, bruised.*	Gen. 3. 15.	שוף
	— Carnebus, *the wounding.* { *pierced*	Ps. 22. 10.	כאר
	{ *treading on*	Ps. 60. 12.	בם
Isa. 63. 1.	— Megeros, *contending.* *conflict*	Ps. 39. 11.	גרה
	Arab., a Ras al Hagus, *head of him who holds.* *take*	Exod. 4. 4.	אחז
	— Ras al Awa, *as in Hercules.* *head*	Isa. 9. 15.	ראש
	Hercules, al Rai, Marsic, *as in Hercules.* Gr., Ophiuchus, *holder of the serpent* (as Afeichus). — Esculapius, Cheleb, *who holds, and Afei, the serpent.* Persian, Affalius, *serpent-holder.* Lat., Serpentarius, *holder of the serpent.*		
	Third Decan. HERCULES, A human figure kneeling on one knee, holding a branch, the other foot over the head of Draco. *Names of the Figure.*		
	Arab., El Giscale, *the strong.* *wounded* {	Ps. 24. 8.	עז
		Isa. 53. 5.	חלה
	Heb., Marsic, *the wounding.* (Sept. and Vulg.) *sword*	Ps. 42. 10.	רצח
Gen. 3. 15.	— Caiam, *punishing* (Arab., *treading under foot*). *chastening*	Job 5. 17.	יכה
Isa. 53.	— Ma'asym, *the sin-offering.*	Isa. 53. 10.	אשם
	— β Kornephorus, *the branch, kneeling.* { *kneeling*	Judg. 7. 5.	כרע
	{ *boughs*	Lev. 23. 40.	פרת
	Arab., a Ras al Gethi, *head of him who bruises. press*	Lam. 1. 15.	גת
Hag. 2. 7.	— Ras al Awa, *head of the desired.*	Isa. 26. 8.	אוה
	— Al Rai, *who bruises, breaks.*	Ps. 2. 9.	רע
	Gr., Engonasin, *who kneels.* Sept. Judg. vii. 5. *goeth*	Job 34. 8.	ארח
	Lat., Hercules, { *who cometh to labour, to suffer.*	Isa. 53. 3, 4.	חלה
	{ *the strong.* *strength*	2 Sa. 22. 40.	יחל

The same star has always been reckoned in the head of Hercules as Ras al Gethi, the head of him who bruises, and Ras al Awa, head of the Desired, and also in Ophiuchus as Ras al Hagus, head of him who holds, and Ras al Awa, head of the Desired. Thus is shown that the two figures relate to the same person, the conqueror of the serpent, the Desire of nations. Hag. ii. 7.

TABLE VIII. C 2

𝔖𝔞𝔤𝔦𝔱𝔱𝔞𝔯𝔦𝔲𝔰.

Prophecies corresponding with the figures and the names.		Texts where the word or its root is used in this sense in the Hebrew Bible.	Hebrew roots.
Ps. 45. 4, 5.	**THE ARCHER, THE GOING FORTH.**		
Mic. 5. 2.	Hebrew name of the Sign, Kesith, *the archer,*	Gen. 21. 20.	קשת
*Gen. 10.13.	*or the bow*	Gen. 49. 24.	
Heb.3.9,11.	Arabic, Al Kaus, *the arrow.* *arrows*	Ps. 45. 5.	חץ
	Syriac, Kesith. *the bow*	Hab. 3. 9.	
Rev. 6. 2.	Coptic, Pi-maere, *the going forth.* *shoot*	1 Sa. 20.36.	ירה
	Greek, Toxotes, *the archer.*		
	Latin, Sagittarius, *the archer, who sends forth*	Gen. 49. 23.	חצי
	the arrow.	1 Sa. 20. 20.	ירה
	Names in the Sign.		
Ps. 72. 7.	Heb., Naim, *the Gracious, the delighted in.*	Ps. 27. 4.	נעם
Ps. 68. 11.	— Nushata, *the going or sending forth.* *went about*	Num. 11. 8.	שט
	Arab., Al Naim, *the Gracious, pleasant.*	Ruth 1. 20.	
	— Al Shaula, *the dart.* marg. *dart*	Joel 2. 8.	שלה
	— Al Warida, *who comes forth.* *comes down*	Ps. 72. 6.	ירד
	— Ruchba er rami, *the riding of the bowman.*	Ps. 45. 4, 5.	
	— Urkab er rami, { *the bowman.*	Jer. 4. 29.	רמח
	{ *the rider.*	Ex. 15. 21.	רכב
*Ps. 18. 10.	— Al Naim, Al Sadira, *the Gracious, who strives.* *laboured*	Dan. 6. 14.	שרר
	Heb., Terebellum, *sent forth swiftly.* *hasty* {	1 Sa. 20. 20.	ירה
		Eccle. 7. 9.	בחל
	Gr., Croton, *the purchaser,* (referring to Libra.) *bought*	Hos. 3. 2.	כרה
	First Decan.		
*Ezek. 1.10.	THE EAGLE, holding the Lyre.	Ezek. 1. 10.	נשר
	Heb., β Shelyuk, *the fishing eagle,* Lev. { *sent forth*	Gen. 3. 23.	שלח
	xi. 17. { *to smite*	Ex. 21. 18.	הכה
	— Sulaphat, *springing up.* *groweth*	Ps. 129. 6.	שלף
Rev. 4. 7.	Arab., Al Nesr, *the eagle,* Lev. xi. 13; *coming straight*	1 Sa. 6. 12.	ישר
	Heb., a Vega, *he shall be exalted.* *triumph*	Exod. 15. 1.	נאה
	Lat., Lyra, *the lyre, or harp.*		
	Second Decan. ARA, The Altar.		
Ex. 20. 24, 25.	Arab., Al Mugamra, *the completing, finishing.* *perfect*	Ps. 138. 8.	גמר
Rev. 8. 3.	Gr., Thusiasterion, *altar.* Sept. Gen. viii. 20. Rev. vi. 9.		
	Lat., Ara, *the same.*		
	Third Decan.		
*Ps. 91. 13.	DRACO, The Dragon, or Serpent.	Ps. 91. 13.	
Isa. 27. 1.	Heb., γ Ethanin, *the long serpent or dragon.* {	Ps. 91. 13. / Exod. 7. 9.	תנין
Rev. 20. 2.	— Grumian, *the subtile.*	Gen. 3. 1.	ערם
	— Giansar, *the punished enemy.* { *punishment*	1 Sa. 28. 10.	ענה
	{ *enemy*	Ps. 139. 20.	ער
	— Thuban, *the subtile* (Arab., *serpent*), (*wise*).	Gen. 41. 33.	בין
	— Rastaban, *head of the subtile, or serpent.* *head*	Gen. 3. 15.	ראש
	Arab., Al Dib, *the reptile.*		
	— a Al Waid, *who is to be destroyed.*	Job 21. 17.	איד
	— El Athik, *the fraudful.*	Ps. 10. 7.	תך
	— El Asieh, *the bowed down.* *stoop*	Job 9. 13.	שחח
	Gr., Drakon, the Dragon, Sept. Ps. xci. 13. Rev. xx., *trodden on.* *tread upon*	Deu. 33. 29.	דרך
	Lat., Draco, Vulg., *the same.*		

In the First Decan, the Persian sphere had a man with a crooked beak on his head, like the eagle-god, the Nisroch of Assyrian sculptures. Nesir, the eagle, might be confounded with Shir, music, and have given rise to the figure of the lyre.

TABLE IX.

Prophecies corresponding with the figures and the names.	Capricornus. THE GOAT, THE ATONEMENT SLAIN.	Texts where the word or its root is used in this sense in the Hebrew Bible.	Hebrew roots.
Gen. 4. 4.			
Exod. 12. 5	Hebrew name of the sign, Gedi, *the kid;* *cut off.* *hew down*	Judg. 6. 19. Dan. 4. 14.	גד
	Arabic, Al Gedi, *the same.* *kid*	Ex. 23. 19.	
Isa. 53.	Syriac, Gedi, *the kid, (cut off,* Syr.)		
		Ps. 19. 5.	חף
*Lev. 16.22.	Coptic, Hupenius, *station of bearing.* { *chamber* / *bear* / *borne*	Lev. 16. 22. Isa. 53. 4.	חפה / נשא
	Greek, Aigokereus, *the goat.*		
	Latin, Capricornus, *the goat, the atonement, sinking down.* *bowed*	Ex. 30. 10. Judg. 5. 27.	כפר פרע

Names in the Sign.

Lev. 16.	Syr., Dabih, *the sacrifice slain.*	Gen. 31. 54.	זבח
	Arab., Al Dabih, *the sacrifice slain.*		
	— Al Dshabeh, *the same,* (also *the slaying,* Arab.)		
	— Ma'asad, *the slaying, destroying.*	Ps. 91. 6.	שד
	— Sa'ad al Naschira, *the record of the cutting off.* *record*	1 Chr. 20. 3. Job 16. 19.	כשר שהד
	Heb., Deneb, *the Lord or Judge cometh.* { *Lord* / *Judge* / *cometh*	Ps. 110. 1. Ps. 68. 5. Ps. 40. 7.	דן / בא

First Decan.
SAGITTA, The Arrow.

*Ps. 38. 2.	Heb., Scham, *destroying.* *desolate*	Ezek. 35. 12.	שם
	Anciently said to be the Arrow that slew the Eagle.		

Second Decan.
AQUILA, The Eagle falling.

Zech. 13. 6.	Heb., γ Tarared, *wounded,* { *torn.* / *he cometh down.*	Jer. 36. 23. Ps. 72. 6.	חער ירד
	Arab., α Al Tair, *the wounding.*		
	— { Al Cair, *the piercing.* / Al Okab, *wounded in the heel.*	Ps. 22. 16. Gen. 3. 15.	כאר עקב
	— β Al Shain, *the bright.* *scarlet*	Josh. 2. 18.	שנה
	Heb., Deneb, as above.		

Third Decan.
DELPHINUS,
Called the DOLPHIN, but in the Egyptian planisphere apparently figured as a vessel pouring out water.

Isa. 44. 3.	Heb., Dalaph, *pouring out of water.* *dropping*	Prov. 19. 13.	דלף
	Arab., Dalaph, *coming quickly.*		
Hab. 2. 3.	— Scalooin, *swift (as the flow of water).*	Job 24. 18.	(ש)קל
	Syr. and Chald., Rotaneb, or Rotaneu, *swiftly running (as water in the trough.)*	Ex. 2. 16.	רחט

The Goat always has the body of a fish in all the Eastern spheres, and in those of Egypt. The Greek sphere has an eagle in the Second Decan, with the end of the arrow; in the Third, the dolphin. In the Persian sphere, in the Third there seems to be both a fish and a stream of water.

TABLE X.

Aquarius.
THE WATER-BEARER, THE POURING FORTH.

Prophecies corresponding with the figures and the names.		Texts where the word or its root is used in this sense in the Hebrew Bible.	Hebrew roots.
Isa. 44. 3. *Num.24.7. Hos. 6. 2.	Hebrew name, Deli, *the water-urn.* bucket {	Num. 24. 7. Isa. 40. 15.	דלי
	Arabic, Delu, *the same.*		
John 4. 14; 7. 37.	Syriac, *the same.*		
	Coptic, Hupei Tirion, *the station of pouring out.*	Isa. 32. 15.	ערה
	Greek, Hydrokoeus, *the pourer forth of water.*		
Hos. 6. 2. Joel 2. 28.	Latin, Aquarius, { *the rising up and pouring forth of water.*	Ezek. 47. 5. Isa. 53. 12.	גאה ערה
	Names in the Sign.		
Acts 1. 11.	Heb., Scheat, *who goeth and returneth.* went about	Num. 11. 8	שט
	Arab., α Scheat er Schad, or Saad al Suud, *who goeth and returneth, the pourer out, stream.* stream	Num. 21.15.	שר
	— Ancha, *the vessel of pouring out, the urn.* bowl	Ex. 25. 29.	נקה
	— α Sa'ad al Melik, *record of pouring forth.* } record	Job 16. 19. Joel 3. 18.	שהד ילד
	Mon, or Meon, *an Egyptian name in the urn, vessel or urn.*	Dan. 5. 2.	מאן
	### First Decan.		
Isa. 44. 3. Isa. 65. 13.	PISCIS AUSTRALIS, The Southern Fish, drinking in the water from the urn.		
Ezek. 47. 9.	Arab., α Fom al Haut, *mouth of the fish.* { mouth	Dan. 6. 22 (or 23). Ps. 104. 25.	פם חיות
	### Second Decan. PEGASUS, The Winged Horse.		
*Isa. 64. 5.	Heb., α Markab, *returning from.* afar	Mic. 4. 3.	רחק
Zech. 1. 8.	— β Scheat, *who goeth and returneth (went about).*	Num. 11. 8.	
Lu. 19.12, 15.	— ε Enif, *the branch.* bough	Lev. 23. 40.	ענף
	Arab., Al Genib, *who carries.*		
	— Homan, *the water.*	Gen. 1. 2.	מים
	— Matar, *who causes to overflow.* plenteous	Deut.28.11.	יתר
Rev. 6. 1; 19. 11.	Gr. and Lat., Pegasus, *coming quickly, joy-fully.* { meetest rejoiceth	Isa. 64. 5. Ibid.	פגע שש
	### Third Decan. CYGNUS, The Swan, Bird of Passage.		
Jer. 8. 7.	Heb., Azel, *who goes and returns.* gaddest about	Jer. 2. 36.	זל
Isa. 64. 1.	— Fafage, *glorious, shining forth.*	Deut. 33. 2.	פע
John 14. 3.	— γ Sadr, *who returns, as in a circle.* round about	Isa. 29. 3.	דר
Mat. 24. 30.	— Adige, *flying swiftly.* flieth	Deut. 28.49.	ראה
Acts 1. 11.	— Arided, *he shall come down.* {	Ps. 72. 6. Isa. 64. 1.	ירד
1 Th. 4. 16.	Arab., Al Bireo, *flying quickly.* flee	Gen. 27. 43.	ברח
	Heb., α Deneb, *as in Capricornus.* judge	Ps. 110. 6.	דן
	Gr., Cycnos, *the swan, circling, returning.* circuit	Job 22. 14.	חג
	Lat., Cygnus, *who comes and goes, circles.* circle	Isa. 40. 22.	

---

† These four names, now placed in Pegasus, appeared properly to belong to the human figure in Aquarius.

The urn alone appears in many of the Eastern zodiacs, with the man in others, as in the Egyptian.

In the First Decan, the Persian sphere had a fish, sometimes having a woman's head, a horse in the Second, and a bird in the Third.

TABLE XI.

Pisces.

THE FISHES, THE MULTITUDES, UPHELD.

Prophecies corresponding with the figures and the names.		Texts where the word or its root is used in this sense in the Hebrew Bible.	Hebrew roots.
Gen. 1. 28. *Ezek.47.9.	Hebrew name, Dagim, *the fishes.* {fish / multitude	Ezek. 47. 9. / Gen. 48. 16.	דג
Gen. 15. 5.	Arabic, Al Haut, *the fish.* beasts	Ps. 104. 25.	חיות
Isa. 60. 4.	Syriac, Nuno, *the fish, lengthened out* {son (*as posterity*).	Job 18. 19. / Ps. 72. 17.	נון
Mal. 4. 2.	Coptic, Pi-cot Orion, *fish of him that cometh.* beast	Ps. 104. 25.	חיות
	Greek, Ichthues, *fish.* Sept. Ezek. xlvii. 9.		
	Latin, Pisces, *fish, multiplying.* Vulg. Ezek. xlvii. 9. spread	Hab. 1. 8.	פשה

Names in the Sign.

John 17. 21.	Heb., Okda, *the united.*	Gen. 49. 6.	יחד
Isa. 41. 10.	Arab., Al Samaca, *the upheld.*	Ps. 37. 17.	סמך

First Decan.
THE BAND.

Hos. 11. 4.	Arab., Al Risha, *the band (bridle).*	Ps. 32. 9.	רסן

Second Decan.
CEPHEUS, a human figure holding a branch.

Jer. 23. 5.	Heb., Cepheus, *the branch.* branches	Lev. 23. 40.	כפה
Jer. 33. 15.	— Cheicus, Caucus, *comes as in a circle.*	Isa. 40. 22.	חוג
	— Regulus, *treading under foot.* Sept. Isa. xxxii. 20. foot	Ps. 8. 6.	רגל
Acts 1. 11.	Arab., α Al Deramin, *coming quickly, as in a circle.*	Eccles. 1. 6.	דרם
	— Al Derab, Al Deraf, *coming in a circle.* round	Isa. 29. 3.	דר
	— β Al Phirk, *the redeemer.* redeemed	Ps. 136. 24.	פרק
	— Al Rai, and Errai, *who bruises, breaks.* break	Job 34. 24.	רע
	This name has by the Arabs been taken as *shepherd,* by the Latins *vociferator,* &c.	Ps. 23. 1. / Isa. 16. 10.	
	Gr., Cepheus, *the Branch,* called by Euripides *the king.*		

Third Decan.
ANDROMEDA, The Chained Woman.

*Isa. 61. 1.			
Isa. 54. 6, 7.	Heb., Sirra, *the chained.* chains	Ex. 28. 14.	שר
Dan. 12. 2.	— Persea, *the stretched out.* spread	Isa. 25. 11.	פרש
2 Sa. 22. 28.	— Adhil, *the afflicted.* poor	1 Sam. 2. 8.	דל
	— β Mirach, *the weak.* faintness	Lev. 26. 36.	מרך
	— Mizar, *the bound.* bind	Deut. 14.25.	צר
Isa. 54. 11.	Arab., Al Mara, *the afflicted.*	Ruth 1. 20.	מר
Isa. 26.19. / Ps. 49. 15. / Hos. 6. 2; / 13. 14.	— Al Moselsalah, {*from the grave, Sheol, Hades.* hell / *delivered.* let go	Ps. 16. 10. / Ex. 5. 1.	שאול / שלח
	— α Al Phiratz, *the broken down.* breaketh	Job 16. 14.	פרץ
Job 19. 26.	— Al Maach, Al Amak, *struck down.* smitten	Isa. 53. 4.	מך
	— Misam al Thuraiya, (*nebula,*) *the assembled, the abundance.*	Joel 3. 11. / Isa. 15. 7.	
	Gr., Andromeda, {*the set free.* liberty / *from death* †. death	Lev. 25. 10. / Ps. 9. 13.	דרר / מות
	— Desma, *the bound* (Aratus).		

† By the familiar change of *d* for *th.*

The fishes in Pisces had, in some Eastern zodiacs, the heads of women. The band of Pisces s often mentioned in the Arabian poem of Antar as a separate constellation. The Greek sphere has Cepheus and Andromeda.

TABLE XII.

𝕷𝖚𝖓𝖆𝖗 𝖅𝖔𝖉𝖎𝖆𝖈;
OR, MANSIONS OF THE MOON *.

Signs to which they belong.	Lunar Zodiac		Texts where the root of the word occurs in the Hebrew Bible.	Hebrew roots.
	Arab., Manzil al Kamar.	{ *mazaloth* *flow*	2 Kgs. 23. 5. Ps. 147. 18.	מזלות כזל
	Sansc., Nakshatra, *set*, Arab. sense. Syr. *full moon*		Prov. 7. 20.	כסא
ARIES,	Al Sheratan, *the wounded, bruised (cut).* Zech. xii. 3.		Lev. 19. 28.	שרט
	Al Botein, *the treading under foot.*		Deut. 32. 15.	בעט
	Al Thuraiya, *the multitude, the abundance.*		Isa. 15. 7.	יתר
TAURUS,	Al Debaran, *the ruling* (Syr. and Arab.). Heb., *by command, word.*		1 Kgs. 19. 9.	דבר
	Al Heka, *the coming.*		Ezra 5. 5.	הך
GEMINI,	Al Henah, *the wounded, afflicted.*		Isa. 53. 4.	ענה
	Al Dirâ, *the seed or branch; arm of a tree.*	{	Gen. 3. 15. Job 38. 15.	} זרע
CANCER,	Al Nethra, *the wealth.*	*plenteous*	Deut. 30. 9.	יתר
	Al Terpha, *the prey.*		Ge. 49. 9, 27.	טרף
LEO,	Al Gieba, *the exaltation* (Arab., *prince*).		Ezek. 17. 24.	נבה
	Al Zubra, *the gathering together.*	*lay up*	Gen. 41. 35.	צבר
	Al Serpha, *the branch.*	*bough*	Ezek. 31. 5.	סרעף
VIRGO,	Al Awa, *the desired.*		Isa. 26. 8, 9.	אוה
	Simak al Azel, *sustaining the branch.*	{ *sprigs*	Gen. 27. 37. Isa. 18. 5.	סמך זל
	Caphir, *the atonement.*		Exod. 39. 35.	כפר
LIBRA,	Al Zubena, *the redeeming.*	*gain*	Dan. 2. 8.	זבן
	Al Iclil, *the completing.*	*consummation*	Dan. 9. 27.	כלה
SCORPIO,	Al Kalb, *the cleaving.*	*cage*	Jer. 5. 27.	כלב
	Al Shaula, *sting or dart.*	*weapon*	2 Chr. 23. 10.	שלח
SAGITTA-RIUS,	Al Naim, *the gracious, delighted in.*	(marg.) {	Ruth 1. 20. Ps. 27. 4.	נעם
	Al Beldah, *hastily coming forth.*	*make haste*	2 Chr. 35. 21.	בהל
CAPRICOR-NUS,	Al Dabih, *the sacrifice slain.*		Gen. 31. 54.	זבח
AQUARIUS,	Sa'ad al Bulâ, *the record of drinking in,*	{ *record* *swallow*	Job 16. 19. Job 20. 15.	שהד בלע
	Sa'ad al Su'ud, *the record of pouring out as a stream.*		Num. 21. 15.	שר
	Al Achbiyah, *vessel of flowing forth.*	{ *hearth* *boil*	Jer. 36. 22. Is. 64. 2, E.V.	אח בעה
PISCES,	Al Pherg al Muchaddem, *the progeny from of old*	{ *young*	Ps. 84. 3. Micah 5. 2.	פרח קדם
	Al Pherg al Muachher, *the progeny of the latter time.*		Job 19. 25.	אחר
	Al Risha, *the band.*		Job 30. 11.	רסן

* The twenty-eight spaces of the heavens through which the Moon passes, one in each day, are called in Arabian astronomy the Mansions of the Moon. These names are given by Ulugh Beigh, also by Alfergani, an Arabic writer cotemporary with Albumazer, and will be found in Hyde's Commentary, Freytag's Arabic Lexicon, &c. The Lunar Zodiac was used in China in the twenty-third century B.C. (See La Loubère, &c.) The Eastern nations have, from all antiquity, made great use of the Mansions of the Moon. A table of them, with their Sanscrit names, showing the stars among which they were placed, is given by Le Gentil, Voy. dans les Indes, 1779. Under different names they are similarly arranged, as are the Chinese, each sign of the Solar Zodiac containing two and a third of these divisions. The Indians have added emblems to them; but these vary in different parts of India. Among the Sanscrit names given by Le Gentil, Ahiliam in Gemini accords with Pi-mahi, the Coptic name of the sign, the brethren. The popular enumeration is twenty-seven, joining Pisces, Rebady, the multitude, with the band; but the scientific is twenty-eight. Among the Chinese names is Mao, in the Pleiades: the resemblance to the Greek Maia points to a common origin of the science of astronomy.

TABLE XIII.

The Galactic Circle.

A WAY RETURNING.

Prophecies.			Texts where the word is used in this sense in the Hebrew Bible.	Hebrew roots.
Ps. 96. 13.	Hebrew, Aroch, the way.	*path*	Gen. 49. 17.	ארח
Isa. 35. 4; 40. 10.	Arabic, Tarik al Lubena.	{ Tarik, *way* / Al Lubena, *white*	Judg. 5. 6. / Dan. 12. 10.	לבן
Mic. 5. 2.	Syriac, Arocea, the way.	*ways*	Dan. 5. 23.	ארחא
John 14. 6.	— Shevil Tevna, way returning.	{ *path* / *return*	Ps. 77. 20. / Dan. 4. 34.	שבל / תב
Heb. 10. 20.				
Hab. 2. 3.	Greek, Galaxias Cyclos, Galactic circle.	*ring*	Esth. 1. 6.	גלגל
Mat. 24. 30.	Latin, Galaxia, the circle, returning.	*wheel*	Ezek. 10. 13.	

Twelve of the decans, or extra-zodiacal constellations, are on this circle or way, in the order here given. The first six having meanings referring to the first coming of the promised seed of the woman, descend from Cepheus, the branch, to the Southern Cross. Thence the Galactic Circle re-ascends to Cepheus, whose other character, the crowned king, becomes peculiarly appropriate, the six ascending emblems having meanings applicable to the return of Him, whose second coming in glory to receive His kingdom is the theme of unfulfilled, as the first is of accomplished prophecy.

(*Prophecies*: John 14. 18; 21. 22. / 1 Cor. 4. 5. / Heb. 10. 37. / Jude 14. / Rev. 1. 7.)

Six Emblems relating to the First Coming.

(Ps. 118. 26.) Cygnus, the swan, coming, going, and returning.

(Isa. 53. / Ps. 22.) Aquila, the pierced eagle.

(Gen. 3. 15.) Ophiuchus, the conqueror of the serpent receiving the wound in the heel.

(Isa. 53.) Victim, in the hand of the Centaur.

(Dan. 9. 26.) Southern Cross, the cutting off of the second Adam.

Six Emblems relating to the Second Coming.

(Zech. 13. 6.)

(Hag. 2. 7.) Argo, Soheil, the coming of the desired, with his people.

(Isa. 9. 6.) Sirius, the prince.

(Ps. 102.16 / Isa. 60. 1; 63. 1.) Orion, coming forth, as light.

(Is. 40.10,11 / Ezk. 37.24) Auriga, the shepherd.

(Ps. 98. 9. / Isa. 59. 20.) Perseus, the breaker of bonds.

(Ps. 93. 2.) Cassiopeia, the enthroning.

Can this arrangement be considered as accidental? Is it not a proof of design? Does it not show a unity of purpose, and what that purpose was,—even to form, in connexion with the unchanging stars, a memorial that God's unchanging ordinance had been declared to the inventors of the astronomical symbols, that to them *God had spoken?*

Plato informs us that many Greek stories were taken from the signification which the sound of foreign words conveyed to their ears. Thus may be accounted for the absurd Greek fable as to milk. The primitive root Gala, a circle or returning way, had the sound of their familiar name of milk, Gala, a word probably derived from another oriental root, Chalav, milk. Another word, Laban, white, also used in Arabic for milk, would assist the mistake, the white circle or way was construed the milky. North American Indians, and even Greenlanders, have given a more poetical meaning to this celestial arch of glimmering light. It was to them the path of the spirits of their ancestors ascending to their heavenly abodes. In early Christian times our forefathers called it Jacob's ladder, on which the patriarch had beheld angels ascending and descending, as they will hereafter on a greater than Jacob. Why, then, should we cleave to the puerile heathen legend, equally incongruous with the nature and the aspect of that sublime wilderness of worlds? the names, not the appearance, having suggested the tale; for there is not the whiteness of milk in the dim effulgence of those faint and far-off luminaries. In such assemblages, such nebulæ, as this Galactic Circle to which our sun belongs, the Creator has congregated the heavenly bodies throughout the almost illimitable universe of stars. The arbitrary groupings which we call constellations exist not in nature, but in the imagination of man.

TABLE XIV.

The Twelve Signs, Sanscrit and Chinese.

	SANSCRIT, As given by Sir W. Jones, Le Gentil, and Prof. Wilson's Sansc. Lex.			Semitic roots.	CHINESE, As given by Martini, Hist. Sin.
ARIES,	Mesha [1], Mecham,	a ram, or an animal thought to be a species of dog.	smitten, as in sacrifice	Isa. 53. 4.	נכח	Pe Yaugh, white sheep.
TAURUS,	Vrisha, Urouchabam,	a bull.	rushing on	Job 15. 26.	רץ	Kin Nieu, golden bull.
GEMINI,	Mit'huna, Mitouam,	a pair.	twins	Cant. 4. 5.	תאם	Shang Hiung, two brothers.
CANCER,	Carcata, Carcallacam,	Cancer.	to encircle		כיר	Kiu Hiai, great crab.
LEO,	Sinha, Simham,	a lion. (A dark lion found in India and Syria.)		Ps. 91. 13.	שחל	Sin, lion.
VIRGO,	Canyà,	a young girl.	gained	Gen. 4. 1.	קנה	Sha Niu, house of Virgo.
LIBRA,	Tolam, Tula,	a balance.	going up	Ezek. 9. 3.	עלה	Tien Tchingh [2].
SCORPIO,	Vrischica, Vrouchicam,	Scorpio.	bruise, crush	Judg. 9. 53.	רץ	Tien Kie.
SAGITTA-RIUS,	Danus, Dhanasou,	a bow. an arrow.	armour	1 Kgs.22.38	ון	Gjin Ma, man-horse.
CAPRICOR-NUS,	Macara, Macaram,	a species of fish, or marine animal.				Mu Thien, mountain sheep.
AQUARIUS,	Cumba, Coumbam,	water-vase. a measure, cab		2 Kgs.6.25.	קב	Pao Piugh, precious vase.
PISCES,	Mina, Minam,	fish. Nuno, Syr. fish.				Shang Yu, two fishes.

[1] The first name is Sir W. Jones's, the second Le Gentil's.
[2] The claws of Scorpio apparently occupy the place of Libra.

The idea of the first sign, the Lamb slain, seems preserved in the name Mecha.

Taum, twin, is recognizable in Mitouam; the Arabic dual of it, in Mit'huna.

The root Car, to encircle, is preserved in Cancer. Sir W. Jones says, Sinha is always and everywhere a lion, as here in the Chinese.

It is to be observed that Virgo is not Ankana, a woman, but Kana, a girl. Here, as everywhere else, in the balance of the zodiac, one scale is *going up*, according to its Arabic name, Al Genubi, the deficient. The price outweighs the purchased or redeemed. In Capricorn, the goat with the body of a fish, the fish-half predominates in the Sanscrit of Jones and Le Gentil, the goat in the Chinese, as in the Hebrew and Arabic; but a more recent Sanscrit lexicon gives Macara as the figure of Capricorn in the zodiac, the forepart a goat, the latter a fish's tail. Carâ, bowing down, Judg. vii. 6, would be the root. In all these, the vase alone is noticed in Aquarius. Shang, two, in the Chinese, corresponds with Sheni, two, in Hebrew. Sir W. Jones says the Indian zodiac was not derived from any other nation, but time immemorial from their own ancestors. If, as many great scholars assert, the Brahmins are descendants of Abraham by his wife Keturah, their astronomy was from him, his fame as a great astronomer being recorded by ancient historians. (See Josephus.) The Hebrew (or Chaldee) roots in Sanscrit are also in the same manner to be accounted for.

Le Gentil thinks the Indian and Chinese astronomy came from Chaldea. Abraham was a Chaldean, and is said by Josephus and others to have taught the science to the Egyptians.

The Siamese worship "the eternal heavens," under the name Sommona Kodom, words which being purely Hebrew testify to such an origin of their astronomy, which they trace from the remotest antiquity.

In the Chronicon Paschale, it is said that Androubarius, a descendant of Arphaxad, taught astronomy to the Indians. The offspring of Abraham were descendants of Arphaxad. In

TABLE XV.

Androubarius there is a root, meaning devoted to God, also son ; it might be the son of one devoted to God, of Abraham. When Alexander took Babylon, Chaldean observations were found for 1903 years back.

In an Indian zodiac given in the Phil. Trans. 1772, Virgo is at the solstice, which was as early as 4000 B.C. In a Buddhist zodiac, there is in Gemini a woman holding a golden cord, indicating the idea of the sign, union. The Chinese very early began their year from 15° Aquarius, where they had observed a winter solstice. This must have been antediluvian. There is a Chinese record of an eclipse of the sun 2150 B.C.

In some Chinese zodiacs, the twelve signs are figured by twelve branches.

Upham speaks of the Tibetian, Chinese, Tartarian, and Mongul zodiacs as resembling each other, and partly also the Mexican, for which he refers to Humboldt.

Humboldt says, "The Chinese, who observed nature carefully, and recorded with accuracy what they saw, have circumstantially noted the path of comets more than 500 years B.C. ;" also, that their historical existence and regular chronology go back to 2400 B.C.

In Mart. Hist. Sin. the Chinese zodiac is given as above, with the claws of Scorpio taking the place of Libra.

Early missionaries report having found in China the mother with the infant in her arms as an object of worship, having a temple, and called the " Queen of heaven."

The Cali Yug, the complete circle or epoch, was the great Indian astronomical period of 3317 years. Yug, circuit, חוג, Job xxii. 14. Cali, complete, כלה, Gen. ii. 1. It began 3102 B.C. Bailly's examination led him to consider it correct, and from actual observations. He says that " the sciences of the ancients were only the fragments of those earlier known to an antediluvian people." To this people he attributes a knowledge of the true system of the world, the return of comets, the exact measure of the earth, the starry nature of the galaxy, and the plurality of worlds, " this people originating the Chinese, Babylonians, Persians, Indians." This opinion corroborates the traditions of the ancient Persians, Arabs, and Hebrews, which attribute the origin of astronomy and other sciences to the family of Seth.

Tables brought by Le Gentil from India coincide with the Cali Yug. The calculations of Bailly have been verified by Playfair, and show that these tables wonderfully coincide with modern science. (Rees' Cyclopædia.)

The Buddhist zodiac commences with Aries figured as a goat, followed by the bull, twins, crab, lion, woman with fruit, balance, scorpion, a bow for Sagittarius, a deer for Capricorn, an urn for Aquarius, and two fishes for Pisces. It is accompanied by figures for the Mansions of the Moon, also by others which may refer to the decans; as, three birds with Scorpio and Sagittarius, and a cobra with the Lion. (See Upham's Buddhism.)

Sir Wm. Drummond says, that in the Buddhist astronomy there is mention of a planet beyond Saturn, which is called Rayu or Rahini.

Upham also gives a Birman zodiac, the ram, the bull, a woman with a musical instrument for Gemini, the crab, the lion, a woman with fruit for Virgo, a man with scales, an animal with eight legs, like a scorpion, the archer, Makara the sea-monster, the vase, and two fishes crossed.

Albumazer, in Gemini, gives a man playing on a flute in the second decan of the Persian sphere.

The Siamese and Indians are said to have cycles and very ingenious periods, and yet to be ignorant of the figure of the earth, the cause of eclipses, and even of the phases of the moon. Their cycles, &c., are therefore derived from ancestors more scientific than themselves.

In deriving the Sanscrit names from Hebrew roots, it is supposed that they were transmitted from Noah, and perhaps Abraham, as proper names of the objects, as such preserved in Sanscrit literature without reference to their radical meaning, as the names Orion and Arcturus, and others, have come down to the nations of the West. Sir W. Jones and others consider the Indian astronomy to be far older than their literature or their history.

" A conjunction of Mars, Jupiter, Saturn, and Mercury was assumed as an epoch by the (Chinese) Emperor Chwen Hio, and found by Bailly to have happened B.C. 449." " The Emperor Chong Kang put to death his two chief astronomers for not giving the right time of a solar eclipse which took place B.C. 2169." (Smythe, Celest. Cycle.)

The miraculous birth of the infant whose figure is found in some ancient zodiacs is indicated in the signification of Kana, or Canya, " a girl of nine years old." (Wilson, Sansc. Lex.)

" In the early Chinese histories the first man, called Pwan-roo, is said to have been produced soon after the period of *emptiness and confusion*. He knew intuitively the relative proportions of heaven and earth, with the principles of creation and transmutation. The first names in the historical line of rulers are Yao and Shun. Yao seems to have been Noah, as a great flood is said to have happened in his time ; and his era agreeing with that of the deluge, Shun may have been Shem." (Medhurst on China.)

The Pleiades.

		Texts where the word or its root is used in this sense in the Hebrew Bible.	Hebrew roots.
PLEIADES { Heb., *the congregation of the Judge.*	}	Ps. 74. 2.	עדה
{ Gr., *the abundance,* Rom. vi. 1.	*abound*	Job 31. 11.	פלל
Arab., Wasat, *the centre.*	*foundation*	Ps. 11. 3.	שת
— Al Thuraiya, *the abundance.*		Isa. 15. 7.	יתר
Sanscrit, Cartiguey, *the daughters of Carteek, circling* (Arab.).			
Carteek was said to be the general of the celestial armies.			
Heb., Arab., Egypt., Atlas, *high, as a mountain.*	*eminent*	Ezek.17. 22.	תל
Gr., Pleione, *abundance.*		Rom. 6. 1.	
— — Maia, *multitudes.*	*many*	Gen. 17. 4.	המן
— — Electra, *the abundance* (with El prefixed).		Jer. 33. 6.	עתר
— — Taygeta, *bound together.*	*bunch*	Ex. 12. 22.	אגר
— — Celene, *the collected together.*	*all*	Gen. 41. 57.	כל
— — Merope, *the weakened.*		Jer. 38. 4.	רפה
— — Asterope, *the light,* Job xi. 17, *that fails, is weak.*		Isa. 35. 3.	
— — Alcyone, { *the centre, foundation,* Ps. civ. 4.	*base*	1 Kgs. 7. 27.	כן
{ *the established,* Ps. lxxxvii. 5 ; lxxxix. 2, 4, 24, 37.			
Lat., Vergiliæ, { *the centre,* Arab. *vertex.*		Gen. 29. 10.	נל
{ of the revolving, *rolled.*			
Heb., Chima, *accumulation.* Arab. sense, *cumulus.*		Job 9. 9 ; 38. 31.	כימה

The group called the Pleiades is, perhaps, the best known of all the constellations. It is a spot of dim light, in which ordinary eyes can distinguish six stars: by some, more are discerned; and by the telescope still more and more, as its powers are increased. Greek tradition tells, that there were originally seven stars distinctly seen, but that at the time of the Trojan war one disappeared, going off like a comet towards the north pole. This group is figured as seven in the Mansions of the Moon of Indian astronomy,[1] though in the story concerning them, the daughters of Carteek are said to be but six, thus indicating the Indian astronomy to be more ancient than their mythology. In the Greek fable, *the seven stars* were called the daughters of Atlas and Pleione. Atlas may mean *high,* Pleione is *a multitude ;* four of the names given to the daughters also mean *multitude, abundance,* as does their Oriental name Al Thuraiya ; two others mean *that which fails ;* the seventh and most remarkable, Al Cyone, is *the base, the foundation, the centre.* It will be seen that in these names there is no allusion to the number seven. Those who gave them to this group of stars saw them to be a multitude. The names signifying multitude seem to have been given to the whole constellation in the Oriental dialects: that of Pleiades, by which it was known to the western nations, conveyed the same meaning. The star which disappeared seems to have been changing or growing dim, when the names Merope and Asterope were given.

Wasat, an Arabic name either of the Pleiades or of their brightest star, transmitted by Ulugh Beigh from early Arabian astronomy, is *the centre.* It thus testifies, like that of Alcyone, to the knowledge of the first astronomers of the long lost but lately recovered fact, that in this group is the centre of that astral system of which our sun forms part. The Latin name Vergiliæ, centre of the revolving, contains the same reference, if explained by its primitive roots. The ancient Greek name Alcyone, now so celebrated in the annals of science, is evidently of Oriental origin, having the Arabic and old Hebrew article Al, prefixed to its root Cyon, *centre.* Its meaning, centre, foundation, anticipates one of the greatest achievements of modern astronomy,

---

[1] Idcler, Le Gentil, Ulugh Beigh, &c.

TABLE XVI.

the discovery that to this point, this centre, gravitates the whole magnificent arrangement of stars called the Galaxy, to which our sun belongs. The latent, long overlooked meaning of these names exists in the dialects of the countries in which it is allowed astronomy had its birth. A most important sanction is thus afforded to the explanation which attributes to the names of astronomy a signification far beyond the idle tales of Indian, Egyptian, Greek, and Latin mythology; a signification discoverable by the primitive roots they contain, and connecting them with the prophecies recorded in the Holy Scriptures.

Ursa Major and Minor,

CALLED THE GREAT AND LESSER BEAR.

It has been remarked by Oriental scholars that the Arab astronomy abounds with allusions to cattle, but without observing that the camel, the peculiar possession of the desert tribes, does not exist among the emblems. Only once, if at all, does even the name occur among the more obscure names of minor stars, as it is said to do in Cancer. Were proof needed that astronomy did not originate in Arabia, this circumstance would afford it. The cattle with which the nomenclature of the stars abounds are the lamb and the kid of sacrifice, the flock of the shepherd, the sacrificial ram and bull of the zodiac, where the western nations still behold them: but besides these are the magnificent emblems of the greater and lesser sheepfolds, with their sheep, long obscured by fable and misconstruction of the names by which they were originally distinguished—names perverted by the Greeks and Romans, but still to be traced in the records of Oriental astronomy. Most people know the remarkable constellation never setting to European climes, called by some the Great Bear, by others the Plough or Charles's wain. In reference to the starry host, the book of Job mentions Ash, saying, " Canst thou guide Ash and her offspring?" where the English has " Arcturus and his sons," according to the confessedly imperfect Greek translation of this most ancient and difficult book. It is not, however, far wide of the real meaning in this place, as Arcturus, though not in the same constellation, appears to lead or govern the three stars where we still find the name Benetnaish, the daughters of Ash, the assembled. The Arabs still call this constellation Al Naish, or Annaish, the ordered or assembled together, as sheep in a fold. The ancient Jewish commentators on Job say that Ash is the seven stars of the Great Bear. In the three stars miscalled the tail, where we find the name Benetnaish, there is also Mizar, a guarded or enclosed place. Another name is Alioth, the ewe or she-goat, near which is the star celebrated in modern astronomy, Al Cor, the lamb, in Arabic also Seya, the lamb, where the small star is now ascertained to revolve, to circle round the large one. Cor originally means to go round, as the lamb remarkably does in the joy of its young existence. This name in this place must suggest the inquiry whether the modern discovery were not known to those antediluvian astronomers, the perfection of whose organs of sight, formed to last a thousand years, might show much that telescopes have shown to their shortlived descendants. Among the other names in this constellation, El Acola also is a fold; Phacad is a watched or guarded place; Dubhè, in Hebrew a she-bear, is still written on our globes. In Arabic Dubah is cattle, and in Hebrew Daber is a fold, either of which might be easily mistaken for Dubhè by the Greeks, and understood as a bear. There is no figure of a bear in the Egyptian planisphere, nor was there in the Persian and Indian spheres, which each had three maidens, no doubt the three daughters of Ash.

The Scandinavian tribes appear to have retained the name; but that they did not invent it may be inferred from the remark of the North American Indian, that those who first called it so had never seen a bear; for what bear ever had a long tail? It is observable that this Indian tribe called the constellation the bear. "Among the Algonquins of the Atlantic and the

Mississippi, the Narragansets, and the Illinois, the north star was called the bear [1]." It is called the chariot of Thor in Danish and Icelandic. By the ancient Britons it was given to their hero Arthur, as Talyn Arthur, the harp of Arthur, was their name for Lyra. With the living animal the Scandinavians were well acquainted, as were the Chaldeans, Hebrews, and Syrians, to whom the remark equally applies.

The appellation Septentriones, the seven which turn, gives rise to a frequent epithet of the north. The Rabbins and Arabs having called these stars Ogilah, going round, as on wheels, a wain in Hebrew and Arabic, may account for that name sometimes applied to them.

In the name of the nymph Calisto, by Greek fable said to be changed into the constellation, we find the Semitic root which we meet again in the west as Caula, a sheepfold. With the idea of a sheepfold [2] in the mind, it needs but to look at these seven remarkable stars to perceive how well is imaged there the fold, and the sheep proceeding from the corner of it, as if following the bright star Arcturus, always said to be the guardian of these stars, whatever they might be called. Arcturus means He cometh, the guardian or keeper. From the root "to come" was also formed Arcas, by the Greeks said to be the name of Ursa Minor. Arcas, by the Greeks said to be changed into the Lesser Bear, was also called the son of the Supreme Deity: the name of the chief star, Al Gedi, the kid, or Lamb of sacrifice, would carry with it that mysterious tradition. In the Persian sphere there are three maidens walking in Ursa Minor, waiting on Him who was to come, as the name Kochab expresses. As in Ursa Major, the Semitic names show that here also was set forth the fold and the flock: the fold, in Scripture metaphor the Church; the flock, the Lord's people. If from Arcas we derive the names of the arctic and antarctic hemisphere, to those epithets we may annex appropriate meanings: the hemisphere in which He came who was to come, of whom the polar star was the emblem, being called the arctic, that in which He came; the opposite, the antarctic, that in which He did not come.

Orion.

Orion, the splendid [3], coming as light, the most brilliant and striking constellation in the starry heavens, has been claimed by the pride of man, from Nimrod, the first of those mighty hunters whose prey was their fellow-man, to Napoleon, whose almost equally extensive empire, won by the sword, was dashed from his grasp, his empire smitten, though not unto death, by the predicted wound from the sword of late-resisting Europe [4]. Where is their glory, where are they now, those kings of nations who said in their hearts, "I will exalt my throne above the stars of God, I will ascend above the heights of the clouds [5]?" The awful depths of unfathomed eternity seem to re-echo, "Where?" Meanwhile the starry emblem of the Mighty One, "who was, and is to come," looks down in dazzling and undiminished lustre on their mouldering dust. Long before Nimrod had founded the first worldly monarchy of bloodshed and oppression, whose ruins now being disinterred tell of its ancient tyranny and utter destruction, this heavenly memorial of prophecy had been consecrated to the glory of a King [6] who shall rule in

---

[1] Bancroft's Hist. of U. S.

[2] The Christian Arabs, interpreting Ash as the *assembly* of mourners at a funeral, called the four stars the bier of Lazarus, and the three of the tail Martha, Mary, and a handmaiden: but the ancient names, cattle, flock, and fold, show that a funeral could never have been the original meaning.

[3] The name is so interpreted by Prof. Lee. Hesiod speaks of the "strong" or mighty "Orion."

[4] Rev. xiii. 3.   [5] Isa. xiv. 13, 14.

[6] The native Irish still call this figure Caomai, the armed king.

righteousness, whose kingdom shall have no end. The names annexed to the constellation, the mighty one, the prince, the ruler, no doubt suggested the original assumption of it, as imaging the first temporal monarch, and the earlier assumption suggested that of later years. But, if earlier, the claim of Nimrod is no better than that of Napoleon. The sycophants of the old Assyrian had no more power to annex a new name to the constellation than the admirers of the recent aspirant for the same honour; no ancient appellation has any more trace of Nimrod than of Napoleon. During the first French empire this starry figure was by some few in France called the constellation Napoleon. When the fallen conqueror was on his way to exile, he is said to have asked a village priest what "those stars" were called. The priest replied, he had never studied astronomy. Such is "fame!" The flatterers of the modern Nimrod were more daring than those of the ancient, who appear to have waited till death had removed their hero from the infirmities and vicissitudes of human life. With what feelings must he have seen the stars once called after his name rise above the prison rocks of St. Helena! If the age of hero-deification was past in his day, in that of Nimrod it seems to have begun to mingle with the earlier and less ignoble worship of the host of heaven. Before Nimrod was a sovereign, "the host of heaven" had been perverted from their original destination of "declaring the glory of God," to the first deviation from the patriarchal religion, that of honouring the symbol with the honour due alone to the thing symbolized.

In the book of Job mention is twice made of Chesil, translated and generally considered to be the constellation Orion; but as the word occurs in the plural, Chesilim, in Isa. xiii. 10, and as there is but one Orion, this name must have a different intention. It always, however, is attributed to Orion, and in its radical meaning of *bound together* well applies to the nebulæ so remarkable in this constellation, stars bound together by the all-pervading law of gravitation. From this most ancient name, and from that of Misam, assembled, applied to other nebulæ, it appears that those who gave them saw what Lord Rosse's great telescope has only lately made plain to modern science. Those ancients knew that these white clouds of light in the far depths of space were *assembled* orbs, *bound together* by the universal law of the universal Lord.

In the modern sphere, the foot of Orion is on the hare, a most unintelligible position; but originally, as may be seen in Egyptian remains [1], his foot was on the serpent. Arnebeth, the hare coming to rend, or tear the vegetable crops, seems to have been substituted for the similar sounding "enemy of Him that cometh." A serpent was figured in this place in Oriental spheres. The foot upon the serpent's head was the distinguishing mark of the seed of the woman, whether as the lamb, the lion, the kneeling Hercules, the conflicting Ophinchus, or Orion "coming forth as light [2]." The victory over the serpent, and the wounded foot, equally indicate him in ancient mythology. The Greeks degrading Orion into a mere hunter, yet gave him divine parentage, and preserved the tradition of the wound in the heel from a venomous creature, which aids in identifying the Mighty One here figured with the promise of the Redeemer who should come " travelling in the greatness of His strength."

---

[1] As the Dendera planisphere. There is a crested bird on the serpent's head in this place, said to be the hoopoe, an emblem of uncleanness among the Egyptians. From this it has been thought the figure of the hare might arise.

[2] By the Egyptians Orion was called the constellation of Orus, both names meaning *who comes.*

𝔑𝔞𝔪𝔢𝔰 𝔬𝔣 𝔱𝔥𝔢 𝔄𝔫𝔱𝔢𝔡𝔦𝔩𝔲𝔳𝔦𝔞𝔫 𝔓𝔞𝔱𝔯𝔦𝔞𝔯𝔠𝔥𝔰.

Prophecies corresponding in word or type with the figures and the names.		Texts where the word or its root is used in this sense in the Hebrew Bible.	Hebrew roots.
Rom. 8. 3. Exod. 12.	Adam, *the likeness, of God.* ARIES, *the lamb, to which the promised seed is likened.*	Gen. 1. 26. Ps. 102. 6.	דמה
Heb. 1. 2; 3. 2.	Seth, *appointed.* TAURUS, *he is appointed to subdue all enemies.*	Gen. 4. 25.	שת
Isa. 53. 3.	Enos, *suffering.* *sorrow* GEMINI, *in the human nature, wounded in the heel.*	Isa. 17. 11.	אנש
Ps. 2. 8. ⎫ Eph. 1. 14. ⎭	Cainan, *gaining or purchasing a possession.* *bought* CANCER, *the purchased possession.*	Deut. 32. 6.	קנה
John 1. 18.	Mahalaleel, *the shining forth of God.* { *shined* LEO, *coming forth to separate good from evil.* { *God*	Job 31. 26. Gen. 14. 22.	הלל אל
Ps. 72. 6.	Jared, *he shall come down.* VIRGO, *the branch or seed of the woman shall come down.*	Ps. 72. 6.	ירד
John 2. 21.	Enoch, *dedicated, as a temple.* LIBRA, *the redemption, by his self-dedication.*	1 Kgs. 8. 63.	חנך
Ps. 68. 20; 49. 15, 16. Gen. 3. 15.	Methuselah, *from death he releases.* { *death* { *let go* SCORPIO, *wounded in the heel, he bruises the head of the enemy.*	Isa. 25. 8. Lev. 16. 22.	מת שלח
Isa. 53. 4.	Lamech, *being smitten.* SAGITTARIUS, *as by the arrow going forth.*	Isa. 53. 4.	מך
Isa. 53. 5.	Noah, *he gives rest.* CAPRICORNUS, *by the atoning sacrifice, of his death.* *comfort*	Ex. 33. 14. Gen. 5. 29.	נח

Such are the meanings of the names of the ten antediluvian Patriarchs. Early Christian tradition has said, that in them is contained the whole scheme of the Gospel. The coincidence of the last eight, with eight of the Signs of the Zodiac, as explained in the preceding tables, is evident. Seth, to whom is attributed the invention of these Signs, seems to have desired to call his descendants by names alluding to the prophecies expressed in them. He might observe that the divinely given name of Adam, *the likeness,* would accord with the divinely ordained sacrifice. The Lamb was the appointed *likeness* of the coming of the second Adam, whose redemption he had typified in the emblems he had chosen: the sign of the Lamb, or Ram, he might therefore connect with the name of Adam. The name which his mother had given to himself would also agree with the next of his emblems. He, whose coming in power the chief of the herd prefigured, was also the appointed. In the following eight names the correspondence is so close as to indicate design. If that design was to follow out the analogy of the Signs, two more names were required: we find them in Shem and Arphaxad, in whom was continued the line of the promised Messiah.

2 Sam. 23. 5.	Shem, *ordained, set up.* { *set* AQUARIUS, *arising, pouring out blessings.* { *made* {	Isa. 41. 19. Exod. 2. 14. 2 Sam. 23. 5.	שם
Ps. 22. 22.	Arphaxad, *supporting the assembly.* { *leaning on* PISCES, *the multitudes united by the band.* { *assembly*	Cant. 8. 5. Ps. 89. 7.	רפק סד

TABLE XVII.

It has been observed that the names of the antediluvian patriarchs, as enumerated in Gen. v. and 1 Chron. i., contain the whole scheme of the Gospel. The assertion has been differently explained by different expositors; all however agree in referring it to the meanings of the names in Hebrew.

All names in all languages have meanings: among the more obvious in English, for example, are Grace, Ruth, Patience, Victoria; among those less so are Robert, meaning strong; George, a tiller of the earth; Anna, gracious.

In this genealogy we have the authority of the context for the intentional application of the name of Noah. We may therefore infer that the intermediate names were also given with some intended application of their ancient Hebrew significations. Their roots are to be found in the Hebrew Scriptures, used in the sense here attributed to them, which, in some instances, differs from the meanings heretofore given, where the texts in which the words are used have not been referred to by those who explained them.

If these successive names be found to form a sentence containing a meaning, it appears probable that the meaning was designedly expressed; if this meaning contain prophecy, it shows that a revelation had been given. That it *does* contain prophecy may be made clear to the English reader as follows:—

> The likeness of God, appointed, suffering.
> Gaining a possession, the shining forth of God, He shall come down.
> Dedicated, from death he releases, being smitten.
> He gives rest, ordained, supporting the assembly.

Each of these four lines in the original would consist of three words. Such is the measure of the Song of Moses, Deut. xxxii., and such that of Lamech in the line of Cain, which has often been cited as the earliest poetry.

The tradition that these names contain the whole scheme of the Gospel is corroborated by the somewhat similar meanings in the names of Cain's posterity. In the line from which the Messiah was to descend, the names are more clearly expressive of the prophecy, and given in such succession as to convey it. In the family of Cain, they are only as it were a faint echo of the promise made to the common ancestor. The eldest son of Cain was called Enoch, dedicated, probably, because, as the firstborn, he was to be the religious as well as temporal head of the family. Such was the birthright which Esau failed to recover, though he sought it with many tears. To the name of Irad, the next in succession, the meaning usually annexed is that of "a wild ass," in Syriac, untamed, in Arabic, hard to subdue, as if inheriting the temper of his grandfather Cain: the next, Mehujael, declaring God, written by the Sept. as they write Mahalaleel, and having nearly the same signification. Methusael, his death is required, may set forth the doctrine taught by the rite of sacrifice. These two last names encourage the hope that the promise of the coming Saviour was not wholly disregarded among the Cainites. The name of Lamech, sixth in the line of Cain, and eighth in that of Seth, has the same meaning in both: whether it had any reference to his homicide is not known. It is considered that with him polygamy began; and he named his offspring not after spiritual, but temporal good. Jubal, fruit of the earth; Tubalcain, worldly possession; Zillah, likeness or shadow, as of the parent; Naamah, gracious.

Had the names of the patriarchs of the chosen family merely individually referred to the promised Redeemer, as did many in later times, their series would not thus have formed a sentence or stanza conveying the prophecies, amplified much beyond what is contained in the promise of the seed of the woman.

If, as antiquity asserts [1], Seth was the inventor of astronomy, his arrangement of the emblems would account for the sequence of the names of his descendants, most of whom he lived to see. The meanings and order of these names therefore furnish corroborating evidence that such was the origin and intention of the signs.

---

[1] Were it proved that Chinese or Egyptian chronology went back further than the date usually assigned to the deluge, there might have been transmitted by Noah the history of his ancestors, or of chiefs and dominions in the line of Cain, especially if connected with astronomical

NOTE ON ENOCH.

Enoch was considered by the ancient Hebrews, Persians, and Arabs as one of the originators of astronomy. The book now extant in his name was found by Bruce in Abyssinia. It has been translated by Abp. Lawrence, who remarks in his preface, that as the writer gives the length of the day as from eight to twelve hours, be must have lived between 45° and 49° N. Lat., and might therefore be one of the ten tribes located in Media. It is certain that in the second century there was such a book, as Tertullian spoke of it. He thought it inspired; but the more learned Origen rejected it. St. Jude had previously adopted the prophecy of Enoch, but not as a book; it might be received from tradition as spoken.

It has been observed that succeeding prophets frequently use the very words of those who preceded them. Moses, in Deut. xxxiii. 2, has been supposed to refer to this prophecy of Enoch, as also Zech. xiv. 5. St. Peter, in his Second Epistle (ii. 17, 18), is considered to allude to the prophecy of Enoch, also Jude 12, 13, 15, where the ideas and even the expressions of the two Apostles remarkably coincide. The prophecy expressly quoted by Jude is to be found in the second chapter of the book translated by Lawrence. This passage, standing alone in its magnificence, luminous in the surrounding obscurity, seems to have been the only genuine record of the words of the patriarch that had reached the writer. There is nothing like it, nothing worthy of it in the rest of the volume, which may well have originated with a Jew into whose hands the Epistle of Jude had fallen. The imagery of the Apocalypse seems imitated in it, but not the prophecies. As the translator observes, none of its attempts at foretelling events after the Christian era correspond with history. The seal of inspiration is therefore wanting to the book, though the inspired Apostle has authenticated this one passage, apparently received by tradition as spoken by Enoch. Whether the book found in Abyssinia is that which Tertullian received but Origen rejected, is not known; but it is generally supposed not to be. Origen speaks of the book with which he was acquainted, as asserting that in the time of Enoch the constellations were already named and divided. The book now extant says, in c. 43, "The angel called the stars by their names, and they heard: they are the names of the righteous who dwell upon the earth." If the book seen by Origen said, "of the Righteous One who shall dwell upon the earth," it would agree with the names of the stars relating to the titles and attributes of the Messiah. There is an Indian tradition that the third from Adam, famous for his piety and the salutary precepts he gave to mankind, was translated to heaven, where he shines as the polar star. Enoch was named in tradition as the *third* with Adam and Seth in the invention of astronomy.

The positive assertion that Enoch was a prophet is founded on the Epistle of Jude. That Epistle, though doubtfully esteemed by some in the time of Eusebius (as it has been in ours), was received by the Council of Laodicea, which, with Origen and Athanasius, held the same books, and no others, to be inspired which are the Canonical Scriptures of the Anglican Church. In addition to this external evidence, the internal is supplied by the test often used as to the other Scriptures. A good man could not have said that he, the writer, was Jude the brother of James, unless he were really so: an evil man, capable of a sacrilegious forgery, could not have written other and highly spiritual parts of the same Epistle. The resemblance to 2 Pet. ii. 17, 18, in verses 6 and 8, 12 and 13, has been explained by supposing both passages to have been taken from the book of Enoch; not that now extant, but that which was known to Origen. A book of Enoch is spoken of in the "Zohar," which was written about the time of the Christian era. It is asserted by many ancient writers that there was a book called the book of Enoch. What the two Apostles quoted as authoritative must have been inspired: but an inspired book would not have perished. Jude does not refer to a book, but to a saying. That prophecy of Enoch might have been traditionally preserved, and inserted in the book called of Enoch, and recognized as prophetic by the inspired writers. The very ancient and widely prevalent tradition that Enoch did write a book, to which in some cases was added that it was preserved by Noah in the ark, is remarkable. May he not have written from the dictation of Adam the four first chapters of Genesis, under the guidance of that Spirit by which Moses might recognize and adopt them?

NOTES ON THE NAMES OF THE ANTEDILUVIAN PATRIARCHS.

The ancient British Triads, stanzas of three lines or measures, containing in each line an important truth, are well known. The same kind of arrangement may be traced in the

data, such as eclipses or conjunctions of the orbs of heaven. Seth has often been supposed by ancient writers to be Hermes Trismegistus.

NOTE ON ADAM.—Some authorities derive Adam from Adamah, red earth; but others from Damah, to be like, and from the same root Adamah, red earth or ground, as being everywhere alike. Flesh-red it is not, but deep brown, not the colour of the Caucasian race, of which Adam is considered the prototype.

NOTE ON METHUSELAH.—Methu, death, a collective noun, as Penu in Gen. xxxii. 31.

primitive poetry of other nations. These significant names of the early patriarchs seem to take a similar form. Thence may have originated the triads of their posterity. There is in these four triads some analogy with the four seasons of the year. The four great astronomical epochs, the two equinoxes and two solstices, then, as now, occurred within the allotted signs of the respective triads. All beauty is a likeness of the perfections of God. The beauty of spring comes; but it is appointed to the suffering of decay. Summer, bringing the wealth, the possession of man, shines forth from God, and comes down in blessing: in autumn, dedicated to death, but to rise again, it is smitten. In winter man rests from his labour; and the ordained sustenance supports the assembled multitudes. Arranged as triads we read—

SPRING	The likeness of God, Appointed To suffering.	. . .	The antediluvian Spring equinox.
SUMMER	Purchasing a possession, The shining forth of God, He shall come down.	. . „ „	Summer solstice.
AUTUMN	Dedicated, From death he sets free, Being smitten.	. . „ „	Autumn equinox.
WINTER	He giveth rest, The ordained, He supports the assembly.	. . „ „	Winter solstice.

NOTE I.
Josephus (Whiston).

" ' The children of Seth ' were the inventors of that peculiar sort of wisdom which is concerned with the heavenly bodies, and their order; and that their inventions might not be lost before they were sufficiently known, upon Adam's prediction, that the world was at one time to be destroyed by the force of fire, and at another time by the violence and quantity of water, they made two pillars, the one of brick, the other of stone. They described their discoveries on them both, that in case the pillar of brick should be destroyed by the flood, the pillar of stone might remain, and exhibit those discoveries to mankind, and also inform them that there was another pillar of brick erected by them. Now this remains in the land of Syria or Seirad to this day." (Book i chap. 2.)

Whiston subjoins an assertion that Josephus confounded Seth with Sesostris, &c.; but late discoveries render it needless to enter on the proof that his opinion has little weight on a subject then so imperfectly understood.

"Let no one, on comparing the lives of the ancients with ours, think that what we have now said is false." "Their food was fitter then for the prolongation of life; and God afforded them a longer time of life on account of their virtue, and the good use they made of it in astronomical and geometrical discoveries, which would not have afforded the time for foretelling the periods of the stars, unless they had lived six hundred years, for the great year is completed in that interval. Now, I have witnesses to what I have said, all those who have written antiquities both among the Greeks and the barbarians; for even Manetho, who wrote the Egyptian History, and Berosus, who collected the Chaldean monuments, and Mœchus, and Hestiæus, and besides these Hieronymus the Egyptian, and those who composed the Phœnician History, agree to what I here say. Hesiod also, and Hecatæus, and Hellancus, and Arcesilaus; and besides these, Ephorus and Nicolaus relate that the ancients lived a thousand years." (Book i. chap. 3.)

NOTE II.
Philobiblion, by Richard de Bury, Bishop of Durham, 1344.

"Catholic doctors have determined that the deep researches of the ancients, before God deluged the original world by a general flood, are to be ascribed to miracle and not to nature; as God granted them as much of life as was requisite for discovering and inscribing the sciences in books, amongst which, according to Josephus, the wonderful diversities of astronomy required a period of six hundred years, that they might be experimentally submitted to observation." (Page 93.)

NOTE III.
From Sir W. Drummond on the Zodiacs of Esneh and Denderah.

"The fact is certain, that at some remote period there were mathematicians and astronomers who knew that the sun is in the centre of our system, and that the earth, itself a planet, revolves round the central fire; who attempted to calculate the return of comets; who indicated the number of solar years contained in the great cycle, by multiplying a period (variously called in the Zend, the Sanscrit, and the Chinese, Ven, Van, and Phen) of one hundred and thirty years, by another period of one hundred and forty-four years; who took the parallax of the sun by a method superior to that of Hipparchus, and little inferior to our own; who fixed with considerable accuracy the distance of the moon and the circumference of the earth; who held that the face of the moon was diversified with vales and seas; who asserted that there was a planet beyond Saturn; who reckoned the planets to be sixteen in number; and who calculated the length of the tropical year within three minutes of the true time. All the authorities for these assertions are stated in my Essay on the Science of the Egyptians and Chaldeans."

"There is nothing, then, improbable, in the report of Josephus, when he says that the descendants of Seth were skilful astronomers, and seems to ascribe to them the invention of the cycle of which Cassini has developed the excellence. The Jews, Assyrians, and Arabians have abundance of traditions concerning the antediluvian astronomical knowledge, especially of Adam, Seth, Enoch, and Ham. It was asserted in the book of Enoch, as Origen tells us, that the constellations in the time of that patriarch were already named and divided. The Arabians say that they have named Enoch, Edris, on account of his learning." (Page 38.)

"Some of the rabbins have said that Cham had learned the science of astronomy and the knowledge of the zodiacal ring." (Page 40.)

"The antediluvian predictions of Josephus were probably astronomical. The Indians have a cycle of sixty years, probably as the decimal part of the great year of six hundred years."

"That the invention of the zodiac ought to be attributed to the antediluvians may appear to some a rash and idle conjecture; but I shall not renounce this conjecture, merely because it may startle those who never thought of it before. Tradition has told several of the Oriental nations that the antediluvians were eminently skilled in astronomy; and tradition has generally some foundation in truth. When Bailly undertook to write the history of astronomy, he found at the outset certain fragments of science, which proved to him the existence of a system in some remote age, and anterior to all regular history, if we except the fragment in the book of Genesis. As all the emblems in the similarly divided zodiacs of India, Chaldea, Bactria, Arabia, Egypt, are nearly alike, it would seem they had followed some common model, and to whom should we attribute its invention but to their common ancestors?"

NOTE IV.

Cassini says, "The period of six hundred years, of which we find no intimation in any records but those of the Jewish nation, referred to by Josephus, and called the grand year, is one of the finest ever invented. It brings out the solar year more exactly than that of Hipparchus and Ptolemy, and the lunar month within one second of what is determined by modern astronomy." He also urges that nothing but the observations of those who lived to see the return of the celestial orbs to the same places could have originated this wonderful period. This argument, again brought forward by Sir W. Drummond, appears to have had weight with him in his conversion to a reverential acquiescence in the authority of those Holy Scriptures he had once undervalued [1]. Cassini, in verifying this ancient calculation, had the use of observations made by means of the instruments of modern science, and from these could ascertain what the patriarchs might know by ocular inspection of the course of the heavenly bodies. In their lives one man might observe twenty or thirty revolutions of Saturn, sixty or eighty of Jupiter, and many more of the inferior planets. In this great cycle of six hundred years, Cassini says, "The lunar month is reckoned at 29 days, 12 hours, 44 minutes, 3 seconds; the solar year at 365 days, 5 hours, 51 minutes, 36 seconds: not that this division was so made in the ancient tradition, as made by computation, but is the result given of the actual completion of the cycle, which might be observed by those whose lives were of sufficient length. After the first completion of the first six hundred years had been witnessed, every succeeding year would furnish another, a new proof its accuracy."

NOTE V.—ON BRITISH TRIADS.

One of these triads appears to imply not only a knowledge of the immortality of the soul, but of the resurrection.

"The Three Restorations in the Circle of Happiness.
"The restoration of original character,
"The restoration of all that was beloved,
"The restoration of remembrance from the origin of all things." (Triads of Bardism.)

---

[1] In his early work, the Œdipus Judaicus, he treats the Scriptures with much disrespect: in his later, particularly his Essay on the Zodiacs of Esneh and Denderah, he expresses his full adhesion to them.

Names of the Sons of Jacob,

ACCORDING TO THEIR BIRTH.

Signs borne on the banners of the tribes of Israel.	ACCORDING TO THEIR BIRTH.	Texts where the word or its root occurs.	Hebrew roots.
AQUARIUS,	Reuben, *behold a son*, the son, arising, pouring out blessings.	Gen. 29. 32.	
PISCES,	Simeon, *heard*, Levi, *bound, united*, } characteristics of the Church.	Ib. 33. Ib. 34.	
LEO,	Judah, *praise to the Lord*, for the coming Messiah.	Ib. 35.	
SCORPIO,	Dan, *judging, ruling*, his people.	Gen. 30. 6.	
CAPRICORNUS,	Naphtali, *wrestling*, sufferings at the first coming.	Ib. 8.	
ARIES,	Gad, *good fortune*, blessings at the second coming, (Arab. use.)	Ib. 11.	
SAGITTARIUS,	Asher, *happy*, the going forth of the Gospel.	Ib. 13.	
CANCER,	Issachar, *recompense, or reward*, of the Messiah's sufferings.	Ib. 18.	
VIRGO,	Zebulon, *dwelling*, as the promised seed at his first coming.	Ib. 20.	
TAURUS,	Joseph, *adding*. Ephraim; *fruitful*, Gen. xli. 52; gathering in the Gentiles.	Ib. 24.	
GEMINI,	Benjamin, *son of the right hand*, called by his mother, Ben-oni, *son of sorrow*, the suffering and triumphant Messiah.	Gen. 35. 18.	
(*Aben Ez. Com. Calmet.*)			

Stones of the Breastplate.

1st Row. Judah,	Odem, ruby, *red*, Isa. lxiii. 2 (*bloodshedding*, Arab. sense). *blood*	Ex. 12. 13.	דם
Issachar,	Pitdah, *reward, price of redemption*.	Num. 3. 49.	פדה
Zebulon,	Bareketh, *shining;* carbuncle. *lightning*	Ezek. 1. 13.	ברק
2nd Row. Reuben,	Nophek, *pouring forth*, as light or water. *flask*	1 Sam. 10. 1.	פך
Simeon,	Saphir, *numbered*, as multitudes, Rev. vii. 9; sapphire. *count*	Ps. 87. 6.	ספר
Gad, 3rd Row.	Jahalom, *which breaks;* diamond. *break*	Ps. 74. 6.	הלם
Ephraim,	Leshem, *tongues*, of fire, Isa. v. 24. *nations, tongues*	Gen. 10. 20.	לשן
Levi,	Shebo, *dwelling;* agate. *dwellest*	Ps. 80. 1.	ישב
Benjamin, 4th Row.	Achlama, *which restores;* amethyst. *recover*	Isa. 38. 16.	הלם
Dan,	Tarshish, *a possession*, Ephes. i. 14. *possession*	Num. 24. 18.	ירש
Asher,	Shoham, *lively, strong* (as a horse, Arab. use); onyx.		
Naphtali,	Jasphè, jasper, *which shall bruise, and be bruised*.	Gen. 3. 15.	שף

The Breastplate of the High Priest, with the Names of the Twelve Tribes and Signs engraven on the Stones; according to the Encampment ordered in Num. ii. (*Josephus, Antiq.*)

1st Row.	Bareketh, Zebulon, VIRGO.	Pitdah, Issachar, CANCER.	Odem, Judah, LEO.	
2nd Row.	Jahalom, Gad, ARIES.	Saphir, Simeon, PISCES.	Nophek, Reuben, AQUARIUS.	Exod. 28. 15—22, compared with Num. 2.
3rd Row.	Achlama, Benjamin, GEMINI.	Shebo, Levi, LIBRA.	Leshem, Ephraim & Manasseh, TAURUS.	
4th Row.	Jasphè, Naphtali, CAPRICORNUS.	Shoham, Asher, SAGITTARIUS.	Tarshish, Dan, SCORPIO.	

NOTE.—Libra was not borne on the banners of any of the Tribes of Israel, Simeon and Levi being united under the emblem of Pisces, but would be on the breastplate.

TABLE XVIII.

Allusions to the Signs of the Zodiac have often been pointed out in the blessing of Jacob [1]; those in the blessing of Moses [2] have been less remarked. Unless these emblems had some signification familiar and important to the hearers, it is not to be supposed that the dying patriarch or the departing lawgiver would have adopted their imagery. If, however, they had been framed by the forefathers of mankind to transmit the primæval revelation, it is consistent that they should again be so employed.

If, as has been shown [3], their import is to be traced in the names of the antediluvian patriarchs, it is the more probable that they should afterwards be used in prophecy. It does not clearly appear whether Jacob and his wives had at first any intention of connecting the names of their children with the signs; but when Jacob changed the name Ben-oni, son of sorrow, to Ben-jamin, son of the right hand, it is probable he had in view the sign of the heavenly twins, which the tribe of Benjamin is known to have borne on its banners, under the accompanying figure of the wolf, whose name means, He cometh.

These names are subsequently consecrated to the purpose of prophecy by the command to engrave them on the stones of the oracular breastplate, and by their place on the gates of the city of Ezekiel and the New Jerusalem of the Apocalypse. While in the names of the earlier patriarchs is found the Redeemer alone, in those of the sons of Jacob there is more of the peculiar people, the Church, then beginning to be set apart, but still, as in the emblems of the signs, in union with the Redeemer. The order in which their father addressed them begins with Reuben. "Behold the Son!" calling on us to look to Him, of whom Isaiah afterwards said, "Unto us a Son is given," and "Look unto Him, and be ye saved, all the ends of the earth." In Simeon and Levi, those that have heard and are joined together, is shown the need they have of union between themselves, and support from Him who sustains them. In Judah, the theme of our praise and the delight in offering it. In Zebulon is set forth that He shall dwell with them, and they with Him. In Issachar, the purchased possession, the reward of Messiah's sufferings. In Dan the salvation of his people is secured by his judging or ruling for them. In Gad, conformed to Him in affliction, they are with Him pierced with many sorrows. In Asher is their blessedness, in feeding on the bread from heaven. In Naphtali they are set free by his wrestling. In Joseph is shown the continual addition to the Church of such as shall be saved. In Benjamin, He who is the man of sorrows, and of God's right hand, closes, as He began, the enumeration. Ephraim, fruitfulness, and Manasseh, forgetfulness of all worldly troubles, equally suit with the place they afterwards occupied in subordination to their father Joseph.

It is not said that the gift of prophecy had been imparted to Jacob before his last illness. Perhaps from the widely diffused tradition of this prophetic effusion an idea as widely received, that dying persons speak prophetically, may have originated.

The prediction first accomplished, that the sovereignty should be vested in the tribe of Judah, is the preliminary mark giving authority to the yet unfulfilled prophecies, both of the Messiah and the tribes. As certainly as the families of the twelve patriarchs divided between them the promised land under Joshua, so certainly shall they again possess it, under Him of whom Joshua was a type. As surely as David the son of Jesse reigned upon Mount Zion, so surely unto that Shiloh, that King Messiah who is also of the line of Judah, shall be the gathering of the nations.

The blessing of Jacob contains prophecies of the Messiah, some of which are equally appreciated by Christians and by Jews. Such is that of Shiloh: but the ancient Hebrews understood far more of these predictions as relating to Him who was to come, than is in general pointed out by commentators. According to the early and most learned Jewish authorities, references to the Messiah are throughout interwoven with those to the patriarchs and the tribes. Some of these annunciations are yet unfulfilled, both as to the final triumph of the Messiah and the destiny of the tribes in their restoration to their own land. Translations, ancient and modern, vary, as in Gen.

---

[1] Gen. xlix.   [2] Deut. xxxiii.   [3] Table 15.

xlix. 26, in which the great majority give Nazir, the Nazarite, where the English has "separate."
Commentators also differ; some, however, have perceived the allusions to the twelve signs, as borne
on the standards of Israel, but have not consi-tently explained or adapted them: not even the
Jewish writers who inform us that they were so borne. However, these ancient authorities
unanimously assert that Reuben bore Aquarius; Joseph, Taurus; Benjamin, Gemini under the
emblem of the wolf; and Dan, Scorpio under that of an eagle, or of a crowned serpent or basilisk.

If these emblems were thus early employed by the family chosen to preserve the worship of
the One true God, the idea of their origin in Egypt, then fast sinking into idolatry, becomes
most improbable. On the descendants of Abraham was ever impressed abhorrence of that
idolatry from which he had been called. What idolaters had invented they might not adopt:
but what idolaters had corrupted they were not always commanded to abandon. The cherubic
forms, afterwards perverted to the purposes of idolatry in Egypt and Assyria, are found in
the four principal signs where the equinoxes and solstices of antediluvian astronomy had
always occurred. These forms could not be of Egyptian invention, for they were set at the
east of Eden. Jewish authorities say that "they were from the beginning in the holy tabernacle
called the face of God." Had the eight intermediate signs been added by the Egyptians, the
chosen family must not have intermingled the devices of man with ordinances of Divine
authority. If they knew that all had been arranged to declare the glory of God and proclaim
the coming Redeemer, the use of them by Jacob, and the recurrence to them by Moses, would
be of obvious utility. Happily would the children of the departed prophet behold them in
the peaceful plains of Goshen. How hopefully in the toilsome valley of the Nile would they
gaze on their own hieroglyphics, of far higher import than those of their oppressors! With
what thankfulness in the weary sands of the wilderness would they repose, encamping every
man under the shadow of his own standard! With what joy would they unfurl those prophetic ensigns to the welcome breezes of the promised land! As the written word of God in
our own day, to some they would still be an unsolved enigma, while to others they would
declare the great salvation. The rebellious seer read in them the ruin of his race: the
triumphant Lawgiver traced the future glories of Him who should be "King in Jeshurun."

It does not appear that the signs were first appropriated to the sons of Jacob by their
father's dying blessing; it rather seems that the children had been named with a reference to
the signs, as is still done in the East: therefore, when Joseph related his dream of eleven
stars bowing down before him, his brethren applied it to themselves, and were offended. This
dream was fulfilled, his second dream was not: his own mother was dead, and his step-mother
also died before his brethren bowed down to him. Jacob appears to have seen, that if the
first was from above, the second was merely natural, and reproved him in consequence.

Beneath the midnight sky of the land of Goshen, the dying patriarch, animated by prophetic impulse and surrounded by reverential listeners, from within the lifted curtain of his
tent might gaze enrapt on the starry heaven, whither by Divine command his father Abraham
had been taught to look for a type of the promised seed. With Leo rising, Aquarius would be
seen about to set, thus figuring the transfer of the birthright from Reuben to Judah. Taurus,
the well-known bearing of Joseph, would be on the meridian; and the place of Scorpio, the
ensign of Dan, though below the horizon, would be pointed out by the head of the Serpent
immediately beneath the Northern Crown. Every intermediate sign would either be visible
or its place indicated by some remarkable star belonging to or above it; as Sagittarius by
Vega, in Lyra, and Capricornus by Cygnus. Reverting from the brilliant orbs on high, beyond
which lay the haven of that salvation for which he had waited, his failing eyes would rest on
the familiar faces around him, the inheritors of that earthly Canaan typifying the heavenly
country which his spirit sought. Full of the glories of Him at once his Saviour and his son, he addresses them under the influence of that Divine Spirit which alone enables man to predict futurity.

NOTE.—The annexed translations, varying but little from the English Version, yet accom-
modated in some degree to the idiom of the Hebrew in its inversions and omissions of connecting particles, if harsh to the ear, aim at conveying some idea of the antique dignity of
the original in the blessing of Jacob, and at shadowing forth the sublimity of that of Moses.

GENESIS XLIX.

1 And Jacob called his sons, and said, Assemble yourselves together, and I will tell you that which shall happen unto you in the latter days. 2 Gather yourselves together, and hear, ye sons of Jacob; and hearken unto Israel your father. 3 Reuben, thou, my firstborn! my might, and the beginning of my strength, the excellency of dignity, and the excellency of power. 4 Poured forth as water, thou shalt not excel, for thou wentest up to the bed of thy father: then didst thou profane; he went up to my couch! 5 Simeon and Levi, brethren! instruments of cruelty in their slaying! 6 Into their council come not thou, O my soul! unto their assembly be not thou united: for in their anger they slew a man, and in their wilfulness they cut off the Prince. 7 Cursed their anger, for fierce; and their wrath, for stubborn: I will divide them in Jacob, and scatter them in Israel. 8 Judah, thou! thy brethren shall praise thee! thy hand on the neck of thine enemies! thy father's children shall bow down before thee. 9 A lion's whelp, Judah! upon the prey, my son, thou art come up: he stoopeth down, he coucheth as a lion, and as a fierce lion; who shall rouse him up? 10 The sceptre shall not depart from Judah, nor a lawgiver from between his feet, until Shiloh come, and unto Him the gathering of the nations. 11 Binding his foal to the vine, and unto the choice vine his ass's colt, he washeth his garments in wine, and his mantle in the blood of grapes. 12 His eyes sparkling more than wine, and his teeth whiter than milk. 13 Zebulon shall dwell at the haven of the sea: and He shall be a haven for affliction, and his side a stronghold. 14 Issachar! a strong ass couching down between the sheepfolds. 15 And he shall see his resting-place, that it is good, and the land, that it is pleasant; and he shall bow his shoulder to the burden, and shall be a servant to tribute. 16 Judging, He shall judge his people, as one of the tribes of Israel. 17 There shall be for Dan a serpent by the way, an adder by the path, biting the horse's heels; and his rider shall fall after. 18 For thy salvation have I waited, O Lord! 19 Gad! a troop shall pierce him: and he shall be pierced in the heel. 20 With Asher, abundant his bread, and he shall give the sweet influences of a king. 21 Naphtali, a hind let loose: he giveth goodly words. 22 Branch of fruitfulness, Joseph, branch of fruitfulness by the fountain! the daughters walk before the bull. 23 The archers have sorely grieved him, and contended with him, and hated him. 24 But his bow shall abide in strength, and his arms shall be made strong, his hands by the hands of the Mighty One of Jacob, from whence the shepherd, the stone of Israel: 25 By the God of thy father, and He shall help thee, and by the Almighty, and He shall bless thee, blessings of the heavens above, blessings of the deep that coucheth below, blessings of the breasts and of the womb. 26 The blessings of thy father have been mighty beyond the blessings of the ancient mountains, the desired of the lasting hills; they shall be on the head of Joseph, and on the crown of the head of Him, the Nazarite among his brethren. 27 Benjamin! the wolf shall rend: in the morning he shall feed on the prey, in the evening he shall divide the spoil. 28 All these, the twelve tribes of Israel, and this, what their father spake unto them; every one according to his blessing blessed he them.

The dying patriarch appears to have addressed each son by name, and then alluding to his appointed emblem, to have pointed out its signification as to the promised Redeemer. To Reuben was allotted Aquarius, the pourer out of blessings, arising as in triumph. *He* was his might and the "excellency" of dignity and of power; but the "excellency" of primogeniture, of being the head of the family, he takes from Reuben, "*Thou* shalt not excel," and afterwards transfers it to Judah. The reason is given in the delinquency of Reuben.

Ver. 5. To Simeon and Levi he allotted Pisces, the united fishes, as brethren. They had slain Shechem, a man, a prince of the land. It has often been pointed out that these two tribes were the enemies of *the* Man, the second Adam, and were instrumental by their "assembly" to the crucifixion, slaying the Prince. The word here rendered prince, is by the Septuagint rendered bull, and by the Vulgate wall. The alteration of a single vowel, in the Hebrew expressed by a single point, allows these variations; and certainly in the time of Jacob the points were not in use. Whether before or after the event, a prediction of the slaying of the Messiah by his own people would not find favour with the Jewish mind. A point would be easily dropt if involving it.

NOTES.

Ver. 7. The original, and as here rendered, allows the anger and wrath to be future, that against Messiah the Prince, foreseen by Jacob.

Ver. 10. Shiloh, the Giver of peace, or the Peace. John xiv. 27. Eph. ii. 14.

Ver. 14. *Sheepfolds.* The word is so rendered Judg. v. 16.

Ver. 16. He, Messiah, shall judge.

Ver. 17. Ancient Hebrew and Chaldee authorities say that Dan bore on his standard a crowned serpent or basilisk, held in the claws of an eagle. The constellation of the serpent by the milky way held by Ophiuchus, in Scorpio, and the reptile under his foot in the zodiac, seem here alluded to. By the serpent wounding the heel, the human nature falls in death.

Ver. 19. By one of the *troop* of Roman soldiers the Messiah was pierced in the side : in being nailed to the cross, He was pierced in the heel. *At last* is the same word as *heel*, Gen. iii. 15.

Ver. 20. " Royal dainties " is in Job rendered "sweet influences." The Rabbins all agree that this is King Messiah.

Ver. 21. *Hind* is of the neuter or feminine gender, as is the *desire* of nations, and wisdom, in Prov. viii., where substituting *it* for *she* would remove difficulties. The Messiah was to take human nature, the nature equally of man and woman. The Hebrew has but two genders, masculine, and all that is not masculine, including feminine and neuter in one.

Ver. 22. The well or fountain may be the river Eridanus. *Daughters*, as in the English margin and the Vulgate, appear to be the Pleiades, which precede the constellation Taurus, the bull, which is known to have been the ensign of Joseph, and afterwards of Ephraim.

Ver. 25. In the remarkable expression "the deep that lieth or coucheth under," there seems again an allusion to the constellation Eridanus, immediately beneath that of Taurus.

Ver. 26. Nazarite. The word rendered *separate* in the English, is in the Vulgate, in Luther's and most other translations, Nazarite. The Jewish writers observe on this passage, that he who is here called a Nazarite cannot be Joseph, who threw himself on the body of his father ; for a Nazarite might not touch a dead body. They understand it of the King Messiah. So understanding it, this is one of the places in which Christ is spoken of as a Nazarite, according to Matt. ii. 23 : the other is Deut. xxxiii., where Moses repeats the words of his ancestor's prophecy.

Ver. 27. *The wolf.* The allusion here is to the figure of the wolf known to be borne on the standard of Benjamin, as representing the sign Gemini. It may be traced in the constellation Sirius, called by the Egyptians a dog. The greater and lesser dog of the modern sphere were called by the Arabs the right and left Prince or Mighty One. The Semitic name of the wolf, Zeeb, is *this* or *he cometh.* *The prey*, that which is appointed, as in Job xxx. 23, at his first coming, the morning ; at his second, the evening, all shall be at his disposal.

Ver. 28. *Tribes*, literally rods, standards. The word is rendered sceptre in ver. 10.

The ancient Rabbis all explain ver. 8 of Messiah. On ver. 11 they refer to Zech. ix. 9. On ver. 8 there is a reference to Job xv. 18 : " as is said by the Holy Spirit by the hand of Job," showing their faith that the Scriptures were dictated by the Holy Spirit, and that Job was inspired.

On Shiloh they say, in ver. 8, "This is the Messiah ; and he shall be over all the world." "The vine is the house of Israel." (Mart. Pug. Fidei.)

" The writers of the Targums allow an original literal sense of a passage, and leave a typical one to prefigure something in the time of Messiah," as Ps. lxxii., of Solomon and the Messiah. On Gen. xlix., Jonathan, Onkelos, and the Jerusalem Targum all interpret Shiloh the Messiah. The latter adds, "whose is the kingdom, and to whom all the kings of the earth shall be subjected." Ahmed Ibn Idris, an Arabic writer, calls this " a prophecy of Isa, upon whom be peace," and renders Shiloh Messias. R. Johanan said that " all the Prophets prophesied only of the days of Messiah :" others that " the Prophets prophesied only of the years of redemption and the days of Messiah." R. Simeon ben Jochai, on Gen. iii., speaks of King Messiah as the son of David, and to be born of a virgin, applying to Him Isa. xi. 2. (Jonathan, with other ancient Rabbis, applies to Him Isa. lii. and liii.) R. S. also says of Him, " God's most holy Son, having put on human flesh, that He may forgive their iniquities," and that "they shall kill Him." R. S. may have understood Gen. xlix. 6 of the Messiah. The Targum of Jonathan says, on Gen. iii., " The children of the woman shall have a remedy (for the wound of the serpent) in the days of Messiah the King." (Nicholl's Conference with a Theist.)

In Martini Pugio Fidei may be seen references to the Jewish books and writers who explain much of the " blessing of Jacob " of King Messiah ; to Him they all agree in referring ver. 8 and 11. On Shiloh they say, " This is Messiah :" also, of Dan, ver. 16, " This, Dan, is Messiah to come, who is to judge as the blessed God." In Beres. Rab. Mose Haddashan is quoted as saying, on Gen. xlix. 11, " When King Messiah comes to Jerusalem to save Israel, He himself shall gird his ass, and ride upon it and guide it himself in meekness to Jerusalem, as it is written Zech. ix. 9." Also, on ver. 10, " The last and final redemption of Israel is here meant." The Targums of Jonathan and of Jerusalem apply all this chapter to the Messiah.

It will be seen from the prophecy of Balaam, Num. xxiv., that the previous prophetic blessing of Jacob was known to him, as he uses its very words in ver. 9. The emblems on the standards of the tribes were before his eyes ; he distinctly alludes to the urn and water of Aquarius, and the lion of Judah. In the order of the encampment given in Numbers ii., these two leading tribes were on the east and on the south, consequently most apparent to the prophet of Midian.

NUMBERS XXIV.

Part of the Prophecy of Balaam.

2 And Balaam lift up his eyes, and he saw Israel abiding according to their tribes.   5 How goodly are thy tents, O Jacob, thy tabernacles, O Israel!   6 As the valleys are they spread forth, as gardens by the river side, as the trees of lign-aloes which the Lord hath planted, as cedar-trees beside the waters.   7 He shall pour water out of his water-vessels, and his seed in many waters, and his kingdom shall be higher than Agag, and his kingdom shall be exalted.   8 God brought him forth of Egypt; he hath as it were the swiftness of the elk; he shall eat up the nations his enemies, and shall break their bones, and pierce with his arrows.   9 He couched, he lay down as a lion, and as a great lion: who shall rouse him up?   Blessed is he that blesseth thee, and cursed he that curseth thee. . .   14 I will instruct thee what this people shall do to thy people in the after days.   15 And he took up his parable and said, Balaam the son of Beor said, and the man whose eyes are open said,   16 He said, which heard the words of God, and knew the knowledge of the Most High, saw the vision of the Almighty, falling, but having his eyes open: 17 I shall see Him, but not now: I shall behold Him, but not nigh: there cometh a star out of Jacob, and there ariseth a sceptre out of Israel, and shall smite the corners of Moab, and bring together all the children of Seth.   18 And Edom shall be a possession, Seir also shall be a possession for his enemies, and Israel shall do valiantly.   19 And from out of Jacob who shall have dominion, and shall destroy the remnant of the city.

NOTES.

It may be observed that Balaam when speaking in his own person uses the name of God in the singular, Al, as in ver. 4, but when speaking of Him as the God of Israel, he calls Him Jehovah: he also, in ver. 16, uses the names Elion, Most High, and Shaddai, the Giver of blessings, or the Almighty.

Ver. 7.   The pouring out of water from the urns or vases here evidently alludes to Aquarius. In the Egyptian sphere the man holds an urn in each hand.   As the second commandment had now been given, it may seem that human figures were no longer on the banners of Israel, if they had ever been.   The Jerusalem Targum, and that of Jonathan, say this is King Messiah: so other Jewish writers. (Gill's Com.)   Agag is supposed to be Gog, Ezek. xxxviii.: so the Septuagint.

Ver. 8.   The Septuagint for Reem has unicorn, the Vulgate, rhinoceros: but modern travellers say there is a large species of elk still called by the Arabs Reem.

Ver. 9.   The first part of this verse is in the words of Jacob, Gen. xlix. 10: the latter part in those of Isaac, Gen. xxvii. 29.   These earlier prophecies appear to have been well known to the surrounding nations.   That now given forth through Balaam was yet more extensively so, as appears from the Persian tradition of the star, and the universal one of the coming of Him who should have dominion.

Ver. 17.   In the book of Zohar it is said, "When the Messiah shall be revealed, a bright star shall arise in the East."   Aben Ezra applies it partly to David and partly to the Messiah, as does Maimonides.   The use made of it by Christians may have induced the Jews to bring in David.   "There shall come a star *out of* Jacob."   The preposition Mem is said by Gill and others sometimes to bear the sense of *unto*.   In this place both senses seem needed; the star, Messiah himself, came *out of*, as well as *unto* Jacob.   The literal star, which led the Magi, came unto the land and descendants of Jacob: of the sceptre, not yet come, the same may be said.   "Bring together."   All mankind are through Noah children of Seth.   So Jarchi observes.   Onkelos has "shall rule over the children of Seth."   He and many other Jewish authorities interpret this of Messiah by name.   Ver. 19 is also in the ancient Jewish writings applied to Messiah.

Ver. 19.   "The city."   The Babylon of prophecy.

Great is the sanction derived to the prophetic import of the signs from the allusions to them in the farewell blessing of Moses to the assembled nation.   Consciously standing on the verge of eternity, no mere device of man could have engaged one moment of fast-fleeting time; but in the prophecies emblematized on those standards of Israel now floating before his eyes he found the pervading theme of his last solemn unveiling of futurity.   They proclaimed the coming of the Deliverer who should bruise the serpent's head.   Where the plains of Moab ended, and the ascent of Abarim, the mount of passing over, rose to the loftier Nebo, the mountain of beholding, stood the divinely appointed leader, his mission fulfilled, his earthly warfare accomplished.   The words of his father Jacob in his mind, the allotted ensigns in his view, he amplified those predictions, dwelling triumphantly on the glorious close, the final restoration of the chosen people to the land of promise, now seen afar off in aerial beauty beyond the intervening flood.

First he invokes on Reuben a heavenly blessing, compensating the deprivation of his earthly birthright: and he then plainly alludes to the man in Aquarius. Turning to Judah, he prays for the speedy coming of Him who was to be of his lineage, and sees the hands of the Conqueror, as in lion-grasp, on the neck of the enemy. To Levi, with whom Simeon is united as the fishes on the ensign, he speaks of the honour of the priesthood, and the union of the Urim and Thummim in the breastplate. In Benjamin he sees alone the glory of the beloved, the son of the right hand. To Joseph, enumerating abundant endowments, he expressly names his well-known ensign, the sacrificial bull, afterwards borne by Ephraim. With Zebulon he rejoices in Him whose goings forth have been from everlasting: with Issachar, that He should dwell in the tents of Shem. In speaking of Gad, he exactly describes the ram whose foot is on the head of the sea-monster, who had provided for himself the first part, "the beginning of months," which the sign Aries was now appointed to be. For Dan he speaks of the ruling; for Naphtali, of the full satisfaction, the blood-bought salvation; for Asher, of the dispensation of peace, the coming swiftly to the earth, as the horse shod with iron and brass, of Him, the God of Jeshurun, who rideth on the heavens in his help.

DEUTERONOMY XXXIII.

1 And this is the blessing wherewith Moses the man of God blessed the children of Israel before his death. 2 And he said, The Lord came from Sinai, and rose up from Seir unto them; He shined forth from Mount Paran, and He came with multitudes of saints: from his right hand a fiery law unto them. 3 Yea, He loved the nations; all his saints in thy hand: and they sit down at thy feet; every one shall receive of thy words. 4 Moses commanded us a law, the inheritance of the congregation of Jacob. 5 And there shall be in Jeshurun a King, in the gathering of the heads of the people together with the tribes of Israel. 6 Reuben shall live, and not die; his men shall not be few. 7 And this to Judah: and he said, Hear, Lord, the voice of Judah! and thou shalt bring him to his people: and his hands mighty unto him, and help from his enemies shalt thou be. 8 And to Levi he said, Thy perfections and thy lights from Him, thy Holy One, whom thou didst prove at Massah, with whom thou didst strive at the waters of Meribah; 9 Who said of his father and of his mother, I saw them not, and his brethren he did not acknowledge, and his children he did not know: for they observed thy word, and kept thy covenant. 10 They shall teach thy judgments to Jacob: they shall put incense before thee, and whole sacrifices on thy altar. 11 Bless, Lord, his substance, and accept the work of his hands: smite through the loins of them that rise against him, and of them that hate him, that they rise not up again. 12 To Benjamin he said, The Beloved of the Lord shall dwell in safety by him; sheltering by him all the day, and between his shoulders he dwelleth. 13 And to Joseph he said, Blessed of the Lord his land, by the precious things of the heavens, by the dew, and by the deep that coucheth beneath, 14 And by the precious things brought forth by the sun, and by the precious put forth by the moons, 15 And by the chief things of the ancient mountains, and by the precious things of the lasting hills. 16 And by the precious things of the earth, and the fulness thereof; and the good will of the dweller in the bush shall come upon the head of Joseph, and upon the crown of the head of Him, the Nazarite among his brethren. 17 The firstborn, his bull, glory for him, horns of lifting up his horns: with them shall he push the nations together in the ends of the earth: and they, the multitudes of Ephraim, and the thousands of Manasseh. 18 And to Zebulon he said, Rejoice, Zebulon, in thy going forth; and Issachar, in thy tents. 19 They shall call the nations to the mountain, there shall they offer sacrifices of righteousness: for the abundance of the seas they shall suck, and treasures hid in the sand. 20 And of Gad he said, Blessed He that enlargeth Gad: as a lion he dwelleth, and teareth with the forefoot the crown of the head. 21 And he provided the first part for himself, for there, in the portion of the lawgiver, was he seated; and he shall come with the heads of the people, to work the righteousness of the Lord, and his judgments with Israel. 22 And of Dan he said, Dan, a lion's whelp: he shall leap from Bashan. 23 And of Naphtali he said, Naphtali, satisfied with favour, and full with the blessing of the Lord: inherit thou the west and the south. 24 And of Asher he said, Asher, blessed with children; he shall be acceptable to his brethren, and dip in oil his foot. 25 Iron and brass thy shoes; and as thy days thy strength. 26 None like the God of Jeshurun; He rideth upon the heavens in thy help, and in his triumph on the sky. 27 The Eternal God thy refuge, and underneath the everlasting arms: and He shall thrust out before thee the enemy, and shall say, Be destroyed. 28 And Israel shall dwell in safety alone: the fountain of Jacob in a land of corn and wine, also his heavens shall drop down dew. 29 Happy art thou, O Israel: who is like unto thee, people saved by the Lord, the shield of thy help, and who is the sword of thy triumph! and thine enemies shall fail before thee, and thou shalt tread on their high places.

NOTES.

Ver. 1.   " Before " has the force of " looking to " or " in prospect of " his death.

Ver. 12.   The ancient Rabbins said, " This is the day of Messiah."   (See Talmud, Gill.)

Ver. 13.   " Coucheth." This remarkable expression is repeated from the blessing of Jacob, as are the fifteenth and sixteenth verses.   It is a Jewish remark, that every prophet quotes from the preceding ones.

Ver. 16.   Here again, as in the prophecy of Jacob, it is *spoken* by a prophet, that He, the Messiah, should be a Nazarite.

Ver. 17.   The word rendered unicorn, rhinoceros, or elk, is rendered lifted up in Zech. xiv. 10; and in Ps. lxxv. 10 the root is so applied to the horn of the righteous, also in Ps. lxxxix. 16, 17.

Ver. 18.   In the going forth of the promised seed, to dwell with men, as in Virgo.

Ver. 20.   The same word is used for the arm of a man and for the fore-leg of an animal. The fore-leg of Aries is on the head of the sea-monster Cetus, or Leviathan, below, showing the predicted bruising the head of the enemy.

Ver. 21.   The beginning of the year, which had previously been at the anniversary of the creation, at the junction of Leo and Virgo, was now, by Divine command, transferred to the new moon of Aries, the portion of the lawgiver, under the type of the lamb slain at the passover.

Ver. 23.   This prophecy remains to be fulfilled, apparently at the restoration of Israel.

Ver. 25.   The rendering of this passage has been disputed; but the word translated strength is so used in Arabic, also in Chaldee, (see Buxtorf,) and is so rendered in the Syriac and Targum (see Lee's Lexicon).

Ver. 26.   " God " is here the singular, El, as is frequent where the second person of the Trinity, about to take into union the human nature, is intended.   In ver. 27 it is Elohim, the Triune God.   For the plurality of Elohim, see Gen. i. 26; xi. 7; Isa. vi. 8.   " R. S. ben Jochai says : Come and see the mystery of the word Elohim.   There are three degrees, and each degree is by itself alone; and yet they are all one, and joined together in one, and are not divided from each other."   (Zohar, Bagster's Comp. Bible.)

Ver. 29.   " Triumph," see Exod. xv. 1.

THE ENCAMPMENT OF ISRAEL IN THE WILDERNESS[1],
AND THE BREASTPLATE OF THE HIGH PRIEST.

The blessing of Jacob had annexed a prophetic importance to these emblems, and had allotted them to the tribes as their standards.   The Supreme Ruler of all things saw fit to direct the encampment of the Children of Israel, " every man by his own standard, with the ensign of his father's house," in their progress through the wilderness.   This their journeying is allowed to be typical of that of the individual soul in its passage through this wilderness of human life, and of the destinies of the Church in its terrestrial existence.   Prophecy, the great proof of the Divine government of the world, and of the fact that God has spoken, pervades the patriarchal and Mosaic records and institutions.   Thus is shown the purpose of Divine dictation in what might otherwise appear unworthy of such superintendence.   The same direction was given as to the placing of the precious stones on the breastplate of the high priest[2].   They are called by names analogous in meaning to those of the ensigns of the tribes.   Thus Odem differently pointed is Adam, flesh, the human nature of the Messiah, who is allowed by Jew and Christian to be typified by the Lion of the tribe of Judah.   The beginning being thus fixed, as in the order for the encampment, the others will follow the same order.   Pitdah, the reward, the price, accords with the reward of Issachar, the possession, in Cancer.   Bareketh, the shining forth, with the dwelling among men in Zebulon and Virgo.   Nophek, the pouring forth, with Reuben and Aquarius.   Sapphire, the number, as in Pisces, who have heard, as Simeon.   Jahalom, which breaks as the diamond, piercing, as Gad, as Aries.   Leshem, the nations, of the fruitful, Joseph and Ephraim.   Shebo, the inhabiting, as in the tabernacle; joined together by redemp-

---

[1] Num. ii.   [2] Exod. xxviii.

tion, as in Levi and Libra. Achlama, which restores, recovers, as Benjamin the spoil. Tarshish, the possession, ruled over, as Dan. Shoham, strong, as Asher, and the horse in Sagittarius. Jasphè, breaking, as jasper is known to do; as Naphtali in wrestling, and Capricorn in being slain. The names used in translations are uncertain or arbitrary.

Eben, a stone, is from the root *Bana*, to build, from which also is *Ben*, a son. Stones build up a house, a dwelling: sons, a house, a family. A stone is thus a type of the Son, the promised Messiah. Stone is first applied in Scripture as typical of the Messiah in Gen. xlix. 24; again in Isa. xxviii. 16. From Ps. cxviii. 22, it is applied by our Lord to Himself, and by the Apostles, Acts iv. 11.

In Exod. xxviii. a command is given to grave the names of the sons of Israel, according to their birth, on two stones of onyx, six on each. Shoham, an onyx, may be considered as intensive of Shem, a name, as a great or strong name. " Name " is often applied to Christ, as in Mal. i. 11, &c.; Acts iv. 12, &c. Shoham may also convey the idea of " this, the multitude," the many. The onyx has many layers or stripes of colour, whence it may have been named and selected to receive many names. Josephus says, " The sardonyx which the high priest wore on his shoulder, displayed a supernatural brilliancy when the Almighty approved the oblations. When in consequence of our supplications He was disposed to grant us a victory, the Essen (or breastplate) emitted a dazzling lustre." The Essen or Hoshen, the *silent*, spoke by the light of its gems. The Chaldee paraphrase on the Song of Solomon says the twelve signs were engraven on the stones of the breastplate, and that they were lucid, like lamps. Maimonides relates, that " the inquirer knelt, while by the increased brilliancy of the stones the answer was read to him by the high priest." Some authorities say that only the ruler or king had a right thus to inquire. The significant names of the tribes and the stones, and their oneness of purpose, the certain approach, the sufferings, and the glory that was to follow, of Him spoken of by all the Prophets from the beginning of the world, show the intention of these apparently arbitrary and minute arrangements. They were prophetic: half of their message is fulfilled in the first coming, half remains to be fulfilled in the second coming of Him they thus prefigured. That the stones on the breastplate of the high priest, and the names engraven on them, had meanings corresponding with each other and with the twelve signs, which ancient authorities say were also engraven on them, has not been equally noticed. That the types and shadows of the Levitical Law were similarly hieroglyphical no scriptural theologian questions.

The fact of Moses having been divinely directed to the use of types, which had been and would be idolatrously perverted, may be understood on the supposition of their having been originally devoted to the glory of the God of Abraham, of Isaac, and of Jacob, and known as such to their descendants. If these emblems each expressed a prophecy concerning the Messiah, made known to the constructors by the earliest revelation, the great honour thus put upon them is intelligible. The prophecies were of God; the symbols contrived to transmit them were of man, but of man living under the manifestation of the prophetic spirit; for we know that Enoch, one of their alleged originators, was a prophet.

In tracing the analogy between the emblems of the constellations and the types of the Levitical Law, it should be borne in mind that this analogy is a natural consequence of the oneness of the subject. The theme of both is the coming of the promised Redeemer, his person and his work. In both the first type is the lamb or young ram. The ancient year of the Hebrews had begun at the traditional anniversary of the creation, where the figure of the lion joins that of the virgin. The civil year of the Jews still commences when the sun is among those stars. By Divine command, the beginning of the sacred year was placed where the sign of the ram or lamb corresponded to the appointment then made of the feast of the passover. Neither solstice nor equinox was then in that sign; neither were its stars visible at night. Only the type there expressed affords a reason for the appointment. The constellation Virgo, figuring the branch, and the woman bearing the seed, would then be seen resplendently in the clear sky of the house of bondage, from which the shepherd of Israel, typified in the accompanying constellation of Bootes, was now leading his purchased flock, represented in the two sheepfolds so long misconstrued as bears. Soon after the going out from Egypt, the bull is ordained for sacrifice[1], in connexion with the consecration of the high priest, the leader and ruler of the people, as the bull was of the herd. This meaning is conveyed in the names of the animal, of the sign, and of its chief star. With the bull two rams without blemish were to be offered. The ram or lamb was equally typical of the great High Priest " who offered himself without spot to God[2]." The two lambs of morning and evening sacrifice accord with Aries and the victim in Libra, one rising when the other sets ; thus keeping constantly in view the Lamb of God, who taketh away the sin of the world, and thus showing that while the Ruler is one, his human nature will appear twice, in the morning and the evening of the dispensation. The altar of incense is then ordained. On the similar starry emblem the victim held and pierced by the Centaur seems about to be placed. On the altar of incense the high priest was to sprinkle the blood of the sin-offering once in the year, on the great day of atonement, the tenth of the seventh month. At that time the sun, among the stars of Scorpio, was over those stars called the Altar. On that great day the sun's place was by the red star Antares, the wounding, wherein is shown the bruising of Messiah's heel, and of the enemy's head. It is said that the Jewish calendar was rectified by reckoning in one year twelve, and in the next thirteen moons. Therefore if on that day in one year the sun was exactly over any star, in the next he would be near it, and in the third return to it again. On the day of atonement there were to be two goats, one slain, the other sent away into a " land of separation," of cutting off, as the unseen state. The death, resurrection, and ascension of the Divine Atoner, are here typified. In the twins of Gemini, one mortal, the other immortal; in the united figures of Ophiuchus, the desired, and Hercules, who bruises the dragon's head; in Capricorn, the falling sacrifice, and Aries, the Lamb that had been slain, but now overcoming as Lord of lords[3], we find among the stars responding emblems. On the fifteenth day of the seventh month the sun would be under the branch held by Hercules, and that in the hand of Bootes, having passed through the sign of which the branch is the leading idea. On that day the Israelites were to make themselves booths or tabernacles of branches[4] : they were to dwell in and be sheltered by Him whose name is the Branch. The star by us called Spica, the ear of corn, the seed, by the Arabs the branch, would be with the sun by day, and at other seasons by night mark its place, at that great feast which showed forth the dwelling on earth of Him who was to come, his tabernacling among men. The two birds of atonement—one killed, the other let go free— also typify the death, resurrection, and ascension of Him who, coming down from heaven, should return thither. With these correspond the constellations Aquila, the wounded and falling eagle, and the eagle of Lyra, risen and triumphing. The slain bird was to be killed over water from a running stream : so the falling eagle is over the water flowing from the urn of Aquarius. Aquila, the wounded, Vega, the triumphant, in Lyra, and Cygnus, the wild swan going and returning, are among the most remarkable of the stars in our sky, and the first to be recognized by learners : would it not be well again to connect with them the death, resurrection, ascension, and coming again of the great object of prophecy, of Him who is equally the subject of the types of the Levitical Law and the emblems of ancient astronomy ?

While in the emblems and names of the signs ten more especially typify the promised Conqueror of the serpent, and two His people, in all the names of the sons of Jacob there is also a secondary reference to the people, the Church, as typified by the Israelitish nation. These names were written on the breastplate[5], it should seem, beneath the emblems or abbreviated

---

[1] Exod. xxix. 1.   [2] Heb. ix. 14.
[3] Rev. xvii. 14.   [4] Lev. xxiii.
[5] It seems probable that in the breastplate only the abbreviations or hieroglyphics of the signs were engraven, in literal obedience to the second commandment. The forms had been desecrated in the service of idolatry, which these abbreviated characters never had been. The horns, or power of wounding or bruising, of the two first signs, the union of the third, the possession in the fourth, the leaping forth in the fifth, the branch and spike in the sixth, the scales brought to evenness in the seventh, the sting in the eighth, the arrow in the ninth, the goat's horns with the fish's tail in the tenth, the water in the eleventh, the different turn of the heads and the band in the twelfth, all avoid the likeness of any thing in heaven or in earth. Like the cherubic heads, they typify the action, not the actor.

characters of the signs. They contain all the letters of the Hebrew alphabet except five, which are interchangeable with those they do contain. If, as Maimonides relates, it was by a supernatural illumination of the gems of the breastplate (with which its name Hushon, *the silent*, agrees), in this manner the high priest would read off the words of the oracle.

In the names given by Divine direction to the child of the prophet Isaiah, and to those of Hosea, we find example and authority for seeking the meanings in other names, especially in those of Divine selection, such as those of the stones of the breastplate, while in the name given to Noah, the meaning of which is recorded as intentionally applied, we find precedent for those of the sons of Jacob.

NOTES.

Hengstenberg, in his "Christology," observes, "The encampment of Israel, Num. ii., has its foundation in Genesis: in chapter xlix. is the key to the arrangement. The same order is observed in Num. vii." "Balaam intentionally refers to Gen. xlix., also Moses in Deut. xxxiii." He thinks *Shilo* is "our peace," or peace-giver, and alluded to in Luke ii. 14.

Memes, "On the Fine Arts of the Jews," remarks, that "where Moses may seem to have adopted Egyptian accessories, it is probable that he returned to patriarchal and even antediluvian forms of worship."

Bunsen rejects the notion of an Indian origin of Egyptian mythology or science. Ancient writers attribute it to the Chaldeans, so more directly from Noah.

NOTE ON JACOB.

The first revelation was too familiar to Isaac and Rebekah not to be borne in mind in naming Jacob, "he shall take hold of the heel," and Esau, "the ordained," (as in 1 Kings xii. 32,) as the firstborn ordained, by that birthright he afterwards sold, to the headship of the family, and so far to the priestly office as to offer the family sacrifices. These names would then bear the meaning, "Jacob shall take hold of the bruised heel of Him, the Ordained to bruise the serpent's head." Esau appears to have been the name of the firstborn till he sold his birthright, afterwards Edom, the red, from the colour of his hair. It is possible that in thus naming his twin children Isaac might have in view the twins of the zodiac, one of whom has a name, Pollux, the ruler, to whom the name Wasat, the appointed or ordained, from the same root as Esau, would also apply. The other twin has a name, Castor, quickly coming, hastening, in allusion to which Jacob, as coming quickly after Esau, might be named, the root of *Jacob* having sometimes the sense of pursuing, coming along a track or way. From the names of his ancestors of the line of Seth, Isaac might have the idea of thus connecting the names of his descendants with the emblems of astronomy, or rather with the great truths those emblems were intended to convey.

The Twelve Signs

AS ALLUDED TO BY JACOB IN GEN. XLIX., AND BY MOSES IN DEUT. XXXIII.

	By JACOB, *Gen.* xlix.	By MOSES, *Deut.* xxxiii.
AQUARIUS, Reuben.	Ver. 4. Poured out as *water*.	Ver. 6. Let not his *men* be few.
PISCES, Simeon & Levi.	5. *Brethren.*	8. Thy *Urim* and thy *Thummim*.
LEO, Judah.	9. A *lion*, &c.	7. Bring him unto his people: let his *hands* [1] be sufficient for him.
VIRGO, Zebulon.	13. He shall *dwell*.	18. Rejoice, Zebulon, in thy *going out* or forth.
CANCER, Issachar.	14 and 15. A *strong ass;* he saw his *resting-place,* that it was good.	18. Issachar, in thy *tents*.
SCORPIO, Dan.	17. A *serpent by the way*.	22. He shall *leap* or *spring* (as the adder).
ARIES, Gad.	19. A *troop* shall pierce him. "He shall be pierced in the heel."	21. He provided the *first part* for himself, &c.
SAGITTARIUS, Asher.	20. The sweet influences of a *king*, Job xxxviii. 31.	25. Thy *shoes* shall be iron and brass.
CAPRICORNUS, Naphtali.	21. A *hind let loose*, released, or sent forth.	23. Satisfied with favour, and filled with the blessing of the Lord.
TAURUS, Joseph.	22. The daughters walk before the *bull*.	17. His glory like the firstling of his *bullock*.
GEMINI, Benjamin.	27. The *wolf* shall tear: in the morning he shall feed on the prey, in the evening he shall divide the spoil.	12. The *beloved* of the Lord shall dwell between his shoulders.

Josephus informs us that the twelve tribes of Israel bore the twelve signs on their banners; and the Chaldee paraphrase, of a still earlier date, asserting the same, adds that the figure of a man was borne on the standard of Reuben, a bull on that of Ephraim, a lion on that of Judah, an eagle on that of Dan. The Targums also attribute to Dan a crowned serpent, or basilisk.

Libra was not borne on any of the standards, Simeon and Levi being included together under Pisces, and the place of Libra and of Levi in the encampment of Israel being that occupied by the Tabernacle.

Part of these prophetic annunciations are as yet unfulfilled, some relating to the final triumph of the "King Messiah," and some to the eventual position of the tribes in the restoration of Israel to their own land. The prediction early accomplished, that the sovereignty should be vested in the tribe of Judah, was the authentication, the seal of the remaining prophecies. As surely as David the son of Jesse, of the tribe of Judah, reigned on Mount Zion, so surely unto that Shilo, that Prince of Peace, who is the root and offspring of David, will be the gathering of the nations.

---

[1] The word equally applies to the fore-paw of an animal, as does the "arm" in ver. 20.

Types of the Levitical Law,

CORRESPONDING WITH THE SIGNS, OR THEIR ACCOMPANYING CONSTELLATIONS.

The paschal lamb (*Se*, Arab. *progeny*, Egypt. *son*), With Aries, the ram or lamb. John i. 29. 1 Cor. v. 7.	Exod. 12.
The young bull, the offering at the consecration of the high priest, With Taurus, the bull. Heb. ix. 11, 12.	Exod. 29. Lev. 8. 2.
The two goats of the day of atonement, With Gemini, the twins, or pair. Heb. ix. 13, 14.	Lev. 16.
The firstborn of cattle to be redeemed, With Cancer, the redeemed possession, under the type of cattle. Col.i.15.	Ex. 13. 12,13; 34. 19, 20.
The cup, or basin, With the cup, crater, in Leo. Matt. xxvi. 39.	Exod. 12. 22; 24. 6, 8.
The firstfruits of corn, With the ears of corn in Virgo. 1 Cor. xv. 23.	Exod. 23. 19; 34. 22, 26.
The crown of the high priest, With the Northern Crown in Libra. Matt. xxvii. 29. Rev. xiv. 14.	Exod. 29. 6.
The high priest making the sin-offering, With Ophiuchus and Hercules in Scorpio. Heb. x. 12.	Exod. 30. 10.
The golden altar, With the altar in Sagittarius. Heb. xiii. 10.	Exod. 40. 5.
The goat of the sin-offering, With Capricornus. Heb. ix. 28.	Lev. 4. 24.
The running water, over which the birds were one to be killed and one let go, With Aquarius. John iii. 5; iv. 14.	Lev. 14. 5, 6.

If any evidence were desired to show that these correspondences are simply from the identity of the subject, redemption by the promised Messiah, it may be found in the absence of any thing referring to the sign Pisces.

The coincidence, more or less complete, between the other emblems of the signs and the types of the Levitical law is consequent on the sameness of the subject, the Redeemer and His work. The law as given by Moses renewed, amplified, and gave additional and most solemn sanction to the first revelation, the original law of the human race.

Here, as elsewhere, it should be observed that the animals of the signs, as well as those of the Levitical law, typified not the person but the actions of Him who was to come; they came and they were sacrificed, by Divine appointment, in atonement for sin.

The first type of the Levitical law was that indicated in the emblem of the lamb or ram in the sign Aries. In that sign it was ordained that the sacred year of the Jews should begin. The new moon in that sign was called the moon or month Abib, the beginning, when the ears of corn began to swell. Then also the firstfruits were commanded to be offered in the temple: they were being so offered at the time of our Lord's resurrection. The bright star Spica, the ear of corn, in Virgo, shone on that solemn hour, when very early in the morning, while it was yet dark, the predicted seed of the woman had become the firstfruit from the dead.

If the supposition be correct that the bright star in Coma, which afterwards faded away, was Messiah's star, the star of Bethlehem, that also shone on the accom-

E

plished prophecy. The moon full among the stars of Libra, the type of the redemption now completed, might dim but would not eclipse it.

It should seem that He who seeth the end from the beginning had overruled to the purposes of prophecy the placing of these emblems in the zodiac. The emblems themselves and their ancient names may be referred to mere human wisdom in their adaptation to the predictions they were intended to transmit, but the correspondence between their purport and the place of the sun when the events so typified occurred, must be the work of the Spirit of prophecy, whether consciously or unconsciously guiding those who so arranged them. When corroborated, in the intervening ages, by the analogous types of the law, the proof that a revelation had been given, that the Lord had spoken, is complete.

The person and work of Christ it is allowed were foreshown in the types of the Levitical law; it might therefore be anticipated that the symbols of the ancient sphere corresponding with them would be again met with in the New Testament. First, of the ear of corn, the seed, our Lord makes use as typifying Himself, His death, His resurrection, and the increase of His spiritual offspring, where He thus speaks, " Verily, verily, I say unto you, except a corn of wheat fall into the ground and die, it abideth alone : but if it die, it bringeth forth much fruit." The word here translated " corn " is rendered in the Hebrew New Testament by the word for seed in Gen. iii. 15. The same emblem is again adopted by St. Paul as to the general resurrection. The accompanying symbol, the palm-branch, employed so often by the prophets [1], was recognized as belonging to the expected Messiah, the Son of David, by the great multitudes who hailed His entry into Jerusalem strewing palm-branches in the way. It may be seen that each human figure in the ancient sphere carried a palm-branch. Baion, in the Greek, as in the Semitic dialects, is " which cometh." Bai is also the Egyptian name of the palm branch.

The divinely appointed emblem of the victim-Lamb was at once applied to Him whom it typified, by the voice that in the wilderness was crying, Prepare ye the way of the Lord, as " the Lamb of God which taketh away the sin of the world." The victim held by the centaur, about to be pierced by the dart in his other hand, prefiguring the weapon that pierced the Lamb of God on the cross, corresponded from the beginning with the sacrifice of Abel and of Abraham, and the paschal lamb itself, which was pierced at the very moment when the Lamb of God expired, rendering all other sacrifice vain. When Christ our Passover was slain for us, the great cycle of the dispensation of types and shadows was accomplished. The very Jews themselves, who reject the one great offering their law so long prefigured, have now no sacrifice. The Levitical law, like the emblems of ancient astronomy, remains to tell to all earth's coming ages that of old the Lord hath spoken.

NOTE.

Two lambs were to be sacrificed for a peace-offering. (Lev. xxiii. 19.) Hyde on the religion of the ancient Persians, remarking that " the symbols of the twelve signs came to us from the most ancient Chaldeans and Phœnicians," adds, that " the Gemini of the Phœnicians were not human figures, but twin kids or lambs." It is therefore probable that the ancient Hebrews so figured that sign, especially as the name by which they knew it, Thaumim, is applied to kids or lambs, as in Cant. iv. 2.

---

[1] Isa. iv. 2; xi. 1.   Jer. xxiii. 5; xxxiii. 15.   Zech. iii. 8; vi. 12.

On the Cherubic Forms

AS CONNECTED WITH THE EMBLEMS OF ANCIENT ASTRONOMY.

	CHERUBIM.		Texts where the root occurs in this sense.	Hebrew roots.
Gen. 3. 24.	Cherub, *thus the Mighty One.*			
Exod. 25.18.	Che, *thus, in this manner.*	*thus*	Gen. 32. 4.	כה
2 Sa. 22. 11.	Rub, *the mighty.*	*mighty*	Isa. 63. 1.	רב
1 Kgs. 6. 24.				

	FACES.			
Ezek. 1. 6.	Man, Adam, *the likeness.*	*likeness*	Gen. 1. 26.	דם
	Lion, Arieh, *coming* (Arab. sense) *as light, a river;* also, *separating, rending.* Ps. lxxx. 12.	*flood*	Amos 8. 8.	אר
	Ox, or Bull, Shur, *coming, stepping forth.*	*steps*	Job 23. 11.	אשר
Rev. 4 7.	or Calf, Eglah, *coming again, as circling.*	*round about*	2 Chr. 4. 2.	עגל
	Eagle, Nesir, *caused to come down. Separating* (Arab. sense).	*directeth*	Job 37. 3.	ישר

Holy Scripture reveals to us the Divine appointment of the cherubim at the east of Eden, over the mercy-seat in the tabernacle, and in the temple of Solomon. Had this appointment not been made, it might be difficult to admit that the use of such figures as those of the constellations, afterwards corrupted to the purposes of idol-worship, could have received the sanction of those "holy prophets who have been since the world began." Coeval with these prophets the emblems of astronomy are traditionally held to have existed, and to have been invented by some of the earliest among them.

As from the cherubic faces most of the idols of the heathen can be shown to have originated, the perversion of the astral figures to the usages of idolatry cannot be urged against their intention. On the authority of the divinely ordained emblems, it may be permitted to infer the similar design and signification of those uninspired symbols that appear to have been constructed after their example.

Whatever those cherubim might be which the Lord placed at the entrance of Eden, whether angelic existences or visionary similitudes, to Adam, Seth, and Enoch they must have been well known, and by them their meaning understood. If from the cherubic forms the figures of the constellations were derived, in order to explain these, the meaning of their originals should be ascertained. It is no where explicitly revealed what these cherubic emblems were intended to typify or to teach. The ancient Jews held that the cherubim in the holy of holies referred to the coming of the God of Israel to Sinai. They asserted, however, that previously these emblems "had always been among believers, in the holy tabernacle from the beginning, when they were placed (tabernacled) before the gate of Eden:" also, that they were known to Noah and Abraham. Thus may be accounted for the prevalence of these forms before the time of Moses in the sculptures of Assyria, Etruria, and Egypt. In consequence of the likeness between the figures of the Assyrian sculptures and those of the vision of Ezekiel, an idea has arisen that Ezekiel might borrow his imagery from those sculptures. But that imagery had a far earlier, a far higher, origin: the similitudes here presented to the prophet had been placed at the gate of Eden, in the tabernacle of Moses, and in the temple of Solomon. When that temple was destroyed, Ezekiel was taught to describe and transmit to posterity their forms, with which, being a priest, he was well acquainted.

These symbolic figures would be to the ancient patriarchs what the types of the Levitical law were to their descendants, shadows of things to come [1]. What then did they shadow forth?

Some Christian writers have attempted to explain the four cherubic faces as showing the human nature of Christ in union with the three persons of the Triune Godhead [2]. By this theory the person of the Father was typified by the bull, for which there is no Scriptural authority. The person of the Son being so typified in sacrifice, this explanation seems at once set aside. By it the eagle was made an emblem of the Holy Spirit, wholly incongruous with that of Scripture, the dove. In the lion, however, they recognized an authorized symbol of the Messiah, the Lion of the tribe of Judah. To Him, and Him alone, the cherubim refer, as their forms and their name abundantly testify.

Others have tried to interpret these "cherubim of glory" of believers, or ministers of the Gospel. Have they not overlooked, that He who appointed these emblems has said, "My glory will I not give to another [3]"? What unprejudiced mind would not revolt from the supposition that the representations of frail, fallible, sinful mortals could be enshrined in the awful sanctuary which it was death for man to enter, save once a year the high priest, in fear and trembling? The tendency of this interpretation is not "to hide pride from man," but to feed that self-importance which grace discourages, but does not eradicate. To whom should these "cherubim of glory" refer, but to the Lord of glory? What should they declare, but that "He that cometh, will come,"—the sacrifice and the sovereign?

The difficulties attendant on the foregoing interpretations are avoided by that which would explain the cherubic emblems as typifying what the promised Deliverer should do, rather than what He should be: not His person, but His actions: His coming, first to suffer, to redeem; again, to judge, to reign. As shown in the human face and that of the sacrificial bull, He was to come in human nature, and to be a sacrifice for sin; as in the lion, coming to rend the prey, and the eagle descending from on high, He was, He is, to come again, to separate good from evil, to subdue all things unto Himself. When Ezekiel saw the cherubim in vision, they were coming, bringing onward the throne, above it the appearance of the Man, the second Adam, the likeness of the glory of God. In the sculptures of Assyria and Etruria, figures compounded of the cherubic forms are walking, coming, as are most of those of the constellations even as now delineated, and more strikingly so in the Egyptian sphere. "He who cometh" is the title of the promised Messiah from Genesis to Revelation. "Behold, He cometh!" was the voiceless proclamation of the herald-cherubim at the gate of Eden: "Surely I come quickly," the annunciation of the Apocalypse. "Even so come, Lord Jesus," is the reply of the believer in all ages.

We are not told whether the name cherub was appointed of the Lord, or whether

---

[1] Col. ii. 17.

[2] This interpretation has chiefly been supported by a passage in the Apocalypse, where the four living creatures having the faces of the cherubim are supposed to say (Rev. iv. 8, 9), "Thou hast redeemed us to God by Thy blood, out of every kindred, and tongue, and people, and nation." But it is to be observed, that "every one of them" is literally "every man of them," the pronoun referring to them being masculine and singular, while the noun, the living creatures, is neuter and plural. These men, the twenty-four elders, then praised the Lamb for having redeemed them, and to their hymn the living creatures said, Amen.

[3] Isa. xlii. 8.

Adam gave the name, as to the animals, from what the object before him indicated. This, as to the cherubim, he could only know by its agreement with the revelation he received.　By the promise of the seed of the woman might be explained the face of the man ; by the rite of sacrifice, that of the bull ; by the second coming announced by Enoch, those of the lion and of the eagle.　Other names are recorded in Scripture, as given by divine command, all expressive and containing their message in themselves ; as Israel, a prince of God : there are also names, as Noah, given on account of their meanings.　The name Cherub may therefore be expected to contain its own message.　No explanation of it is given in Holy Writ.　When first mentioned it is as *the* cherubim[1], as if equally well known to the writer and the readers of the record.

Adam appears to have given names to the animals brought to him from the actions he saw them perform, or saw they were fitted for.　These names were probably those preserved in the Hebrew, Arabic, and other ancient dialects.　The animals whose faces formed parts of the cherubic images were no doubt seen and named by him.　Names given by man as denoting actions, would be intelligible to man as expressing actions : figures suggesting those ideas were accordingly used in the forms of the cherubim ; they spoke to man in his own language.　Adam saw each of these three animals *coming*, with different modifications of that leading idea.　Thus the bull came stepping on the earth ; Arieh, the lion, sprung swiftly forward ; Nesir, the eagle, came descending from the clouds of heaven.

The four cherubic forms were early appropriated, as emblems, to the four Evangelists.　To St. Matthew was given the man, because of beginning with the genealogy of the supposed father of the Messiah, whose heir he became through his mother Mary. To St. Mark was given the lion, some say because he alone mentions the wild beasts being with Christ in the wilderness.　To St. Luke the ox, a sacrificial animal, as most explicit on the subject of the incarnation of Christ at his first coming to be a sacrifice for sin.　To St. John the eagle, because he early relates Christ's declaration to Nathanael of the glory of the second coming.　Thus Jerome and Ambrose divide them ; but Augustine says he prefers " the tradition " which gave the lion to Matthew and the man to Mark.　Neither of these traditions lays any claim to inspiration : their chief importance is in showing that neither the interpretation which would make the cherubic forms symbolize the Holy Trinity, nor that which would lower them to emblematize human beings, was prevalent in the primitive Church.

To the opinion that they in any way referred to the Divine Saviour, the Mighty One who should come, it has been objected that " the living creatures " in Rev. iv. " give glory " to Him that sitteth on the throne : but so does, or ought to do, man bearing the likeness of Him who made and who redeemed him.　The likeness, whether in flesh or in spiritual existence, is not the reality, but the shadow ; and the shadow may well bow down before the substance.　Before the shadow, the image, we may not bow : in so doing, the Israelites in the wilderness, and Jeroboam in Samaria, were guilty of idolatry.　These emblems were not ordained to be worshipped, but to instruct, to foreshow the two comings of Him who was to come, in whom should dwell the fulness of the Godhead bodily, as the God of Israel dwelt between the cherubim.

---

[1] Gen. iii. 24, where the definite article is omitted in the E. V.

Symbols of the Constellations.

THE TWELVE SIGNS.

		Texts where so used.
ARIES,	The lamb, of innocence, meekness. Exod. xii. 3.	Isa. 53. 7. Lu. 10. 3.
TAURUS,	The bull, of power, rule. Exod. xxix. 1.	Ps. 22. 12. Isa. 34. 7.
GEMINI,	Gemini, of union, entwining, twins. Lev. xiv. 22.	Cant. 6. 6.
CANCER,	The crab or scarabæus, of holding or binding.	Gen. 49. 11.
LEO,	The lion, of victory. Gen. xlix. 9.	Ps. 7. 2.
VIRGO,	The ear of corn, of seed or offspring. Exod. xxii. 29.	Deut. 26. 2.
LIBRA,	The balance, of weighing. Lev. xix. 36.	Isa. 40. 12. Dan. 5. 27.
SCORPIO,	The scorpion, of wounding. 1 Kings xii. 11.	Ezek. 2. 6.
SAGITTARIUS,	The arrow, of going forth. Ps. xlv. 5.	Zech. 9. 14.
CAPRICORNUS,	The kid of sacrifice. Lev. xxiii. 19.	Exod. 12. 3.
AQUARIUS,	The water of cleansing. Lev. viii. 6. Isa. xxxv. 6, 7. John iv. 11.	Isa. 44. 3.
PISCES,	The fishes, of multitudes. Luke v. 6. John xxi. 6. Matt. iv. 19.	Eze. 47. 9, 10.

Such are the meanings of the names, such the distinguishing qualities of the objects, such the use made of them as symbols in all times and countries. An exception, however, must be made as to the crab or sacred beetle of Egypt, the scarabæus. The Semitic word Sartan applied to the sign is the binding, the holding fast, as the crab its prey, the scarabæus its nest, its progeny. The foal of the ass borne on the standard of Issachar was to be *bound* to the vine, as the Church to the true Vine. The Egyptian scarabæus has by some been interpreted as symbolizing the sun at the summer solstice, where in the splere that figure is frequently placed, because it was said to pass half the year above and half below the ground; by others it has been held to typify, like the butterfly of the Greeks, the immortality of the soul, part of its existence being passed upon or under the earth, part soaring above it in the boundless heaven. In this view the scarabæus becomes an emblem worthy of the series with which it is connected. It is often seen in Egyptian remains[1] ascending with expanded wings, with human figures below in attitudes of admiration, so, like the Grecian Psyche, emblematizing the human soul freed from the body, rising to celestial life and endless happiness. The resemblance of the Egyptian mummies to the chrysalis has often been noticed; and the idea of thus preserving the human body for the expected resurrection may have thence originated[2].

Of the remaining thirty-six symbols, the Decans, the 1st, the 16th, and the 35th are the woman, every where a prophetic type of the Church.

Cassiopeia,	As the Church enthroned in glory.	Isa. 54. 11, 12. Rev. 19. 7, 8.
Virgo,	„ the Church in which the promised seed is born.	Isa. 7. 14.
Andromeda,	„ the Church in bonds, from which the promised deliverer releases her.	Isa. 49. 24.

In the 3rd, 4th, 6th, 18th, 22nd, and 34th the man represents the promised seed, the Redeemer,

Perseus,	As coming to break the bonds of the Church.	Mic. 2. 13.
Orion,	„ coming in glory.	Isa. 63. 1.
Auriga,	„ the good shepherd. John x. 11. Ps. xxiii.	Isa. 40. 11.
Boötes,	„ the keeper of the flock. Ps. cxxi. 3.	Ps. 121. 5.
Ophiuchus,	„ bruising the head of the enemy, receiving the wound in the heel.	
Hercules,	„ the deliverer kneeling as wounded, but about to crush the head of the dragon.	Isa. 53. 10.

---

[1] For instance, on the sarcophagus of Alexander in the British Museum.
[2] Herodotus was told by the Egyptian priests, that after 3000 years the dead would rise again.

		Texts where so used.
	As the flock of the Good Shepherd, the Lord's people are represented in the 10th, 11th, and 12th; and in the 33rd by the ancient Christian emblem of the Church, the fish.	
Ursa Minor,	The lesser flock, of the suffering Church, resting on the Lamb that was slain. Mic. vii. 14. Ps. lxxvii. 20 ; lxxviii. 52.	Lu. 12. 32.
Ursa Major,	The flock of after times, looking to Orion coming in glory, and following Arcturus their keeper and guardian going before. Isa. lx. 7. Jer. xxiii. 3.	Joh. 10. 16.
Argo,	The company of the Prince, the desired, the seed.	Cant. 6. 13.
Southern Fish,	The Church refreshed by the pouring forth of the Holy Spirit.	
	The enemy appears in the 2nd, 7th, 13th, 23rd, 25th, and 36th,	
Head of Medusa,	As finally subdued. Ps. lxviii. 21.	Gen. 3. 15.
Lepus,	„ trodden under foot.	Ps. 91. 13.
Hydra,	„ with the cup of wrath resting on him.	Ps. 75. 8.
Serpent,	„ wrestling, but overpowered.	Isa. 27. 1.
Draco,	„ encircling the centre of the sphere.	Rev. 12. 4.
Cetus,	„ bound, under the foot of the Lamb that had been slain.	Rev. 20. 2.

Each of these symbolical figures is performing a typical action, an action suited to the nature of the object it represents. The southern fish might seem to be an exception, for fishes do not drink; but water is to be drunk, and must here be considered the symbol. That of which the fish is the type, the multitude of the Church, is here shown drinking in the water of life, as promised by her Lord to the woman at the well of Samaria.

However well known may be the general forms of the twelve signs of the zodiac, they are often in some particulars incorrectly represented, thus obscuring their leading ideas; as, in heraldic terms, Aries, the ram or lamb, should be *couchant*, while the bull and lion should be *passant*. Aries should be holding in his fore-foot the band that unites the two fishes of Pisces, and also that with which the sea-monster or leviathan is bound ; the bull rushing on as if overthrowing, dispersing his adversaries. In the twins, the first holds an arrow, the second a palm-branch. The crab has been hopelessly corrupted, apparently from the scarabæus, the sacred beetle of the Egyptians, but preserving the idea of holding fast a possession. The lion is coming, leaping forth, his foot over the head of the serpent Hydra. The virgin holds in one hand a palm-branch, in the other an ear of corn. The scales should be uneven, the northern exalted, the southern depressed. The sting of the scorpion should be reverted, as in wounding ; the arrow coming forth ; the goat or kid sinking down, and having the body of a fish ; the man pouring forth the water, standing, risen ; the fishes bound together and looking different ways. These emblems, even in some of the ancient Oriental zodiacs, lose their characteristics.

Typical actions, and the representations of actions, speak all languages ; of them it may well be said, there is neither speech nor language, but their voice is heard among them ; and such we find in the Twelve Signs. The woman *upholds* the branch and seed ; one scale *weighing* down the other ; the sting of the scorpion *reverting* to the heel ; the foot of the conqueror *bruising* the head ; the arrow being *sent forth* from the bow ; the victim-goat *bowing down* ; the water being *poured* forth ; the fishes *bound* together ; the ram *holding* in his forefoot their band, and that of the enemy below, whose head he is *bruising* with the other foot ; the head of the bull represented as *rushing on* ; the twins *entwining* each other ; the claws of the crab, or scarabæus, *holding* the possession ; the lion *leaping forth* to rend the prey ; all being actions expressing the prophecy to which they refer.

The decans, or other constellations, also each represent an action developing or extending the meaning of that represented in the sign to which they severally belong.

1. In Cassiopeia the liberated woman is *setting free* her hair.
2. The head of Medusa is being *carried* as in triumph by the armed man.

3. Perseus, the breaker, is *breaking* the bands of Andromeda, the chained woman, and *carrying* the head of his conquered enemy.

These actions exemplify the chief purport of the sign Aries, in which they are placed, showing that He who was Himself pierced, bruised, or broken, shall break the bonds of His Church, and bruise the head of His enemy.

4. With Taurus, the ruling, Orion *comes* in splendour and in strength, his foot *treading* upon the enemy.

5. Eridanus, the river of the Lord, *flows* on.

6. Auriga, the shepherd, carries one of his flock in his bosom.

Here are expressed the victorious coming, the flowing forth, the superintending care of the Prince, the Ruler, the Shepherd of His people.

7. Lepus, representing the enemy in Gemini, is *trodden on* by Orion, while the two dogs or wolves are *coming quickly*, being named

8. The Prince, and

9. The Redeemer, whom they typify.

So showing the two comings of Him, who in one person is David's Lord and also his Son; and they accompany Orion, to whom they are always said to belong.

10. Ursa Minor, the lesser sheepfold, whose stars revolve round the pole, the cynosure, called by the Arabs the kid, thus showing that they belong to Him on whom they wait, the Lamb of God, typified from the beginning of the world in the ordinance of sacrifice.

11. In Ursa Major, the greater sheepfold, the sheep are *following* Arcturus, their keeper and guardian.

12. Argo, the company of travellers, is *following* Canopus, their prince and their guide.

13. In Leo, Hydra, the subdued enemy, is *trodden under foot*.

14. The cup of wrath is *poured out* on him, and

15. The bird of prey is seen *rending* his flesh.

16. In Virgo the seed is *borne* by the woman.

17. The centaur is *piercing* the victim.

18. Bootes or Arcturus, the guardian of the flock, is *going* before them.

19. In Libra the cross is placed under the feet of the centaur, who is *coming* as towards it.

20. The crown above his head seems *threatened* by the serpent, while

21. The victim is being *pierced*, the altar, the cross, and victim showing the price of redemption.

22. In Scorpio the serpent is struggling with Ophiuchus.

23. Ophiuchus is *wrestling* with the serpent, *bruising* the head of the scorpion, receiving the wound in the heel.

24. Hercules *kneeling* from having received the wound in the heel, *threatens* to bruise the head of the great serpent, Draco.

25. Draco, the dragon, accompanying Sagittarius in his going forth, is *wreathing* himself round the pole.

26. The altar under Sagittarius *flames* as it receives the victim.

27. The ascending eagle in Lyra *goes forth* as in triumph.

28. In Capricornus the arrow of death is *sent forth*.

29. Aquila, the falling eagle, *descends* as smitten.

30. The dolphin is *raised, lifted up*.

31. In Aquarius, Cygnus, the swan, is *returning* from afar.

32. The winged horse is *coming quickly*.

33. The southern fish is *drinking in* the water of life.

34. With Pisces, Cepheus, the branch, as the king is firmly *standing* crowned on high.

35. The chained woman is being *liberated* from her bonds.

36. The enemy lies *bound* under the foot of Aries, which *holds* the band.

When it is seen that every explanation here given of the action in each emblem is borne out by the meaning of the ancient names, the unity and consistency of the original design will be made evident. So explained the emblems annexed to the stars of heaven do indeed "declare the glory of God."

" A threefold cord is not quickly broken."—Eccles. iv. 12.

" In the mouth of two or three witnesses every word shall be established."—2 Cor. xiii. 1.

The emblems, the names, and the prophecies agreeing present such a threefold cord, such witnessing.

Emblems.	Names.	Prophecies.
The ram,	ARIES, the ram, *coming forth*.	Isa. 63. 1. Mic. 5. 2.
or lamb,	Taleh, the lamb, *sent forth*. El Nath, Natik, the slain, the pierced.	Gen. 22. 8. Zech. 12. 10.
The bull,	TAURUS, the bull, coming to *rule*.	Isa. 32. 1. Mic. 5. 2.
The twins,	GEMINI, the twins. Thaumim, the *united*. The union of the Divine and human nature.	Zec. 6. 12, 13.
The crab, or scarabæus,	CANCER, holding the possession. Sartan, who holds or *binds*.	Gen. 49. 11.
The lion,	LEO, leaping forth. Arieh, *rending*.	Ibid. Rev. 5. 5.
The virgin,	VIRGO, the virgin, or woman. Bethulah, *virgin*.	Isa. 7. 14.
The scales,	LIBRA, weighing. Al Zubena, *redemption*.	Ps. 130. 7, 8.
The scorpion,	SCORPIO, the conflict. Akrab, scorpion, or *conflict*.	Isa. 63. 3. 5.
The archer,	SAGITTARIUS, the arrow-bearer. Kesith, archer, or bow. Al Kaus, *arrow*.	Ps. 45. 5.
The goat, or kid,	CAPRICORNUS, the goat, or atonement, sinking down. Gedi, the kid, *cut off*, (Arab. sense.)	Isa. 53. 7. Dan. 9. 26.
The water-bearer,	AQUARIUS, the rising up and pouring forth of *water*.	Isa. 44. 3.
The fishes,	PISCES, the fishes, multitudes, as *fish*.	Ezek. 47. 9.

This threefold cord of the emblems, the names, and the prophecies in which those emblems and names are found, *binds*, as it were, their evidence to revelation. . That God has spoken admits of evidence, is open to proof. Something of presumption seems to attend seeking or even bringing forward evidence that *He is*. That great foundational truth we have by tradition. Once taught to look for Him, we see Him in His works; else, like those beasts of the field who are said to be deficient in the power of raising the eyes to heaven [1], we might fail to recognize those traces of His Divine Presence. So witnessed to, we learn from these ancient emblems that God had spoken, had given the prophecies they embody. Could man know of himself, what is here prefigured, that One whom his co-temporaries should call " the Lamb of God " should be slain, pierced, when the sun should be in the stars they had called the lamb, the slain, the pierced? Could man of himself foresee, that fifteen hundred years before that time, and more than two thousand from the time when these emblems are known to have been in use, the people among whom that One should be born would begin to slay a lamb in every family at that precise period in every returning year?

Surely we may say, God had spoken. Needs there any other evidence that HE IS?

[1] It is said that cows and sheep probably never saw a star, not having the muscle which elevates the eyes.

Types of the Apocalypse,

CORRESPONDING WITH THE EMBLEMS OF THE CONSTELLATIONS.

The Lamb who had been slain, With Aries, Capricornus, the victim held by the centaur.	Rev. 5. 6; 7. 17.
The four living creatures before the throne, With Leo, Taurus, the man in Aquarius, the eagle above Scorpio.	Rev. 4. 6, 7, 8.
The white horse and the crowned archer, With Sagittarius.	Rev. 6. 2.
The golden altar, With the altar in Sagittarius.	Rev. 8. 3; 11. 1.
The dragon, With Draco.	Rev. 12. 3, 9.
The serpent, With the serpent held by Ophiuchus.	Rev. 20. 2.

The woman crowned with twelve stars,
    With the woman in Virgo;
    With the woman in Andromeda, when fleeing from the face of the serpent;
    With the woman in Cassiopeia, when as the bride, the Lamb's wife.
	Rev. 12. 1, 5.
	
	Ibid. 14.
	
	Rev. 19. 7, 8;
	21. 9.

"Having on His head a golden crown," "On His head were many crowns," With the Northern Crown.	Rev. 6. 2; 14. 16; 19. 12.

It has been observed by those who would refer the origin of all religions to the constellations, that in the imagery of the Apocalypse may be traced some correspondence with the stellar symbols. With the explanation here given that these emblems typify the progressive manifestations of "the Great One," who is, and was, and is to come, this is not surprising; visions, typical forms, impressed on the eye, mental or bodily, of the seer were from the beginning made the means of conveying the knowledge of future events to the prophet who was to declare them. Those seen by Daniel are, as it were, the key, the foundation of those seen by John. Neither the beasts of Daniel nor those of the Apocalypse were real existences, but images presented to the prophet's sight. He who explained the vision to Daniel told him that the beasts typified empires, and the horns kings. The distinguishing quality of the beast seems to be that it knows not God; its other characteristics depend on its form, one configuration expressing ferocity, others swiftness or voracity. The woman with wings like a stork and the four horses of Zechariah were visionary, not actual existences; so were the star-crowned woman and she who rode the seven-headed beast in the Apocalypse. Among these visions brought before St. John, some coincide with those presented to the minds of the ancient prophets, and others with the typical actions and forms of the Levitical law. The candlestick of Zechariah, or lamp-stand with seven lamps, is the forerunner of the seven seen by St. John, having no analogous figure in the constellations. The Lamb as it had been slain, in the midst of the throne, answers to Aries, Capricornus, and the victim, and to the rite of sacrifice from Abel downwards.

The four cherubic forms, as found in the four cardinal signs, are seen by John as separate living creatures, typifying the two comings of Him before whom they stand. As the man He had come, as the sacrifice He had made atonement for sin, but He was yet to come, separating good from evil, as the lion rends the prey, descending as the eagle from heaven. When both comings were future, the four symbols were united; when one was past, they were separated.

The golden altar before the throne, in the Apocalypse, responds to that below Sagittarius; the dragon whose tail drew the third part of the stars of heaven, to that which wreathes around the northern pole. He that sat on the white cloud had on his head a golden crown; so Cepheus, the never-setting king of the arctic sky, is represented. The white horse on which goes forth the crowned rider, conquering and to conquer, agrees with that called Pegasus, always said to be white. The black horse, whose rider has a pair of balances, suggesting Libra, may be likened to that of Sagittarius; the red or blood-coloured horse, to whose rider was given a great sword, to the Centaur armed with a spear.

The woman equally symbolizes the Church in the constellations and in the Apocalypse. The woman crowned with twelve stars [1], bears, like the virgin of the zodiac, the promised infant; she is threatened by the serpent enemy as Andromeda; as the bride adorned for the marriage supper of the Lamb, she appears in Cassiopeia the enthroned in glory. Still, though the same figure is used, the likeness is only general. The woman of the Apocalypse has no branch, no ear of corn; she is not chained in her affliction, she is not enthroned in her beatitude. The dragon of the Apocalypse is bound, he of the constellations is trodden under foot. The starry crown is vacant, while on the head of the triumphant King of kings in the prophecy are many crowns. The unity of the subject appears in the resemblance of the symbols. Those of the Apocalypse, appointed by Divine wisdom, may throw light on those used by man to transmit the revelation which had been made to him.

How could the magnificent and mysterious symbols of the Apocalyptic visions, transcendent in sublimity, unfathomed in manifold meaning, fulfilling and fulfilled, how could they be copied from the simple emblems of ancient astronomy? Who can think that these spiritually significant images could be derived from the familiar forms of the starry emblems? Such might well embody the figures of that first revelation, so concise in its world-involving vastness, so plain in its announcements of infinite and eternal import, "He shall bruise thy head, and thou shalt bruise his heel." But the future, the everlasting triumph of the risen and victorious Messiah, and the brilliant happiness of His redeemed people, required, as they have found, imagery of unearthly splendour to set forth the glories of His celestial kingdom in eternity to come.

The emblems of the constellations, their line which is gone out through all the earth, and their words to the end of the world, when read by the light of revelation, may be understood by the child in age as well as in capacity; but the brightest imagination lags, the highest human intellect fails, in attempting to follow the flights of the Apocalyptic eagle [2].

---

[1] These twelve stars appear to represent the twelve prophetic lights symbolized by the twelve signs, and also conveyed by the names of the twelve stones of Rev. xxi., when explained by the Semitic roots, as is shown in the annexed table, the references after the names of the stones being to texts in which the root is used in the sense here attributed to it.

[2] In attempting to refer the symbols of the Apocalypse to those of the Constellations, Dupuis acknowledges he can give no explanation of the chapters between the fifth and the twelfth.

Prophecies of the Messiah,

CORRESPONDING WITH THE TWELVE SIGNS OF THE ZODIAC AND THE TWELVE PRECIOUS STONES OF THE FOUNDATIONS OF THE HOLY CITY OF THE APOCALYPSE (Rev. xxi.).

		Predictions of fulfilment.
ARIES, The ram, or lamb, his foot on the neck of the enemy.	**I.** As the Lamb as it had been slain, bruising the head of the enemy. Exod. xii. 11. Ps. cx. 1. Rev. v. 6. Beryl, the Son. Ps. ii. 12. Ascended. Gen. ii. 6.	Gen. 3. 15. Isa. 27. 1. Heb. 1. 13.
TAURUS, The bull as rushing on.	**II.** As subduing His enemies. Gen. xxii. 17. Ps. ii. 9; xviii. 47; xlv. 5; cx. 1. Isa. xi. 4. Topaz, dash in pieces. Ps. ii. 9.	Ps. 72. 9. 1 Cor. 15. 25. Heb. 2. 8.
GEMINI, The twins, the united.	**III.** As reigning in the Divine and human nature. Num. xxiv. 17, 19. Isa. xxxii. 1. Jer. xxiii. 5; xxxiii. 15, 21. 1 Cor. xv. 25. Chrysoprasus, the united (chain). Cant. i. 10. Bruising, breaking. 2 Sam. v. 20.	Isa. 9. 6, 7. Zech. 6. 12, 13. Rom. 15. 12.
CANCER, The crab holding the possession.	**IV.** As possessing the reward of His sufferings, the multitudes of the redeemed. Gen. xxii. 17, 18. Ps. ii. 8. Isa. xl. 10; liii. 10, 11. Jacinth, He shall possess. Gen. xiv. 19.	Isa. 40. 10. Heb. 2. 9. 10. Rev. 7. 14.
LEO, The lion rending the enemy.	**V.** As executing judgment, separating good from evil. Enoch, in Jude 14, 15. Gen. xlix. 8, 9. Ps. xxi. 8. Dan. xii. 2. Amethyst, He destroys. Ps. lii. 5.	Dan. 7. 9, 10. Rev. 20. 11, 12. Matt. 25. 31 —46.
VIRGO, The woman bearing the branch, the seed.	**VI.** As the seed of the woman, the Son, the branch, coming forth. Gen. iii. 15; xxii. 18. Isa. vii. 14; ix. 6; xi. 1. Jer. xxiii. 5. Zech. iii. 8; vi. 12. Jasper, He shall bruise and be bruised. Gen. iii. 15.	*Fulfilled.* Matt. 1, &c.
LIBRA, The scales of purchase.	**VII.** As redeeming, purchasing. Deut. xxxii. 6. Job xix. 25. Exod. vi. 6, 7. 2 Sam. vii. 23. Ps. xlix. 7, 15; lxxii. 14; cxxx. 7. Isa. lxii. 12. Sapphire, number. Deut. xxxii. 8. Ps. lxxxvii. 6.	Luke 1. 68. John 3. 16, 17.
SCORPIO, The scorpion bruising the heel.	**VIII.** As paying the price of redemption, His obedience and sufferings. Gen. iii. 15. Ps. xl. 6—8. Isa. liii. Chalcedony, the affliction, Ps. x. 8, of the Lord. Ps. cx. 1.	Luke 24. 46, &c. 1 Cor. 5. 7.

IX.

SAGITTARIUS The archer sending forth the arrow.	As going forth, and sending forth His word. Gen. xlix. 10. Ps. xlv. 5; lxviii. 11. Rev. vi. 2. Emerald, He that keepeth thee. Ps. cxxi. 3—5.	Matt. 10.5; 28. 19. Acts 1. 8.

X.

CAPRICORNUS, The goat. the sacrifice sinking down.	As dying, and making atonement by his death. Gen. iv. 4; xxii. 8. Exod. xii. 5. Lev. xvi. 15. Isa. liii. 5. Dan. ix. 26. Sardonyx, the Prince. Isa. ix. 6. The Lord. Ps. cx. 1. Smitten. Isa. liii. 4.	Matt. 27, &c. John 19.30.

XI.

AQUARIUS, The water-bearer, water rising in the vase, and poured forth.	As arising, ascending, and pouring out blessing. Hos. vi. 2. Ps. xvi. 9, 10; lxviii. 18; cxviii. 16, 17. Lev. xiv. 5, 6. Isa. xliv. 3. Sardius, the Prince. Isa. ix. 6. Who goes forth. Job xxviii. 8.	Matt. 28. 7, &c. Acts 1. 9.

XII.

PISCES, The fishes, bound together.	As uniting and upholding His Church. Gen. xv. 5; xxii. 17; xlix. 10. Isa. xlix. 6; li. 5. Ps. ii. 8. Chrysolite, He binds (as in chains). Cant. i. 10.	Acts 2. 47; 4. 33, &c.

" Other foundation can no man lay than that which is laid, which is Jesus Christ [1]."
Not the Apostles, but the revelations concerning Christ contained in the names of the
precious stones, on which their names were written, garnished that foundation.   The
twelve stars of the crown of the woman, the Church, in Rev. xii. 1, and these twelve
precious stones, were alike, in that both were lights.   These stones contain eleven
varieties of the diamond, and one expressly typical stone, in which are united rock-
crystal, which breaks other substances, and red clay, liable itself to be broken, showing
forth the Divine and human nature of Christ in union.   For this purpose then were
these beautiful earth-stars created; they tell of light shining in darkness, incorruptible,
unchangeable, everlasting; they garnish the foundations as the stars of the firmament
the over-arching of the new Jerusalem, the city that hath foundations, the building of
God, not made with hands, eternal in the heavens [2].

Significant names were given by Divine command under the old dispensation, and St.
Paul lays much stress on the " interpretation " of the name and title of Melchizedek,
therefore the names here given by inspiration must be supposed also to have signification, and to be capable, by " interpretation," of imparting instruction.   Twice in the
Apocalypse there is reference made to the *Hebrew* names of things spoken of; therefore
as the Greek names of these stones explained by the Greek do not seem to convey
instruction, they are here referred to their Hebrew roots.   So interpreted they reflect
the twelve lights of prophecy transmitted by the twelve signs, the starry heralds of the
coming day, whose meridian glory shone on the Holy City which St. John was privileged to behold.

---

[1] 1 Cor. iii. 11.   [2] 2 Cor. v. 1.

ON THE

PLENARY INSPIRATION OF THE SCRIPTURES,

AS CONNECTED WITH THE NAMES OF ANCIENT ASTRONOMY.

In the use here made of the coincidence between the names of astronomy and the words in which the Hebrew Scriptures are transmitted to us, it is not only considered to be proved that these Scriptures were inspired, that the prophecies came in old time by holy men of God, speaking as they were moved by the Holy Spirit, but also that the words in which they were expressed were suggested to their minds by the same authority, the same divine overruling influence. The proof is to be found in the existence and accurate fulfilment of prophecy. It is further assumed that we now have those words preserved to us, with slight and unimportant variations, by means of the care taken of them by the Jews, those faithful guardians of the prophecies they failed to interpret, they having counted the number of each letter in each book, an enumeration still to be seen in their Talmudical writings. Nevertheless, as the addition of a letter in one place would compensate for the omission in another, there are variations, for the most part such as in English would be occasioned by a superfluous letter inserted or omitted, or perhaps by the addition or omission of an article or a conjunction. Seldom do any variations occur in an important passage, and none are supposed or used in the derivations here given.

Having therefore the Hebrew Scriptures in such a state of verbal preservation, the original meaning of the names of astronomy, of which the roots there occur, may be ascertained. It is especially confirmed when the same word or its root is found in the name of the emblem or of its stars, and in the prophecy where that emblem is used as a type.

These writings must have been in perfect preservation when Christ Himself, referring to them as of supreme authority, said " the Scripture cannot be broken," thus authenticating their verbal accuracy and plenary inspiration [1]. Again, to the 110th Psalm, to a single word of it, and that involving a seeming difficulty, our Lord appeals, and His appeal silences His opponents. Desirous as they were to confute Him, they never thought of questioning the plenary inspiration or the correctness of their sacred books, which were then, and now are, those received by the Reformers, and alone acknowledged divine by the Anglican and other Protestant Churches. Our Lord also in many other places speaks of different books of these Scriptures as of indubitable authority; as of that of Daniel, predicting the time of His coming and the destruction of Jerusalem, in Matt. xxiv. 15, where He quotes the precise words of the prophecy, " the abomination of desolation," the idol of the Romans, their military eagle. Thus He gives His sanction to the verbal accuracy as well as to the authenticity and genuineness of that book ; a book whose importance has caused it to be

---

[1] See Prof. Gaussen on plenary inspiration ; Haldane on verbal inspiration, &c.

attacked by those who have not fully examined its evidences, or who are unwilling to admit any evidence whatever of that supernaturality of our religion, without which it becomes a mere system of morals.   Had these "Scriptures," as held sacred by the Jews and forming the Protestant canon, contained any uninspired books, or any falsehood of any kind, He who was "The Truth" must have denounced it.   Frequently condemning the teaching of the scribes, He never accuses them of corrupting the Scriptures of which they were the keepers; or had any undesigned corruption stolen upon the oracles of God, He who knew all things must have seen and exposed it.   Should it be imagined that in the original writings unimportant words might be left to the writer to supply, the question arises what words are unimportant.   Mere human intellect, however desirous faithfully to transmit the prediction that had been indicated, might not have chosen the precise word required for the exact fulfilment of it.   The accomplishment of the prophecy depended on the accuracy of every word.   The Lamb of God, like that of the passover, was to be pierced, but not a bone of either was to be broken; the omnipotent and omnipresent Spirit of prophecy held the hands of the Roman soldiers; they pierced, but might not break.   It may be said that these words are evidently important, but how could the unassisted mind of man discriminate between the vesture, the one mantle, and the many garments, the lot and the dividing, circumstances so apparently trifling, yet so remarkable in the fulfilment of the prediction?

In the original Scriptures not only were the words suggested to the mind of the writer by the Holy Spirit, but by superintending providence they have been most marvellously preserved, as may be seen by the vital importance of single words to the accomplishment of prophecy, the stamp and seal of revelation.   The Jew is still before us "a proverb and a by-word among the nations," nor is "one stone left upon another" of the temple that its conqueror was so solicitous to preserve.   The great apostasy forbids to marry, and "silly women are led captive," as its melancholy cloisters have witnessed for so many ages.

If plenary inspiration be granted, yet restricted to prophecy, it should be observed that neither the passage of which our Lord speaks as Scripture that cannot be broken, nor that of which He says David *in spirit* called Him Lord, is prophetic.

On any lower view of the inspiration of the Hebrew Scriptures little sympathy could be expected with the investigation of the support they afford to the theory of the prophetic import of the names and emblems of ancient astronomy.   On any lower estimate of the integrity of the Hebrew text it would be difficult to account for the coincidence between those names and emblems with the words and figures found in the prophecies with which they correspond.   If it be doubted whether the first revelation of God to man is recorded without failure in the written word, it will not be easily admitted that these antique symbols are indeed memorials of it.   If, however, it be admitted that the original words of prophecy, written or spoken, were impressed by the Holy Spirit on the mind of the human agent, and that they have reached us without important variation, the coincidence with Scripture of the names and emblems will support their similarly prophetic signification.

The manner in which these words could be so impressed has been discussed, and the inquiry denounced as presumptuous; still analogies may have been given in the ordinary course of nature to help our conceptions of the extraordinary.   Persons of fine musical ear can easily sing with a melody heard on an instrument for the first time.   If about to sound a false note, there would be an inward perception of "wrong;" and the true would come with a delightful feeling of "right."   So, under the Divine influence, might the tongue of the prophet, as "the pen of a ready writer," sweetly, safely flow on with the stream of inward harmony that governed it.   Again, it is often alleged that there is a style peculiar to each writer of the Holy Scriptures, and that therefore the words they use could not have been given to them. Those who urge this objection seem to recognize this peculiarity in translations; it must therefore be in the ideas, not in the words. If the inspiration of the ideas be questioned, what becomes of the authority of the Bible?

Here again an illustration from the science of music may assist. The melody will be the same, though performed on different instruments. There is certainly a tone, a colouring, as it were, that distinguishes the princely Isaiah from the herdsman Amos, the lowly John from the highly-educated Paul, easier felt than defined. Or may it not be exemplified by the sunlight passing through a coloured medium, casting a different hue on the object it enlightens, but not changing its form or properties? The gold of morning on the sea does not dim the transparent brilliancy of its wide-flowing waters. The rosy hues of evening on the snowy mountain-top do not disguise the splendid purity of its wintry summits. So the light of inspiration may shine through the atmosphere of the individual mind, tinged but not obscured by its peculiarities, which may colour, but do not alter what those rays illuminate.

With the plenary inspiration and accurate transmission of Scripture the signification of the names and emblems of ancient astronomy is closely connected, not as depending on, but as bearing testimony to it. If they embody prophecy, there had been a revelation : if they correspond with the revelation recorded in Scripture, they testify to its existence and to its purport. If in subsequent prophecy are found similar ideas, often expressed in the same words, these emblems accorded with the mind of the Giver of revelation : they should therefore be valued by us as reflecting, though not directly transmitting Divine light. They may be received as the commentary of good and wise men on the preceding revelation. The only express record of that revelation is in the early part of Genesis. In this book are divisions, each commencing with nearly the same form: " These are the generations." It has been supposed that the earliest might be derived from Enoch, Seth, or even Adam [1]. To these patriarchs the invention of astronomy has been attributed by the ancient Hebrews, Persians, and Arabians. Thus may be accounted for the coincidence of parts of the written word afterwards given by Moses, with the names and emblems of that science.

Those who treat this earliest history of man as " a myth," an allegory, violate the reverence due to the words of Him, one of whose splendid attributes, frequently claimed by Himself, is truth. His very enemies said, " We know that Thou art true." He, the manifested, the incarnate Truth, referred to this history as a fact, saying of man, " He created them male and female ;" and of the enemy, that he was a murderer from the beginning, a liar, and the father of it.

Those who allege that our Lord in these allusions might accommodate His words to the prejudices of His hearers, offer Him an affront on which the consciences of His adversaries did not allow them to venture. Standing in His august presence, they were forced to admit, that teaching the way of God in truth, He regarded not the person of men. Would it have been teaching the way of God in truth, to speak of that as fact which was a fable, a myth, an allegory? Let no names of men, however influential, induce us to disparage Him who has called Himself " the way, the truth, and the life."

Our Lord Himself having thus authenticated the relation of the fall in Genesis, it is again repeatedly and more circumstantially adverted to by the Holy Spirit, speaking by the mouth of Paul. Could He, the Spirit of truth, who was to guide into all truth,

---

[1] See Dr. Pye Smith's Lectures, &c.

make or permit such reference to a myth, an allegory? When Paul used an allegory [1], he called it such; but to this history he appeals as recognized fact. With this history the emblems of the constellations coincide; the seed of the woman and the serpent in various figures pervade the sphere; in the primary prophecy it is written, "*He* [2]," the seed of the woman, "shall bruise thy head, and thou shalt bruise his heel." In the emblems the seed of the woman is figured by the ear of corn held in a woman's hand, marked by a bright star called Spica, and Subilon, the ear of corn. When figured as a man, one foot is on or over the head of the serpent, the other is held up as wounded; in that of Orion is found the name Saiph [3], the bruise or bruising, the very word of the written record. Thus every word must have been what it is, to account for and agree with the emblems and their names.

The proof of the plenary inspiration of the Old Testament Scriptures derived from our Lord's words, as given in the Gospels, seems to require proof of the similar inspiration of those Gospels.

Prophecy requiring verbal inspiration to display accurate fulfilment, those Gospels must have been so inspired, for they contain our Lord's predictions. He had foretold, what then seemed most improbable, the total destruction of that Temple which even the enemy was solicitous to preserve. How literally that prediction was fulfilled is well known: not one stone has been left upon another. The forewarned Christians fled over the mountains, and were saved, ere the enemies had completed "to cast a trench around the city, compassing it round, and keeping it in on every side." The failure of a single word might have marred the warning and cost those precious lives; but the Scripture could not be broken, and that Scripture was their guide. The same faithful record contains those words which give the sanction of our Lord Himself to the Jewish Canon. By the literal accomplishment of that prophecy the three first Gospels were authenticated, as verbally inspired, to their own generation; the fourth by our Lord's prediction, then also wholly improbable, that neither on the mountain of Samaria nor at Jerusalem should they worship the Father.

By the equally literal accomplishment of His other prophecies every subsequent age has received additional authentication of these books. False Christs soon arose. Mahomet coming in his own name was received. "Wars and commotions, earthquakes, famines, and pestilences" have yearly testified to the precision of the prediction and the accuracy of the record. "Heaven and earth shall pass away," but His "words shall not pass away:" therefore they must have been recorded with unfailing exactness. We are told He spake many more words than are written; but all that are written He spake. We may therefore rest in the conviction, that whether it be the Scripture to which He appealed, or that in which the appeal is recorded, as He said, "The Scripture cannot be broken."

"Plenary inspiration" is here used as implying that the whole, and every word of the Original was inspired, and that every one of those words is and always has been and shall be in the world, some words being preserved in some MSS., and some in others, to be sought out by human industry and scriptural examination.

---

[1] Gal. iv.

[2] *He:* not only is the pronoun masculine, but what is less liable to corruption, the verb also, thus leaving the Vulgate without excuse in translating the pronoun *ipsa, she.* The woman's foot is no where on the serpent's head, the man's every where. See Lee's Lex.

[3] The rendering of Suph, the root of Saiph, as bruised, is confirmed by the two Arabic senses, stricken or wounded, and bitten; also by the corresponding Chaldee, to bruise.

ON THE IMMORTALITY OF THE SOUL

AS KNOWN TO THE ANTEDILUVIAN PATRIARCHS, AND TO THE ANCIENT HEBREWS, AND INDICATED BY THE EMBLEMS OF ANCIENT ASTRONOMY.

IT has been asserted that the immortality of the soul was not revealed in the Hebrew Scriptures, or to the early patriarchs. But what is well known is not the subject of revelation; it is referred to incidentally, and as needing no confirmation [1]. Such reference to the immortality of the soul may be pointed out, where it is said that Abraham expired, and "was gathered to his people [2]." His soul was gathered to the "general assembly of the first-born, of the spirits of just men made perfect [3]," to Abel and to Enoch, but his body slept not with theirs; it was buried in the cave of Machpelah, where were none of the bodies of his forefathers, where only that of his wife Sarah was laid. No explanation was given, for none was needed. Those who wrote and those who read and heard knew that their God, the God of Abraham, was the God of the living; for that "all live to Him," they knew full well. In after times the Lord Himself announced, "Aaron shall be gathered to his people [4]." There in the lonely sepulchre on the summit of Mount Hor was his body buried, in that utter solitude which still surrounds the desert mountain-top, unvisited but by the step of pilgrims from a far-off land, still testifying to its profound silence, its inviolate sanctity of seclusion. Again, the Lord said to Moses, "Die in the mount whither thou goest up, and be gathered to thy people, as Aaron thy brother died in Mount Hor, and was gathered to his people [5]." So far was Moses from sharing the sepulchre of any of his fathers, that no human eye ever beheld that tomb of mystery [6], wherein the Lord Himself buried the exanimate corpse of His servant. Whether he appeared in the body or in the spirit, he was seen, a living person on the mount of transfiguration. In after times arose the sect of the Sadducees, whose denial of the doctrine of the existence of the spirit proves that others held it. And good reason had the disciples of Moses to hold it, for he solemnly addresses God as "the God of the *spirits* of all flesh,' when the spirits clothed in flesh heard and trembled before Him [7].

As the man of the constellations typifies the human nature of the Messiah, so the woman typifies the Church, from Abel to the last of the elect of God who shall be born of woman and added to the number. The promised Messiah was to be born in or

---

[1] Gen. xv. 15.   [2] Gen. xxv. 8.
[3] Heb. xii. 23. Gill says, "The people of God, 'the spirits of just men made perfect,' the souls of all the saints who had departed before him." Clarke says the same.
[4] Num. xx. 24.
[5] Num. xxvii. 13. "Thou shalt *lie down*," in Deut. xxxi. 16; the word is so translated Job xiv. 12, a verse which ought to be read interrogatively: "Shall he not arise?" thus affirming, not contradicting, his resurrection. "*With* thy fathers," *even as* thy fathers: so rendered in Job ix. 26, this expression referring to the body, as "gathered to thy people" to the spirit. "Thou shalt *go* to thy fathers in peace," Gen. xv. 15, again referring to the disembodied spirit.
[6] Deut. xxxiv. 6.   [7] Num. xvi. 22; xxvii. 16.

of the Church, as well as of the woman. The figure of the woman in the sign Virgo symbolizes the Church; that in the first decan, preserved in the Egyptian planisphere, the woman, the virgin-mother. The woman in Andromeda, chained and prostrate as in the bonds of death and the grave, threatened by the enemy, but about to be delivered by Perseus, the breaker of bonds, again shows forth the Church. Here she is beheld in her fallen and suffering state, subject to death, but, as her name Moselsalah indicates, to be set free from Hades, Sheol, the separate, the invisible state. Here, then, those early patriarchs, newly become subject to death, and awfully impressed by that beyond, have typified the existence of the soul through and after death; for Andromeda in the emblem is not dead, dies not in the mythic story. In Cassiopeia, the enthroned, "the daughter of splendour," the Church appears, symbolizing the all-glorious bride of the King Messiah, the assembly of the spirits made perfect, the Church beyond death and in resurrection glory.

Whether under the starry emblem as Perseus and Andromeda, or in the mythological tale of Hercules and Hesione, the tradition is equally preserved.

The immortality of the soul and the general resurrection are implied in the prophecy of Enoch. The judgment is to be upon *all*, all the ungodly of all generations, when the Lord cometh with myriads of His saints.

To the patriarch Job and his contemporaries the constellations were evidently well known[1]: as familiar objects he alludes to them, and as the great things of God, past finding out. The Divine voice again names them as beyond the rule of man: "Canst *thou* bind the influences of the Pleiades?" of that central group of suns which is now found to *influence* the whole arrangement of our nebula, round which the galaxy, the system to which our sun belongs, is believed to revolve, obeying its sweet, its gracious *influences*. So wonderfully are the discoveries of real science anticipated by the words of Divine revelation, words only gradually comprehended as science is gradually developed. Again, it is said, "Canst thou loose the bands of Orion?" dissolve the wonderful attraction which binds together the magnificent multitude of suns that are at last discerned in the streak of light in that splendid constellation. The creature cannot: the Creator could. He bound, and He could loose. In both these allusions the universal domination of the force of gravitation is implied. While that world-compelling law was unknown their meaning was not understood, their sublimity was unappreciated.

That the great Arab prophet Job[2] lived before Abraham appears to be the opinion of the greatest scholars, before the distinction between the Ishmaelitic Arabs and the original, the Hamayaritic tribes: his testimony to the patriarchal faith is therefore earlier[3] than that of the expression that Abraham expiring was gathered to his people. It seems, also, now a prevalent opinion that Moses wrote the two first chapters and the last of the book of Job, giving his sanction to the authority of the intermediate portion, and to the whole as inspired Scripture, that intermediate part

---

[1] Job ix. 9; xxxviii. 32.

[2] No doubt seems ever to have been entertained as to the personality of Job, and the truth of his history, till the time of Maimonides. His objections are *not* to the evidence of the facts, but solely to the view thence derived of the providential government of God. He finds no flaw in the historical or traditional accounts; his objections are not to the proofs, but to the thing proved. Therefore, though many other learned men have taken his view of the case, it would be set aside in any court of justice.

In the epilogue to Job in the Septuagint it is said, "*Job is Jobab.*" That name occurs in Gen. x. 29, before the time of Abraham; another Jobab is named, Gen. xxxvi. 33, as being king, reigning in Edom, which does not apply to Job.

[3] According to Dr. Hales, 180 years before Abraham. See also Abp. Magee, Patrick, Sherlock, Lowth, &c.

being the composition of Job himself, under the influence of the Spirit of prophecy. Such guidance was indeed needful to such a prophecy as is admitted to be contained in the nineteenth chapter: " O that my words were now written, O that in a book they were engraven! that with a pen of iron and lead, for ever in the rock they were hewn out[1]!" Then follow the Divine words worthy of such everlasting preservation: " For I know that my Redeemer liveth, and in the after time He shall stand on the earth, and after my awaking[2], this body destroyed, yet in my flesh shall I see God: whom I shall see for myself, and mine eyes shall behold, and not a stranger, fulfilled my hopes within my bosom." This rendering of the latter verse seems most agreeable to the ancient translations and the marginal corrections of the English Bible.

Whichever version is followed, the prophecy that the Redeemer should stand on the earth, the dust of the earth, remains uninjured—words indeed worthy of everduring remembrance.

Celebrated as is this testimony to immortality and resurrection, the fourteenth chapter contains what is scarcely less decisive. After describing the apparent resurrection of a withered plant by the effusion of water, the prophet follows out the analogy with the death of man[3]. "*And*[4] man shall die and shall waste away, and man shall expire, and where is he? The waters fail from the sea, and the flood decayeth and drieth up: and man hath lain down, and shall he not arise? before the failing of the heavens[5] shall not they awake? and shall not they arise from their sleep? O that Thou wouldst hide me in the unseen state! Thou wilt shelter me till the passing away of Thine anger! Thou wilt set to me a time, and remember me! Even if a man die, shall he live? All the days of my appointed time will I wait (*trust*), till my change come." By thus reading the apparent assertion in ver. 12 as an interrogation, and taking ver. 14 as implying an assertion, the whole analogy is carried out, and the argument becomes conclusive. Shall the plant revive, and shall not man? Yea, assuredly he shall. This persuasion was not peculiar to Job. Eliphaz[6] says of the wicked man, "He believeth not that he shall return out of darkness." And Elihu[7] comforts Job with the expectation of resurrection, when he shall be delivered from " going down into the pit," or into corruption, when God shall " bring back his soul," or person, " to be enlightened with the light of the living."

Such was the faith of Arabia, before the generation of the sons of Noah had passed away, Shem, by some identified with Melchizedek, having lived to see the birth of Isaac, and apparently the trial of Abraham.

The faith of Job was, then, that of the family of Seth, represented by Shem, the name of whose ancestor Methuselah[8] bore testimony to the revelation of life beyond death, and by Arphaxad, the last whose name transmitted the series of prophecies, from which the twelve signs were constructed.

As the history of ancient Israel proceeds, is found Hannah[9], poetess and prophet, incidentally declaring her faith in the resurrection. " The Lord causeth to die and to

---

[1] Job xix. 23.
[2] This word is so translated in Ps. lvii. 7, 8, and many other places.
[3] Job xiv. 10.   [4] Not *but*.   [5] Ps. cii. 26.
[6] Job xv. 22.   [7] Job xxxiii. 28, 30.
[8] The name Methuselah is thus to be explained: Methu, death, a collective noun with *vau* formative postfixed, as Penu in Penuel, Gen. xxxii. 31. See Table XVII. Schlegel, who considers patriarchal tradition the origin of all mythology, thinks that the translation of Enoch was the natural end of man, death being *not* natural, but penal; also that the primitive race of men were of " giant" frame, and that by bodily strength they built the Cyclopean walls, &c. (Philos. of History.)
[9] 1 Sam. ii. 6, 10.

live, to go down to the grave" (Sheol, the unseen state), "and He shall raise up." That she spoke by the Spirit of prophecy is shown where she says, "He shall give strength to His King," when as yet there had been no king in Israel; and that "He shall exalt the horn of His Anointed," the power of His Messiah.

What can be more explicit than the testimony of David, in the sixteenth Psalm, saying, "My flesh also shall rest in hope, for Thou wilt not leave my soul in hell" (again Sheol, the unseen state)? a prediction in its primary sense belonging to Him for whom the Apostle claims it, but also applicable to every believer. In the forty-ninth Psalm it is written, "Like sheep they were laid in the grave, death shall feed on them; and the upright shall have dominion over them in the morning," the morning of the resurrection. "But God will redeem my soul from the power of the grave, for He shall receive me." The result of the philosophy of Solomon was, "The spirit shall return to God who gave it[1]." Then, as St. Paul has said, "Esaias is very bold," when he saith[2], "Death is swallowed up in victory:" "Thy dead men shall live:" "Awake and sing, ye that dwell in the dust; for thy dew is as the dew of herbs, and the earth shall cast out the dead."

What can be clearer, simpler, more positive, than the declaration of the prophet Daniel? To the well-known promise he adds the time, when "many that sleep in the dust of the earth shall awake[3]."

If, as has been objected, the laws of Moses were enforced by temporal and not eternal motives, so are the laws of England, so must be all human laws; for the human lawgiver cannot administer the destinies of the invisible state, nor can man behold them. If less is said of those motives by subsequent prophets than might be expected, their mission was not, like that of uninspired teachers, to recall well-known truths to the mind, but to give forth prophecy, the test and sanction of that revelation which had declared those truths. As surely as Nineveh and Babylon should fall into irretrievable ruin, so surely shall man arise, for ever freed from the power of death. As surely as Judah and Israel should go into captivity, and man into the bondage of the grave, so surely shall they be restored, and the children of men return, the sleepers in the dust of the earth awake, "some to everlasting life, and some to everlasting shame and contempt."

As certainly as the seed shall spring up to the harvest, so certainly shall the natural body, sown in corruption, be raised a spiritual body in incorruption. Thus, in the very image adopted by St. Paul, was shown to the first who should pass through death the hope of life and immortality beyond it, the seed, the ear of corn in the hand of the woman proclaiming to the first of redeemed transgressors, "As in Adam all die, so in Christ shall all be made alive."

NOTE.

The Apocryphal books, such as the Wisdom of Solomon, or Ecclesiasticus, even if only written by Alexandrian Jews, a little before or a little after the Christian era, show that the national belief of the Jews included the immortality of the soul and the resurrection of the body[4]. In the Wisdom of Solomon it is said, "God created man to be immortal, and made him to be an image of His own eternity[5]:" in Ecclesiasticus, "Of the twelve prophets let the memorial be blessed, and let their bones flourish again out of their place[6]." These writers have been called Platonizing Jews: but though Plato might teach the immortality of the soul, he knew nothing of the resurrection of the body implied in the last quotation.

[1] Eccles. xii. 7.　[2] Isa. xxv. 8; xxvi. 19.　[3] Dan. xii. 2.
[4] See Horne's Introd.　[5] Wisd. ii. 23.　[6] Ecclus. xlix. 5.

ON THE BOOK OF JOB

AS CONNECTED WITH THE EMBLEMS OF ANCIENT ASTRONOMY.

WHO was Job?

It is said in the epilogue to the Greek translation of Job that Jobab is Job. Two of the name are mentioned in Genesis. The second is said to *reign as a king* in Edom. Gen. xxxvi. 33; but there is no trace of the kingly office in the book of Job; the manners and language lead to supposing him an Arab Sheik or Emir.

When did he live?

The first Jobab, mentioned in Gen. x., was fourth in descent from Shem, Abraham being the eighth. If this were Job, he was before Abraham probably more than a hundred years, and living in the lifetime of Shem. In the book are allusions to the Deluge, though none to any subsequent event, and Job uses the very words of Genesis relative to the creation of man in several places. That history, whether traditional or written, was evidently well known to him, but there is no allusion to any later events.

Many learned men have considered the book of Job as the most ancient in the world. Those who think that part of the book of Genesis was arranged by Moses, under the guidance of inspiration, from previous records, also inspired, and left by the Prophets Enoch and Noah, in the four first chapters, from the authority of Adam, written by Enoch, and the five following to the twenty-eighth verse of the ninth chapter by Noah, would place the book of Job after this part of Genesis in point of antiquity.

The subsequent chapters, beginning with chapter x., may have been by Abraham, those from chapter xxv. to xxxvii. by Jacob: the remainder either by Joseph or Levi, the immediate ancestor of Moses, always, however, subject to the guidance of that Holy Spirit who spake by Moses, and who enabled and authorized him to authenticate these ancient records. They became the first book of Moses without ceasing to be the early Scriptures of mankind, with which Job was evidently acquainted.

The opinion of many great authorities is, and has been, that when Moses resided for forty years in Midian he was divinely directed to give his sanction to the writing left by Job himself, and to prefix to it, what only revelation could make known, the part which Satan had in his affliction, adding that account of his death which concludes it. It has been said by competent judges that the narrative style of Moses may be recognized in the two first chapters and conclusion of the last, and that the intermediate part is too unlike the poetical style of Moses to be attributed to him.

How is it known that the book of Job is to rank with the other Scriptures as the inspired word of God?

It was part of the Jewish canon when our Lord gave His sanction to that canon.

What is the purpose of this book?

To record and make known a most wonderful miracle, the Voice from heaven, that God had spoken, magnificently, solemnly, as He spake from Mount Sinai; and again at the baptism of our Lord, at His transfiguration, at His manifestation to the Greek strangers, at His final entry into Jerusalem. When the Lord had spoken to Adam and Eve and to Abraham, it appears to have been to them alone. His voice out of the whirlwind was the first heard openly and with witnesses.

Was not this the great patriarchal revelation, as that at Sinai was the Mosaic?

By the mouth of Job came the clearest prophecy of the Redeemer's standing in the after time upon the earth, and by the Voice from Heaven the declaration of the unfathomableness of the wisdom of God, and the unsearchableness of His providence.

When from the depth of heaven shone forth splendour from God in terrible majesty, and those who beheld it feared before Him, the Creator of the universe spake of the mysteries of its unfathomable antiquity, of its progressive developments, so tasking, baffling human science to follow even afar off. That divine voice named Chima and Chesil, Ash and Mazzaroth, as things that are, but beyond the reach of man, subject to the Creator's will; these are not the astronomy of Job, they are the astronomy of revelation. The same voice speaks of the "ordinances of heaven," "the dominion thereof upon the earth." Was there not here implied gravitation and motion, the centripetal and centrifugal force? By these "ordinances" it is now known that Chima [1], the Pleiades, has 'dominion" not only over the earth, but over the sun round which that earth revolves; not only over the sun, but over the galaxy of suns to which he belongs, as their centre, ruling them as a circle.

By these ordinances also are the *bands* of Orion fixed on the multitudes of associated suns that form his robe of light, their mutual attraction, their *bands* to each other so recently divined by modern science, and thus indicated in this ancient revelation. Leaving the early celestial grandeurs of pre-existent creation, from which human intellect shrinks dismayed, the divine Monitor descends to the familiar earthly objects [2] with which

---

[1] Dr. Hales, in his Chronology, would deduce the age in which Job lived from the supposition that by the sweet influences of the Pleiades, "Chima," the spring equinox was meant. So supposing, he deduces from the precession of the equinoxes, that B.C. 2337, which he holds to be about 187 years before the birth of Abraham, the spring equinox took place in or near the Pleiades.

In the word Chima, the *accumulation*, as *of stars*, there is no relation to the equinox. In those climates, the *abundance*, the *multitude* of the spring did not wait for the equinox; the corn in the time of Moses was in the ear at the passover. Before the age of Noah the equinox had not reached the Pleiades; it is now far beyond them. The Hebrew word *maedanoth*, translated in the English "sweet influences," in the Greek "*bonds*," in the Latin *rays* or *brightnesses*, may be from the same root as *Eden*, pleasure, sweetness, or by a Chaldee usage from Adun, ruling, influencing; the English has given both senses. That the Pleiades have any *influence* on the spring is merely a poetical fable of after times, when their helialical rising, seen in the sweet morning dawn, announced the spring to Greece. They have no *influence* on it, though they accompanied it in the days of Greek poetry. While it is true, according to modern science, that the Pleiades, *graciously*, for good, *influence* the motion of our whole astral system, it is not true that they influence earth's seasons, nor has that influence any reference to chronology. The Divine voice spoke truth, a wonderful long-hidden truth, it could speak only truth—therein could be no allusion to fiction.

According to Buxtorf the early Hebrews understood *maedanoth* as *bonds*.

[2] "Behemoth, whom I made with thee," one of the present creation, often understood to be the elephant. The Greek and Latin name, Elephas, exactly renders Job xl. 19, "He is the *chief* of the ways of God," as it contains the Semitic root, Eleph, the chief, the leader. It has been difficult to apply to the elephant the expression "He moveth or setteth up his tail like the cedar?" Schultens renders it of the trunk. which moves majestically, as a cedar before the wind. The radical meaning of the word rendered tail is given as *extremity*, applying as well to the trunk as to the tail; and it may have a signification of enclosing or encompassing, also peculiarly suitable to the trunk. [Of

Job was surrounded, and asks, shall he who knows not these below presume to question the decrees of Him who formed and governs those above?

The astronomy of Job may be traced in the twenty-sixth chapter. He knew what modern science shows, that the omnipotent Creator "hangeth the earth upon nothing," and acknowledges that He by His Spirit hath garnished the heavens, and "His hand hath formed the crooked serpent," as in the stars of Draco winding round the Pole, that "north which He stetcheth over the empty space," a part of the heavens now perceived by telescopic examination to be comparatively void of stars, beyond the congregated orbs that crowd the Galactic Circle. To Job and his friends, Chima and Chesil, Ash and Mazzaroth, needed no more identification than the Lion and the Raven, the Horse and the Eagle, with which they are contrasted. To them these constellations were evidently known by name and by sight, and as much of their "ordinances" as is conveyed by the names was probably known by tradition. From the book of Job it may be inferred that the science of antediluvian astronomy was familiar in the land of Idumea, where the light of antediluvian revelation shone so clearly, testified to not only by the Prophet himself, but by the friends his acquiescing auditors.

There has been a frequent mistake as to the radical meaning of the word *Goel*[1], Redeemer, used by Job in the great prophecy, chap. xix. It is thought to mean avenger. Avenger, as in Num. xxxv. 12, is a secondary sense of that word, its primary and general meaning being to restore, to bring back an original good condition. Job was not comforted by looking for vengeance on those who had destroyed his wealth; none came; but he knew and hoped in the great restoring Redeemer, who should stand upon the earth in the after-time, fulfilling his hopes within his bosom[2].

An objection[3] has been made against the great antiquity of the book of Job, from the similarity of some of its sentiments and expressions to others in the Psalms and Proverbs; but if this book were most ancient, the writers of the subsequent books must have been well acquainted with it; their minds would have been imbued, as ours ought to be, with the Scripture. If Moses indeed brought the history of the trials, the patience, and the happy end of Job to the Israelites, on the verge of their long wanderings in the wilderness, how precious it must have been in their sight, a spiritual manna for their daily food!

Having long been the Scripture of the Arabs, by the sanction of their lawgiver it became such to the Hebrews. By the sanction of our Lord Himself it is such to us.

Of the Leviathan * it is not said, " whom I made with thee." The description is too grand, too terrific for the crocodile as now existing. It has been thought to be of some extinct species: might it relate to one of those fossil monsters, the Ichthyosaurus for instance, to whom the description seems suitable? Might a knowledge of what these wonderful remains had been, form part of the science of those antediluvian sages whose astronomy astonishes their descendants?

The Lord had appealed to the marvels of creation above and around, the ordinances of heaven, the living inhabitants of earth,—did He now appeal to the stony relics of long-past ages to show what fearful creatures had preceded man on earth, and been swept away to give him dominion, asking, what could man have done had such been his contemporaries?

[1] See the use of it, as to redeem, in Lev. xxv. 24, 25, and many places; also Lev. x. 56.

[2] See "Immortality," &c. p. 66.

[3] Another objection has been urged as to the naming of Satan. But in this book he is always called *the* Satan, or adversary, while in the later books, the 1st of Chronicles and the 109th Psalm, he is named Satan, without the article, as if by long use Satan, the adversary, had come to be understood as a proper name.

---

* A writer in Tait's Mag., May, 1857, on the Testimony of the Rocks, expresses the opinion that the Leviathan of Job "may have been one of those great formations of which happily only the bones remain."

PROPHECY,

AS CONNECTED WITH THE EMBLEMS OF ANCIENT ASTRONOMY, FOR WHICH A PROPHETIC IMPORT IS CLAIMED.

WHAT is Prophecy? It is the declaring beforehand what shall happen. Man may guess, but no more. Mere human intellect, the very highest, but guesses, and seldom guesses aright. Neither Socrates nor Plato foresaw that universal empire of Rome, as already prefigured in the visions of Daniel.

Does prophecy exist, and where? It exists in books proved to have been known long before facts occurred which are there described as in after times to happen. When those facts came to pass, these descriptions and annunciations were ascertained to be prophecy. Thus it is also proved that they must have come from a Being superior to man; from One knowing the end from the beginning. It is certain that the books of Moses were translated into Greek and paraphrased in Chaldee while the Jewish nation yet possessed Jerusalem. In those books, preserved by the Jews with reverential care, there will be found an exact picture of all that has befallen them since their lapse into idolatry under their later kings, madness and blindness, famine and pestilence, and failure of rain [1], their removal into all the kingdoms of the earth, where they should serve, not worship, but be made servants to gods of wood and stone [2]. The Jew is at our door, we have but to say, Behold!

Our Lord's prediction, that not one stone of the edifice He looked on should be left on another, is similarly exact, similarly indisputable, and its fulfilment similarly conspicuous to the present time. Babylon and Nineveh are in their predicted desolation, while of them it is not, it might not be said, that not one stone should be left on another. But to this prophecy also we have but to say, Behold! The record of the prediction concerning Jerusalem, as given in the Gospel of St. Luke xxi. 6, was written and circulated some years before the events which prove its Divine origin. In these books, thus authenticated by the accomplishment of their announcements, are found the other prophecies with which the names and emblems of ancient astronomy correspond. Many of these are fulfilled in the first coming of our Lord and Saviour, to suffer, to die, and to arise. Others remain to be fulfilled when He shall come again, as the King who shall rule in righteousness [3].

When a prophecy has two senses, both fulfilled, it is seen to be more marvellous, more beyond human intellect, more certainly divine [4]. The first prophecy as recorded in these books, the chief theme of the emblems of astronomy, told that the Seed of the woman should be bruised in the heel, as He literally was by the nailing on the cross; also, as the word for heel sometimes signifies, that it should be in the after time [5]. When

[1] Deut. xxviii. [2] Deut. xxviii. 64. [3] Gill, Alford, &c.
[4] Bp. Horsley. [5] Ps. cxix. 33, 112.

four thousand years had elapsed it came to pass. When Noah foreshowed to his un-dutiful son the future destiny of his descendants, he only declared, he did not imprecate the curse on Canaan, " Cursed, Canaan [1]. Servant of servants shall he be to his brethren." And truly he has been, and wofully is, he now : Canaan, the bought and sold, the human merchandise [2]. But the merciful alleviation is quickly announced : " Blessed the Lord God of Shem, and Canaan shall be *His* servant," the servant of the Jehovah Elohim of Shem.   How eagerly, how affectionately the Negro race receive the Gospel, let our missionaries make known [3].

" God shall enlarge, expand, persuade Japheth."   He shall expand him over the dwellings of Shem, as the English in India.   He shall persuade him, as He has per-suaded him of the truth of the Gospel of Christ, of Him, the Lord God, who should dwell in the tents of Shem, when in the person of the Messiah He should take flesh of the lineage, and in the dwellings of Shem [4].   Again this wonderful prophecy, so doubly fulfilled and fulfilling, closes with the redoubling of the consolatory assurance, " Canaan shall be His servant." Though to Noah God thus revealed futurity, neither of the Deluge nor of this remarkable prophecy are there any traces in the emblems of astronomy. Thus it seems evident that they were constructed before that time: the Seed of the woman is their only subject, the salvation of the fallen race by faith in the promised Redeemer their only object.   To their inventors the Lord had spoken, or they could not so have prefigured the great sacrifice of which the earth was to be the altar.   To the whole earth their voice was to go out, their words to the ends of the world.

The Israelites were positively forbidden to make to themselves the likeness of any thing in heaven as well as on earth, to bow down to them and worship them, by the Divine voice in the thunder of Sinai.

" To themselves."   The cherubic images were appointed for the people, not by them. By not observing this distinction the Jews so soon violated the commandment whose awful sound still hung upon the echoes of the fearful mountain.   When they demanded Elohim, gods, to go before them, the cherubim of gold ordered for the tabernacle were not yet fashioned, yet the form of the cherubim was well known to them by tradition if not by sight.   Aaron made *one* molten calf, apparently to represent those primeval consecrated symbols, and said of it, " *These*, thy Elohim, O Israel," and proclaimed a feast to Jehovah.   For this sin, but for an Intercessor, the nation had been consumed. In the emblems of the sphere it is seen that the existence and future incarnation of that Intercessor were indicated and already traditionally known to those who so needed Him.

Thus do these emblems show that God hath spoken, and thus from of old " the heavens have declared the glory of God ;" and of all succeeding generations may we not say with the great Apostle of the Gentiles, " Have they not heard ? yea, verily, their sound went into all the earth, and their words unto the ends of the world."   From the sculptures of Babylon and Nineveh, as from those of Etruria, Egypt, Mexico, and

---

[1] If any verb be supplied, it should be *is*, or *will be*.

[2] The word Canaan means *merchandise*.

[3] Townsend, the devoted missionary to the interior of Africa, whose acquaintance with the native language (Yoruba) is astonishing, related that meeting a party of Africans, strangers, they stopped him, and said, " We would be very glad if white men would come and tell us about God."   The missionary pointed to the sky, saying, " There is God : ask Him."   They all fell on their knees, raising their clasped hands towards heaven, and saying, " O God, send us white men to teach us about Thee ! "

[4] Onkelos, on this text, says, " God shall cause his Shechinah, or glorious majesty, to dwell in *the tents* of Shem."   So Jarchi and many Christian writers.

India, we see that the nations had so heard, but also we see how soon they perverted the message of salvation to the fables of idolatry. Sacrifice was taken to authorize murder; the divinely appointed cherubic images became gods of wood and stone, of silver and of gold. So still in martyrdom for religious opinions, and the image and picture-worship of apostate Christendom, it is seen that even the revelations of God can be used as the occasion of sin and suffering to mankind. The cherubic emblems seem to have stood amid the ancient world, like the tree of knowledge in the garden of Eden, as a test of obedience. If they have been corrupted into idols, so have imaginary representations of the objects of Christian veneration, yea, even of Him who spake in the terrors of Sinai, forbidding us to bow down to the likeness of any thing, even of things in heaven, even of the human nature of Christ, the reality of which His disciples worshipped when on earth, and believers worship now in the heaven of heavens.

Thus did these emblems silently prophesy of the first coming, to make an atonement for sin, of Him whose yet future coming to reign they still set forth. If those who constructed them were uncertain of the time of His suffering, as we are of "the glory that should follow," still they knew, for they have prefigured, that He should come, should suffer, and should reign. These emblems are reflected in the traditions of all nations; all in their hour of midnight darkness saw these stars of dawn. Some might be led to look to the Sun of righteousness whose arising they announced; too many, alas! mistook the heralds of the King's approach for independent magnates, and fell down before them in forbidden worship.

After the fulfilment of one part of their message, their words, which had gone out to the ends of the earth, were lost in the echoes of earth's confusion, of persecution, heresy, and apostasy. They had prepared the nations to expect the first coming of the King Messiah, the Prince of Peace : half their mission was accomplished. May there not be an approaching revival of attention to their long-lost import, to those characters of light in which is written the speech where even yet "night unto night showeth knowledge;" again proclaiming, "Behold, He cometh"? "Surely I come quickly," was said eighteen centuries ago. Eighteen centuries has the Church in her weary wilderness trusted in that promise, looked confidingly for that coming, and to every one of her members it has been fulfilled. He has come to them in the hour of death ; His presence has illuminated the shadowy valley, shining as really and as brightly as it will do when every eye shall see Him together, when His appearing shall be as the lightning which "cometh out of the East, and shineth even unto the West." Even so, Come, Lord Jesus.

NOTE.

Albumazer, in his enumeration of the Decans, says, that "they were known all over the world and had caused long speculation, and that many had attributed to them a divine and even a *prophetic* virtue[1]."

---

[1] Dr. A. Clarke quotes from Maimonides, that, according to Jewish tradition, the first man who introduced the worship of the stars asserted that it was derived from *prophecy*.

ON THE ORIGINAL LANGUAGE

TO WHICH THE NAMES OF ANCIENT ASTRONOMY ARE REFERRED.

THE philology of those who do not entirely and implicitly receive the Holy Scriptures as the revelation of God, appears, to those who do so receive them, as confused, as vain, and as baseless as their theology. Those who thus receive them appeal to those earliest records for vestiges of that original language in which Adam named the creatures brought before him, and in which he conversed with Eve and with their offspring. These vestiges remain in the names given in those first ages of the world, and in the reasons assigned for them. These words, or their roots, are found, in the sense there attributed to them, in all the Semitic dialects, and in many others derived through the children of Ham and Japheth; they may therefore be held to belong to that primitive language [1]. In the time of Noah this language appears in the names of his sons and the prophecy concerning them. Such roots pervade the subsequent books of the Old Testament, and more or less the dialects of all nations, consistently with what is written, that the confusion of Babel was in the *lip*, the pronunciation. Each wandering tribe of similar *lip* would deduce new shades of meaning from old roots, and in some cases, by repeated changes of letters, "leave not a wreck behind" of the original word. Nevertheless many of these primitive roots have survived time and change, and appear in various dialects, ancient and modern, barbarous or polished, to attest a common source of the language and of the race. The verb "to be," Ehcych, as in the Hebrew of the first verse of Genesis, with its many prefixes and terminations, is perhaps the most widely diffused. It is frequently to be found in the names of the Supreme Being; as in the Greek Theos, and the Mexican Teotl, He who is, the Eternal, transmitting the divine truth recognized by the elevated intellect of Plato, that God alone *is* [2]: a sublime revelation made a thousand years before by the voice of God Himself to the Jewish lawgiver, and previously to the early patriarchs; for " by His name Jehovah was He not known to them"? as according to many ancient Jewish and learned modern commentators He said to Moses, concerning His revelations to Abraham, Isaac, and Jacob [3]. That name, so revered by the Lord's people in all ages, is translated for us by the Holy Spirit in the Apocalypse: " He which is, and was, and is to come," the word containing in itself the distinguishing letters by which the three times or tenses of the verb " to be " are denoted.

Where similar sounds in different dialects are found to express the same ideas, the word or root may be claimed as belonging to the primitive language.

Such primitive and widely diffused roots are found in the names of the stars and the

[1] For instance, the names of Cain as " gain," and Seth as " set up," are in constant use, in English as well as in Hebrew and Arabic.
[2] Of other names given by the Greeks, Socrates said that Zeus and also Dis, meaning "living and giving life," was the offspring of some great intellect.
[3] Exod. vi. 2. Being read interrogatively by Maimonides, &c.

emblems that contain them. The most familiar examples are perhaps Arcturus, and Orion, from Arab, to come; Aldebaran, from Debar, to rule; and Sirius, from Sir, a prince, and to reign, as a title of dignity pervading both the East and the West.

Dr. Donaldson in "The New Cratylus," says, "Language was originally one." Vowels and other servile letters have been, in the course of time, added or omitted; as in the Etruscan, Esl, peace, may be referred to Sala, peace, in Hebrew, &c., and Æsar, God, to Sur, Isur, who rules. Æsar is also used in Irish for God. In the Islandic, Æsæ and Asar have the same meaning; also the Indian Eswara, the Scandinavian Æsa and Æsar, and the Egyptian Osàr, or Osiris, the prince, as in Isa. ix., and in the name of Sarah, princess. Our familiar household word "sir" thus evidently belongs to the original language of mankind.

The Semitic tribes, long stationary, preserved their language nearly in its primitive form. The children of Japheth, who early commenced the migrations that were to place them in the tents of Shem, varied more in pronunciation and inflexions, but retained many of the original roots of two or three consonants, by which the long-lost languages of Babylon and Assyria are now interpreted[1]. These roots, though seldom if ever occurring in Arabic writers, are to be found in Arabic lexicons, and are considered to belong to the ancient Hamayaritic dialect.

In the Sinaitic inscriptions, which have of late excited much interest, a rough semblance of the square Hebrew character is evident. The words, as far as deciphered, are imperfect Hebrew, of which the roots are common to the Hebrew and Arabic. The figures of animals, the ass, the horse, and the goat, may represent the standards of Issachar, Asher, and Naphtali. The more frequent recurrence of that of the ass may indicate that there was encamped the tribe of Issachar. From the coarse writing and irregular spelling, it might seem that " the mixed multitude " who followed the Israelites were the carvers. Many of them would be Egyptians, and might have learnt in the quarries of their native land the methods of executing such works, which it baffles modern science to explain. These inscriptions, if so made, would not be early enough to throw light on the primeval language. The words given as names in Genesis, used in the sense there annexed to them, being recognized in all the dialects of mankind, are the true relics of that primitive language. The ancient names of the stars may also be considered as remains of the same, as fragments testifying to the origin, the intention, and the beauty of the once perfect but long dilapidated edifice, " whose maker and builder was God."

The original language of mankind should not be called Hebrew or Arabic, or by any other name of national dialect. These are, as it were, sisters, daughters of that given to Adam and transmitted by Noah. To that original language, by means of the roots preserved in the Semitic dialects, the names of astronomy are here referred.

---

[1] "The language of Assyrian and Babylonian inscriptions is not strictly Hebrew, Chaldee, or Syriac, but presents many points of analogy with those dialects both in its grammatical structure and in its elemental words." (Vaux on Nineveh, &c.)

Bunsen (Egypt) says, "Language and mythology are the two keys to the history of nations."

Lord Kingston, in his great work on Mexico, says, "Many Hebrew words may be found in the dialects of the Indians, among the rest, Abba, father."

Bel, or Belus, meaning Lord or Ruler, is to be met with from India to Scandinavia as the name of a deity, in Irish and in Punic, in Babylon and Assyria.

Sir W. Jones traces Chaldaic roots in Persian, Zend, and Sanscrit.

Gin, the native Australian for woman, is nearly the same as the Greek Gune. Matar is said to be Taheitan for kill.

ON THE CONNEXION OF THE GREEK WITH THE

SEMITIC DIALECTS.

To the consideration of Greek scholars, who are not also orientalists, it may be submitted that though in modern elementary books a tolerably consistent view may be afforded of the Greek mythology, yet, as has often been shown, the most contradictory accounts were given by the ancient writers themselves. The earlier the writer, the more unlike are those relations to the generally received notions. By Plato we are told that the Greeks adopted or translated the " barbarian names," and founded stories on the meaning in their own language. This assertion is sufficient to authorize the explanation of the Greek fables relative to the constellations from the import of the names in the oriental and to them " barbarous[1]" dialects. That Jupiter, the commonly called father of the gods, was a king of Crete, where his tomb was still recognized, and that Minerva was the mother of Prometheus, are extreme cases. To Cadmus, whose name means the man of the east, the Greeks themselves attributed their first literature; though it is said he came from Egypt, it does not follow that he was born there. His name refers him rather to that eastern race, the Phœnicians, that people to whom Homer, by the name of Phæacians, ascribes such wonderful civilization in the days of the Trojan war[2]. Their very name signifies exquisitely polished and educated[3]. From them the Greeks learnt arts and sciences, and from thence Pythagoras brought those correct notions of astronomy and even geology, which are the astonishment of modern times. To such an origin then let not the Greek scholar scorn to refer the names and consequent histories of the constellations[4].

As popular instances of the light to be thrown on the difficulties of ancient classical literature by a reference to Semitic roots, may be mentioned the application by Sophocles of the epithet *morian* equally to Jupiter and to the olive tree. The word Morah occurs in Mal. ii. 5, as reverence, reverential *fear*—both the deity and the consecrated olive were to be reverenced. The olive was held sacred, as may be seen from the use made of it in the East as a pledge of peace—a usage supposed to have been derived from the branch brought by Noah's dove[5]. From Neh. viii. 15 we find that olive branches were

---

[1] The word barbarian in a Greek mouth meant simply *foreign*.
[2] See Lyell.
[3] As in Prov. xxix. 21, and in the Arabic.
[4] The Egyptian priests told Herodotus the Greeks were " people of yesterday."
[5] Gen. viii. 10, עלה, sometimes rendered branch. (Ainsworth.)
The Targum of Jonathan adds, " which it had taken from the Mount of Olives;" olives being said not to grow in Armenia.
Ancient heathen authors make mention of birds sent out by Sisithres (Abyrenas); Plutarch

among those commanded to be used in the Feast of Tabernacles, and of this tree Solomon made two cherubim before the oracle [1]. It was also consecrated among divinely appointed emblems.

There is another similar difficulty which has embarrassed commentators on the Greek tragedies—the epithet *crocean* blood, which some moderns interpret *yellow*, supposing blood to turn yellow by fear, with various other whimsical attempts at accommodation. The Greek word Krokos has no root in that language; of such Plato says they are derived from the barbarians. The Hebrew and Arabic Kerah or Kerach is bound together, involved, as the chives of the crocus flower, whence saffron is made, and as the flower itself is. The chives and the medicinal saffron made from them are certainly yellow, but the flower of the saffron crocus is purple, and in the East there are crocuses of a deep red, blood colour; such are mentioned in the letters from the Crimea in 1855 [2]. These then are the crocuses to which Æschylus likens the blood of Iphigenia.

When Homer says the gods called the eagle Percnos, he gives the exact equivalent of one sense of the usual oriental name Nesr, the eagle, who rends asunder. Perek is to tear in pieces [3] in the Semitic dialects.

There is a famous Latin enigma, *Lucus*, a grove, *à non lucendo*, because there is no light in it, at which every schoolboy is amused. Luk or Luch is *fresh, cool, moist, green*, as may be seen by the use of the word in Deut. xxxiv. 7, and Gen. xxx. 37; in Arabic it is applied to a stream of water *fresh* from the hill. Again, *mosaic*, as applied to works of art, has the meaning of Mosae, a *work*. The word occurs in 1 Kings vii. 33, stone worked, made up, in opposition to the natural state. The much-disputed origin of the word Mass, the Roman Catholic service, may also be explained from the same root, a *work* done [4].

It has been advised to seek assistance from the Scandinavian dialects in some Greek difficulties. What has been found there will have been from the primitive roots they contain, and would be more readily found in the Semitic, from which the Cadmean derived them, especially as the Ionic is said to afford such examples. To the Semitic dialects, therefore, let not the Greek scholar [5] refuse to resort for otherwise un-

---

saying that Deucalion sent a dove out of the ark, and Lucian speaks of a golden dove on the head of a statue at Hierapolis, supposed to be Deucalion's. (Dr. Gill.)

" The dove returned with an olive leaf plucked off, an emblem of peace between God and the earth; and from this circumstance the olive has been the emblem of peace among all civilized nations." (Dr. A. Clarke.)

Elah, the word used in Gen. viii. 11, for leaf or branch, may have originated the Greek Elaia, and even the European olive.

" A *dove* distributing *leaves* was the hieroglyphic emblem of *languages*." (Prescott's Mexico.)

[1] 1 Kings vi. 23.

[2] In a line quoted in the " Amber Witch," and attributed to St. Augustine, the epithet *red* is attached to crocus. A lady in the south of England has now some such growing in the garden, brought from the Crimea. For " yellow blood," see notes to Conington's Agamemnon.

[3] Zech. xi. 16.

[4] Polydore Virgil says Missa is a Hebrew word.

[5] " Ignorance of the Greek language is at this day highly injurious to the study of the Latin, without which the dogmas, either of the ancient Christians or Gentiles, cannot be comprehended. The same may be credibly supposed of the Arabic in many astronomical treatises, and of Hebrew in reading the Holy Bible. Clement V. providently meets these defects; wherefore, we have taken care to provide for our scholars a Hebrew, as well as a Greek Grammar." (Philobiblion, a Treatise on the Love of Books, by Richard de Bury, Bishop of Durham, A.D. 1344. Inglis's Translation, p. 72.)

" There (in books) we survey the antarctic pole, which eye hath not seen, nor ear heard; and with delectable pleasure we admire the luminous way of the galaxy, and the zodiac painted with celestial animals." (Ibid. p. 88.) A record of the tradition as to the Southern Cross is here indicated.

attainable explanations of the perplexities of Greek mythology, or to refer for the antique and oriental appellations of the stars and constellations [1].

---

[1] Being told by Plato also that the Greeks founded fables on the meanings that these "barbarian" names might bear in the Greek language, thus is authorized the explanation of the traditions relative to the constellations from the sense the foreign names might convey to Grecian ears; for instance, Arcas, in the Semitic dialects, meaning coming, or who cometh, was taken as Arkos, a bear. Cynosura, the pole-star, from Cyn or Con, the centre, and Zar, to bind together, as the constellations, they whimsically interpreted a dog's tail, no dog being figured near that place among the stars. This name has been attempted to be accounted for by that of a promontory near Athens, above which the pole-star might be seen on entering the harbour. A promontory cannot easily be forced into a likeness to a dog's tail, but might well be named as a landmark from the fixed pole-star shining over it.

In the Cratylus is discussed the question, How and why were names given? Nothing can be more unsatisfactory than the answers. The Hebraist will reply, to express the nature of things. When the philosophers again ask who gave them, the Biblical student will say, Adam and his immediate descendants. Socrates then says, "The men who first founded names seem to have been no mean persons, but conversant with high subjects;" also, that "to the East we must look for the solution of many difficulties." Thus did these greatest of Greek authorities agree in referring "the Greek to the Semitic dialects."

"Rosenmüller, in his *Scholia*, is of opinion that the Cherubim described by Ezek. i., and as placed at the east of Eden, were adopted by the nations as symbols of sacred things and places which it was not lawful to approach; the sphinxes of the Egyptians, the dragons of the Greeks, and the griffins of the Indians and northern nations of Asia, being similar to the Cherubim of the Hebrews." (Blackburn's Nineveh.)

In the Cratylus Socrates says, "The barbarians are more ancient than we;" and from them he says the Greeks got many names not explicable by the Greek. He seems to find no difficulty in the insertion or change of a letter. *Pur*, fire; *udor*, water: and *kunos*, a dog, are instances he gives of these "barbarian" names, and as used by the Phrygians. As the Phrygians are supposed to have been a colony or dependency of the Assyrian empire, and as Semitic or fraternal Hamite roots are found to pervade and assist in deciphering the language of Assyria, Phrygian names may yield their meaning to the same system of interrogation. Phrygia would be fruitful, or flourishing offspring, as the root is used in Cant. vii. 12 (13); Ilion or Ilium, high, as in 1 Kings ix. 8; Troy, high hill or mountain, as in Dan. ii. 25; Priam, the parent, Paris, son or offspring, one of the progeny, as in Gen. xxx. 2; Hecuba, the female, as in Gen. i. 27; Hector, who smites and is smitten, as in Exod. xvii. 5.

Æschylus is vindictively eloquent on the meaning of Helen, as destructive. One meaning of the Semitic root Hele is "to utterly confound," as in Job xii. 17; but as another is "to be dazzlingly bright," it is probably from this she was named. This passage in Æschylus, however, tends peculiarly to show the connexion of the Greek and Semitic dialects.

Some modern critics, ignoring the Hebrew origin of the writers of the New Testament and the acknowledged Semitic origin of the Greek language, speak of the Greek of the New Testament as "made up of barbarous and corrupt dialects," seeming to mean the Hebrew, Chaldee, Syriac, Arabic, &c., not taking into consideration that the sense of the original root of all these dialects is what those writers had in view and intended to convey.

It has been remarked, that a standing memorial of the miracle of the gift of tongues remains in the Greek of the first Epistle of St. Peter, so unanimously praised by scholars. It has also been said, "It needed inspiration to prevent faulty grammar in the herdsman of Tekoa and the fisherman of Galilee," and their writings prove they had it. What have been called by some solecisms in the Greek of St. John, are by others held to be intentional, to convey a doctrine, as in ch. xvi. 13, the personality of the Holy Spirit.

FABLES OF GREEK AND ROMAN MYTHOLOGY
ANNEXED TO THE CONSTELLATIONS.

THE virgin of the zodiac was said to be the mother of Prometheus, a divine person, who suffered for the love he bore mankind, whom he taught not to fear death, by means of the hopes which he gave them. Libra was the balance of Jupiter, in which he weighed the fates of men. The scorpion was sent to wound the heel of Orion, who was an offspring of the gods. Sagittarius, Capricornus, and Aquarius were said to relate to deeds done by Hercules, a son of the Supreme Deity, who laboured for the good of mankind, and died by the poison of his serpent enemy, but was afterwards taken up into heaven as a god. Of the fishes of Pisces men were born. Jupiter was once in the form of the bull, and he was worshipped under that of the ram, over whose head is Deltoton, the triangle, by the ancients considered a sacred, mysterious, and divine emblem, showing the name of God, and placed by Jupiter in the heavens. The twins were one human and the other divine; one the son of man, the other of Jupiter. The crab was sent to bite the foot of Hercules. Leo was said to be a lion slain by Hercules, in whose skin he was always clothed; thus connecting him with the animal he was said to have slain. Others, however, said that this lion was by Jupiter made king of all beasts.

In the other constellations we find the same traces of the original idea. Beginning with those belonging to Virgo, we see that Coma was understood to be the hair of a human head. The centaur was slain by Hercules, the suffering but divine son of Jupiter. Hercules, Boötes, or Arctophylax was the same as Arcas, a son of Jupiter, and was the guardian of those stars called a bear, but by the Semitic names the fold and flock. The cross was considered a sacred symbol by the ancient Persians and the Egyptians. The crown was said sometimes to belong to Vulcan, a god and the son of the Supreme God, suffering from a hurt in the foot; sometimes to Ariadne, called the wife of Bacchus, whose name may mean " he cometh quickly," another son of a god. The victim was one offered by the gods. The dragon was slain by Hercules, who was said sometimes to be the same person as Prometheus and Esculapius, all sons of God labouring for the good of man. Hercules dying on earth of the venom of the serpent[1] became immortal in heaven. Ophiuchus, the serpent-bearer or conqueror, was considered to represent the same person as Orion, Hercules, and Esculapius; Orion and Hercules being wounded in the foot, and Esculapius always bearing a serpent in his hand. Lyra, the lyre of Orpheus or of Apollo, sons of deities, but also called the eagle, whose form Jupiter had assumed. Cygnus, the swan, whose shape had also been taken by him. Ara, the altar on which the gods swore, and Piscis Australis was a fish in some way belonging to the gods. Aquila, an eagle either slain by Hercules, or that in which Jupiter had appeared. Sagitta, the arrow with which Hercules killed the

---

[1] Hugh Miller (Testimony of the Rocks) remarks that the Ophidian or Serpent order, "illustrative of extreme degradation," appears in all ancient mythologies, "representing man's great enemy, the Evil One."
Columbus found among the Caribs in Guadaloupe wooden statues with their legs enwreathed with serpents. (Southey's West Indies.) It is remarkable that Hercules, so celebrated as a serpent-slayer, was not among the "chief gods of Greece and Rome."

G

eagle tearing Prometheus. The dolphin was that of Arion, whose name means "he who cometh." Pegasus, a horse belonging to the gods, and ridden by a son of a god, Bellerophon, whose name means "the lord, the restorer;" or by Perseus, the deliverer, or breaker of the bonds of the chained woman: this woman was called Andromeda, daughter of the king Cepheus, exposed to be devoured by the sea-monster, from whom Perseus delivered her, whose wife she became. Cassiopeia, wife of the king, sitting on a throne, black but beautiful, having offended the deities, but raised to heaven as a constellation. In these two last figures we clearly trace the Scripture type of the Church, the bride of Him who delivered her from the power of sin and death, and afterwards raises her to a throne of glory, to which the name Cassiopeia refers. Eridanus, the river of the lord, sometimes called the river of Orion. Auriga, a human figure, sometimes called Erichthonius, said to be of divine origin, to be lame [1], to have had legs like serpents, and to have had a serpent found in the cradle with him. Canis Major is said to be the dog of Orion or of Jupiter. Canis Minor also a dog of Orion. Argo, a miraculous vessel, and endued by one of the gods with the power of speech, which bore a company of voyagers, some of them said to be of divine parentage. Ursa Major, said by some to be the mother of Arcas, by others the nurse of Jupiter. Ursa Minor, Arcas, the son of Jupiter, the same person as Arctophylax, of whom there was a tradition that he died and came to life again on earth, and was then taken up to heaven. Hydra, a serpent slain by Hercules, of whose venom he died. Crater, a cup belonging to the gods, of which, as well as of Corvus, nothing definite seems to have been known by the ancients, nor why these two figures were united with the serpent Hydra among the constellations.

The mythologies of the nations were not mere inventions, but combinations of most widely varying traditions, whence the inconsistencies that pervade them. The Greek poets seem to have thought themselves at liberty to interweave even "barbarian" legends with those of their own country, as Herodotus [2] tells us was done by Æschylus. From Egypt they seem to have borrowed the story of Latona [3], whose name means "she who brings forth," as the Mylitta and Alitta of the Assyrians.

The connexions [4] here pointed out are only a part of what might be adduced, and probably will suggest others to the classical scholar, but they may suffice to show the resemblance of the fables of Greek and Roman mythology to the meaning here attributed to the astronomical figures to which they are referred, thus affording an important corroboration of the argument that such was the original intention of those emblems ; that intention being to proclaim to all coming time that the seed of the woman, the Divine Conqueror of the Serpent, should be born and die, should suffer and be exalted, that He had been promised and foretold from the very beginning of the world, that God had spoken.

---

[1] The lameness attributed to Auriga and to Vulcan may be referred to the circumstance that the human figures of the emblems are represented holding up one foot, as wounded, *bruised*.

[2] B. 2. 150.

[3] "As the Python pursued Latona to devour her offspring, so the serpent held by Ophiuchus appears aiming to devour the infant of Virgo." Thus justly observes Dupuis. The worship of Latona, and her magnificent temple in Egypt, further connect her with the woman of the zodiac ; as does the additional fable, that her offspring, the infant Apollo, immediately slew the serpent, whose name Python is the word translated "adder" in the 13th verse of the 91st Psalm.

[4] "The surest and best characteristic of a well-founded and extensive induction is, when verifications of it spring up, as it were, spontaneously into notice from quarters where they might be least expected, or from among instances of that very kind which were at first considered hostile. Evidence of this kind is irresistible, and compels assent with a weight that scarcely any other possesses." (Herschell on Nat. Phil. p. 170.) This remark equally applies to the mythologies of Egypt and Assyria, &c., as to those of Greece and Rome.

THE NAMES OF THE TWELVE CHIEF GODS OF ROMAN AND GREEK MYTHOLOGY.

EXPLAINED FROM THEIR PRIMITIVE ROOTS, AND REFERRED TO THE CORRESPONDING SIGNS.

			Texts where the root of the name is used in this sense in the Hebrew Bible.	*Hebrew roots.*
ARIES,	Roman, Vulcan, *who goes or comes forth.*	go	Gen. 24. 58.	הלך
	Greek, Hephæstus, *who sets free.*	free	Job 3. 19.	חפש
TAURUS,	R., Jove, a corruption of Jehovah, *who was, and is, and is to come.* (Etruscan.)		Exod. 6. 3.	יהוה
—	Jupiter { *he who is, Jah,* Ps. lxviii. 4.	the Lord	Exod. 15. 2.	יה
	{ *the creator or originator, Patar.*	opening	Exod. 13. 2.	פטר
	Gr., Zeus, Theos, and Dis, *who is*[1]. { be		Gen. 18. 24.	יש
	{ is		Gen. 28. 16.	
GEMINI,	R., { Apollo, *the Judge.*	Judge	Job 31. 11.	פלל
	Gr., { Phœbus, *the shining,* Job iii. 4 ; *who cometh and goeth.* Apollo and Diana were twins.		Hab. 2. 3.	בא
CANCER,	R., Juno, *gracious,* Prov. xi. 16.		Ps. 77. 9.	חן
	Gr., Hera, *who bears,* Isa. vii. 14.		Gen. 16. 11.	הרה
LEO,	R., Mars, Mavors, Mamers, *breaking, wounding.*	manslayer	Num. 35. 6.	רצח
	Gr., Ares, *the same.*			
VIRGO,	R., Minerva, *who heals.*		Isa. 30. 26.	רפא
	Gr., Pallas { *set apart (as the Virgin),* Exod. viii. 22.		Ps. 4. 3.	פלה
	{ *who considers, is wise, weighs.*		Isa. 26. 7.	פלס
	{ *who judges.*		Deut. 32. 31.	פלל
—	Athene, *who gives (the branch).*	gave	Gen. 25. 6.	נתן
LIBRA,	R., Vesta, *salvation.*		Ex. 14. 13.	ישועה
	Gr., Hesta, Hestia, or Hesia, *the same.*			
SCORPIO,	R., Ceres, *the wounding (as ploughing).*		Job 1. 14.	חרש
	Gr., Demeter, *wounding,* Gen. xxxvii. 26, *of the coming or returning.*		Esth. 2. 15.	תר
SAGITTA-RIUS[2],	R., Diana, *the feminine of Dan, ruler.*	Lord	Gen. 42. 33.	דן
	Gr., Artemis, *who cometh,* 2 Sam. xii. 4.	the twin	Cant. 4. 5.	תאם
CAPRICOR-NUS,	R., Mercury, *from afar,* Job xxi. 16 ; *recurring, as in a circle* (Arab.).			
	Gr., Hermes, *cut off, or who cuts off.*	destroyed	Ex. 22. 20.	חרם
—	Cyllenius, *pierced, slain.*	wounded	Isa. 53. 5.	חלל
AQUARIUS,	R., Neptune, *expanded, spread out as water.*	open	Isa. 41. 18.	פתח
	Gr., Poseidon, *diffused, spread out* (Arab.).	spread	Hab. 1. 8.	פשה
PISCES,	R., Venus, *gracious,* Ps. lxxvii. 9.	full of grace	Ps. 45. 2.	חן
	Gr., Aphrodite, *who is fruitful,* Gen. viii. 17 ; { much plentiful.	{ fruitful	Exod. 36. 5.	די
			Gen. 8. 17.	פרה

The Latin names are given from Ennius as those of the twelve principal gods of Rome, called *Dii Consentes*[3], consenting or agreeing, as in their relation to the twelve signs. The Crab was said to be sent by Juno to bite Hercules in the heel; the Scorpion to have been sent by Ceres to sting Orion. In the Indian zodiacs, a woman holds the scales of Libra, and Sagittarius is called the bow or the arrow, whence the archeress Diana might have been imagined in that sign. The figure of Andromeda in Pisces might suggest Venus, and Virgo was already there. Thus are accounted for the six female divinities of the twelve chief gods. The Greek names are from two lines by an unknown Greek poet. (Robinson's Archæologia.)

---

[1] Plato, in Cratylus, pronounces that such is the meaning of these names, saying that the name "Zeus is the offspring of no mean intellect."

[2] The arrow-bearing figure in Sagittarius has been by the ancients identified with the arrow-bearing twin in Gemini.

[3] The Roman explanation, that these gods *consented* in counsel with Jupiter, seems an afterthought. Ceres does not appear in the Homeric synod: Hestia is not even named by him.

The Greeks and Romans, the Assyrians, and other ancient nations, had twelve principal objects of worship, gods and goddesses, apparently derived from the twelve signs; those of the Romans, as has been said, being called Dii Consentes, a name, though explained as consenting to the counsels of Jupiter, more probably given as coinciding in that origin, and in resemblance to those signs.

The most remarkable agreement is perhaps in the stories concerning Minerva, the virgin daughter of Jupiter without a mother, so celebrated in Homeric verse. A tradition of the first created woman seems here mixed up with those derived from the sign Virgo. By authorities less familiar than that of Homer she is said to be also a mother, the mother of the conqueror of the serpent, the sun-god Apollo, as Isis of the Horus of Egypt; by some, of Prometheus, the divine and suffering benefactor of mankind. The ægis encircled by serpents, which she wore on her breast, was the trophy of a victory gained, not by herself, but by Perseus, a son of Jupiter by a human mother, over Medusa, whose name means "the bruised," "the trodden on." The olive-branch was another of her attributes, connecting her with the branch-bearing virgin of the zodiac, whose offspring was to bruise the serpent's head. Her name Minerva might convey the meaning of "who is to be reverenced," as well as "who heals;" but her Etruscan name Menefra would be "who is to bring forth." The signification, *who heals*, would account for her being called the goddess of medicine, among other things. These names were unknown to the Greeks, by whom she was called Pallas, "who judges," from the same root as Apollo; also Athene, "she who gives," and Parthenis, "who brings forth," a name equally applicable to the human female and the woman of the zodiac. From this root Parah, the Romans derived Virgo, a woman, and Virga, a branch, by the common Etruscan change of *p* to *v*. Minerva, then, is to be referred to the virgin mother of the zodiac.

Vesta, or Hestia, may be found in Libra [1], the name signifying salvation, the Vestal Virgins dedicated to her service being probably derived from the preceding sign.

Ceres, drawn in a car by two dragons, the serpents of the sign Scorpio, under the name of Tellus, the earth, sent forth the scorpion to wound the heel of Orion, as in the sign it wounds that of Ophiuchus, one of whose names is Triptolemus, said to be taught by Ceres to plough the ground, the names Ceres and Demeter meaning to wound, bruise, *crush*.

Diana, who rules, as the moon the night, Artemis, who cometh, the arrow-bearer, the twin-sister of Apollo, said to have taken refuge from the Titans in the form of a mare, corresponds with the equine form and bow and arrow of Sagittarius.

The ibis-headed Mercury in Egyptian zodiacs is found standing on Capricornus the fish-goat. He is sometimes imaged as sitting on a fish, sometimes with a goat at his feet. The Greek name Hermes is " who cuts off, or is cut off," agreeing with the idea of sacrifice, as does that of Cyllenius, which has nearly the same meaning. He was said to carry away the souls of the dead. Like Apollo, he was the son of Jupiter by a human mother. The Roman name Mercury, and the Etruscan Turm, returning from

---

[1] This sign seems to have been confounded with the preceding or that which follows, the Virgin of the zodiac being sometimes represented with a balance, and called Astræa, the goddess of justice. The Scholiast on Virgil says that anciently there were but eleven signs, the claws of Scorpio, called Chelæ, taking the place of Libra. Cali being an implement of any kind, as the scales, might cause this confusion. Ovid and Virgil both adopt this notion, which obviated the difficulty which must have embarrassed those who held that Zodion or Zodiac meant a circle of living creatures. In the Indian zodiac the scales are held by a human figure; but the sign is called Tula, or Tolam, the balance, the suspended or held up. In Greek the sign is called Zugos, the yoke or beam of the balance, certainly not a living creature.

afar, as in a circle, were interpreted by them as the messenger of the gods, but had a higher reference: the Divine Messenger, the Son of the Supreme, should come, go, and return.

Neptune, the ruler of the water; Poseidon, spread out, as his ocean-realm.   The constellation Pegasus, the horse, whose head joins that of Aquarius, the water-bearer, accounts for the fable that Neptune assumed the figure of a horse, and for horses being sacrificed to him, also for his presenting the war-horse to mankind, a gift held even by the heathen inferior to that of the olive of Minerva, the emblem of peace, derived from the branch in the hand of the virgin of the zodiac, symbolizing Him who is the Prince of Peace.   The neighbouring constellation of the dolphin was said to be the dolphin who brought to Neptune his spouse Amphitrite.

Venus with her son Cupid in the Titan war took refuge in the form of fishes.   The name Venus, kindness, graciousness, accords with the union of the two fishes in Pisces; Aphrodite, fruitful in offspring, with the meaning of the name of the sign, the multitudes.

Vulcan, the spouse of Venus, who comes forth, but is hurt in the foot, accords with Aries, He who comes, as also by his Greek name Hephæstus, the setter-free.

Jove, a corruption of the sacred name of the Jewish Scriptures, and Jupiter, He who is the Creator, or Originator, in Greek Zeus, Theos, Dis, He who is, the chief deity of the two nations, had, it was fabled, once borne the form of the bull; and to him bulls were sacrificed.

Apollo, the judge, and Phœbus, the shining, the conqueror of the serpent, and son of Jupiter, twin-born of a human mother, may be traced to the divine twin Pollux, the judge, the mighty one, of Gemini.   He was sent down on earth to keep the sheep of King Admetus, to whom he granted life on the death of a substitute; this name Admetus is said to be the only trace of that of Adam in Greek fable.   His wife Alcestis was rescued from death by Hercules, the suffering son of Jupiter, who in the sign Gemini was reckoned the twin with Apollo, and who died by the venom of the serpent he had conquered.   Thus in this story are remarkably combined various traditions concerning the promised "seed of the woman."   *The king*, a frequent epithet of Apollo, to whom no kingdom is assigned, may be from the tradition that this infant should be the " King who should rule in righteousness."

Juno may be traced to Cancer, the crab, which she was said to have sent to wound the foot of Hercules, afterwards placing it in the heavens as this constellation.   As Cancer signified possession, typified by cattle, so she was the patroness of wealth and fecundity, and in the Titan war hid herself in the form of a cow.   In Juno, the often disobedient but ever chaste spouse, we trace the Bride, the Church, bound in the chain as Andromeda, seated on the throne as Cassiopeia; so in the infant, the victim, and the conqueror, we trace the coming Saviour.   Her Latin name is "the gracious, or loved;" her Greek name, " who bears."

Mars, born of Juno without a father, according to some, but of Jupiter, according to others, strong and unconquerable, has his attributes in common with the lion.   His names, whether Mars, Mamers, or Ares, may all be derived from the same root, to break, wound, slay, whence his Homeric epithet, the homicide: also the fable of his being wounded in the Trojan war.

The tradition of a son of the Supreme God, born of a human mother, conquering the serpent, yet dying by its poison, pervades the stories of these twelve chief gods of Greece and Rome, as it is the theme of the twelve signs to which they are here referred.

Thus also we find the Dii Consentes, the twelve principal deities of the Romans, following out the circle of the signs, and *consenting* to the message of prophetic truth which these emblems had been formed to convey.

That six of those deities are feminine, while in only one of the signs a woman's figure appears, is a variation in accordance with the still prevalent tendency of human nature to set up a female divinity, a queen of heaven.

The Romans are considered to have adopted some of these names from the Etruscans, whom the colonists under Æneas found an ancient and civilized people : others, as Jupiter, they appear to have brought with them from their Asian home. It is said that the Jupiter of Etruria was called Tinia, or Tinis, also that the Romans had learnt from them the names Jove and Jave. As is often the case in names, Tinis may only express one of the attributes of deity, from a primitive root, to endure, be lengthened out, as in Ps. lxxii. 17, expressing eternity, or from another root might mean the giver, but Jave and Jove are evidently derived from Jah and Jehovah.

Among the Etruscan remains lately brought to light, there are figures like those found at Nineveh by Layard, combining three of the cherubic forms : a human head on the body of a lion with eagles' wings. Both these figures, Etruscan and Assyrian, are walking, coming.

Gems bearing Etruscan characters or emblems are mostly cut into the form of the Egyptian scarabæus, the sacred beetle, equivalent to the figure of the crab in Cancer. This is one of the frequent resemblances of Etruscan to Egyptian remains : not that these nations descended from, or perhaps even borrowed from one another, but had all one common source, the family of Noah. The Etruscan Apollo holds a branch, as do many of the figures, divine or priestly, of the Assyrian sculptures. The branch and the cherubic emblems, received through that family, pervade all mythology, and point to that origin, to which the twelve great gods of Greece and Rome, as well as the twelve signs of the zodiac, are here referred.

Though not numbered among the twelve great gods, Castor and Pollux were peculiarly venerated Roman divinities. The Helen of the Iliad claims them for her brothers, but the Romans regarded them with superhuman awe. Both Greeks and Romans in some way connected them with the starry twins, their dazzling helms always crowned by a star. Both now immortal and divine; but one had been born mortal, and the divine twin had shared his immortality with him. There is tradition here far beyond the reach of astronomy. Nothing in the stars of Gemini could suggest it. Prophecy alone can account for it. There was to be a mysterious union of Divine and human nature in One who was to come, the theme of prophecy and the prototype of the emblems of those constellations that perpetuated it. One sense of the name of the branch-bearing twin, Pollux, is the *wonderful*, the *strong*. Such seemed to be the feelings with which the Romans regarded these Dioscuri, these divine youths. Their mother's name, Leda, is she who brings forth [1], the universal appellation of the woman of the zodiac.

Janus, also not included among the twelve chief gods, received especial Roman veneration. His temple was to be shut in universal peace ; when the blessing was come there was no need to pray for it. His name signifies [2] peace, rest, cessation ; resting, as the sun at the winter solstice, ceasing, as the year, thence to recommence. Twelve altars, and altars of twelve stones were dedicated to him, referring evidently to the twelve signs. That temple was shut, for the last time, at the birth of Him " who is our peace," at that winter solstice with which Janus was associated He

---

[1] Mic. v. 3.   [2] Gen. 1. 17 (Arab. sense).

was born. That the Divine Word was then to take into communion with Himself a created nature seems symbolized in the figure of the sign where then was the winter solstice; the victim kid, the sacrifice for sin, typifying the Redeemer, is there united with the fish, the well-known symbol of "his body, the Church."

Another object of wide-spread worship, the Bacchus of the Romans, and Dionusos of the Greeks, was also not of the twelve. The name Bacchus is from the root Ba, he cometh (as in Bootes), and Acha, smitten, wounded. Dionusos from Dios, the divine, and Nusos, wounded. In the Syracusan dialect Nusos is said to have meant lame [1], wounded in the foot. Dire was the perversion of prophecy in the Bacchanalian and Dionysian festivals of abandoned profligacy. Women bearing branches, the well-known emblem of Him who was to come, the Desire of nations, attended the figure of the divinity, others carrying aloft the foreleg of an animal, kid or lamb. This unexplained symbol seems to have originated from the Oriental word Zeroah [2], the foreleg, suggesting the similar sound Zerah, the seed, the offspring. The serpents also, borne as in triumph by the Bacchantes, can only be accounted for by the tradition, that He who should come should be the conqueror of the serpent [3].

Hercules [4], or Heraclas, though the most famous of the serpent-slayers, and said to be celebrated as such in every ancient mythology, does not appear in the circle of the twelve chief gods of Greece and Rome. A constellation is named after him, but it is not in the zodiac, though his name has there been applied to one of the twins. Whether there were one, two, four, or forty-four of the name was uncertain; and he was so extensively worshipped as to be called the god of many nations. Labouring and suffering for mankind, extirpating the seven heads of the abhorred, the hydra, he did yet more: bringing back from the tomb the faithful wife of King Admetus, and his friend Theseus from Tartarus itself, he was the conqueror of death and hell. The constellations of Perseus and Andromeda set forth the prophecy so early recorded in the name of Methuselah, and transmitted in the story of Hercules freeing Hesione, the saved one, from the sea-monster figured in Cetus, who like Andromeda becomes the bride of the deliverer, to be, as Cassiopeia, enthroned in glory by the side of Cepheus, the branch, there placed on high as the crowned king. If such gleams of divine truth still pervaded the darkened atmosphere of heathenism, shall they not be joyfully recognized as illuminating the dreary retrospect of those ages of idolatrous obscurity?

---

[1] Hederic. Lex.   [2] Deut. iv. 34.   [3] Gen. iii. 15.

[4] The eight Dii Selecti of the Romans, deities of the next order, were Saturnus, Janus, Rhea, Pluto, Bacchus, Sol, Luna, Genius. They were not referred to any of the twelve signs, nor indeed to any of the other constellations.

The Dii Minorum Gentium included almost innumerable other objects of worship. They were apparently adopted from other nations. Among them were reckoned Hercules, and Castor and Pollux, which, however, were named as the twins in Gemini. Pan also, sometimes called the greatest of the gods, was among them. *Pan*, from its Greek signification, was often understood as *universal*, the god of all; but having the horns and legs of a goat, he might have originated from the sign Capricorn: if so, the name, from its Semitic root "to turn," might refer to the winter solstice passing into that sign about 2000 years B.C., when the sun turned again, began to return.

THE TWELVE LABOURS OF HERCULES[1],

AS AGREEING WITH THE SIGNS.

THE slaying of the Nemean lion, with Leo.
The victory over the queen of the Amazons, with Virgo.
The battle of the centaurs and slaying the boar of Erymanthus, with the Victim held by the
    centaur in Libra.
The hydra killed by Hercules, who dies by its poison, with Scorpio.
The birds of Stymphalis shot by Hercules, with Sagittarius.
The stag, or goat, slain by Hercules after a year's pursuit, with Capricornus.
The pouring of the river through the Augean stable, with Aquarius.
The seizing the horses of Diomedes, with Pegasus in Pisces.
The voyage in quest of the golden fleece, and the deliverance of Andromeda, with Aries.
The conquest of the bull of Crete, with Taurus.
The infant Hercules, and his mortal twin-brother Iphiclus, strangling the serpents, with Gemini.
The taking the flocks and herds of Geryon, with Cancer.

The resemblance that has been observed between the twelve labours of Hercules and
the signs of the zodiac has sometimes led to the supposition that the signs were formed
from the stories relative to these labours. But ancient authorities differ widely as to
the history, and even the personality of Hercules, questioning whether there were one,
or three, or six heroes of the name. They disagree also about the nature and order of
the so-called twelve labours, while the figures and succession of the signs have come
down unaltered and undoubted; this permanent and unvarying series must therefore be
the original from which the uncertain and fluctuating fables have been copied.

The mythological Hercules has been considered as a personification of the sun, and
his twelve labours as denoting its progress through the signs in the annual course. It
seems that the fables insensibly grew out of the traditionary explanations of the starry
emblems, given to the wonder-loving Greeks by the Phœnician mariners, or transmitted to them from their Phœnician or Egyptian ancestors.

From this allegorical personage, the sun-god, may have been named that hero whose
descendants, the Heraclidæ, have a real historical existence. As in more recent ages
Odin, the successful leader of northern invasion, has been confounded with the god

---

[1] "The author of the Hymns of Orpheus seems to identify Hercules with the sun.
Porphyry, who was born in Phœnicia, assures us that the name of Hercules was given to the
sun, and that the fable of the twelve labours expresses the progress of the sun through the
twelve signs of the zodiac. The Scholiast of Hesiod says, 'The zodiac in which the sun performs
his annual course is the career of Hercules in the fable of the twelve labours; and by his
marriage with Hebe, goddess of youth, whom he espouses, after having finished his career, must
be understood the renewal of the year after every revolution.'" (Dupuis, Origine des Cultes,
p. 108.) G. S. Faber quotes ancient authorities to prove that Hercules was sometimes represented as contending with a serpent, whose head is under his heel. Silius Italicus describes a
temple of Hercules, very ancient in his days, at Gades in Spain, in which was no image or similitude of the gods, but on its door was sculptured that labour of Hercules in which he slew the
serpent Hydra.

Odin, of Scandinavian mythology, whose name he bore. So the human hero and the deified allegory may have been interwoven in the poetic traditions of Grecian antiquity.

The story of the divine Hercules, the son of the Supreme God, who came on earth to labour, to suffer, and to die, has too many points of resemblance to the great theme of prophecy, the promised Conqueror of the serpent, not to be at once referred to primeval revelation shedding a twilight ray on the darkness which covered the Gentile earth. The sun of this world, though its glorious image was too soon desecrated by idolatry, yet in some measure connected the perversion with the truth. The sun-god Hercules preserved many of the characteristics of the Sun of righteousness who was to arise.

He was said to have contended soon after his birth with two serpents, which he strangled. His subsequent victory over the one serpent, the Lernean hydra, at once carries us back to the original promise; but for the story of two enemies at once we must seek some other source. We may find it in the constellations of Hercules kneeling on one knee, as from the wound in the heel, while his foot is over the head of Draco, and the united emblem of Ophiuchus, the serpent-bearer, sometimes called also Hercules, who not only holds the serpent with which he is in conflict, but has his foot on the head of another enemy, the scorpion, from whom he seems about to receive or to have received the predicted wound in the heel. Had the emblems been taken from the fable, these two human figures would have been infantine like those of Gemini; but the fable being derived from the emblems, finding them placed soon after the commencement of the ancient year, where Virgo holds in her arms the promised infant, might refer the struggle to the beginning of the hero's career. Two serpentine emblems accompanying the human ones in the constellations may be thus accounted for: that two periods of time, the wounding and the victory of the promised Deliverer, were to be represented in one symbol.

Other achievements attributed to Hercules refer to other of the constellations beyond the zodiac; but it is always asserted that there were twelve principal ones, called by way of distinction the twelve labours, though different authorities relate different stories to make up the number. It seems, however, by all agreed that the first labour was the conquest of a lion: the summer solstice, the commencement of the ancient year, having receded from Virgo into Leo, here the sun-god naturally began his progress. Did the fable more closely follow the order of the signs, the victory over the queen of the Amazons, corresponding with the sun's passage through the sign Virgo, should come next; for Libra there seems to be taken the adjacent constellation of the centaur piercing the victim, alluded to in the slaying of the boar of Erymanthus, and the victory over the centaurs said to occur in the course of that adventure. For Scorpio [1] we find the hydra, by whose venom the hero afterwards died, killed by Hercules with the assistance of his friend Iolas; in which may be traced the union of the two constellations, Hercules and Ophiuchus [2], belonging to this sign. In Sagittarius, with the neighbouring constellations, Aquila [3] and Sagitta, the hero is destroying with his arrows the ravenous birds of the lake Stymphalis. In Capricornus the stag or goat of Diana, which Hercules pursued for a whole year, has often been recognized; to which sign the winter solstice had early receded. In Aquarius is seen the origin of the story of the cleansing of the

---

[1] It is possible that the scorpion was an early corruption of the serpent, from the name of the sign, the conflict, suggesting that of the scorpion; nevertheless, the scorpion is a most suitable type in this place, and is perhaps alluded to in Ps. xci.

[2] In the name of his twin-brother Iphiclus, Ophiuchus may be traced.

[3] The ascending and falling eagle will bring to mind the type in Lev. xiv. 4.

Augean stable by turning a river through it; but as the human figure was never, among its many names, called Hercules, it is evident the sign was not invented from the story. The seizing of the horses of Diomedes, and their consecration to Jupiter by the labouring hero, appears to take the constellation of Pegasus in the place of Pisces. In Aries we find Cetus, the sea-monster from which Hesione was said to be delivered by Hercules, her name meaning "saved from affliction," as that of Andromeda, from whence the story was probably derived. Aries was said to be the ram whose golden fleece Hercules went with the Argonauts to obtain. In the belly of that sea-monster Hercules was said to have remained "three days and three nights" by Lycophron [1], who, living at the court of Ptolemy Philadelphus, had access to the translation of the Hebrew Scriptures made for that sovereign, whence he might obtain the knowledge of the typical prophecy of Jonah. From the Jewish translators he might learn its application to Him who was to come, called in the same Scriptures the Sun of righteousness, and thus being by the poet connected with the sun-god Hercules. In Taurus is seen the bull of Crete. In Gemini the branch in the hand of that twin sometimes called Hercules seems to have connected with this sign the story of that garden of the Hesperides, so remarkably preserving the tradition of Eden and the forbidden fruit, the serpent and the Conqueror. In Gemini we also trace the reason why the divine Hercules was said to have a human twin-brother, called Iphiclus. This name never having been annexed to either twin of the constellation shows that the sign did not follow, however it might originate, the fable. The acquisition of the flocks and herds of the triple-headed king Geryon [2] well corresponds with the interpretation of the sign Cancer, as setting forth the purchased possession, the flock of the good Shepherd, the peculiar people of the King who shall rule in righteousness, in whose person dwelleth the whole fulness of the Godhead bodily, in whom alone is declared the glory of the triune God.

Great authorities have observed that wherever in Greek mythology there is a fable concerning a son of Jupiter, there may be traced, as its foundation, a prophecy of the Messiah [3]. This observation is remarkably exemplified in the stories concerning Hercules, as may be seen in those relative to the twelve labours, here shown to correspond with the symbolizations of the signs and constellations belonging to the signs. Hercules and his labours are seldom thought of, except during the study of those ancient authors still made part of modern European education. In after life few remember and fewer care what he or they might signify, but the twelve signs of the zodiac are in the memory of all. Every elementary book with but a single page devoted to astronomy contains them. Surely a great step in the promotion of Christian knowledge will be gained, if these wide-spread, almost universal symbols can be shown, when rightly interpreted, to declare the glory of God in the work of redemption; if the fables derived from them of the labouring, suffering, dying, and deified sun-god of mythology are used as testifying to their original in revelation, even as the broken reflection on the descending current to the stedfast rays of the luminaries above it.

---

[1] Æneas Gazeus, a writer less known, also says, "Hercules is reported to have been, when shipwrecked, swallowed up by a whale (κῆτος)." Much has been said as to the species of fish by which Jonah was swallowed. The Hebrew merely says דג, a fish: the original meaning of Ketos is equally general, being merely the Greek writing of Chayith, an animal, used for a marine animal in Ps. civ. 25. Many of the apparent difficulties in ancient literature, as well as in the Scriptures, would in like manner be removed by adverting to the Semitic root of the word.

[2] Geryon may have had the first syllable from Kir, the last of Cancer, as his dog with two heads has probably been taken from the two dogs in the preceding sign, and its name, Orthos, from the usual root ארח, who cometh.

[3] Bp. Horsley, &c.

THE SPHINX,

AS CONNECTED WITH THE SIGN VIRGO.

THERE are typical actions recorded in Scripture, in which there is evident allusion to the sound of the name, as well as to the nature of the object employed : and sometimes the reference is to the sound alone; as, for instance, in the ancient usage recorded in the history of Ruth, when the man who refused to take the widow and the inheritance together pulled off his shoe, or sandal, in Hebrew *Nayal*, and gave it to Boaz in token of transferring to him his right to the inheritance, in Hebrew *Nahal*[1], of the deceased. It has been observed by the modern decipherers of Egyptian hieroglyphics that the figure of the sandal has some relation to the country of Egypt. As Nahal also signifies a valley down which the stream runs, and sometimes the stream itself, and as the great similarity of the ancient Egyptian to the Hebrew seems now acknowledged, this hieroglyphic may be thus accounted for.   The ancient names of the river Nile, as Sihor, the dark ; and Oceanus, stretched out, expanded, as the river in its overflowing; and Egyptus, covering [2], as the land by inundation, whence the country itself was called Egypt, the covered, and the Nile was represented as veiled.   Ethiopia being inundated also, was called Cush, also meaning covered.   This great peculiarity of Egypt, the inundation, has always been considered to be alluded to in the celebrated figure of the Sphinx, a human head with the lion's body.   The name Sphinx in the ancient dialects means " the pouring out [3]."   This figure has been said by different ancients to relate to the creation of the world [4], to the inundation, and to the summer solstice, at which the Nile begins to rise, but how and why they say not.   There is a tradition that the creation was at the summer solstice.   Four thousand years before Christ this solstice took place where the junction of Leo and Virgo is marked by the bright star Denebola [5].   By referring the figure of the Sphinx to the junction of the signs of Virgo and Leo, these three traditions are reconciled and explained.   The Krio-Sphinx, or ram-headed lion, is common in the monuments of Egypt.   The ram's head on the lion's body may be accounted for by the junction of Aries and Leo in one object of veneration, both typifying the same person in the intention of their inventor, though

---

[1] Or Nachal.   [2] 2 Sam. xv. 30.

[3] As in Deut. xxxiii. 19, where it is translated "abundance," in the blessing of Zebulon, who bore Virgo upon his standard.   The Sphinx of Egypt must have been familiar to the Israelites, and its relation to the inundation.

[4] Macrobius says that the Egyptian astronomers taught, that at the creation the sun rose in Leo and the moon in Cancer.   Julius Africanus says that Petosiris and Necepsos, ancient Egyptian philosophers, also taught that at the creation the sun was in 15° Leo, and the moon in 15° Cancer.   These signs are still in astrology called respectively the houses of the sun and moon.

[5] A name meaning "the Lord who cometh quickly," where a figure of a youth bearing a branch may be seen in the Egyptian planisphere.

not in the mythology of Egypt, for there the ram Ammon was adored, while the lion was little known, except in their lion-headed idols and in the figures of astronomy [1].

The lately-found remains of Assyrian sculpture throw much greater light on this investigation than those of Egypt. In a purer style of art, they indicate a less corrupt state of morals and even of religion. The earlier of them seem to belong to the period of transition from Sabianism, the undue veneration for the host of heaven, to an idolatrous worship of images representing them. The images then becoming the idols of Assyria are the four principal constellations combined ; these referring to the four faces of the divinely-appointed emblems of the cherubim.

The Andro-Sphinx, a man's head on a lion's body, coincides with the discovery that the great Sphinx of the desert holds in the fore paws a shrine containing the figure of a young man, representing, it should seem, the promised deliverer, the hoped-for progeny of the virgin. Some however have thought that the Sphinx was a youth, and not a woman.

The Sphinx of the pyramids, if female, would refer to the woman in the sign Virgo, as united in the starry emblems with that of Leo [2]. If male, as the Andro-Sphinx else-where met with, it still expresses the prophecy: it is there the seed, the infant, the son, who is emblematized in the man as the sacrifice, in the lion as the conqueror. He is so typified in the two-faced cherub of Ezekiel xli. 18, 19, which is understood by Jewish authorities to have been the same as those of Divine ordination in Exodus xxvi. and 1 Kings vi., on the curtains of the tabernacle and on the walls of the temple. According to Al Makrisi (who gives no explanation of it), the ancient name of the Sphinx is Bel-hit; it may be explained " the Lord who cometh [3]:" the modern Abou-houl, father of sand, is also masculine.

By the Greeks the Sphinx was said to be born of Chimera, a monster formed of three of the starry emblems, the lion, the goat and the serpent; whose name is taken from Chema, heat, of fire and of wrath; thus furnishing an additional instance of the derivation of the wildest and most incoherent of the Greek fables from the names and figures of the constellations.

In the prophecies annexed to the multitude of sparkling orbs shining in their clear midnight sky, the Greeks perhaps found that insolvable enigma [4] which they made it characteristic of the Sphinx to propound: this part of the story might arise from the tradition of the hidden meaning belonging to the mystic emblem of the Egyptian Sphinx. The Greek fables concerning it take no notice of the enshrined youth, perhaps then as now generally buried in the sand, the discovery of which however has strengthened the evidence connecting the Sphinx with the sign Virgo.

---

[1] The Egyptian union of the ram and the lion in one image shows a tradition of Him at once the appointed victim and the future conqueror. In the book of Revelation He is at once " the Lamb as it had been slain," and "the Lion of the tribe of Judah." Not that St. John adverted to the hieroglyphic, but that the hieroglyphic was taken from the emblems of the zodiac embodying the earliest prophecies, with which the latest are in accordance.

[2] Layard thinks the figure of a female sphinx is sometimes met with in the Assyrian sculptures. It seems still undetermined whether the great sphinx of the desert represents a woman or a youth ; in either case it is equally referable to the first revelation. As in the sign Virgo both the woman and the promised offspring are to be found, both aspects of the Sphinx may have had the same origin.

[3] Deut. xxxiii. 21.

[4] This enigma is said to have been the question, What is the animal which goes on four legs in the morning, two at noon, and three at night? Œdipus replied, " Man, crawling as an infant, walking erect in manhood, and in old age with a staff." It is possible that the infant of Virgo, the man in Ophiuchus, and the branch-bearing Hercules of the constellations might have given the hint of her riddle.

THE SIBYL,

AS CONNECTED WITH THE SIGN VIRGO.

THE name Sibyl, for which no satisfactory derivation has otherwise been given, signifies in the Semitic dialects "who carries," "the bearer [1]." A nearly similar root is an ear of corn [2], and also a branch [3], thus identifying this mythological personage, the bearer of the golden branch in the Æneid, with the figure of Virgo, the seed-bearer in the zodiac. The Sibyl was always said to be a prophetic virgin: the Cumean may have been so called originally from Chimah, the desired, afterwards corrupted to Coma, one of the names of the infant borne by the virgin of the zodiac.

The story of the first acquisition of the Sibylline books in the early annals of Rome may be chiefly poetical fiction, but it is an historical fact that books called Sibylline were long preserved at Rome with the utmost veneration. Being destroyed by fire about a century before the Christian era, the Romans sent delegates to Asia, to the islands of the Archipelago, to Sicily, and to Africa, where it was understood that these prophecies were yet extant. They collected about a thousand verses, out of which the learned at Rome made a selection, probably of such as most agreed with their recollections of those that had perished [4]. The verses thus selected formed those Sibylline books to which Cicero, as an augur, had access, and of which he says "that they were rather calculated to extinguish than to propagate superstition:" consequently their subject was not the idolatrous religion of Rome. Cicero also informs us that they predicted a king who was to arise about that time, whose sovereignty was to be universal, and under whose rule the world should be at peace. A farther insight into the subject of these ancient prophecies is gained from Virgil's celebrated poem called Pollio. The remarkable coincidence of some of its imagery with the prophecies of Isaiah has been beautifully developed in our English masterpiece of verse, Pope's Messiah. This resemblance may be accounted for by the researches of the Romans having been directed to Asia Minor, where these prophecies were first delivered and were well preserved. But there are other images introduced in the Pollio, also occurring in ancient prophecy, but of which Isaiah did not furnish the original. Isaiah does not speak of the time when the Prince of Peace shall be born. The other Hebrew prophecies which declare the time of the accomplishment of the great sacrifice do not fix that of the Messiah's birth; yet the expectation was prevalent all over the East that He should come about that time (perhaps from the seventy weeks of

---

[1] Isa. xlvi. 4, 7.   [2] Job xxiv. 24.   [3] Isa. iv. 2.   Zech. iv. 12.
[4] Bp. Horsley on Prophecies of the Messiah among the heathen. In what language were the first Sibylline books written? It seems that the delegates translated into Latin the prophecies which they collected.

Daniel): and it seems that the Sibylline verses confirmed the general anticipation. After an introduction declaring that the age spoken of by the Cumean Sibyl was now arrived, the poet seems not merely to relate her predictions, but to speak in her person, saying, " The great order of ages is born again in its completeness." This assertion remarkably coincides with the circumstance stated as an astronomical fact, that " when the moon was new in Aries, in the year of the world usually considered as that of our Lord's incarnation, her conjunction with the sun took place at the time of the true equinox," thus completing one magnificent cycle of the heavenly movements, and commencing another not yet concluded [1].

The Sibyl seems next to say, " The virgin comes who shall bear the promised progeny of heaven, who shall revive the worship of that Deity, long hid beneath the idolatries of the iron age, whose early reign, whose age of gold, he shall restore."

The peace of Brundusium, concluded under the consulate of Pollio, gave occasion to the poet there to seek the commencement of the predicted reign of blessedness, and to express the hope that in the young Octavius, then for the first time assuming the title of Cæsar, was to be found the promised pacificator. Again he takes up the Sibyl's strain, attributing to him that power of atoning for the sins of the world which had never been believed of any mere man, and that removal of human fears, which had been made a characteristic of Prometheus, the divine and suffering benefactor of the human race.

Astronomical emblems are then brought forward by their astronomical names: Capella, the she-goat; and Aries, the ram; and the fall of the serpent, in terms resembling those of the original promise to Adam.

There is then a clear distinction drawn between the early period of Messiah's reign, when there should be " wars and rumours of wars," and the happy completion of it, when " nation shall not lift up sword against nation, neither shall they learn war any more," when famine and pestilence shall cease, " when the earth shall bring forth her increase," when " instead of the brier shall come up the myrtle-tree," " and the desert shall rejoice and blossom as the rose."

The early Romans were little skilled in any language but their own; therefore the Sibylline books which they were accustomed to consult must have been translated at least into the ancient Latin tongue. May not the celebrated spondaic hexameter, that magnificent line, the marvel of Latin poetry, " Cara Deum soboles, magnum Jovis incrementum," have existed in those early records, preserved in the memory of those conversant with them, and retained by the exquisite taste of Virgil to give the dignity and authority of antiquity to his work? A corroboration of this conjecture offers itself in the word Soboles, an offspring, a shoot or branch, a word containing the same primitive root as the branch, the seed of prophecy, while Sibylla would be the seed or branch-bearer. It might be that the ancient Latin verses spoke of the promised infant by this name [2],

---

[1] In French astronomy of the last century, as La Loubère, &c.

[2] When the Emperor Constantine delivered his oration to the Christian Church, to point out that the expected infant in this celebrated Eclogue was Christ Himself, it is supposed he only enlarged on what was then a prevalent idea. This opinion, long disregarded, Pope revived, Horsley advocated, and many have since adopted. Virgil seems to have been a good astronomer, and aware that the accomplishment of the great cycle was at hand. He also appears to have known that universal peace was to accompany the birth of the great one who was to come from the East, and was right in fixing its commencement with the peace of Brundusium, in the consulate of Pollio. As even Christian expositions of prophecy have too often done, he however mingles up the glory and blessedness of the second coming with the humiliation and suffering accompanying the first.

which occurs as an Arabic name in the sign Virgo, and amongst the fixed stars as Subilon, a name of Canopus.

As in the case of Hercules, so in that of the Sibyl, ancient authorities differ as to whether there were one or more. Plato spoke but of one, while the Romans enumerated ten, apparently supposing a separate prophetess to have lived in every place where they found the prophecies.

One of these Sibyls was named from the ancient Sabine town of Tibur, where Hercules (a personification of the prophecies of the promised seed, the theme of the Sibylline verses) was peculiarly worshipped. If these verses contained any explicit assertion, that he who was to reign was also to suffer, it could not be expected to appear in the application to Octavius : but when Virgil in the sixth Æneid again introduces the Sibyl, he represents her as applying to Æneas predictions of sufferings that should precede and be merged in glory. These in the Pollio he brings forward as concerning the state of mankind. Here, carried by the Sibyl, may be recognized the branch, the sacred golden branch that had power over the infernal regions, when carried thither in the hand of Mercury, said to be a son of the Deity, procuring " liberty to the captives, and the opening of the prison to them that are bound." When in that of the pious hero, propitiating towards him the powers of the invisible world, this branch is likened by the poet to the mistletoe, whose name means the " sent forth," the self-springing " plant of renown," held in veneration by the northern nations, sought out and cut off by the Druids with mystic ceremonies, evidently derived from the universal tradition, that the Seed, the Branch, He who was to come, the Desire of nations, was to be cut off, but not for Himself, and should be born out of the common course of nature, as the mistletoe was long supposed to be produced. When the Spaniards met with that extraordinary tradition in the sacred records of Mexico, they were led to trace the Hebrew word Messiah in the name of the woman-born deity Mexitli, a derivation which, however possible in the strange and manifold corruptions to which unwritten languages are liable, must not be pressed here; for it will not bear the test by which all the accompanying derivations have been tried, which is, that when written in Hebrew letters they present the very word, or at least the root required, according to which they are interpreted. The name Deiphobe, given by Virgil to his Sibyl, would in Greek signify *fearing God*, and might give rise to the story of her fleeing from Apollo [1]. That of Amalthea, elsewhere attributed to her, would be from the Semitic root, *she who labours* or *travails*, who shall bring forth. From these circumstances of the story of the prophetic and long-lived Sibyl, we gather that among the nations there existed the memory of the revelation made to Adam, as it is figured by the seed-bearer of the zodiac, and in corresponding words by Isaiah and Micah. The branch, by which the promised seed is so often typified by the prophets, is by them nowhere spoken of in connexion with the woman, though in the name and history of the Sibyl, as in the figure of the constellation, we find it to be so. It is also met with in one of the names of the bright star in Virgo, Al Zimach, which is the very word used as branch by Isaiah, Jeremiah, and Zechariah. Thus we find additional evidence, were such needed, that the virgin of the zodiac was intended and long understood to set forth the tradition so widely diffused among the descendants of him to whom it was first given, concerning the seed of the woman, the " Branch of the Lord's planting."

We learn from the researches of Layard, that the figure of a woman, which might be

---

[1] If from a Semitic root, it would be " she who flees away, goes wandering."

referred to the same origin as the story of the Sibyl, occurs among the later Assyrian remains: a woman with a star upon her head, a branch or flower, and sometimes a serpent in her hand, a lion under her feet. This figure seems plainly derived from the promise to Adam, and its record in the starry emblems. Among the earlier sculptures of Assyria no female figure has been met with; they present at first only the various combinations by which human perverseness corrupted to idolatry those divinely-appointed emblems of the cherubim at the gate of Eden. As this corruption increased, they turned from Him who was to come, the Seed of the woman, to the woman herself, as we have seen even in Christian times, in the worship of the blessed mother of Christ and her images, in the "great apostasy." In the latter days of the Assyrian empire a female idol was worshipped, under the name Mylitta, or Alitta, meaning "she who brings forth," from the word used by Isaiah and Micah. The branch or seed may have been originally the chief emblem in the sign Virgo, the woman supporting it only an adjunct. That the early Assyrian worship of the host of heaven did not include the woman's figure, agrees with this supposition.

The mistranslation in the Latin Vulgate, which would make the woman (*ipsa*) bruise the serpent's head, is wholly contrary to the Hebrew original, and to the Septuagint, as also to the figure in the sign, where are found the branch, the seed, and the woman, but not the enemy. There is no serpent here. He by whom Paradise was lost shall not enter that Paradise of God, regained by the victory of the promised Seed of the woman.

NOTE.

"An oracle which declared that nature was about to bring forth a king to the Roman people," as Suetonius records, "had become known in Italy sixty-three years before the Christian era." Faber adds, "It is probable the words, whether traditionary or in the Sibylline books, were 'a king to the world.'"

Virgil, agreeably to the feelings of the Romans, avoids the word "king," which might have existed without offending them in the original books brought to the king Tarquin. Bp. Horsley considers that Cicero admits that this prophecy was in the Sibylline books with which he was acquainted. Had it not existed in the ancient books, then not so long destroyed but that their contents must have been remembered, it would on that account have been rejected. The constellation Cepheus, with the accompanying fable, had long and widely testified to the same future event as the traditional prophecies scattered among the heathen. The first time the title "king" is found in the Scripture records in connexion with the expectation of the seed of the woman, the branch, is in the prophetic blessing of Jacob, where to Asher he speaks of the "*sweet influences of the King.*" Then, in the prophecy of Balaam, *the shout* or *proclamation of the King* is said to be among Israel, and *the exaltation of his King* is predicted [1]. Again, in the blessing of Moses, "He," the Lord, "was," or shall be, "King in Jeshurun [2]," among his upright people.

In the days of the prophetess Hannah, when as yet there was no other king in Israel, the title of king seems familiarly known as belonging to the Anointed, the Messiah [3]. David repeatedly announces a higher King than himself [4]. Isaiah and Jeremiah foretel Him, *the King, the Branch*, predicted and borne by the mythic Sibyl. That Sibyl, she who *bears* or *carries*, was evidently a personification of the virgin of the zodiac, of the woman of the primeval prophecy there recorded.

[1] Num. xxiii. 21; xxiv. 7.
[2] Deut. xxxiii. 5.
[3] 1 Sam. ii. 10.
[4] Ps. ii., &c.

ON THE SIGN VIRGO.

In this sign the woman bearing the seed is every where recognized; even where the prophecy was forgotten the emblem remained.

Our Lord at His solemn manifestation to the Gentiles, when the inquiry of the Greeks who came saying, "We would see Jesus," was answered by the voice from heaven, spoke of Himself as the corn[1] (or seed) of wheat, which dying should arise, and "bring forth much fruit." So highly sanctioned is the interpretation which explains this emblem as representing the seed held by the woman of the first prophecy. Thus understood it does indeed "declare the glory of God," His great glory in redemption.

It is evident that Eve supposed her firstborn to be the promised seed; for she said, "I have gotten a man, the Lord[2]." It is not said how or when she was undeceived; but it seems to have been before she called the next son Abel, vanity. Neither Sarah nor Rebekah fell into the error of Eve: the hope of the wives of Israel was to be the ancestress, not the mother of the Messiah. Such was the honour regretted by the daughter of Jephthah, when the maidens of Israel went yearly to lament with her over its renunciation. The affliction, almost to despair, of Hezekiah in the prospect of dying childless was from the same cause: he feared lest he should not be the ancestor of the Messiah, perhaps even lest the promise of "the seed of David" should therefore utterly fail[3].

In all tradition, in all mythology, the woman of the zodiac was always a virgin, and almost always a virgin-mother. Bethulah, the maiden, is her name in Hebrew, Adarah, the pure virgin, in Arabic. Such was the Astrea of Greece and Rome, and such the mother of Krishna in India. Isis, the "thousand-named" goddess of Egypt, identified by Eratosthenes with Virgo, might seem to be an exception: but by some of those names she is daughter or sister of Osiris, though always the mother of Horus, 'He who cometh."

The figure of the woman in the zodiac did not represent the mother of mankind, neither did it prefigure Mary the daughter of Heli[4]. It is the virgin daughter of Zion,

---

[1] The Hebrew New Testament translating "corn" by the same word used as "seed" in Gen. iii. 13, this was probably the word our Lord here used, as no doubt the Greeks who came up to worship at the feast understood the language of the country.

[2] It seems now admitted that the particle *eth*, here rendered *from*, is no more to be so translated in this place than where it occurs twice previously in the same, and twice again in the next verse. The Targum of Jonathan renders the words of Eve, "I have gotten a man, the angel of the Lord."

[3] Josephus.

[4] Adam Clarke's Com., Bloomfield's Greek Test., Gill, &c. Mary is called the daughter of Heli in the Talmud. T. Hieros. Sanhedrim, fol. 25; Gill's Com.

H

the Church, which Paul would present "as a chaste virgin unto Christ[1]," re-appearing as the woman crowned with twelve stars in the Apocalypse. To that Church the Messiah was born, as the virgin of the sign bears the branch and the seed.

The woman holding an infant, below Virgo, in the Egyptian planisphere, is evidently that "first decan of Virgo" spoken of by Albumazer, corresponding with the prophecy of Isaiah, "Behold, a virgin shall conceive, and bear a son." Not till the end of the fourth century after the accomplishment of that prophecy was it ever imagined that the virgin-mother of the promised Messiah, *the* virgin[2] of prophecy, should be also the mother of any mere human offspring. That notion was then treated as a heresy, arising among Arians, and by the great body of the Church at once rejected. When the far greater error of the undue glorification of the blessed Mary was denounced by Protestants, that exploded notion was after ten centuries revived. But error should not be combated by error: the truth is strong, and shall prevail.

Great names in the Protestant Church have declared against that supposition. The apparent difficulties in the first chapter of Matthew are thus met: the Jews called the first offspring, whether of man or beast, *firstborn*, even if none followed, and it was holy to the Lord[3]. The Greek word of which *firstborn* is the translation is rejected from the text by many Bible critics[4]: that rendered *till* does not exclude the time beyond, as may be seen where it occurs in Matt. xxviii. 30, and where our Lord promises to be with His disciples *unto*, or *till*, the end of the world, and certainly His presence will not be then withdrawn. In the celebrated sermon "On the Lineal Descent of Jesus of Nazareth," Dr. South speaks of Joseph as the last male heir of the royal line of David. As such apparently the angel addressed him, "Thou son of David," an appellation after the death of Joseph given to our Lord Himself, by some perhaps as supposed the son of Joseph, and due to Him as the son of Mary; for by her father Heli Mary was the heiress[5] of the line of Rhesa, the younger son of Zorobabel, the line of the elder son Abiud having terminated in Joseph. All tradition agrees that Joseph was an aged man at the time of the angelic annunciation. According to the customs of the Jews, he must have been previously married; but he must have died childless, else his offspring, and not the son of Mary, would have been the rightful king of the Jews[6]. That title was given Him by friend and foe, by Pilate and Nathanael. If "brethren and sisters" are mentioned in connexion with Him, it is well known that then, as now[7], any near relations would be so called. Tradition has also said that the Virgin Mary had two sisters, of course younger than herself, and that James, "the brother of the Lord," was the son of one of them. If our Lord had been indeed dead, James might have been called the king of Israel: but the disciples knew their King was living, and those who believed it not put James to death, perhaps on account of that possibility.

Had James been, as some have suggested, a son of Joseph, he, and not the son of Mary, being indeed the rightful king of Israel, our Lord, who was "the Truth," could not have allowed that title to be given to Himself untruly. The Pharisees recognized His descent, when they expressed the fear lest if all believed on Him the Romans would take away their place and nation. It was the king, not the

---

[1] In the Douay Bible the woman in Rev. xii. is called the Church.
[2] Dr. Owen and Bp. Middleton point out the article as emphatic in Matt. i. 23.
[3] Exod. xiii. 2.   [4] Tischendorf, &c.
[5] It is supposed Mary went to Bethlehem, Luke ii. 5, because she was an heiress. (Bloomfield's Greek Test.)
[6] "The Jews themselves say he was nearly allied to the kingdom." (Gill, from Sanhedr. fol. 43.)   [7] Layard, &c.

teacher, whom the Romans would oppose. By Divine pre-ordination those very Romans proclaimed His title on the cross, a spectacle to men and angels. When He, the King of the Jews, and of the universe, crowned with His first but not His only crown, was lifted up, according to the typical prophecy [1], on the predicted hill of Zion, He said to His desolate and soul-pierced mother, "Woman, behold thy son;" and the beloved disciple took her to his own home. Is it not evident she had no other son? So said the voice of tradition, so the voice of nature when not made dumb by prejudice. Without such prejudice it might well be asked how any woman, above all any mother, could admit the possibility that the most highly honoured, the blessed among women, could have a thought, a feeling not devoted to Him whom she knew to be at once her son and her Saviour, that Holy One whose helpless infancy was nourished at her bosom and supported in her arms? Did He not need, would He not obtain, all that the most intense and exclusive maternal tenderness could give? What other might share it with Him? Will not every woman who looks to Him, whom not having seen she loves, believe that the blessed mother, who hourly saw Him in His infant dependence on her care, would find her love of Him an absorbing sentiment, devotion mingling with natural affection? So have spoken instinctive feelings in every age. When by the most Protestant of painters or poets has she been represented with another infant in her arms, another offspring at her knee? And Joseph, the venerable guardian of the highly favoured mother and the holy child, was it not the sufficing happiness of his old age to watch over that mysterious treasure, Incarnate God, committed to his charge, the long-announced and earnestly expected seed of the woman, who should bruise the serpent's head?

The often-discussed word *Almah*, in Isa. vii. 14, is doubtless derived from Alam, hidden, as were oriental maidens, especially among the Jews in ancient times. Jerome appeals to the Punic usage of it as meaning a pure virgin. Lee also says that those who have disputed it have done so for party purposes. He points out the definite article in Isa. vii. 14 as emphatic: *the* virgin of prophecy. Had it not been so understood from very early times, even from the days of Noah, how could the whole heathen world have had the tradition of the Divine Deliverer, the Virgin-born, or the Son of the Supreme by a human mother? The sign Virgo has thus from the most remote antiquity witnessed to the miraculous birth as well as to the mission of the seed of the woman who should come "to make an offering for sin [2]," and "to bring in everlasting righteousness."

NOTE.

South's Sermon on the Lineal Descent of Jesus of Nazareth.

"The royal line of David by Solomon being extinct in Jeconiah, the crown and kingdom passed into the immediately younger line of Nathan (another son of David) in Salathiel and Zorobabel, which Zorobabel having two sons, Abiud and Rhesa, the royal dignity descended of right upon the line of Abiud, of which Joseph was the last, who marrying the Virgin Mary, which sprung from the line of Rhesa, the younger son of Zorobabel, and withal having no issue himself, his right passes into the line of Mary, being the next of kin, and by that means upon Jesus her son, whereupon He was both naturally the Son of David, and legally the King of the Jews, which latter is accounted to us by St. Matthew, as the former is by St. Luke, who delivers

[1] Numb. xxi. 8.
[2] As figured in the accompanying constellation of the centaur piercing the victim, and the following sign Libra.

down the pedigree of Mary, the mother of Jesus and daughter of Heli, though Joseph her husband stands there named, according to the known way of the Jews computing their genealogies." (Vol. iii. 277.)

Dr. South thus shows that Joseph was the only surviving heir of the elder royal line of the house of David, through Abiud, the elder son of Zorobabel. He says, " From thence there arises *this* unanswerable argument, both against the opinion of those who affirm Joseph to have had children by a former wife, as also against that old heresy of Helvidius[1], who against the general and constant sense of the Church denied the perpetual virginity of Mary, affirming that Joseph had other children by her, after the birth of Jesus."

NOTE ON LUKE.

Gill says on Luke iii., " This is the genealogy of Mary, the daughter of Heli. The mother's family was not mentioned in the genealogies of the Jews."

Dr. Clarke is of the same opinion : " Jesus, son of Mary, reunited in Himself all the blood, privileges, and rights of the family of David, in consequence of which He is emphatically called ' the Son of David.' His lineal descent from David was not even by His enemies disputed." " The opinion of Julius Africanus preserved by Eusebius (Hist. Eccles.) was this : Jacob and Heli were brethren by the mother, so that Joseph and Mary were cousins ; but according to Jewish usage Joseph was reckoned the heir of Heli. Africanus said he received his account from the relatives of our Lord." " When a family ended with a daughter, the Jews inserted her husband in the genealogy." (Clarke's Com.)

Matthew speaks of literal sons, Luke of heirs.

NOTE ON VIRGIN-BORN.

A French Protestant writer says, " Among the Gauls 100 years B.C. an altar was found with the inscription " To the virgin who is to bring forth."

Univ. Hist.—" The Taurians had human sacrifices to a virgin," the Diana of Euripides, Iphig. in Taur.

" It was said in the sacred books of the Chinese that a virgin should bring forth a son to the *west* of China." If, as Dupuis infers, the dogma was invented from the constellation, why was such an interpretation put upon the figure of a woman *suckling* an infant, by all mythology said to be virgin-born ? how but by tradition of the prophecy ? He has well shown that the mythologies of the Gentiles corresponded with the names and figures of the stars and constellations, but not why they were so named and figured.

The Ven. Bede, " in libro temporibus," says that " Easter, to whom the Saxons sacrificed, was Astarte." The name of this Saxon goddess is sometimes written Eostre, the starry, the *bright*, as Astarte, from the Hebrew and Arabic root found in Zoharah, the evening star. At *Easter*, so named from the Saxon festival, the stars of Virgo are *bright* in the evening sky.

Hyde, de Rel. Pers., quotes from Abulfaragius, that Zaradusht (or Zoroaster) taught the Persians that in the latter times a virgin should bring forth a son, and that when he should be born a star should appear, and should shine and be conspicuous in the midst of the figure of the virgin. It is then said that he commanded his disciples, the Magi, when they should see the star, that they should go forth where it directed them, and offer gifts to him that should be born.

Krishna, an Indian incarnation of the Divinity, is said in a Sanscrit dictionary compiled two thousand years ago, consequently before the birth of Christ, to have been born of a woman. He is frequently figured as wrestling with a serpent while it bites him in the heel, also sometimes triumphant, with his foot crushing its head. He is also said to have slain in his boyhood the serpent Caliya. Thus is proved the wide diffusion of the prophecy, that a Divine person, conflicting with and conquering the serpent, should be born of a woman, without a human father.

---

[1] Helvidius was the disciple of Auxentius, an Arian bishop in the East, excommunicated A.D. 368.

ANCIENT ARABIAN AND PERSIAN TRADITIONS.

SHEIK Sadi, the author of the celebrated Gulistan, says, "God gave to Adam the robe of honorary purity, to Edris (Enoch) pre-eminence in teaching, a victorious soul to Noah ; he hung the toolsan of dignity from the head of Hûd[1]; he girded Abraham, the friend of God, with the sword-belt of attachment ; he wrote the diploma of sovereignty in the name of Ismael ; put the seal of royalty on the finger of Solomon, the shoe of intimacy on the foot of Moses, the turban of pre-eminence on the head of Jesus." Sadi lived more than a hundred years, dying in 1296. He spent thirty years in study, thirty in travel, thirty in devotion and retirement.

This great poet's constant aim seems to have been the inculcation of true wisdom ; for example, the following fable. "Young man, attach not thy heart to this world or its creatures, but to God, who is the supreme good. No son of Adam had a longer life than the sage Lokman. When the angel of death came to him, he found him weaving a basket in an osier-ground. He asked, ' O wise Lokman, why didst thou never build thyself a house ? ' ' Azrael,' replied the sage, ' he must be a fool who would do so while thou wert pursuing him.' "

The great Persian poet Ferdusi, who was born in the year 916, studied the works of the Guebres, or fire-worshippers, whose lawgiver Zerdusht, or Zoroaster[2], was by some supposed to be the prophet Daniel, or at least to have been one of his disciples. From Ferdusi's chief work, the Shah-nameh, or hero-book of Iran, a history in verse, collected from the ancient chronicles of Persia, this passage is given. "At this time," the reign of Gushtasp, or Darius Hystaspes, "sprang up in Iran a tree, of which the leaves were counsel, and the fruit was wisdom. An old man appeared on the earth, in his hand the staff of Aud (the same as Hûd), and blessed was his footstep. His name was Zerdusht, and his arm smote the ill-working Ariman. To the shah of the world he spake thus : ' I am a messenger of heaven, and will show thee the way of the Lord. In Paradise I have kindled my fire-offering, and the Creator said to me, Take this flame with thee : behold the heaven above and the world

---

[1] Hûd, said to be an antediluvian prophet, is supposed to be Enoch. The name means lignified, glorious, happy. His history, mingled with fables, may be found in the Koran. By other authorities he has been supposed to be Eber or Heber, Gen. xi. 15.

[2] Syro-Egyptian Society, Feb. 8, 1853. Dr. Camps on the Zend Avesta:—"According to the Dabistan, Zerdusht, or Zoroaster, appeared as a religious reformer in the reign of Gushtasp V., by most historians ancient and modern identified with Darius Hystaspes. This makes him cotemporary with Haggai and Zechariah, and a few years later than Ezekiel and Daniel."

It was said by the translator of the Zend Avesta, M. Anquetil Du Perron, that the Zend was the old language of Media, and that the books preserved in that very ancient language were the genuine works of Zerdusht, or Zoroaster, and written in the fifth or sixth century before Christ. So the learned Professor Rask.

Dr. Camps asserted his conviction that " Zerdusht, or Zoroaster, had earned for himself a fair and just title to the name and character of a reformer and philosopher." (Athenæum, No. 1322.)

Was not Zoroaster merely an epithet, Zerdusht the name ? Zoroaster would be the bright, glorious, or splendid stranger, and therefore might be applied to more than one eminent personage. Zoroaster is said to have taught the future incarnation of the Deity, a general resurrection, and the destruction of the world by fire.

beneath; I produced them without water and without earth. See man, whom I have made, and know that no one is like me, who am the preserver of all. Now that thou knowest all this to have come from me, honour me as the Creator of all. From him who speaketh with thee receive faith, and teach his ways and his laws, as the great Architect teaches thee. Choose wisdom, use all things earthly as trifling; and learn that faith is the true life, and without it majesty is worthless.' Gushtasp and Serir[1] listened to his words, also Zohrasp at Balk. The great and wise of all places came to the shah to seek conversion, the idol-worship was suppressed, and the worship of fire founded in its stead. The fire-temple at Bersin was erected, and worship and holy rites were there established. A holy cypress of Paradise he planted before the door of the fire-temple; and it was written on its high-sprouting branches how Gushtasp had declared for the true faith, and placed this tree in testimony that his soul was growing up in the right way."

In the sixth chapter of Ezra, Darius acknowledges "the true faith," ordering sacrifices to be offered to the God of heaven, and prayers to be made for the life of the king and of his sons. Confucius lived about the same time, and may have been one of "the great and wise who came to seek conversion" from the instructions of Zerdusht, whose words, as given by Ferdusi, retain a strong resemblance to the Hebrew prophets, especially to those prophecies of Isaiah relating to Cyrus, which it seems probable the prophet Daniel would expound to those princes, Cyrus and Darius, whose prime minister he was. (See Dan. vi. 28.) In the Zend Avesta, ascribed to Zoroaster, it is asserted that the ancient Persians divided the zodiac into twelve constellations with names corresponding to those now in use; they had also a division corresponding to the mansions of the moon.

NOTE ON ZOROASTER.

Hyde De Vet. Rel. Pers., quoting from Abulfaragius, says that Zoroaster the Persian, in the time of Daniel the prophet, predicted to the Magi, or Astrologers of Persia, the future appearance of a star which would notify the birth of a mysterious child, the Almighty Word which created the heavens, whom He commands them to adore. "It is elsewhere said that Zoroaster predicted that this star should appear in the figure of a virgin," *the* Virgin, for the Arabic in which Abulfaragius wrote has no indefinite article. It has been by some supposed that the Zend Avesta, the books of Zoroaster here referred to, have been interpolated since his time; yet as these interpolations are confessedly very ancient, should this mention of the place where the star was to appear be supposed to be one of them, it would nevertheless tend to show that in the figure of the Virgin it did appear, supposing the interpolation to be subsequent to the event.

The great Arabian astronomer, Albumazar, in describing the signs and their decans, speaks of Virgo as having two parts and three forms, but does not specify what they were. He only goes on to say that "in the first decan, as the Persians and Egyptians, the two Hermes, and Ascalius and the first ages teach, a young maiden arose, whose Arabic name is Adrenedefa, a pure and immaculate virgin, holding in her hand two ears of corn, and seated on a throne, nevertheless nourishing an infant, who has a name in Hebrew, Thesus, signifying to save, which we in Greek call Christ, who rises with that Virgin and sits upon the same throne. If the seed, the ear of corn, was the original emblem of the sign, the woman and the infant may well have been the first decan. Their figures are now to be seen in the Egyptian planisphere, under that of the woman carrying the ear of corn, as Virgo. Koma, in Hebrew, corn in the ear, might be the original name in Coma, and marking the head of the Infant, the Desired. The very ancient name Awa, the Desired, seems to refer to it as the Desired, but several of the others, as the ear of corn, the seed, the desired seed of the woman.

Gaffarelli says, "of all the pictures of the signs on the Arabian sphere that of the Virgin is the most wonderful." The Arabs call Virgo and the infant the mother of Christ and her son.

Dupuis says, "In the Bibliothèque Nationale there is an Arabian MS. which contains the Twelve Signs, with an infant by the side of Virgo."

In a criticism on the Dabistan, it is observed, "the ancient Persian religion," probably referring to the early Sabian, "was founded on transcendental notions of the Deity, rather acknowledging the influence of, than worshipping the stars," "then the seven planets as mediators." To this ancient creed Zoroaster added the belief in an evil principle, and in the promise of an incarnation of the Deity, he also foretold the destruction of the world by fire, and a general

---

[1] Serir, Cyrus.

resurrection. These doctrines the second Zoroaster would hear from the prophet Daniel, while the first of the name, said to be cotemporary with Nimrod, would know them by immediate tradition from Noah, Dan. vii. and xii.

From what genuine remains we have of Zoroaster in the Greek are taken these, the very words of Zoroaster himself: "God is the first of all things, incorruptible, eternal, unmade, without parts, unlike any other being, perfect, wise." Univ. Hist.

Anquetil du Perron gives these words also as of Zoroaster: "Man shall one day be delivered from death; the resurrection of the body must be preceded by the conversion of the whole world to the faith of Zoroaster."

When Zoroaster is interpreted as saying, "God has the head of a hawk," he probably alluded to the eagle face of the cherubic images, and perhaps to the perversion of them which gave rise to the Oriental idol Nisroch, whose figure of a man with an eagle's head so often occurs in the Assyrian sculptures.

"The Magi among the ancient Persians held a good and an evil principle: the good they called Yezdan, or Ormusd, the Creator, the Eternal; the evil they called Ahriman." (Univ. Hist.) If these names are explained, according to the principles of Rawlinson, &c.; from Oriental roots, Yez-dan is Yez, or Yeza, who causes to come forth, as in Gen. i. 12; Dan, the Lord, as in Ps. cx. 11. Ormusd, Or, light, as in Ps. civ. 2, &c.; and Masda, the shedder of blessings, as a form of Shaddai, the name by which God revealed Himself to Jacob, Gen. xxxv. 11, otherwise rendered Almighty. Ormusd was therefore the pourer-forth of light. Abriman, from Abram, to be subtile, the epithet of the serpent that tempted Eve, the evil one in Gen. iii. 1. The names would accompany the tradition from Noah downwards, as would also the annexation of the truths of religion to the starry emblems, too soon perverted in Sabian worship, as afterwards to idolatry.

Trench, in the Hulsean Lectures, speaks of the ancient Persian religion as the noblest and least corrupted of those of the ancient world.

The ancient Arabs very early corrupted their ancestral astronomy into Sabaism, the worship of the host of heaven. The Hamayarites chiefly worshipped the Sun; the tribe Misam, Al Debaran, Tai, Soheil, or Canopus: it was said to bring happiness to all on whom it shone, probably from its name, the Desired. Mahomet's grandfather is said to have tried to persuade the Korish to leave their images and worship the star Sirius, adored by the tribe Kais. Some tribes worshipped Al Moshtari, the planet Jupiter; others, as Asad, worshipped Otared, or Mercury. The Arabs had seven celebrated temples dedicated to the seven planets. One in the chief city of Yemen to Al Zoharah, the planet Venus; the temple of Mecca, where Mahomet destroyed 365 idols in one day, was said to be dedicated to Saturn. These idols may have been one for each day in the year, from stars rising on those days. They however continued to acknowledge One Supreme God, Allah Taàla, God Most High. They professed to worship in the stars, not the orbs, but angelic intelligences governing them, mediating between God and man. They attributed their religion to Noah, from whom, no doubt, they had the astronomical foundation of it. (Univ. Hist.)

THE STAR OF BETHLEHEM.

ABOUT 125 B.C. a star so bright as to be visible in the daytime suddenly appeared; and this, it is said, induced Hipparchus to draw up his catalogue of stars, the earliest on record, which is supposed to be transmitted to us by Ptolemy.

Other stars have in like manner appeared and disappeared. Was that mentioned as being in Coma, the head of the infant accompanying Virgo, in the time of Ptolemy, and afterwards gradually disappearing, indeed the star which led the Magi to Bethlehem? Its peculiarity would be, that 1400 years before[1], its place over the very centre of the future possessions of the descendants of Jacob had been predicted. The prediction of Balaam was double, and doubly fulfilled: that Messiah, the bright and morning Star, should come out of Jacob, from Jacob's posterity; and also that a literal star should come forth at or over the land of Jacob's inheritance, to announce as arrived the time of that greater coming, the first appearance of the Desire of all nations.

It is said in the Zend Avesta, that Zoroaster, who taught astronomy to the Persian Magi, had told them, when they should see a star appear in the figure of the virgin, they should go and worship the Great One, whose birth it announced. That they did so we know from the inspired Word. If Zoroaster were, as is supposed, the disciple of Daniel, he would be acquainted with Daniel's prophecy of the seventy weeks of years, which it appears fixed the time of the Messiah's ministry: he would know that at thirty years of age that ministry must be entered on. If he were acquainted with the traditions of antediluvian astronomy, he might know if the now invisible star in Coma was one of those which have appeared and disappeared from time to time, and he might have a record of its period. It has now been invisible some 1700 years: did it shine on Abraham when the Lord bade him look toward heaven, and said, "So shall thy seed be?" Had it shone on Seth and Enoch, when "the family" of Seth, dividing and naming the stars, had called this constellation "the head of the Desired," the promised seed of the woman? An awful question arises: if so, will it shine again? Will it be connected with the sign of the Son of Man, announcing His second coming? We must not inquire *when*: the times and the seasons are not for us to know.

The bright star which appeared between Cepheus and Cassiopeia in the years 945, 1264, and 1572, the last time being observed by Tycho, the great Danish astronomer, is considered to have probably been the same star at its periodical return of about three hundred years. That which appeared in 1604, in the constellation Ophiuchus, was observed by Kepler. He even conjectured that it might have been the star of Bethlehem; but it was not vertical over Jerusalem and Bethlehem, which the star in Coma was. The star of Kepler was near the ecliptic, being just over the planets Jupiter and Saturn, then in conjunction. The star of prophecy was to appear out of, over, or *with*[2] Jacob. The Magi knew it, and came to the metropolis of the inheritance

---

[1] Num. xxiv. See Hyde de Vet. Rel. Pers., Bp. Horsley on the Prophecies of the Messiah, Gill's Commentary, Smyth's Celestial Cycle, Trench on the Star of the Wise Men, &c.
[2] The preposition or prepository letter (ב) is rendered "at" in Gen. iii. 24; "at" or over the east of Eden.

of Israel to seek " the King of the Jews." Once in every twenty-four hours it was vertical over that spot; and the Magi knew at that hour it might appear to go before them, and "stand" over the place where the young child was. In the midnight of the winter solstice, at the time of the birth of Christ, the sign Virgo arose[1]. As the season advanced, it would be on the meridian at that time, and the star in Coma would be vertical, apparently *standing* over the predicted spot long enough to mark it during their visit of homage. As the fugitives from trans-atlantic bondage follow the north star without map or guide, and reach the shore of freedom, so the Magi might follow the predicted star by observing its position at midnight: when it became vertical[2], stood as it were over Jerusalem, they stopped. The slight difference in position between Jerusalem and Bethlehem[3] they are said by an Oriental tradition to have recognized by beholding the reflection of the star in a well[4]. By the reflection of the sun in the well of Syene it is known the line of the tropic was determined, and by its declension the lapse of years since the well was dug. Was this the well of which David retained such a loving remembrance, of which he longed to drink? The Scripture, however, says nothing for or against this possibility.

From the very ancient book of Job it is seen that the light of early revelation still shone clearly in the land of Idumea; for not only the great patriarch and prophet[5] himself, but his three friends partook of it. In the neighbouring lands of Moab and Midian that primeval light was not yet wholly obscured, though idolatry had perverted the daughters of Moab. Balaam evidently knew and believed the immortality of the soul, and the blessedness of the righteous after the death of the body. The light so vivid in the time of Job still shone on him; and however unworthy the recipient, through the prophecy he was employed to utter its rays descended on the long current of ages, even to the time of the Magi, and brought to the feet of the infant Saviour those firstfruits of the Gentile world. Balaam needed not to announce His coming; all antiquity was looking for " the Desire of nations," the promised seed of the woman, the conqueror of the serpent, as foreshown by the constellations and the prophecy they figured: but he announced that the time and place of His manifestation should be declared by the arising of another star at the time of His birth, and over the locality of His future kingdom. Seth is said to have previously given forth the same prediction. Whether a new creation or the return of a periodical star, its time, as now that of comets, being calculated by those wonderful first astronomers, only Divine Wisdom could foretell as was foretold that at its appearance He should be born, the expected Messiah, " the King of the Jews."

---

[1] " It is a fact independent of all hypotheses, that at the precise hour of midnight on the 25th of December, in the ages when Christianity appeared, the celestial sign which mounted on the horizon was the virgin of the constellations." (Dupius, Orig. des Cultes.)

[2] The Magi, forewarned that the star must appear "over Jacob," over his inheritance, would see that the star in Coma passed over the centre of that inheritance: but as it would also appear to pass as vertically over every part of it that was nearly in the latitude of Jerusalem, they could not at once fix on the spot of the Messiah's birth, therefore they went to inquire; the latitude, as it were, being given by the star, the longitude by the prophecy.

[3] " Bethlehem indeed became that which its name had promised from the first, 'the house of bread,' even 'the living bread which came down from heaven;' and 'Ephratah' was truly the fruit-bearing field." " We have too many of these significant names to have the right to suppose them merely accidental." (R. C Trench, Star of the Wise Men.) Trench speaks of this star as shining in " calm and silent splendour, a star, as we may well believe, larger, lovelier and brighter than any of the host of heaven." He adds, " We have many allusions," in ancient Christian writers, "to the surpassing brightness of this star;" and he quotes from Ignatius, " At the appearance of the Lord a star shone forth brighter than all the other stars." Ignatius may have so heard from those who had seen it. From Prudentius it is also quoted, that not even the star of morning was so fair. Trench adds, " This star, I conceive, as so many ancients and moderns have done, to have been a new star in the heavens."

[4] They came to a well associated with a beautiful tradition. It is that the Magi, who had lost the guidance of the star, sat down beside this well to refresh themselves, when one of them saw the reflection of the star in the clear water of the well. He cried aloud to his companions, and "when they saw the star they rejoiced with exceeding joy." (Scotch Mission.)

[5] Lee's Job.

The star that shone over Bethlehem in splendid reality had illuminated in prediction and in tradition the whole ancient world. A star is the symbol of divinity in the newly discovered Assyrian remains, as it has long been known to be in the mythology of Egypt[1], Greece, and Rome.

Prophecy is the greatest of all miracles, an immortal, an everlasting miracle, a sign for all ages and all nations, given with the first revelation to the first of men, and with continually brightening and increasing evidence formed to close around the last.

NOTES.

Gill, on Balaam :—A star shall דרך walk its course from Jacob, or above or over the land of Israel.

"Magi was a Persian word, but the Hebrew root Gehe, high, of dignity, explains it. 'Wise concerning God,' is said of them by Porphyry : by Xenophon they were said to be appointed by Cyrus to sing hymns, and sacrifice at the dawn of day. Zerdusht, or Zoroaster, the author of the sect of the Magi, or wise men, and who appears to be a Jew by birth, and to be acquainted with the Old Testament, spoke of the birth of Christ to his followers, and told them when He should be born a star should appear and be seen in the day, and ordered them to go where that directed, and offer gifts and worship Him." Also "the prophecy of Balaam was known to them." Gill refers to Abulfaragius. Hyde quotes the same from Abulfaragius.

"It is said" (see Wolf. Bib. Heb. p. 1156) "that Seth the son of Adam gave out a prophecy that a star should appear at the birth of the Messiah." "Some have thought that Virgil, (Ecl. ix. 47) speaks of this star, as 'Cæsaris astrum.' There is a star so called often on antique gems, &c., of Julius Cæsar. That which Pliny mentions (Nat. Hist. lib. ii. c. 25) he calls a comet, and describes as dazzlingly bright, with a silver beard." "The Jews still expect a star to herald Messiah." "The Jews in an ancient book of theirs (Zohar) say more than once that 'when Messiah shall be revealed, a bright and shining star shall arise in the East.'" (Gill's Commentary.) "The Jews still expect a star to be seen at the coming of the Messiah." (Alford.)

Suetonius and Tacitus both mention an old and constant opinion prevailing in the East, that at this time Judea should prevail. Tacitus adds, that it was contained in ancient and sacred books. (Alford.)

Bloomfield's Greek Test. on Mat. ii. :—"We cannot doubt that the Magi were acquainted with the Hebrew prophecies." Benson, on the Chronology of the Life of Christ, would place the visit of the Magi about February 13, J.P. 4710.

Trench thinks their journey took about three months. Their doctrines are said to have been derived from Abraham, to have become corrupted, and to have been again purified by Zoroaster, who derived his evident knowledge of the Hebrew Scriptures from Daniel.

Ancient writers call the star "exceedingly brilliant."

Alford thinks "The narration does not imply any thing miraculous in the appearance of the star, but something in the course of nature." (If so, the miracle is in its being predicted.) He says, "A remarkable conjunction of the planets of our system took place a short time before the birth of our Lord, in the year of Rome 747." He then enumerates three conjunctions of Jupiter and Saturn in that year: "at the two latter, in October and November, the two planets were seen so close as to appear but as one star." But there was no prediction of these conjunctions; and such have taken place before and after, as, for instance, the far more remarkable one from whence the Chinese annals were reckoned[2]. Such conjunctions have been much spoken of by astrologers, but no great events seem to have been marked by them; and unless prophesied of, as was the star of Bethlehem, they could not have signified the birth of the King of the Jews. One such in 1463 was by Abarbanel the Jew supposed to announce the coming birth of the Messiah. Kepler, however, says that while the conjunction of Jupiter and Saturn took place in the year of Rome 747, yet in 748 another one happened of Jupiter, Saturn, and Mars, so weakening the argument; for if one announced the birth of Christ, the other did not.

"That the Jews understood this prophecy of Balaam to refer to the Christ they gave fearful witness. The false Christ who under Adrian took up arms for the last terrible struggle with Rome gave himself out as the Messiah whom Balaam had foretold, and assumed the name of Barchocab, or the son of the star." (R. C. Trench.)

---

[1] "Among the Egyptians a star was said to be the symbol of the Divine Being." (Adam Clarke.)

[2] A conjunction of Saturn, Jupiter, Mars, and Venus with also the moon took place 2012, and was observed and recorded in China. (Martini, Hist. Sini.)

THE SOUTHERN FISH,

IN AQUARIUS.

In the Greek word ΙΧΘΥΣ, Ichthus, has been found an anagram of "Jesus Christ, Son of God, Saviour." It is well to see Christ wherever we can; but it is best to see Him where Scripture points Him out. No where in Scripture is he typified by a fish; but He Himself applies the symbol to those who should believe, being, as it were, caught by the Gospel net: so, when in calling Peter and John He says, " I will make you fishers of men," and again, in Matt. xiii. 47, the net of the Gospel encloses good and bad fishes, in neither place can the figure possibly apply to Himself, but well typifies His Church.

In the Old Testament must primarily be sought the intention of the emblems of the constellations. There we find that to Adam was given dominion over the fishes of the sea, as to the second Adam over the inhabitants of the earth. In Ezek. xlvii. 9, 10, the type is unquestioned; the fish are the converts to the Gospel. Habakkuk also speaks of " men as the fishes of the sea."

Ichthus may well be derived from *Chayith*, the name used for marine creatures in Ps. civ. 25. In the Southern Fish, in the name Fom al Haut, there is the same root, as also in the Arabic name Al Haut, or Hut, the fishes of Pisces. These are in Hebrew called Dagim, from *multitudes of offspring*, a meaning equally applicable to the symbol and to the Church as described in Isa. lx. and in Rev. vii. 9, &c., which it symbolizes.

The fish, then, " bringing forth abundantly " typifies the visible Church; the woman, the invisible, the true, the spiritual Church. The fishes " pass through the paths of the sea," as the Church through the water of baptism. The Church drinks in the influences of the Holy Spirit, as the fish of Aquarius the water poured into its mouth. The literal fish does not drink: this figure is therefore wholly typical, but surely of the recipients, not of the Giver of the water of life.

In the days of persecution the early Christians frequently made themselves known to each other by the fish engraven on their rings, signifying that they were baptized believers. It was also sometimes sculptured on their tombs, as is to be seen in the catacombs. So the beautiful token of their faith, the passion-flower, was worn by them for the same purpose, as representing the "instruments of cruelty," the crown of thorns, the nails, the cross itself: but they neither worshipped the flower nor the fish, nor with any " likenesses " of them hazarded the infringement of the second commandment. With them the fish was a symbol, but never was perverted to an idol, though in the fish-god Dagon the progressive corruption of the emblems of the constellations, first to Sabaism, and then to idolatry, has long been recognized. Dagon is now believed by Layard to have been one of the great gods of Assyria. It appears to have been a combination of the human form in Aquarius with the fish beneath [1].

---

[1] Kwanghi, the goddess of mercy, is in China represented as riding on a fish. (Bingham's China.) She is called the Queen of Heaven, and has an infant in her arms. (Fortune's China.)

In the Mexican zodiac, a figure crowned with the sun, between a fish and a quadruped, is said to represent the first winter solstice; probably the southern fish in Aquarius and the kid in Capricornus.

THE HEBREW ALPHABET,

AS CONNECTED WITH THE CONSTELLATIONS.

"A few ideas differently combined form all the objects of sense, as the letters of the alphabet form words."—*Berkeley, Principles of Human Knowledge.*

"Names are pictures of things, each letter having some resemblance to the thing named."—*Plato in Cratylus.*

The words given as names to the Hebrew alphabet may furnish examples, each letter contributing an idea, and the name thus defining the object.

Constellations.		NOUN, Name of the figure of the Letter.	VERB, Of the action expressed.	Reference to texts where the root is so used.
Taurus,	א	Aleph, Bull, Ps. 8. 7 . .	To Lead . .	Gen. 35. 15.
Gemini,	ב	Beth, House, Gen. 7. 1 .	„ Contain . .	Gen. 2. 1.
Cancer,	ג	Gimel, Camel, Gen. 24. 11	„ Recompense . .	Isa. 35. 4.
Leo,	ד	Daleth, Door, Gen. 19. 6 .	„ Lift . .	Amos 6. 3.
Virgo,	ה	He, Being, Gen. 1. 28	„ Be . . .	Ex. 3. 14.
Libra,	ו	Vau, Hook, Ex. 27. 10	„ Join . .	Ex. 27. 10.
Scorpio,	ז	Zain, Armour, 1 Kgs. 22. 38 .	„ Encompass . .	1 Kgs. 22. 38.
Sagittarius,	ח	Cheth, Animal, Gen. 1. 30	„ Live . .	Gen. 3. 20.
Capricornus,	ט	Teth, Slain Victim, Isa. 53. 7	„ Sink down .	Ps. 9. 16.
Aquarius,	י	Yod, Hand put forth, Ex 7. 19	„ Send out (Arab.) .	Obad. 11.
Pisces,	כ	Caph, Hand grasping, Ex. 4. 4	„ Hold . .	Ex. 33. 23.
Aries,	ל	Lamed, Ox-goad, Judg. 3. 31 .	„ Teach . .	Deut 4. 5.
Eridanus, the river,	מ	Mem, Water, Gen. 7. 17	„ Expand (Arab.), multiply . .	Ezek. 7. 11.
Southern Fish,	נ	Nun, Fish (Syriac) .	„ Lengthen out . .	Ps. 72. 7.
Band of Pisces,	ס	Samech, Band holding up, Ps. 71. 6.	„ Sustain . .	Isa. 63. 5.
Pleiades,	ע	Ayin, Eyes, Isa. 6. 5 . .	„ Be acted on .	Ps. 66. 7.
Hyades, mouth of Taurus,	פ	Pe, Mouth, Deut. 32. 1 .	„ Open . .	Lam. 3. 38.
Orion,	צ	Zaddi, Coming onwards, Ps. 68. 7	„ Advance . .	Hab. 3. 12.
Belt of Orion,	ק	Koph, Band girding, Isa. 3. 24	„ Bind . .	Isa. 3. 24.
Sirius,	ר	Resh, Head, Ps. 110. 7 . .	„ Originate, be first .	Ps. 118. 23.
Procyon,	ש	Shin, Tooth, Gen. 49. 12	„ Repeat, be second .	1 Kgs. 18. 34.
Southern Cross,	ת	Thau, Boundary, Gen. 49. 26 .	„ Bound, finish, limit .	Ps. 78. 41.

There seems no natural reason for the order in which the letters of the alphabet are placed. The order still generally prevalent appears to be derived from the Hebrew. If this order were taken from the previously existing arrangement of the prophetic types in the constellations, a reason is presented. The names of the Hebrew letters, it will be seen, agree in signification with those of the constellations, of which names or descriptive epithets they are the initials [1]. Most of the Oriental alphabets are similarly arranged; that the ancient Arabic was so may be seen from the numeral powers of the letters. The invention of letters is attributed to the family of Seth by ancient Jewish and Arabic writers[2], as well as of the emblems of the sphere.

It is well known that the ancient Jews distinguished the Twelve Signs by the twelve first letters of their alphabet. They are said to have applied the remaining letters to other constellations, probably to those which, as is shown above, agreed with them in meanings and initials. The ancient Persians also marked the Twelve Signs with the twelve first letters: as the modern Persians are said to do[2]. The sixteen Runic characters are said to be named after constellations, and dedicated to divinities.

NOTE ON RUNIC.

The Runic character or Runes have sufficient resemblance to the Samaritan and other ancient Oriental alphabets to indicate that they were derived from a common original. Great antiquity is attributed to them. Mallet shows that they were used by northern poets long before the Christian Era. By these ancient authorities they were said to have been invented by Odin. Odin was a title of dignity, as Don in modern times; it was applied to the Supreme Deity from the earliest ages. It was assumed by Sigge, hero, conqueror, and bard; about 70 B.C. he introduced and used the Runes, and to him the invention is sometimes ascribed; but Olaus Rudbeck believed them to have been communicated by Magog, son of Japheth, to Tuisco, the German chief, about A.M. 1800. Mallet thinks the name Runes derived from an ancient Gothic word, to cut; but from their admitted antiquity and their use as the vehicle of poetry, it is more probably from ranah or runah, Heb. and Arab., to sing, as in Job xxxviii. 7.

---

[1] "The constellations were formerly denoted by the Hebrew letters, beyond twenty-two to forty-four with two combined, after that, with three; and the letters were instead of animals." (Gaffarelli.)

[2] References to these authorities may be found in Dr. Gill's Commentary on the Scriptures. These meanings of the names of the letters generally agree with those in Gaffarelli, Curios. Lit., who refers to Reuchlin and Bellarmine, also to Rab. Kapol, mentioned by Southey as having written on the "Astral Alphabet," and said by Gaffarelli to have been the greatest Jewish astronomer.

ON THE ANTIQUITY OF THE SQUARE CHARACTER
OF THE HEBREW.

IT is acknowledged that the Jews brought this beautiful character back with them from the Babylonish captivity, previous to which they seemed, during the reigns of the Kings of Judah, to have used, on their coins at least, a character more nearly resembling the Samaritan. In the remains of the Babylonish empire, in which science and art were cultivated from the earliest period of its settlement, a very different character is now found and read, without any record of its origin other than the universal tradition that Seth was the inventor of alphabetic characters. From Seth, through Noah and Abraham, it seems very easy to trace their existence with the Hebrews, and among all the other children of Noah. In their migrations some tribes perverted, and many finally lost, this most precious invention. The Hebrews even are said greatly to have deteriorated it; whether before or after the time of Moses there appears no decisive evidence. If the original character were used by Moses, if it were traced on the tables of the law, still it is possible that in the sacred books alone it remained in perfection; their ordinary character had perhaps the same resemblance to it that the writing of the illiterate in this country may have to our printing type.

Every where the first character preserves some attempt to represent the horned head of the Bull, the Leader, the Aleph (the trace of whose name still remains to us in the name of the chief of beasts, the elephant), though in the Samaritan and Western alphabets it is inverted. The y of the Hebrew, the O of many other languages, is still to be traced in the name of the eyes, and in the picture which the letter presents of the organ of sight, the Hebrew representing both eyes, most other alphabets only one, either full as O in the Jewish coins, or in profile, as in the Samaritan. The Syriac and modern Arabic, being confessedly more recent inventions or adaptations, like our short-hand, cannot be appealed to as any authority, though their Aleph may represent one horn, their O or Ayin, one eye, as does our European O. In the square characters each is an abbreviated picture of the object from which it takes its name. The Rabbins have preserved the tradition that such was their intention. In the lapse of centuries, and the corruption of Hebrew learning into Talmudical fables, it is possible some slight change has taken place; they have, however, preserved the key that will unlock all; they refer to an Astral Alphabet, perverted indeed to the service of astrology, but pointing to the true origin of the Ancient Alphabet. In some cases, as in the Irish, the wandering tribe had apparently lost all but the tradition that the sounds of the human voice had once been designated by certain marks, and had, therefore, to re-invent them for themselves, and a weak invention we find they lighted on. In Irish it is said to be initial letters of the names of the trees of the country. The Ogham and the Runic, &c.,

are imperfect substitutes for the original arrangement of the leading ideas of the human mind under the forms of visible objects embodying them, which we find in the ancient or Hebrew character. That those visible objects had previously been selected to express ideas of the same nature in the twelve signs of the Zodiac and ten other constellations closely connected with them, will be seen in the preceding table [1].

The more nearly any alphabetic character approaches to the *picture* of the original objects from which the letters are named, the more ancient it should seem to be. If Seth be, as tradition has called him, the father of letters, and the author of the square character, whether preserved by the Hebrews or the Chaldeans, its portraits of the things it names are easily to be accounted for. Adam had been divinely incited to name visible objects by names conveying the ideas those objects were fitted to convey, as may be seen by the ancient Hebrew names preserved in the early books of Scripture.

If the Sinaitic inscriptions be coeval with the Exodus, they show that some letters resembling those of the square character were then used perhaps by that " mixed multitude " who went up with Israel out of Egypt. Since the Babylonish arrow-headed or cuneiform character has been read, all idea of the Jews having learnt the square character in Babylon may be given up.

NOTE ON BABYLONIAN.

Sir H. Rawlinson now says that even that character has been originally pictorial; this is not more difficult to imagine than that our modern English character was such, which nevertheless may be shown to be the case. While the Hebrew letter Aleph, א was always held to represent the head of a Bull, in most languages the likeness is traceable; the European A is the head and horns inverted. One of the Egyptian hieroglyphics read as A is the head of Apis, the Bull, with the globe between the horns.

---

[1] The Beth of early alphabets seems to represent a booth; in later ones, as our own, a two-storied house, B; or it might be, a double-roofed one only.

MEANINGS OF THE HEBREW ALPHABET,

FROM ANCIENT JEWISH AUTHORITIES.   (GAFFARELLI, Cur. Lit.)

					Texts where so used.
א	Aleph,	Significat viam, sive institutionem .	A way, or a beginning [1].		Job 33. 33.
ב	Beth,	Denotat domum	A house . . .		Job 1. 13.
ג	Gimel,	Retributionem	Retribution . .		Gen. 50. 15.
ד	Daleth,	Ostium	A door . . .		Gen. 19. 6.
ה	He,	Demonstrationem	Demonstration . .		Gen. 47. 23.
ו	Vau,	Uncinum retortum	A nail bent back .		Ex. 26. 32.
ז	Zain,	Arma	Armour . . .		1 Kg. 22. 38.
ח	Heth or Cheth	} Terrorem	Terror . . .		Gen. 35. 5.
ט	Teth,	Declinationem	Declination . .		Ex. 15. 4.
י	Jod,	Confessionem laudis . . .	Confession of praise .		Gen. 29. 35.
כ	Caph,	Volam	Hollow hand . .		Gen. 40. 11.
ל	Lamed,	Doctrinam	Doctrine . . .		Deut. 4. 1.
מ	Mem,	Aquas	Water . . .		Gen. 1. 6.
נ	Nun,	Filiationem	Filiation . . .		Gen. 21. 23.
ס	Samech,	Oppositionem	Opposition . . .		Ezek. 24. 2.
ע	Ayin,	Oculum	An eye . . .		Num. 14. 14.
פ	Pe,	Os	A mouth . . .		Ex. 4. 10.
צ	Tzaddi,	Latera	Sides . . .		Gen. 6. 16.
ק	Koph,	Circuitum	A circuit . .		Ps. 19. 6.
ר	Resh,	Paupertatem	Poverty . . .		Prov. 10. 15.
ש	Shin,	Dentem	A tooth . . .		Ex. 21. 24.
ת	Thau,	Signum	A sign . . .		Ezek. 9. 4.

Somewhat of a symbolical and even a sacred character seems given to the alphabet by the use made of the allusion to Alpha and Omega in the Apocalypse. Alpha is plainly the Aleph of the original alphabet, as in the ancient Oriental alphabets, *the leader, chief, first,* the beginning. The Omega of the Greeks supplied the place of Thau, the last letter of the ancient series, originally figured as a cross, like our modern T, t. The word Thau means in those dialects *a mark,* as in Ezek. ix. 4; a boundary, as in Gen. xlix. 26. By dropping the prefix Th, it gives the sound of Omega. The Arabic sense of the word Thau is a mark in the form of a cross, with which the Arabs marked their animals.

The first and last letters being thus used symbolically in Scripture, it seems probable that every intermediate letter had some similar purport, agreeing with that of the constellation to which they belong.

Faber says that some of the ancient Rabbins thought the present Hebrew character was the

---

[1] Aleph is translated "teach," as *leading* in the *way.*

original, called Assurith, "blessed," because God wrote it in the tables of the law. The Jews could not have adopted it from the Chaldeans; for at Babylon, as in Assyria, the arrow-headed character appears to have been exclusively used. Some Arabic writers attribute the invention of the Hebrew character to Seth, as well as many of the ancient Jews.

Plato (in Cratylus) seems to recognize the fact that each letter conveys an idea, as that L is the opposite of hardness, R a rushing on, motion, and that i attenuates, also saying that " a name as well as a painting is an imitation."

In the Hebrew the mother-vowels and other serviles give the ideas in most frequent requisition. The absence of the distinction between servile and radical confuses Plato's argument as to the Greek. In Arabic the distinction is recognized, though apparently seldom mentioned in grammars. It is traceable, with few variations, in all languages, as in English [1] the vowels and the letters L, M, N, S, T, Y are serviles. The ideas conveyed by the Hebrew serviles, when used as serviles, may be thus expressed. Aleph *originates*, Beth *incloses*, He *is*, Vau *connects*, Yod *individualizes*, Caph *grasps*, Lamed *transfers, passes on*; Mem *adds, increases*; Nun *diminishes*; Shin points out what *follows*; Thau *bounds, confines*.

It is said by Alfred Jones on proper names : "The Jews considered Enoch as the inventor of letters, and that Noah had in the ark a book of 'visions and prophecies' of Enoch."

Names are not mere arbitrary combinations of letters. In the original language they expressed the nature of their subject, an idea by each letter. The names recorded in the earliest chapters of Genesis prove that the first given names were intended to describe that to which they were given. Cadmus is said to have brought sixteen letters from Phœnicia, probably Hebrew consonants, omitting the Shin, *sh*, a sound unknown to Greece. To Cadmus, whose name means the man of the East, it is confessed Europe owes the alphabet. In the ancient Cufic, as in the modern Arabic, and in the Greek and Roman characters, some resemblance may be traced to the Hebrew and Samaritan.

Silvestre de Sacy places the existence of the Arabic alphabet now in use two hundred years earlier than the usual date, about 325 of the Hegira. "The passage from the Cufic to the Neshki seems not to have been sudden, and before the Cufic was a character resembling both." Forster infers that the Neshki or modern Arabic character, like the Hamayarite, belonged to a prior and primitive alphabet, and that selection, not invention, was the office of alphabet-makers of after-times.—Forster's One Primitive Language. The Hamayarites are said to have had an alphabetic character as early as the time of Job. (Univ. Hist.)

Bonomi says that Rawlinson is of opinion that " all the signs of Assyrian inscriptions had once a syllabic value, as the names of the objects they represented, but to have been subsequently used, usually in the initial articulation, to express a mere portion of a syllable; also, that the Babylonian and Assyrian languages are decidedly Semitic." (Bonomi's Nineveh.)

Col. Mure considers the Greek alphabet[2] of Phœnician Semitic origin, as proved by the analogy of the four first letters with Aleph, Beth, Gimel, Daleth. (Ancient Greek Language and Literature.)

---

[1] Athenæum, August, 1856.—Mr. Nasmyth, speaking of a connexion between the Assyrian and English alphabets, Dr. Hincks said it was established that A was the head of a bull and T a cross; Rawlinson said the cuneiform character was a series of pictures. B was a house, and in the Hamite character represented by a square. Barsip, also Hamite, probably " weedy lake." May it not rather be Bars sippa, the tower of the lip, the confusion of the lip, there taking place. *Meat*, what is *eaten*, is an instance of *m* being servile in English.

[2] Forster's One Prim. Lang. says, " The Celtiberian alphabet resembles the Semitic." The alphabet of man, like his language and his religion, was originally one.

THE SOUTHERN CROSS.

THIS remarkable constellation is said to suggest to every one the idea of a cross, particularly when in attaining the meridian its upper and lower star are perpendicularly, on it.   Though now no longer visible in the north temperate zone, it was seen there from the time of Adam and Seth to that of the Christian era.   It seems impossible that a constellation of such brilliancy and distinctness should have been omitted in the early arrangement of the emblems, though gradually declining in altitude from a considerable elevation, till the topmost star disappeared under the horizon of the latitude of Jerusalem, about the time of the awful sacrifice it prefigured.   This fact, and this alone, reasonably accounts for the ancient tradition, that whenever the south polar constellation should be discovered, it would be found to be in the form of a cross[1].   The ancient Persians celebrated a feast of the cross a few days before the sun entered Aries, when this constellation would be brilliant among the stars of night. Its disappearance may be thus briefly explained.   Owing to the greater thickness of the earth at the equator, that part of the earth comes every year a little sooner to what are called the equinoxes, the points where the ecliptic crosses the equator ; consequently the north pole moves every year a little farther on in the circle it describes in the northern sky.   Thus it has gradually receded from the Southern Cross.   This movement being known to be about 50″ in a year, the place of the stars in ancient times can be ascertained by it[2].

It is well known that the cross was a sacred emblem in the Egyptian mythology. The Arabians and Indians also, before the coming of Christ, venerated this emblem.   There is in the British Museum a large silvery cross, taken from the mummy of an Egyptian priest.   Sozomenes, A.D. 443, relates that " there was found in the temple of Serapis the sign of the cross, surrounded by hieroglyphics, which meant the life to come." The last letter in the Hebrew alphabet, *thau*, was originally in the form of a cross ; and its name means boundary, limit, finishing[3], as of the Messiah's work, as when He said, " It is finished."

When this constellation began to sink below the horizon in the north temperate zone, and its form was no longer apparent, its memory seems there to have been lost, and its place among the decans to have been supplied by the division of some other emblem. Ptolemy substituted the half-horse, to make up the number of the constellations to forty-eight : an injudicious contrivance still preserved on our globes.   Others, by reckoning as separate constellations the Pleiades and Southern Crown, and making the number forty-nine or more, threw into confusion the original arrangement of three decans to each sign.

Dante, who was a great astronomer as well as poet, supposes himself at the antipodes of Jerusalem, and describes what he would have certainly seen there, these " four stars never beheld but by the early race of man."   Humboldt conjectures he had seen them on Arabian globes : but at the time he wrote southern voyagers had brought the report of them, though as yet they had seen but four.

---

[1] Dupuis, &c.   [2] Humboldt's Cosmos, Herschel, &c.   [3] As in Gen. xlix. 26.

" In the fourth century the Christian anchorites in the Thebaid would see the Southern Cross at an altitude of 10°." " It will again appear in the northern latitudes, but after the lapse of thousands of years[1]."

In a recent letter from Australia, a working man writes home with much admiration of the Southern Cross, calling it "our constellation," " the constellation of Australia." May the omen be fulfilled !

Still, it should be borne in mind that even this emblem, so dear to the heart of the Christian, has been, like the brazen serpent of old, made an object of almost idolatrous veneration. That serpent must have been lifted up on a cross, no other form would support it, even as our Lord Himself was lifted up, that whoso looketh on Him may live : but when the people offered incense to it, it must be broken, as Nehushtan[2], a mere piece of brass. To this resplendent starry symbol no desecrating honours appear to have been offered. Regarded as a memorial of our faith, it may be very precious to our expatriated brethren, and remind them that the crucified Saviour will be present, according to His promise, where " two or three" of them are gathered together in His name, in those Australian wilds, as He has been to their northern ancestors from whose sky its splendours have so long departed.

From the calculations of modern astronomy we learn that the constellations of our sky, at least the principal ones, if we were transported to the nearest fixed star, would be seen in the same grouping as from the earth. This fact is peculiarly interesting as to the Southern Cross. May not the sacrifice offered on earth upon the cross extend to the universe of starry worlds? it should seem so from what St. Paul says, " Making peace through the blood of His cross, by Him to reconcile all things unto Himself, by Him, whether things in earth or things in heaven."

NOTE I.

" The cross was the symbol of worship of the highest antiquity in Egypt and Syria, said to signify the life to come. Champollion interprets it *support*, or Saviour." " It is among the ruins of Palenque with a child held up to it in adoration." (Prescott's Mexico.)

NOTE II.

Kennicott thought that " instruments of cruelty in their habitations" (Gen. xlix. 5) related prophetically to the cross of Christ : the nails, the scourge, and spear might be included. The cross occurs here as the third decan or accompanying constellation of Libra. On the breastplate of the high priest the name of Levi and the sign Libra appear to have been engraven on the same stone. In the third decan of Libra the Persians, according to Albumazer, had the name Arbedi, one sense of which is " to cover," as in Prov. xxx. 22. This might well be derived from the traditionary revelation, that on the cross the charity, the love, the sacrifice of the Redeemer should *cover* a multitude of sins. The Southern Cross is immediately below the victim, the atoning sacrifice.

NOTE III.

Should any one wish to follow, on the modern celestial globe, the position assigned to this constellation in former ages, it will be necessary to reckon back the precession of the equinoxes to the time required, as altering the boundaries of the signs, the position of the colures and of the pole of the earth. While the pole of the ecliptic, in reference to which the stars are divided, is fixed, the pole of the equator has a motion

---

[1] Humboldt.
[2] 2 Kings xviii. 4. The author of the Apocryphal book of Wisdom says, " The pole, Num. xxi. 8, was a sign of salvation."

in consequence of that of the equinoxes. About 6000 years since it would point to the brightest star in the tail of the dragon, which must be considered as the pole-star, in trying to rectify the globe for that time. This must be done for N. lat. 36° or there-abouts, which the traces of ancient astronomy have been thought to indicate as that where the earliest observations were made. Such being the situation of the sources of the river Euphrates, this supposition agrees with what is said in Genesis ii. as to the original habitation of mankind, the fountains at least of great rivers apparently not having been altered by the deluge. The Southern Cross will then be found to rise about 16° above the horizon when on the meridian; this altitude gradually lessening, its highest star will be seen to have disappeared from the latitude of Jerusalem about the time of the crucifixion of our Lord.

NOTE IV.

" In consequence of the precession of the equinoxes the starry heavens are continually changing their aspect from every portion of the earth's surface. The early races of mankind beheld in the North the glorious constellation of the Southern Hemisphere rise before them, which, after remaining long invisible, will again appear in these latitudes after the lapse of thousands of years. At Berlin, and in the northern latitudes, the stars of the Southern Cross, as well as α and β Centauri, are receding more and more from view. The Southern Cross began to become invisible in 52° 30′ north lati-tude, 2900 years before our era. According to Galle it might previously have reached an altitude of more than 10°. . . . I am indebted to the communications of my friend Dr. Galle, by whom Le Verrier's planet was first discovered in the heavens, for all the calculations respecting the visibility of southern stars in northern latitudes." (Hum-boldt, Cosmos.)

" The constellation of the Southern Cross has acquired a peculiar character of import-ance from the beginning of the sixteenth century, owing to the religious feelings of Christian navigators and missionaries who have visited the tropical and southern seas, and both the Indies. The four principal stars are mentioned in the Almagest, and were regarded in the time of Adrian and Antoninus Pius as parts of the constellation of the Centaur. At the time of Claudius Ptolemæus the beautiful star at the base of the Southern Cross had still an altitude of 6° 10′ at its meridian passage at Alexandria, whilst in the present day it culminates there several degrees below the horizon. In order, at this time (1847), to see α Crucis at an altitude of 6° 10′ it is necessary, taking the refraction into account, to be 10° south of Alexandria in the parallel of 20° 43′ north latitude. In the fourth century the Christian anchorites in the Thebaid desert might have seen the Cross at an altitude of 10°. Dante says in the celebrated passage in the Purgatorio:—

> ' Io mi volse a man destra, e posi mente
> All' altro polo, e vidi quattro stelle,
> Non viste mai fuor ch' alla prima gente.'

And Amerigo Vespucci, who at the aspect of the starry skies of the South, first called to mind this passage on his third voyage, boasted that he now looked on the four stars never seen till then by any but the first human race."

This constellation is mentioned by Christian missionaries and navigators as " a won-derful cross more glorious than all the constellations in the heavens."

Acosta mentions that in the Spanish settlements of tropical America the first settlers were accustomed, as is now done, to use the Southern Cross as a celestial clock, reckoning the hour from its vertical or inclined position.

Humboldt says, "the Persian, Kaswini, and other Mahomedan astronomers took pains to discover crosses in the Dolphin and the Dragon." This has probably been to account for the feast of the Cross observed in ancient Persia.

Humboldt says of the Divina Commedia, "The philosophical and religious mysticism which vivifies the grand composition of Dante assigns to all objects besides their real existence an ideal one, it seems almost as if we beheld two worlds reflected in one another." " The ideal world is a free creation of the soul, the product of poetic inspiration."

ANCIENT NAMES OF THE SUN, MOON, AND EARTH,
EXPLAINED FROM THEIR PRIMITIVE ROOTS.

Prophecies, &c., corresponding with the names.			Texts where the word is used in this sense in the Hebrew Bible.	Hebrew roots.
	THE SUN.			
Gen. 1.14. *Mal. 4. 2. Rom.15 8 Heb. 8. 2.	Heb., { Shemish, *minister (as of light)*.	*sun* *ministered*	Isa. 60. 20. Dan. 7. 10.	שמש
	{ (Chald. and Syr.)			
Isa. 18. 4. Jer. 31.35.	— Chres, *giving heat.*	{ *sun* { *burning*	Judg. 8. 13. Deut. 28. 22.	חרס
Acts 26.13 1 Co. 15.41	— Chamah, { *causing motion.* Arab. sense, *troubling.* { *disturbing.*	*sun* *hot displeasure*	Cant. 6. 10. Deut. 9. 19.	חמה
*Ps. 72. 5; 84. 11.	Arab., Shemish, Chres, Chamah, as above.			
*Ps. 19. 4; 89. 36.	Copt. Pi-othiri [1], *the sender forth of heat*, as Ra.		Deut. 7. 4.	חרה
Ps. 136. 8.	Egypt., Ra, *giving out heat.* Arab. sense, *heat, kindled.*			
	Sansc., Suraya, as Ra. Aditta, *glorious.*	*glory*	Hab. 3. 3.	הוד
	— Heli, *shining.*	*shined*	Job 31. 26.	הל
	Cingalese, Irida, as Ra.			
1 Cor. 15. 41.	Scandinavian, Sonne, *shining*, Arab. sense.	*scarlet*	Josh. 2. 18.	שני
	Gr., Helios, as Heli.			
	Lat., Sol, *which shines*, with *s* prefixed.	*shine*	Job 41. 18.	הל
	Irish [2], Sam, as Shemish.			
	— Greian, as Chres.			
	— Re, as Ra.			
	— Sol, as Sol.			
	THE MOON.			
*Deu.33.14 *Ps. 8. 3.	Heb., Yareah, *sent forth.*	{ *as rain* { *moon*	Hos. 10. 12. Josh. 10. 12.	ירה ירח
Isa.60.19; 30. 26.	— Lebana, *white.*	{ *white* { *moon*	Exod. 16.31. Cant. 6. 10.	לבן
Ps. 72. 7; 104.10; 89. 37.	Arab., Al Kamar, *the red moon*, Arab. sense.	*foul*	Job 16. 16.	חמר
	— Lebana, as above, *white.*			
Job 31. 26.	Copt., Pi-cochos, *who circles*, Arab sense.	*circle*	Isa. 40. 22.	חרג
Ps. 121. 6.	Egypt., Aah, *connected.*	*brother*	Job 30. 29.	אח
	Sansc.,Chandra,fromChadi, *shines*, Arab. sense, *shoot out*		Jer. 50. 14.	ידה
	— [3] Hima and Soma, *associated*, (*s*).	*with*	Gen. 18. 23.	עם
	Persian, Mah, as Aah.			
	Cingalese, Handou, as Chandra.			
	Scand., Mone, Mond, Monat, *numbering.*		Dan 5. 26.	מנא
	Gr., Mane, as Mone; Selene, *which shines*, (*s*).	*shineth*	Job 25. 5.	הל
	Lat., Luna and Lunus, as Lebana (Levana).			
	Irish, Luan, as Lebana.			
	THE EARTH.			
*Gen. 1. 10.	Heb., Aretz, *broken, bruised.*	*brakest*	Ps. 74. 14.	} רצץ
Gen. 6. 11, 13; 18 18.	Chald., Arya, the same.	*bruised*	Isa. 42. 3.	
Deut. 32.22.	Arab., Aradt, the same.			
Job 38. 4, 6.	Egypt. ?			
*Prov. 8. 31.	Sansc., Gauh, *broken.*	*brake*	Job 38. 8.	נח
Ps. 102. 25.	Scand., Hertha and Erde, as Aretz.			
Isa. 45. 2.	Gr., Ge, as Gauh.			
Jer. 51. 15.	— Era, as Arya.			
Hos. 2. 22.	Lat., Terra, as Arya.			
Hab. 2. 14. Matt. 5. 5. 2 Pet. 3 10. Rev. 20. 11.				

. The asterisks mark where the root of the name exists in the prophecy.

---

[1] Pi is the masculine article, Egyptian and Coptic, appearing in the Greek names.
[2] The Irish are on the authority of Thaddeus O'Connellan.
[3] The Chinese character for the moon, reduplicated, forms that for *companion, associate.*

ANCIENT NAMES OF THE PLANETS,

EXPLAINED FROM THEIR PRIMITIVE ROOTS.

Prophecies, &c., corresponding with the names.		Texts where the word is used in this sense in the Hebrew Bible	Hebrew roots.
	URANUS.		
	Burman, Rabi, Rahini, *failing*, Arab. sense. *afraid*	Isa. 44. 8.	רהה
	SATURN.		
Heb.4.1–9 Deu.12.10 Isa.11.10.	Heb., Sabbatei, *resting.* *rest*	Gen. 2. 2.	שבת
*Isa. 58.12. Ez. 16. 53.	or, — Sabbath, {*dwelling.* *dwell* {*restoring.* *restoreth*	Deut.12.10. Ps. 23. 3. Isa. 58. 12.	שב
*Ex. 33. 14. Isa. 58. 12.	Arab., Zohal, *hiding, sheltering.* *shadow* — Refan, *resting.* *slack*	Judg. 9. 15. Josh. 10. 6.	צל
*Mal. 4. 2. *Deu.32.39	Copt., Refè, Refan, Remphan, *restoring.* *healeth* or	Exod.15.26.	רפא
*Isa. 53. 5. Acts 1. 6.	Egypt., Seb, as Sabbatei. Sansc., Aspujat, as Sabbatei. — Sani, Arab. sense, *hiding, defending.* *shield* Persian, Kivon. *Chiun*	1 Sam.17.7. Amos 5. 26.	צנה כיון
Ps. 31. 20. *Isa. 16. 3.	Scandinavian, Satur, *hiding.* *protection*	Deut.32.38.	סתר
Exod. 34. 7.	Gr., Phainon, *covering, hiding.* (Arab. sense, *rest.*) *forgive*	Gen. 50. 17.	אנא
*Ps. 17. 8.	— Kronos, *quiet.* *cool* Lat., Saturn, *hiding*, as Satur.	Prov.17.27.	קר
	JUPITER.		
*Jer. 23. 6. Acts 3. 14; 7. 52.	Heb. Zedek, {*just*, Isa. xlv. 21. *righteous* {*true*, Isa. xli. 26.	Isa. 53. 11.	צדק
Nu. 24.19. Deu. 1.15.	Arab., Al Moshtari, *having dominion.*	Job 38. 33.	משטר
Mic. 5. 2.	— Gad, *good fortune.* Copt., Picheus, *glorious*, Arab. sense. or		
Jer. 10.10. John 14.6.	Egypt., Ammon, *true.* *truth*	Isa. 65. 16.	אמן
Col. 1. 15.	Sansc. Brahaspati, {*originating.* *create* {*revealing*, as below.	Gen. 1. 1.	ברא
Eph. 5. 23.	— Urishaspiti, *chief, head.* *first* Scand., Thor, *who breaks or bruises; cut*, Arab. *razor*	Exod.13.13. Num. 6. 5.	פטר תער
Ps. 22. 28. Acts 5. 31.	Gr., Phëton, or Phaeton, *coming.* *came* — Dis [1], *second.* Chald., *du, two.*	Isa. 41. 5.	אתא
Ex. 3. 14. John 8.58.	Lat., Jupiter, {*who is.* *Jah* {*revealing, interpreting.*	*Ps. 68. 4. Gen. 40. 8.	יה פתר
	MARS.		
Ex. 12.22. *Isa. 63. 2.	Heb., Adom, *red, bloodshedding.* *blood*	Josh. 20. 3.	דם
Rev. 19. 13.	— Madim, *made like blood*, Arab. sense. *wounded* Arab., Melekh, as Melokh. Pers., Azar, *blood-flowing*, Arab. sense. *distress*	Gen. 35. 3.	צרה
Gen. 3. 15.	Copt., Molokh, *broken, bruised.* *wring* or	Lev. 1. 15.	מלק
Isa.53.4,5. Zec.13.6.	Egypt., Khons, *wounded.* (Hercules.) *smitten*	Isa. 53. 4.	נכה

[1] The Greeks seem to have mistaken *dis*, the *second* planet, for *Dis*, the God.

Prophecies, &c., corresponding with the names.	MARS (continued).		Texts where the word is used in this sense in the Hebrew Bible.	Hebrew roots.
Mat. 28. 18.	Sansc., Khonda, as Khons.			
	— Angareka, *wounded*.	*stricken*	Isa. 53. 4.	נגע
	— Mangala, *the same*.			
Isa. 49. 25.	Scand., Tuisco, *striving*.	*strove*	Gen. 26. 20.	עשׁק
	— Tyr, Tys, as Mars.			
Heb. 12. 3.	Gr., Pirois, *bruising or*	*bruised*	Isa. 42. 3.	} רצץ
	— Puroeis, *fire colour*.			
	— Ares, as Mars.			
	Lat., Mars, *bruised or breaker*.	*brakest*	Ps. 74. 14.	

VENUS.

Prophecies	VENUS		Texts	Hebrew roots
⊦Isa. 60. 19.	Heb., Nogah, *bright*.	*shining*	Isa. 4. 5.	נגע
Cant. 6. 10.	— Hillel, *very bright*.	*Lucifer*	Isa. 14. 12.	הלל
Rv. 20. 11; 21. 5. }	Arab., Al Zoharah, *bright*.	*shine*	Dan. 12. 3.	זהר
Isa. 14. 12.	Copt., Surath, *morning twilight*.	*morning*	Cant. 6. 10.	שׁחר
	— Athor, *coming or bringing light*.	*light*	2 Sam. 23. 4.	אור
Isa. 60. 3.	Egypt., Athyr, as Athor.			
Cant. 1. 5; *6. 10. }	Sansc., Sikra, *dawn, twilight*.	*dawning*	Josh. 6. 15.	שׁחר
	— Sivah, *bright*.	*brightness*	Dan. 2. 31.	זיו
Cant. 4. 1–7.	Scand., Freya or Frigga, *fair, bright*.	*glorified*	Isa. 60. 9.	פאר
	Gr., Heosphorus, Hesperus, *beautiful*.	*garnished*	Job 26. 13.	שׁפר
Ps. 97. 11.	— Phosphorus, *light-bringer or beautiful*.			
	— Aphrodite, *who is fruitful*.			
	— Hera, *who bears*.			
	Lat., Lucifer, *light-bringer*. Vesper, as Hesperus.			
Cant. 4. 10.	— Venus, *lovely*.	*grace*	Prov. 1. 9.	חן
Eph. 5. 27.				

MERCURY.

Prophecies	MERCURY		Texts	Hebrew roots
*Job 23. 6. Ps. 24. 8; *98. 9. }	Heb., Catab, { *powerful, strong.* { *who cometh.*	*power* *cometh*	Num. 14. 17. Ps. 96. 13.	כח בא
John 14. 3. Acts 1. 11. }	— Cochab, *coming as in a circle*.	*star*	Num. 24. 17.	כוכב
Ps. 2. 8; *72. 8. Rv. 19. 15. }	Arab., Otared, *coming*.	*to have dominion*	Num. 24. 19.	רדה
Rev. 1. 7.	Copt., Thaut, *coming*.	*come*	Deut. 33. 2.	אתא
	or			
⊦Ps. 113. 4.	— Pi-ermes, *that cometh*.	*moveth*	Gen. 9. 2.	רמשׁ
Hab. 2. 3. Heb. 10. 37. }	Egypt., Thoth, as Thaut.		Isa. 6. 1.	רס
2 Th. 2. 1, 8.	Sansc., Bouta, or Budha, *coming*.	*coming*	Mal. 3. 2.	בא
Ps. 110. 2.	Scand., Woden, *coming*.	*passed*	Job 28. 8.	עבה
Rev. 1. 14.	Gr. Stilbon, *who is bright*.	*white*	Dan. 12. 10.	לבן
	or			
	— Hermes, as Pi-ermes above.			
Mark 8. 38.	Lat., Mercurius, { *strong*, Arab sense.	*Lord*	Dan. 2. 47.	מרא
John 14. 3.	{ *coming again, recurring, circling,*			
Jude 14.	{ Arab. sense.			
2 Th. 2. 8.				
Rev. 22. 20.				

AUTHORITIES.

Burmese, Sir W. Drummond, &c. Hebrew, Buxtorf, Seb. Munster, Gaffarelli, &c. Arabic, Freytag's and Wilmet's Lexicons, &c. Coptic or Egyptian, Montucla, Histoire des Mathématiques; Bunsen's Egypt, &c. Sanscrit, Wilson's Lexicon, Sir W. Jones, &c. Scandinavian, Verstegon, &c. Greek and Latin, various poets and astronomers. Recently discovered Egyptian names, Mr. W. Elllis. D is always rendered by T in Egyptian: the other slight changes in thus referring these names to Semitic roots are according to Bunsen's Vocabulary, &c.

"Some tablets have recently (1856) been discovered in Egypt, containing planetary inscriptions in the demotic character. These tablets were discovered by Mr. Stobart, and examined by Mr. Brugsch, of Berlin," From this account are taken the annexed names of the planets. Mr. Ellis, of the Greenwich Observatory, has ascertained that the tablets contained planetary positions according to the Egyptian calendar, extending from A.D. 105 to A.D. 132.

				Texts where the roots occur.	Hebrew roots.
1. SATURN,	Hor-ka,	{ Hor, *planet*.	*traveller*	2 Sam. 12.4.	ארח
		{ Ka, *slow*.	*heaviness*	Isa. 61. 3.	כהה
2. JUPITER,	Hor-sat, or Hor-p-sat,	{ Hor, *planet*. { Sat, *just, true*, Arab. Sadak, as Zedek.			
3. MARS,	Hor-tos, or Hor-tas, *bruising*.		*thresh*	Isa. 28. 28.	דש
4. VENUS,	Pe-neterti [1], *bright, fair*, Cant. iv. 1.		*glorious*	Exod. 15. 6.	נאדר
5. MERCURY,	Sewek, or Sowek, *coming quickly*.		*run*	Isa. 33. 4.	שק

The names in the previous Tables were conjecturally given by Bunsen, Birch, and other Egyptologers, but rather as names of planetary deities than of the planets; still when they resemble the ancient Hebrew, Coptic, or Sanscrit, it may be supposed they also were names applied to the planets at different times and in different places, especially as the leading idea of the other names is contained in them. The affinity between the ancient Egyptian and the Semitic dialects seems admitted. Bunsen says, "The cradle of Egyptian mythology and *language* is Asiatic."

Diodorus Siculus says, "The motions and periods and stations of the planets were well known to the ancient Egyptians."

Edinburgh Review on Delambre's Ancient Astronomy.

"We find five of the planets mentioned so early as the time of Eratosthenes, more than a century before the Christian Era. He speaks of ' Jupiter or Phainos, large. Phaëthon, not large. The third is Mars, or Puroeides, the colour of fire, not large. Phosphorus or Venus, of a white colour, and the largest of all the stars. The fifth Mercury, or Stilbon, brilliant but small.' Phaëthon, says M. Delambre, can only be Saturn.

"Achilles Tatius, who wrote a commentary on Aratus about 300 years B.C., speaks thus of the names and order of the planets among the Egyptians. 'It is by euphemism that the Egyptians call Saturn Phainon, *apparent*, seeing it is the most obscure of the planets; the Egyptians also call it Nemesis. The second planet is Jupiter, which the Greeks call Phaethon, and the Egyptians Osiris. The third is Mars, which among the Greeks is Puroeis, and among the Egyptians the star of Hercules. The fourth is Mercury, Stilbon among the Greeks, and the star of Apollo among the Egyptians. The fifth is the planet Venus, which the Greeks call Heosphorus.'

"Here it is observable that Eratosthenes and Achilles Tatius interchange the names of Jupiter and Saturn. Cicero calls Saturn, Phainon; Jupiter, Phaethon; Mars, Puroeis; Mercury, Stilbon; and Venus, Phosphorus and Lucifer.

"Aristotle de Cœlo, says, 'Those Italians who are called Pythagoreans affirm that *Pyr* is in the centre, and that the earth being itself one of the stars circling or revolving about that centre produces night and day.'

"Plutarch considered Pyr as synonymous with Helius, and mentions Pythagorean teachers as maintaining that the earth revolved round the sun.

"Mene was an early Greek name of the moon."

"The star which is called at once by the names of Phainon and Kronos occupies always as its place the one next to this; next, that bearing the name of Phaethon, called also by the title of Zeus; then Pyrois, which is called both by the names of Heracles and Ares; and next Stilbon, whom some call sacred to Hermes, but others to Apollo; after whom the star called Phosphorus, whom some call the star of Aphrodite, and others the star of Hera."—From the Treatise (falsely) ascribed to Aristotle. De Mundo, Cap. ii.

---

[1] According to Bunsen's vocabulary, Pe was an Egyptian name or epithet for heaven, the fair, the bright, the beautiful, like the Greek Ouranos, the place of light. But the Hebrew and Arabic, Shamayim, the set up, Exod. xl. 8, as in order, well ordered, gives a higher and more scientific definition of the nature of those heavens whose order and wonderfully balanced regularity are brought to light by the researches of modern astronomy, and yet seem taken for granted in this most ancient appellation. Pe-neterti would be the glorious, or glory of heaven.

NAMES OF EGYPTIAN GODS,

EXPLAINED FROM THEIR PRIMITIVE ROOTS, AND REFERRED TO THE CORRESPONDING PLANETS AND SIGNS.

THE EIGHT GODS OF THE FIRST ORDER.

			Texts where the word or its root is used.	Hebrew roots.
SUN,	Ra[1] (Helios), *raying* forth light and heat.	Arab. sense		ירה
MOON,	Neith, *sent forth, caused to come.*	came	Deut. 33. 21.	אתא
MERCURY,	Aroeris, *coming and coming again.*	traveller	2 Sa. 12. 4.	ארח
VENUS,	Mut, *the mother;* Leto and Latona, *who brings forth.*			ילדה
	Buto, *the daughter.*	daughter		בת
MARS,	Khem, *red, angry.* (Pan, *as wrathful?* or	{ fury	Gen. 27. 44.	חם
	brown, hairy?)	{ brown	Gen. 30. 32.	
JUPITER,	Sat, now ascertained to be a name of Jupiter.			
SATURN,	Kneph, or Ka, *slow.*	heaviness	Isa. 61. 3.	כהה
URANUS,	Amun, *concealed,* as frequently unseen.			

The mythology of the Egyptians had the same source as that of the other nations, the primitive revelation, which in the figures of the constellations was perverted first into Sabianism, and thence into idolatry. Osiris, the man, the prince; Isis, the woman; Horus, the promised seed, He who cometh. These primary objects of prophecy, with what was there said of them, originated the various forms of Egyptian divinities and all their many names; the serpent, not worshipped, was continually figured as an accompaniment. "He shall bruise and be bruised," was the distinction of the expected Great One. The word Saph[2], to bruise or wound, is nearly related to Sapha, a lip. An Egyptian divinity[3], generally a child, is represented with the finger on the *lip,* the promised offspring who shall bruise and be bruised. Others, to the utter mystification of all explainers, have a pestle and mortar, implements of *bruising,* on their heads; the woman, as well as the man having them, as the mother of Him who should be bruised and shall bruise the serpent's head. Many carry a flail, the instrument with which "bread-corn is *bruised.*" The plough-share is an Egyptian emblem, it occurs near the Pole in the planisphere of Dendera. The Heb. name of it is Ath (Isa. ii. 4), meaning which comes, from Atha, to come; also, it *bruised* the ground, as expressed in the word charash, to *plough,* to *crush* the ground.

The head of the ram (or male lamb of sacrifice) is frequent on the body of a man or a lion, a corruption of the Cherubic forms[4].

---

[1] For these names see Wilkinson and Bunsen.

[2] Doubts as to this word seem to be set aside by Rom. xvi. 20, the Vulgate of Gen. iii. 15, and two Arabic senses of it, to wound and to bite.

[3] Generally named Harpocrates, which may be rendered who cometh, who is to be cut off; from *ara,* who cometh, as in, 2 Sam. xii. 4, and *carath,* cut off, Jer. xi. 19, with the masculine article, Pi, inserted.

[4] The cherubic heads predominate in the forms of the Egyptian idols, but the ibis-headed Mercury is frequently seen. Ibis means *he shall come:* the bird called ibis *came* after the inundation, and was the foe of the serpent, for which it has been supposed that it was venerated, but also probably originally as a symbol of Him who was to *come* to be the conqueror of the serpent. Ibis is written in hieroglyphics Ib or Eb, without the Greek termination *is,* thus nearer to *iba,* he shall come.

The hawk substituted for the eagle, apparently unknown in Egypt, the lion, the bovine face often of a calf or cow, and the high plumes on the heads representing the wings, are evidently derived from the cherubic figures.

Dupuis says, "The Egyptians worshipped the hawk for the sun, the ibis for the moon.

"Astronomy was the soul of all their religious system.

"The Egyptian priests gave the designs for the statues of the gods from the spheres, the astronomical figures of the heavens." (Orig. des Cultes.)

" Chæremon and the most learned priests of Egypt were of opinion with the ancient Egyptians that the only gods were the sun, moon, and planets, and also the other stars which compose the Zodiac, and all those which by their rising or setting mark the divisions of the signs, their sub-divisions, the horoscope and the stars which preside over it, which they call powerful chiefs of heaven; these ancient Egyptians also regarded the sun as a great god, architect and ruler of the universe, explaining all their religious fables by the stars." (Dupuis.)

Lucian says that the Egyptian religion was entirely founded on the sky.

In the mythology of Egypt is thus to be traced the universal tradition of the woman who should bear the seed, and her Infant, the God who should be born, and who as man should suffer and die. We learn from Herodotus that Isis and Osiris were the only gods worshipped in Egypt, Horus appearing to have been worshipped in Osiris; but he also says the Egyptians had three orders of divinities, of course inferior to those who were alone worshipped. The first order, of eight, of which he only says that Pan and Latona were among them; the second order, of twelve, of which Hercules was one, and which had some connexion with the twelve months of the year; he does not say of how many the third order consisted. These orders are said to be planetary and astral. As Plato says that the Egyptians confessed that they did not originate but adopted the names they used, and that they attributed their astronomy to the Chaldeans, in that dialect, or its cognate Hebrew and Arabic, the meanings of those names should be sought.

THE TWELVE GODS OF THE SECOND ORDER.

		Texts where the word or its root is used in this sense in the Hebrew Bible.	Hebrew roots.
ARIES,	Seback, who subdues, Egyptian [1], most anciently with a ram's head, who takes *captive*, as Mesartim, *the bound*, in Aries.	Gen. 14. 14.	שבה
TAURUS,	Mau, Mu, or Mui, sometimes with a bull's head, and called, *victorious, strong.* Sometimes called En-pe, *leader of heaven*, perhaps when the spring equinox was in Taurus. *steady*	Exod. 17.12.	אם
GEMINI,	Atmu, or Atum, with a youthful human head, *the twin.* He is called Nefer and Nefru, *the branch. blossom*	Gen. 25. 24. / Isa. 5. 24.	האם / פרח
CANCER,	Pecht, a goddess with a cat-head, called Mut, *mother*, and Menhi, *many* (Arab. sense). *number*	Dan. 5. 26.	מנה
LEO,	Tefnu, the lion-headed goddess. *smiting*	Nah. 2. 8.	תף
VIRGO,	Nutphè, the mother of the gods, the mistress of heaven, represented as suckling a child. *infant*	Gen. 34. 29.	טף
LIBRA,	Ma, *truth, justice.* *truth*	Isa. 65. 16.	אם
SCORPIO,	Khunsu, called Hercules, sometimes holding a palm-branch. Chons, Copt. *strength.*		
SAGITTA-RIUS,	Muntu, Mandulis, hawk or eagle-headed. The constellation of the Eagle is in the sign Sagittarius, *sending forth*, as *arrows.* *shoot*	Jer. 50. 14.	ידה
CAPRICOR-NUS,	Tet, Thout, Hermes, ibis-headed. A human figure with ibis-head stands on Capricorn in the Dendera zodiac. *He shall come, he cometh.* *came*	Gen. 49. 10. / Deut. 33. 2.	יבא / אתא
AQUARIUS,	Seb, a human figure, with a goose on his head, perhaps referring to the water, *who turns, returns*, as the solstice. *returned*	Gen. 8. 3.	שב
PISCES,	Hather, Athor, Aphrodite, *the fruitful, abundant.* A goddess with a cow's head. *abundance*	Isa. 15. 7.	יתר

---

[1] Bunsen.

" The Egyptians divided the year into twelve parts. In this they affirm the stars to have been their guides. They first invented the names of the twelve gods, and from them the Greeks borrowed them." Herodotus.

" Herodotus expressly states that twelve, the number of these gods, was sacred, probably taken from the twelve months of the solar year." (Bunsen's Egypt.) Bunsen attributes to them "an astral import."

According to ancient lexicons, the Egyptian name of Hercules was Khons. The constellation Hercules is in Scorpio.

As Herodotus reports that Isis and Osiris alone were worshipped all over Egypt, the multitudes of other names and figures called divinities, which perplex modern investigators, were only deified attributes, or these two deities under different aspects. Isis, the woman, she who should bear the promised Seed; Adam had named the woman Isha or Isa, whence Isis; Virgo was called Isis in the time of Eratosthenes. Osiris, the Prince, the Ruler, who was to die and rise again; he was sometimes called the spouse, sometimes the brother of Isis. The infant held by Virgo, when considered as the offspring of Isis, was called Horus, he that cometh, a divine person, born of the woman. Such was the early tradition of the Egyptians of this ancient patriarchal faith, the religion of their ancestor Noah. Then followed the deification of the first order of eight gods, apparently the sun, moon, and six planets; then the second order of twelve, the signs of the Zodiac; after these the third, of seven, which might be the sun, moon, and five planets, after the Uranus was forgotten.

THE THIRD, CALLED THE OSIRIS ORDER.

What were the gods of the third order seems very uncertain. If they were the planets, or rather, as is said, guardian genii of the planets in the order of the days of the week, said to be of Egyptian origin, they may be thus arranged :—

			Texts where the word or its root is used in this sense in the Hebrew Bible.	Hebrew roots.
SUN,	Osiris, as the sun-god, the Ruler.	chief	Gen. 21. 22.	שר
MOON,	Isis, as " mistress of the moon," the *woman*.		Gen. 2. 23.	אשה
MARS,	Harpocrates, *who cometh, the cut-off*.	{ wayfarer { cut off	Jud. 19. 17. Dan. 9. 26.	ארח כרת
MERCURY,	Aroeris, or Hor-her, or Horus, hawk-headed, *coming and returning*, as the eagle.			
JUPITER,	Set, Sat, as Zedek, *just*, *true*.			
VENUS,	Nephthys, sister of Isis, *opening, bringing the morning*.	break forth	Jer. 1. 14.	פתה
SATURN,	Anupu, or Anubis, *resting*, Gen. v. 20. *coming*.	rest cometh	Exod. 23. 12. Ps. 96. 13.	נוח בא

These seven are said by Herodotus to proceed from the first order (the eight). The five great gods of this order, not the sun and moon, but the five planets, are said to have been born on five successive days, discovered in that order and on those days. When the days of the week were named the Uranus was forgotten.

"Sirius the Egyptians called Anubis, and worshipped him under the form of a dog or Schachal." *Warning like the barking of a dog*, one sense of the root being *to bark* (" Latrator Anubis," Ovid.), *foreshowing, warning*.

The hawk, the Egyptian substitute for the eagle, was an emblem of the sun as ascending and descending in heaven. The Ibis became an emblem of the moon, as coming, returning, יבא.

Here may be traced the rise of Sabaism, the worship of the host of heaven, and the gradual perversion into the gross forms of idolatry for which Egypt became a proverb among the nations. The sun was identified with Osiris, the moon with Isis, the prophetic types of Him who was to come to be the light of the world, and His Church the assembly of the called, His bride, also called His sister-spouse, thus accounting for the confusion in the relationship of Isis and Osiris, like that of the Jupiter and Juno of the Greeks[1].

With regard to the great antiquity by some writers, ancient and modern, attributed to the monarchy of Egypt, nature, interpreted by geology, seems to bring it within the bounds of that claimed for other ancient nations. The French scientific men who accompanied Buonaparte, believed they had ascertained from the depth of the silt or deposit of the inundation, that the Nile had flowed rather less than 6000 years. Beneath that deposit is the sand of the neighbouring desert, and beneath that again marine formations; though Wilkinson and Newbold seem to have assigned greater depth to the deposits of the inundation, yet Hugh Miller[2] speaks of this "chronology" as in "legitimate connexion with the recent introduction of the human species." All geologists seem now agreed that there are no earlier traces of mankind[3]. The theory that derives the Egyptian mythology from prophecy, refers it to the revelation to Adam, from whom few now dispute that the whole human race descended. One proof among many others being the similar tradition among all nations of the seed of the woman, the conqueror of the serpent.

"Chæremon sought to command the Genii in the name of him who is seated on the Lotus, carried in a ship, *who appears different in each sign of the Zodiac*." In the Egyptian planisphere of Dendera some figures with mystic attributes are seated on the Lotus, and others are as coming in boats. The Brahma of Indian mythology sits on the Lotus. The word Lotus, from its Semitic root, would mean *concealed*, as the water-lily beneath the water, the flower in the bud, the promised Deliverer not yet come.

"Champollion read on the Zodiac of Dendera the title of Augustus Cæsar, on that of Esneh the name of Antoninus." Such may have been the dates of the buildings, as the figure of the Ibis-headed Mercury, or Capricorn, where the head of the goat joins the body of the fish, may indicate; but the headless horse, as the ascending node of the ecliptic (the wintry solstice) is figured, being placed beyond, shows a much earlier era for the Zodiac.

Dupuis, who calculated the date of the planisphere from 4000 B.C., appears best to have understood it. The Zodiac now used is that of Ptolemy's time, rather later than that of Augustus; but Canterbury Cathedral and other buildings on which our ancestors inscribed it are not therefore of that age. The Egyptians[4] depicted the ancient Patriarchal Zodiac as it had come down to them, adding emblems that belonged to their own time.

---

[1] The Egyptians gave to every deity a consort, hence the multiplicity of goddesses.
[2] Testimony of the Rocks.   [3] Typical forms, &c.
[4] Sir G. Wilkinson says, "We do not see them in their infancy as a nation." "Of this we may be certain, that neither the Hindoos borrowed from the Egyptians, nor the Egyptians from the Hindoos."
"The Asiatic origin of the Egyptians accounts for any analogy with the Oriental nations." Reviewer adds, "Nothing has ever yet been discovered to illustrate the position of the Egyptians when they emigrated into the valley of the Nile."

THE TWELVE GREAT GODS OF ASSYRIA.

PRESIDED OVER BY ASHUR, THE KING OF THE CIRCLE OF THE GREAT GODS.

			Texts where the word or its root is used in this sense in the Hebrew Bible.	Hebrew roots.
THE SUN,	Ashur, *the Prince.* Suraya is a name of the sun in Sanscrit.	*prince*	Dan. 10. 13.	שר
AQUARIUS,	Anu, as Janus, *resting,* as the sun at the winter solstice, in Aquarius at the Deluge and the foundation of the Assyrian empire.	*rested*	Nu. 10. 36.	נוח
PISCES,	Uncertain, perhaps Dagon, as the *multitudes* of fish.	*fish*	Gen. 1. 26.	דג
		multiply	Gen. 48. 16.	
ARIES,	San, from the Semitic Se, *a lamb*	*lamb*	Exod. 12. 4.	שה
TAURUS,	Merodach, *subduing.*	*subdue*	Gen. 1. 28.	מררה
GEMINI,	Yav, *shall come.*	*came*	Gen. 19. 1.	יבאו
CANCER,	Bar, *producing,* as the multitude of cattle.	*rank*	Gen. 41. 5.	ברא
LEO,	Nebo, *sent forth, coming* (*Lord,* Egyptian).	*shall come*	Hab. 2. 3.	בא
VIRGO,	Mylitta, or Alitta, called the mother of the great gods, *bringing forth.*	*bare*	Gen. 4. 1.	ילדה
LIBRA,	Uncertain, name not clearly read, 1853.			
SCORPIO,	Bel, *the lord,* Ophiuchus.	*Bel*	Isa 46. 1.	בל
		master	Exod. 22. 8.	בעל
SAGITTA-RIUS,	Shamash, *ministering,* Egyptian, Chald.	*ministered*	Dan. 7. 10.	שמש
CAPRICOR-NUS,	Ishtar, *wounding,* Arab. sense.	*smiting*	1 Sam. 5. 10.	שתר

LAYARD'S NINEVEH, 1853, p. 351.

"An inscription now in the British Museum commences with an invocation to the God Ashur, the supreme Lord, the king of the circle of the twelve gods. Then follow the names of these divinities. They are the same as those on the black obelisk belonging to the son of the king represented on this slab, although they are not placed in the same order. These divinities may preside over the twelve months, corresponding with the same circle in the Egyptian mythology, with which it is possible they may hereafter to a certain extent be identified. The first named is Anu (?), the last Ishtar, probably Astarte, or the moon; not Venus, as some have believed." The difference in the order may have been an accommodation to the birth of that prince and to his horoscope. From this authority the names are here given.

The Assyrians seem to have worshipped one Supreme God, whom they called Ashur, the prince or ruler, in which sense it was also applied to the Sun, as in the above table. This name, therefore, as Layard says, also enters into the names of the kings and even of private persons. Different nations had different names for the Supreme Deity; by the Babylonians called Nebo, the sent forth, or, who shall come forth.

"On cylinders the figures of the deities standing on animals are frequently seen in act of adoration before the Supreme God in the circle." "The Supreme God was sometimes represented under a Triune form." (Layard.)

Human figures with tails have been discovered among the sculptures of Nineveh, as in Egyptian remains. There are two Semitic words for tail, Zenab, which divided Ze-nab, would convey the idea *this cometh,* or, shall be sent forth; and Alyah, having the same sense from a different root.

Dr. Grotefend says, "On the Assyrian cylinders every thing, as far as possible, is represented by stars." He derives the mythology of the Assyrians from a primæval worship of the starry host. Layard also says, "Originally the Assyrian religion was a pure Sabeanism, worshipping the heavenly deities."

Many figures of divinities standing on a lion or a bull have a star on their cap. These are very early. Two human-headed lions, with human arms, have in one hand a goat or stag, in the other a *branch*. He frequently speaks of a sacred tree, and occasionally of a branch. In the fir-cone, so frequently held by the divinities, &c., *The Seed* may be recognized. Layard speaks of the Nineveh inscriptions as a dialect of the primitive tongue, thus authorizing the search for primitive roots in the names of the deities.

It seems from Biblical authority that the ancient name of Assyria was Ashur [1]. It is probable that the Cherubic names, Shur, the bull, and Nesir, the eagle, suggested the names of the empire as well as those of the images they venerated. It is observed that in Assyrian and Persepolitan remains, wherever the eagle is represented it is as victorious. In Persian remains the bull is always represented as subdued, about to be slain, *sacrificed*, by Mithra, as an incarnate deity, whose name may be from the ancient root, *ar*, to come, He who shall come, as from the tradition that He who was to come, the Mighty One in human nature, should offer himself as a sacrifice.

A "sacred tree" appears among the traces of Assyrian worship. It has been conjectured to be a traditional representation of the tree of life; but there is no fruit on it. It is more like "the branch," the universally preserved emblem of divinity, of Him who should come, the recognized emblem of the Messiah, and borne by the woman of the zodiac, with the ear of corn, the seed.

Layard gives representations of two slabs, on one of which "the sacred tree" appears in the middle, with on each side the figure of Nisroch, the eagle-headed human figure, the idol god before which Sennacherib was slain. He holds in his right hand the fir-cone, the symbolic seed, and in his left "the usual basket." The basket, that which carries, from a Semitic root *sebil*, one of the Oriental names of the woman in Virgo, appears to refer to that sign. On the other slab, the sacred tree again in the midst, has two kneeling bearded human figures, with eagle wings, and the cap with horns emblematizing power, these figures appear to be offering homage to the tree or branch. Layard thinks "the sacred tree" something of the honeysuckle kind, if so, it is a plant always rather *a branch* than *a tree*. These figures so placed may embody a tradition that the Cherubic forms represented the same person as the sacred tree, the branch, and the seed, carried, borne by the woman. Other similar human figures carry in one hand an antelope, the kid of sacrifice, in the other the branch, "the holy tree."

The name Nimrod has been derived from the Semitic root *marad*, to rebel, and it has also been said that his character in ancient tradition of being the first rebel and apostate thence originated. But of his rebellion the Scripture says nothing. He is there characterized as a mighty hunter, by which the derivation of Nimrod from Nimehar, swift, and Adar, to come or pass [2], seems authorized. In Hab. i. 6, Nimehar occurs as swift, hasty, and in ver. 8, Nimar, as a leopard, a swift animal. Nimar is the word translated leopard in Dan. vii. 6. The figure, said

[1] Gen. x. "Out of that land he went into Assyria." So Onkelos, and the Targum of Jonathan, saying, "He, Nimrod, reigned in Assyria." Assyria is called the land of Nimrod. But Josephus and Jarchi held it was *Ashur* went out, &c. Nineveh, a pleasant habitation. (Gill.) Dr. A. Clarke prefers *he*, Nimrod.

[2] Dan. iv. 28.

to be of Nimrod, in the Assyrian sculptures, holds an animal, which, but for the lion-like mane, would be a leopard, and thus by the name Nimar suggest both the name, Nimrod, and his character of swiftness as a hunter. The animal is evidently not struggling, as if in combat, nor dead, as if subdued, but is there as an attribute, a hieroglyph of the name of him who holds it.

Interesting indeed are the coincidences between the Assyrian records as now develop-ing, and the historical and prophetic books of Scripture; but the traces of the early revelation, the faith of Adam and of Noah, furnished by the sculptures, are even more interesting and important. The discoverers are of opinion that the emblems, having such remarkable affinity with the Cherubic forms, were not originally idolatrously worshipped, but that upon mysterious veneration of the symbol was gradually engrafted that species of worship of the image forbidden in the second commandment. The bowing down there prohibited is that of Abraham in courtesy to the children of Heth [1], whom certainly he did not *worship* in the sense of the word understood as divine worship, but rather in the sense in which it is used in the Anglican marriage service, and as a title of certain English magistrates. The word rendered *serve* may include taking care of those images, burning lights before them, and similar acts of *service*.

This gradual falling into the sin of idolatry and its moral corruptions from the use of likenesses "made to themselves," even when in imitation of those symbols divinely ordained, the Cherubim, will show the reason of the awful chastisements inflicted on the first violators of the second commandment, even when they professed to intend to see in their image of the golden calf only a repetition of the divinely ordained Cherub. It may also enforce the wisdom of Protestant Reformers in banishing all "likenesses" from their temples.

NOTE ON CHERUBIC FORMS.

At one time Layard conjectured that Ezekiel having seen these Assyrian figures, might from them describe the figures of his visions. But Ezekiel says of them, "I *knew* they were the Cherubim," and as a Jewish priest he must have been well acquainted with these forms, which had recently been in the temple of Solomon, and long before in the tabernacle of Moses. Ancient Jewish writers say that they were "in the tabernacle from the beginning," and so known to Noah, Abraham, and the children of Israel before they went into Egypt. Many modern com-mentators are of the same opinion. "They were held to be the same figures with those at the gate of Eden." Gill also observes, "They are always represented as vehicles on which He sits or rides." The Jews frequently speak of "the mystery of the Cherubim." "In the glory of them Christ will come a second time." Dr. A. Clarke says, "The word Cherub never being employed as a verb, it is justly supposed to be a word compounded of the particle of resemblance Ke (or Che), like to, or like *as*, and Rab, he was great," &c. The Teraphim are thought to have been of somewhat similar forms. (Judg. xvii. 3, &c.) As also the images stolen from Laban by Rachel, and the Penates of the ancients, images having *faces*, as the Hebrew, *peni*, faces.

---

[1] Gen. xxiii. 12.

NAMES OF THE STONES

ON THE FOUNDATIONS OF THE HOLY CITY,

IN THE ORDER IN WHICH THEY ARE GIVEN IN Rev. xxi. 19, 20,

REFERRED TO THE HEBREW ROOTS.

		Texts where the word or its root is used in this sense in the Hebrew Bible.	*Hebrew roots.*
VIRGO,	Jasper, *He shall bruise and be bruised.*	Gen. 3. 15.	שפה ¹
LIBRA,	Sapphire, *number.*	Deut. 32. 8.	שפיר
SCORPIO,	Chalcedony, *the affliction, poor,* חלך, Ps. x. 8. *of the Lord.*	Ps. 110. 1.	אדן
SAGITTARIUS,	Emerald (Smaragdos), *He that keepeth,* שטר, Ps. cxxi. *his people.* *troop*	Amos 9. 6.	נדר
CAPRICORNUS,	Sardonyx, *the Prince,* Isa. ix. 6., *the Lord,* דן, { Ps. cx. 1. } *smitten*	Isa. 9. 6. / Isa. 53. 4.	שר / נכה
AQUARIUS,	Sardius, *the Prince,* as above, *who goes forth.* *passed*	Job 28. 8.	ערה
PISCES,	Chrysolite, *binding as a chain,* חרץ, Cant. i. 10., *raising up.* *went up*	Gen. 2. 6.	עלה
ARIES,	Beryl, *the son,* בר, Ps. ii. 12. *ascended*	Ps. 68. 18.	עלה
TAURUS,	Topaz, *breaking, dashing in pieces.*	Ps. 2. 9.	נפץ
GEMINI,	Chrysoprasus, as *who breaks,* חרץ, *bruised.* *gold dust* *breaking forth*	Zech. 9. 3. / 2 Sam. 5. 20.	הרץ / פרץ
CANCER,	Jacinth, *He shall possess,* *possessor*	Gen. 14. 19.	קנה
LEO,	Amethyst, *destroying, beat down.* *destroy*	Ps. 52. 5.	נתץ

Christ is often figured as a stone [2], a precious stone; also as the foundation [3]. In the names of these divinely-selected stones of the foundations [4] of the Holy City, if there are meanings expressing the same prophecies which suggested to the first astronomers the names of the twelve signs, shall we not here recognize the plan which gave the same colours to the rainbow of the sky and to the diamond of the mine, and adopted them equally as symbolizing Divine truth? The same graceful form belongs to the bell-polypus of the solar microscope and to the forest-canopying convolvolus of the South American wilderness. The gigantic fossil fern and the animalcule invisible to the human eye, the desert flower and the deep-sea shell, have harmony of form and beauty of colouring analogous with each other; and may we not expect the types and figures chosen by Divine direction, and revealing Divine purposes, to have similar harmony in diversity, similar marks of unity of design in variety of execution? In recognizing these correspondencies and following them out, shall we not find edification in developing the latent perfection, the manifold wisdom of the written Word [5]?

---

[1] Parkhurst gives a root in this form. Buxtorf gives שיף, *to bruise.* The Arabic sense is to bruise, as by biting. (See Lee's Lexicon.)

[2] Gen. xlix. 24; Isa. viii. 14; xxviii. 16; 1 Pet. ii. 4. 6. 8; Ps. cxviii. 22; Matt. xxi. 44.

[3] 1 Cor. iii. 11; Isa. xxviii. 16.

[4] Isa. liv. 11.

[5] These stones are "applicable to Jesus Christ, the one and only foundation." (Gill.) So says Matthew Henry; but neither of these commentators say in what manner. "The Jews speak of the tabernacle above being built on twelve precious stones." (Gill, from Zohar.) It will be remembered how the gold of Australia is found by breaking, crushing, *bruising,* and that in the Levitical Law *gold* is the frequent type of Christ or his attributes, as in Exod. xxv. 11, &c.

ON THE SIGN CAPRICORN.

THE figure of the Fish-goat and names appropriate to it are found in all ancient zodiacs. Indian, Egyptian, Assyrian remains all agree in so representing it. Idle fables of old, and still idler explanations in modern times, have confused but not obliterated this wonderful record of ancient prophecy. The kid of sacrifice is here united with the fish, the emblem of the Church. The fish, with its abundance of spawn, typifying the multitude of believers, inhabiting the waters, which typify time, swiftly coming, never staying, swiftly going by, is a most expressive emblem of "the great congregation." It has been erroneously applied to the Lord of that congregation, because the Greek word, Ιχθυς, a fish, contains the initial letters of words applicable to Christ: but that Greek word is derived from the Hebrew חיות, living things, used as fishes in Ps. civ. 25. The beasts typifying nations are so called in Daniel, chap. vii., &c. The noun is feminine (or neuter), and no where applied to an individual man.

This emblem has in modern times been supposed to indicate the winter solstice as happening in that sign; but it was not there till long after the fish-goat had been figured in ancient astronomy. What, then, did it signify?—like the other signs, it embodied a prophecy of Him whom the kid of sacrifice, from the fall of man downwards, had typified, and here shown as united to the Church, His body[1], whose nature He should take into union with Himself. It also indicated the time when He should assume it: when the solstice took place among those stars He should be born on earth. Born at the winter solstice, from that hour the days began to lengthen; light began to prevail over darkness when He, the true Light, came to enlighten the world.

Much confusion has prevailed on the subject of the day of our Lord's birth, particularly in the Eastern Church, which long continued to use the imperfect and bewildering Greek methods of computing time. But it was not so in the Western, where the calendar had been rectified by Julius Cæsar, and the winter solstice shown to happen on the 25th of December. It has now receded to the 21st, the shortest day at this time[2].

This sign is then to us a monument of prophecy fulfilled, of which the Western never had any doubt, but obscured by the uncertainties and miscalculations of the Eastern Churches.

Commenting on Psalm cxxxiii., St. Augustine says, "The dispensation of man became less and less, which was signified in John; the dispensation of God in our Lord Jesus Christ increased. And this is shown even by their birthdays; for, as the Church hath delivered down, John was born when the days begin to diminish" (June 24th, the summer solstice), "but the Lord was born when now the days begin to increase" (December 25th, he says). This date he frequently refers to as undoubted.

St. Augustine was fifty-seven years old, when the archives of Rome were destroyed by the Gothic invasion, previous to which he seems to have inspected them.

The doubt and ignorance of the Eastern Church on the true day of the birth of Christ is shown by the title of a homily of St. Chrysostom, preached in Antioch on the 5th of December, in the year of the common era 386. It is this: "Homily for the

---

[1] 1 Cor. x. 17.
[2] In China, an observation of the solstice when in Aquarius, is still preserved.

K

Birthday of our Saviour Jesus Christ, which was unknown until a few years since, when some persons coming from the West made it known, and publicly announced it." The Roman archives were still extant and might be consulted, and to them St. Chrysostom appeals ; and in them the very day of Christ's birth was shown by the register.

NOTE I. (ON LUKE II.)

The Chronological Introduction to the History of the Church, by Dr. Samuel Farmer Jarvis, Historiographer to the Episcopal Church of the United States, is here referred to, in which work it is shown that the birth of Christ took place December 25th, Julian period 4707, on the 5th day of the 9th month, A.U.C. 747, and in the year in which Augustus closed the temple of Janus for the third time.

"There went out a decree from Cæsar Augustus that all the Roman world should be written up, enrolled, as in the census of modern days; but it appears that the census of Syria was not sent up to Rome till Cyrenius was governor of Syria. It would then be entered into the Augustan register, which, though now lost, was undoubtedly seen by Justin, by Tertullian, by St. Augustine, who refer to it, as does Chrysostom, as extant in their time, and easily inspected. When Augustine was fifty-seven years of age, the city of Rome was sacked by the Goths under Alaric, after which this record was lost. In it was the name of Mary, and of the birth of Christ at Bethlehem, and it should seem as born on the 25th of December, as that day was always at Rome commemorated as the day of our Lord's birth; it was then more precisely the winter solstice than now, owing to the precession of the Equinoxes. At first, the Eastern Churches, whose method of reckoning time differed, and who had no such record as the Augustan register, were uncertain in their commemorations of it, but gradually conformed to Roman authority."

NOTE II.

The early Eastern Church, which was in doubt about the time of our Lord's birth, had no means of ascertaining the date with precision. Clemens Alexandrinus mentions with great contempt the errors of those who placed it in April or May. (A.D. 194.)

Justin Martyr, in the year 150, referred the whole Roman Senate to the census made at Bethlehem, as a sure proof of the date of Christ's birth, "which," he says, "ye can learn from the enrolments completed under Cyrenius, your first procurator in Judæa." Justin was at Rome; he could himself consult the archives, and must have done so, or he would not have so referred to them. Eastern Christians could have no such opportunity, but it was easy for any Christian of the Western Church to consult the archives; these were preserved in the Palatine and Ulpian Libraries, and the house of Tiberius, all of which in the fourth century were collected in the baths of Diocletian. They were destroyed when the city was sacked by the Goths under Alaric. During the period of their existence we have the testimony of Christian writers who appeal to them.

First, Tertullian, who against Marcion writes, "concerning the census or enrolment of Augustus, which the Roman archives preserve, as a faithful witness of the Lord's nativity." To the same archives he appeals for the narrative of our Lord's crucifixion sent by Pilate to Tiberius. Again he says, that being reckoned of the root of Jesse, He was therefore enregistered, privily, by Mary, for He was of the country of Bethlehem, and of the house of David, as among the Romans she is described in the census, "Mary, from whom Christ is born." Tertullian held that the 25th of December, then the winter solstice, was the day of our Lord's birth.

St. Ambrose argues that the census was designed by Infinite Wisdom as a solemn and indubitable record of the great event, the birth of Christ at Bethlehem, so fulfilling prophecy. St. Augustine has left thirteen sermons on the festival of the Nativity, in every one of which he calls it, as then observed on the 25th of December, our Lord's birthday; in one of them he says that our Lord Jesus Christ not only chose the virgin from whom He should be born, but also the day on which He should be born, the winter solstice.

He also asserts that Christ was conceived and suffered in the same month, as is shown by the day of His nativity, which is perfectly well known to the Churches, "being," he says, "the 25th of December[1]."

NOTE ON "CENSUS."

In the Commentary of St. Ambrose on the Gospel of St. Luke, the aim is to show that Augustus acted only as an agent of the Almighty ; that the birth of Christ at Bethlehem was the

---

[1] Dr. Jarvis, Chron. Introd. to the History of the Church, on the true dates of the birth and death of our Lord.

important object to be accomplished, and that the Census itself was designed by Infinite Wisdom as a solemn and indubitable record of that great event.

Epiphanius speaks of "the cavern" at Bethlehem as the spot where it occurred.

Though the Eastern Church was uncertain as to the day of our Lord's birth, not so the Western Church. There the facility of examining the Roman record of the enrolment spoken of by St. Luke, ch. iii., seems to have held that Church to the 25th of December, which at the time of His birth was the winter solstice. When this testimony was brought before the Eastern Church, the Western date was quietly and universally adopted. It was generally observed throughout the Christian world before the council of Ephesus (A.D. 431), and since then by all parties, all churches.

Those of the Eastern Church who at first observed it on the 6th of January are thought to have done so as the *Epiphany*.

The Eastern Church having no such records to appeal to, as those kept at Rome, appealed to and consulted by the writers of the Western Church, fell into confusion as to dates.

Bianchini, 1716, has observed that the table of dates of Hippolytus A.D. 220, (found 1551,) fails from not noticing the precession of the equinoxes.

St. Augustine in his first sermon on the Nativity of John the Baptist, after observing that the Church keeps but two birthdays, those of St. John and of Christ, says that John was born on the day of the summer solstice, "on the 8th day before the calends of July, and from this day the days are diminished, but Christ was born on the 8th day before the calends of January, and from that day the days increase." In his comment on the 133rd Psalm, he repeats these assertions, saying, "as the Church hath delivered down," and adds, "hear John himself confessing, 'He must increase, but I must decrease [1].'"

Pope Telesphorus, A.D. 127, at the suggestion of St. Cyril of Jerusalem, caused a scrutiny to be made as to the birth of Christ, and the 25th of December was fixed upon.

NOTE ON THE SIGN CAPRICORN.

At the winter solstice in this sign, figuring the fore part of the kid of sacrifice joined to the body of a fish, He who was to come, was symbolized in the figure attributed to the constellation, united to Himself by His human birth, in His body, the Church. Then the day, and it might be the very hour of the winter solstice saw the arising of the promised Sun of rightcousness, even as the sun of this world then began to ascend in his course through the signs emblematizing the manifestations of his great prototype.

While all the positive evidence that can be collected is for this day being indeed the day of the birth of Christ, only guesses and conjectures, chiefly occasioned by the gradual recession of the equinoxes, are against it. How fine an emblem, how beautiful an analogy would they destroy, and for what? but that so many commentators and chronologists love darkness better than light!

The increasing light and warmth, the returning life attending the sun's arising from the winter solstice, ought every returning year to make us feel what with our lips we acknowledge, 'Unto us a child is born, a Saviour, which is Christ the Lord.''

On the midnight of this day not only did the constellation Virgo with the branch, the seed, arise, but it was followed by the Northern Crown [2], the only constellation really resembling what it is called, passing vertically over Bethlehem.

NOTE ON SOLSTICE.

In the early ages of astronomy the winter solstice did not take place in Capricorn, but when the solstice reached that sign He whom it typified was to be born. The Spirit of prophecy alone could declare this; but whether He had made it known to those holy men to whom tradition attributes the invention of the signs is not declared in Scripture. In the ancient emblem, the Kid or Lamb of sacrifice is united to the body of the fish, the type of the Church. When the sun, at the winter solstice in those stars, reached the point from whence he should begin to arise and commence a new and still brightening course, cheering and enlightening the world, then the promised Sun of righteousness began to rise on the earth. Ancient authorities having said the incarnate Word was born on the day of the winter solstice, then called the 25th of December, on that day the Christian Church has long kept it. Though the solstice has now receded to the 21st, perhaps on the 25th the day first perceptibly increases; therefore the memorial is still applicable.

---

[1] Dr. Jarvis, p. 538, where it is also said, " In Tertullian's book against Marcion, he uses these words : 'Finally, concerning the census (or enrolment) of Augustus, which the Roman archives preserve as a faithful witness of our Lord's nativity.' Again he says, Christ 'was euregistered, namely by Mary (for He was of the country of Bethlehem, and of the house of David), as among the Romans she is described in the census, Mary from whom Christ is born.'"

[2] It is asserted by ancient writers that Nimrod caused a diadem to be made for himself in imitation of it.

ON THE SIGN ARIES.

FROM all antiquity this sign has been figured as the sacrificial Lamb or Ram, and names meaning wounded and slain have been annexed to its principal stars [1]. So it has been figured, and so named, by nations who never heard of the Jewish Passover, and long before that observance was ordained.

The Jewish, and apparently the patriarchal calendar, was kept regular by ocular demonstration of the new moons, and by reckoning twelve months to one year, and thirteen to the next. The twelfth moon was called Abib, supposed to be from the swelling of the grains of young corn; the thirteenth, Nishan, or second, reduplicated year or month. The first record of the reckoning by months is that of Noah, by number [2]. By the time of Moses, the name Abib seems to have been in use; it is used by Moses, Exod. xiii. 4, as well known to those he addressed. The spring equinox had at that time receded into the sign Aries, but no allusion to it is made in the institution of the Passover; by the time of the coming of Him whom the Passover typified, it had receded to the spot where are still to be found the star named El Nath or Natik, the pierced, wounded, or slain, and the mansion of the moon, Al Sheratan, the bruised, wounded. The emblem and the names existing before what they indicate took place were prophetic, and are among the many proofs from prophecy that God is, and hath spoken. He commanded Moses so to fix the ordinance of the Passover, that during the darkness at the crucifixion, the star so named would be seen close to the sun and the whole of the constellation Aries [3], He who cometh, would appear around it. Man could not arrange this coincidence, man could not predict it, but God by Moses prefigured it; the lamb was yearly slain for 1500 years, when the sun was among those stars, but the equinox had not yet receded thither; seasons, months, and years may vary, but the solstice and the equinox never; different stars are behind the sun at those moments in the lapse of centuries, but man cannot mistake the day when the shadows no longer lengthen, but begin to contract, nor that when day and night are equal. These universally perceptible and unalterable anniversaries, by divine appointment marked, foreshowed the two great events in the history of man, the birth and death of the Messiah.

The day appointed for His death had been the day when His incarnation was announced to the blessed Virgin. So the Western Church held for 400 years without hesitation, for during nearly that time the Roman records were preserved, and were open to that investigation which it is evident the early Latin Church, and by their own account

---

[1] In the ancient Egyptian circular zodiac of Dendera the sign is figured as the Lamb, being without the horns of the Ram.
[2] Gen. vii.   [3] Part II. p. 9.

Augustine and Tertullian had made in them. The Greek Church had no such facilities of examining the authentic records, and the Greek computation of time was all confusion till the Julian Calendar had been adopted; still the true date of the crucifixion was less disguised by the Greeks than that of the nativity, but the wish, almost the necessity, of so keeping Easter as to make the day of crucifixion Friday, and of the resurrection Sunday, caused differences of opinion that led to persecution and bloodshed.

It should seem that He who seeth the end from the beginning had ruled to the purposes of prophecy the placing of these emblems in the zodiac. The symbols themselves, and their ancient names, may be referred to mere human wisdom in their adaptations to the predictions they were intended to record, but the correspondence between their purport and the place of the sun in them when the events so typified should occur must be the work of the Spirit of prophecy, whether consciously or unconsciously guiding those who so arranged them. The sun was in Aries, where the Lamb of sacrifice was typified in the stars at the vernal equinox, when the Lamb of the Passover was killed for every family of Israel, and the Lamb of God hung on the cross, shedding the blood that speaketh better things than that of Abel. The witness in heaven of the Lamb of the Zodiac, corroborated, perpetuated in the intervening time by the corresponding types of the Mosaic law, yet stands in proof that God had spoken. To Him alone belongs the knowledge of the times and seasons of fulfilment, even when prophecy is most gloriously explicit. He only could so direct the observance of the passover at the moment when the event it typified should take place. He only could have ruled the purpose of the inventors of astronomy, to place the emblematic sign where the sun should be when the event typified should arrive.

By divine command to Moses, the first ordinance of the Levitical law, the slaying of the Paschal Lamb, was to be when the sun was in Aries, in the figure of the Lamb, or young ram, in the time of Moses being in the month called Abib, when the firstfruits, the earliest ears of corn, were gathered; then the new moon, so called, was beginning to take place among the stars of Aries; fifteen hundred years afterwards, the sun's place was in the head of Aries at the full moon of that month. On the morning of the resurrection of our Lord, the firstfruits of earth's harvest were offered in the temple; and the bright star in Virgo [1] called Spica, and Subilon the ear of corn, had shone on that solemn hour when the seed of the woman arose, the firstfruits from the dead. The star in Coma, then bright, though now long lost to view, which has been thought the star of the Magi [2], also shone on that accomplishment of prophecy; the moon, full among the stars of Libra, the sign typifying the now completed redemption, might dim, but not eclipse its radiance.

Wherever the zodiac is found, it always begins with Aries, even among those nations who have commenced their year at other parts of its circle, as the Chinese in 15° Aquarius, the Jews, their civil year in 1° Virgo. The lunar zodiac also invariably began in Aries. At the time when the Chinese made use of both these zodiacs, no natural epoch, neither solstice nor equinox, occurred in Aries; none such took place there when Moses appointed the sacred year of the Hebrews to begin with the new moon of the month Abib. 1490 years afterwards the spring equinox had receded from Taurus to the head of Aries, the sun was at or near the stars called El Nath and Natik, the wounded, the slain; the moon in the lunar mansion Al Sheratan, the bruised, the wounded, names transmitted by the Arabs, unconscious or careless of their meaning. Then the

---

[1] Page 16, Second Part. [2] Page 104, Second Part.

Lamb of God was slain, and the sun was darkened at noonday, where the Lamb of the signs had so long prefigured the awful sacrifice.

The sun's place at the time of the crucifixion was undoubtedly in the head of Aries at any part of the time by which chronology varies. Whether exactly over, or only near the stars called Al Sheratan, El Nath, and Natik, they would be hid by his rays. The *sign* was adapted to the senses of mankind, rather than to the calculations of mathematicians.

We are not told in Scripture that it was by divine direction the inventors so placed that sign, but tradition names among them the prophet Enoch, by whose prevision a coincidence might be prepared, which no unassisted human intellect could have anticipated. If Abel's sacrifice gave the type, the position of the sign gave the time of its fulfilment; only the Spirit of prophecy which foretold by Enoch the coming of the Lord to execute judgment could so have indicated it.

NOTES.

Tertullian, addressing the Roman rulers, says, " you have in your archives the relation of that phenomenon," the darkness at the crucifixion. Also that Pilate had announced "all these things concerning Christ to Tiberius Cæsar [1]." He says elsewhere, reasoning with the Jews concerning the seventy weeks of Daniel, that the Messiah had been cut off as had been foretold under Tiberius Cæsar, Rubellius Geminus and Fufius Geminus being consuls, in the month of March, in the season of the Passover, on the eighth day before the calends of April (March 25), on the first day of unleavened bread, in which it had been commanded they should kill the Lamb.

Lactantius, writing about 312, confirms this testimony, saying that Christ was crucified " in the fifteenth year of Tiberius, the two Gemini being consuls."

St. Augustine asserts that it was most certainly known that the annunciation and the crucifixion both took place on the 25th of March, also that He was born on the 25th of December, in the thirty-third year of the reign of Herod. Sabinus and Rufinus being consuls. He also says, that from the giving of the Holy Spirit at Pentecost to the ides of May in the consulship of Honorius and Eutydianus 365 years are found, by the enumeration of the consuls, to have been completed.

The list of consuls as corrected by Victorinus, a great mathematician, who was at Rome A.D. 455, gives the Gemini as the consuls under whom our Lord was crucified.

Dr. Jarvis gives these dates. In March, year of Rome, 747, Augustus shuts the temple of Janus. Birth of Christ, 747. Universal peace. Baptism, January 6, year of Rome, 777. Crucifixion, March 26, 780. Ascension, May 6, 780. Aged 33 and 3 months. Crucified on the anniversary of the Annunciation.

NOTE ON THE PASSOVER.

"If it was said by the Gentile authorities that our Lord ate the Passover on *Thursday* evening, the Jews would say it was *Friday* evening. Evening came before morning." But it was the *true* time, astronomically.

When Victorinus and others say the passion of our Lord commenced on the Thursday evening, they mean by His agony in the garden, when His sufferings began, and when the Jewish nation's day of preparation began with its evening. But it was the *true* Passover day, beginning with the evening.

The Greek Church held in opposition to the Latin, that the Passover was kept two days together in the year of our Lord's crucifixion. Many learned men have held the same opinion[2]. It is thus explained: Maimonides says the feasts of the Jews were sanctified not by a calendar, but by the heavens. In the Talmud of Babylon, and by Maimonides it is recorded that " the senate, on the 30th day of the month, sat in the outer court of the temple; if no approved witnesses came to say that they had seen the new moon, the next day was called the 31st of the preceding month, and the feast appointed accordingly. If afterwards credible witnesses reported having seen the new moon on the 30th, the senate was bound to alter the appointment.

---

[1] Phlegon on the Olympiads records the darkness, saying, "stars were seen in the heavens."

[2] Munster, Scaliger, Casaubon, &c. In this case the Eastern Church on this point may be the best authority from the local traditions.

This they did not always do, and the nation[1] sometimes differed as to the time of keeping the passover." Of course the new moon having been seen, the first day was astronomically correct; on that day, beginning with the evening [2], our Lord ate the passover with His disciples. In its morning, He, the true Lamb of God, was nailed to the cross at the exact time when the lamb of the daily offering was slain in the temple, on the passover day. The lamb of the evening sacrifice was slain when the sun began to decline; then the noon-day darkness fell on the nation who were slaying the lamb of the passover, while the true Lamb of God was dying on the cross. At the ninth hour, when the evening sacrifice was wholly consumed, incense was burnt on the golden altar; then our Lord resigned His Spirit, His sacrifice was completed, and the vale of the temple, before which the priest was officiating, was rent in twain.

The difficulty here removed, the Jews and other objectors often bring forward in argument.

NOTE ON THE NAMES IN THE SIGN ARIES.

The Greek word, *ars*, a lamb, though not used for this sign, yet by the roots to which it may be referred, meaning coming quickly, connects the Latin Aries with the Semitic Taleh and Amroo by the similar sense of coming forth. The Egyptian name in this sign, Ammon, signifies true, faithful, the appointed, the established, the steadfast, as is shown by the Noetic or Hebrew root אמ. The hieroglyphic name for the first decan is *set, appointed*. The truthfulness of the lamb does not characterize the ram. The ancient oriental names are all the lamb, and the figure in the Dendera zodiac having no horns is also the lamb, but the Egyptian idol called Ammon had horns, which are found on medals of Alexander, as claiming a divine origin from Jupiter Ammon. The Greeks and Romans also fell into this corruption of the original emblem, giving the horns and the name of the ram to the lamb of ancient astronomy.

Ars and Aries from the root *ar*, mean to come, or flowing forth as light or water; *kir* in *krios*, to come as in a circle. The termination *es, os*, or *us*, might be from the Semitic or Noetic root חש, to *hasten*, come quickly.—Isa. viii. 3.

In words apparently synonymous it has often been shown that there are shades of meaning. In Taleh the shade of meaning is *coming forth from above* as the dew; in Amroo and the Chaldee Emmer, it is *coming forth as a branch;* Amin, a branch, being especially a palm-branch, the well-known emblem of Him who was to come, recognized as such, when strewed before Him at His entry into Jerusalem. Amnos, another name of a lamb not found in the sign, meaning truthful, is the Lamb of the Gospel; while Arnion, who cometh, is the Lamb of the Apocalpse.

It is to be remarked that the Syriac name of the sign, Amroo, is the word used in the Syriac Gospel of St. John [3], being from the root Amar, to spring forth as a branch, a *palm*-branch.

Tametouris Ammon, the Coptic, supposed to be the ancient Egyptian, is translated by Montucla, the reign of Ammon; the S in the root Shur, dominion, being changed to T, as in Taurus, &c. Ammon, as is well known, was the Egyptian ram or lamb[4].

The English name lamb, contains a Noetic root lam, meaning mild, gentle. Ram is the root we find in Abram, high or great, whence were named Romulus and Rome.

Mesartim, the binding, the place of binding, or of those that are bound, refers to the fishes of Pisces, whose band is continued to and held by the forefoot of Aries, and Cetus the sea-monster, the band round whose neck is also so held.

El Nath is used by Chaucer as the name of a spring star.

El Natik, the pierced or slain, applies equally to the lamb of Abel's sacrifice and the Lamb of God, whom it prefigured.

Deltoton, the Triangle, was said by the ancient Greeks to contain the name of the deity, and to be a most divine emblem.

Albumazer records that the first Decan of Aries in the ancient Persian and Indian spheres, was a throned woman called the daughter of splendour, evidently Cassiopeia.

Shedar, who sets free, is in Arabic peculiarly applied to a woman setting free her hair; such appears to be the action of the figure of Cassiopeia.

Dupuis says, "the Persians called the sign Aries the Lamb; when the sun entered Aries they had a feast called Neurouz, a few days before they had the Feast of the Cross [5]."

NOTE ON THE DATE OF THE ANNUNCIATION.

The great French astronomers of the eighteenth century wrote thus;—" Le jour suivant la conjouction moyenne de la lune au soleil, année de la naissance de Jésus Christ, 25 Mars, qui

---

[1] Maimonides and the Gemara.   [2] Gen. i.
[3] John i.   [4] Page 9, Second Part.
[5] Probably the constellation of the Southern Cross, visible at that time, in that latitude.

selon l'ancienne tradition de l'Eglise, rapporté par St. Augustine, fut le jour même de l'incarnation de Jésus Christ, fut aussi le jour de la première phase de la lune, et par conséquent il fut le 1 jour du mois selon l'usage des Hébreux, et le premier jour de l'année sacrée qui par l'institution divine devoit commencer par le premier mois du printems, et le 1 jour d'une grande année dont l'epoque naturelle est le concours de l'équinoxe moyen et de la conjonction moyenne de la lune avec le soleil. Ce concours termina donc les periodes luni-solaires des siècles précédens et fut une époque d'où commença un nouvel ordre des siècles."—La Loubère.

NOTE FROM DR. CUDWORTH'S "TRUE NOTION OF THE LORD'S SUPPER."

"The Greek Church held in opposition to the Latins that the passover was kept the year of our Saviour's death on two days together. Many learned men, as Munster, Scaliger, Casaubon, &c., have since closed with the Greeks. How might this legally be done? and the true answer must be derived from the manner of determining the beginning of their months in use at that time, which was according to the phasis of the moon, for they had then no calendar as a rule to sanctify their feasts, but they were sanctified by the heavens, as the Misnah speaks. This is clearly stated by Maimon (Kiddush Hacchodesh), who having spoken of the rules of observing the phasis adds that these were never made use of since the Sanhedrim ceased in Israel after the destruction of the temple. Since that time they have used a calendar calculated according to the middle motion of the moon, except the Karaites, whom they abhor for giving it up. The manner of reckoning by the phasis is thus described in the Talmud of Babylon (500 A.D.), in Rosh Hashanah, and by Maimon in Kiddosh Hachad. In the great or outer court of the temple, there was a house called Beth-juzek, where the senate sat all the 30th day of the month to receive the witnesses of the moon's appearance; if there came approved witnesses on the 30th day, then the chief men of the senate stood up and pronounced, Mokaddosh, it is sanctified, whereupon notice was given to all the country. But if when the consistory had sat all the 30th day there came no approved witnesses, then they made an intercalation of one day in the former month, and decreed the following 31st day to be the calends, and yet notwithstanding if afterwards witnesses credibly testified having seen the phasis in due time, the senate was bound to alter the beginning of the month and reckon it a day sooner, from the 30th: here we see how the difference of a day might arise about the calends of a month, on which the feasts depended. Now it was a custom among the Jews, in such doubtful cases, to permit the feasts to be solemnized, or passovers killed, on two several days together. Maimon affirms, that in the remoter parts of the land of Israel, they kept the feast of the new moon two days together, nay in Jerusalem itself, they kept the new moon of Tisri, which was the beginning of the year, twice, lest they should be mistaken in it; and in the Talmud (Gemarah Rosh Hashanah, c. i.) we have an instance of the passovers being kept two days together, because the new moon was doubtful, nay, the Rabbinical Jews themselves still keep the passover two days together *iisdem ceremoniis*, as the learned author of the Jewish Synagogue reports, and Scaliger also, not only of that, but also of the other feasts; ' Judæi post institutionem hodierni computi eandem solemnitatem celebrant biduo, propterea quod mensam incipiant à medio motu lunæ. Itaque propter dubium conjunctionis luminarium, Pascha celebrant 15 et 16 Nisam, Pentecosten 6 et 7 Sivan, scenopegia 15 et 16 Tisri, idque vocant festum secundum exsiliorum.'

"Thus our Saviour might eat the passover, and yet Himself be offered up at the very time when the Paschal lambs were sacrificed at the temple; the third hour, nine in the morning, the time of offering the lamb of the daily offering. He was nailed to the cross; at the sixth there was darkness until the ninth; on the passover day they anticipated the killing the evening sacrifice, which on other days was done at half-past two, and offered at half-past three, but now on account of the number of Paschal lambs to be slain, was done as soon as the sun began to decline, because the blood of the daily sacrifice must be sprinkled before that of the Paschal. The darkness therefore when the blood of the evening sacrifice and Paschal lambs was offering may be considered as a token that they were now rejected. At the ninth hour, when the incense was to be burnt on the golden altar, which was done when the sacrifice was wholly consumed, Jesus expired, and the vale of the temple was rent, before which stood the golden altar where the priest was officiating. The following sabbath St. John calls a *high day*; the same word is used by the Septuagint, Isa. i. 13, for the calling of assemblies, namely, on the first and last days of the solemn feasts, which plainly points out this sabbath as being the first day of unleavened bread, and consequently that the passover had been eaten on the preceding night. The next day when our Lord rose from the grave was the second day of unleavened bread, sixteenth Nisam, on which the wave sheaf [1], the first-fruits of the harvest, was to be presented before God. On the morrow of the seventh sabbath, Pentecost, the wave loaves were offered. Exod. xxiii. 16, ' firstfruits of thy labours.'

"The Jews have often with this difficulty perplexed the Christian opponent."—Christian Observer, 1803.

---

[1] Applied to the Resurrection by Kennedy, Astr. Chro., alluded to by St. Paul.

MAZZAROTH

PART III

MAZZAROTH;

OR,

THE CONSTELLATIONS.

"Canst thou bring forth Mazzaroth in his season?"—Job xxxviii. 32.

THIRD PART.

Days of the Planetary Week,

AS NAMED AFTER THE SUN, MOON, AND FIVE PLANETS.

Roman Names.	English and Anglo-Saxon Names.	German and Scandinavian Names.	Scandinavian Names of Planets or Deities.		Texts where the word or its root is used in this sense in the Hebrew Bible.	Hebrew or Noetic roots.
s Solis,	Sunday.	Sonntag.	Sonne, Arab. sense, *shining.*			שׂי
Day of the Sun.	Sunnen-dæg.			*scarlet*	Josh. 2. 18.	
s Lunæ,	Monday.	Montag.	Mone*, and Monath, *companion,*			אח
Day of the Moon.	Monan-dæg.		moon, &c.	*brother*	Job 30. 29.	
s Martis,	Tuesday.	Dienstag.	{ Tyr, *who tears.*	*wounds*	Num. 6. 5.	חער
Day of Mars.	Tiwes-dæg.	Tyersdag, Icelandic.	{ Tuisco, *who delivers, saves.*		2 Kgs.19.19.	ישׁח
s Mercurii,	Wednesday.	Mittwoche.	Woden, { *coming,*	*passed*	Job 28. 8.	עדה
Day of Mercury.	Wodnes-dæg	Wodens- or Odinstag.	or Odin { *or ruling.*	*Lord*	Ps. 110. 1.	דון
s Jovis,	Thursday.	Donnerstag.	Thor, { *giving light.*	*light*	Gen. 1 3.	אור
Day of Jupiter.	Thowres-dæg	Thorsdag.	{ *who bruises.*	*wounds*	Num. 6. 5.	חער
s Veneris,	Friday.	Freitag.	Freiya, *fertile, bearing fruit.*		Gen. 8. 17.	פרה
Day of Venus.	Frig-dæg.	Freyasdag.		*fruitful*		
s Saturni,	Saturday.	Sonnabend.	Sater, *hiding, sheltering.*	*hide*	Ps. 17. 8.	סתר
Day of Saturn.	Sætur-dæg.					

* In deriving Moon from אם, מ servile must be prefixed, and ן postfixed, as frequently occurring, and exemplified in the English word *mine*, where the pronoun I takes both these additions, as also in the Greek μηνη.

It appears from the most ancient records, that among all nations the period of seven days was used from time immemorial. It is traced in the account given of the Deluge in the book of Genesis[1], and in the scarcely less ancient book of Job[2]. By the Hebrews, Arabs, and Persians the seven days were distinguished, as in the history of the creation, by numbers, as day one, &c., —a form considered to be of the highest antiquity. It may be seen in the Syriac calendar[3], as used by the ancient Hebrews, the Syrians, Arabians, Persians, and Ethiopians: "one from the Sabbath, two from the Sabbath, &c., till the sixth, eve of the Sabbath; and the seventh the Sabbath, the *rest*." The Assyrians, Babylonians, Egyptians, Chinese, and the nations of India, were acquainted with the seven-days' division of time, as were the Druids. It has been traced in the interior of Africa, and among the American nations of the west. The word week[4], חן, a returning period, first occurs in Gen. xxix. 27: that it there meant the seven-days' week may be seen by a reference to Judges xiv. 12.

There is nothing in nature to account for this division of time by sevens. Those writers who refer it to the moon's motion round the earth seem never to have observed that the new moon always falls about one day later in the week in each lunation: there being twenty-nine days

---

[1] Gen. viii. 10, 11.   [2] Job i. 6, and ii. 1, where the Hebrew is *the* day.
[3] Bp. Marsh, Michaelis.
[4] Week, Woche, German, &c., from חן, an ordinance, Exod. xii. 14. 17, and Day, Dæg, Dæg, Dies, from ידי, which appears and makes appear, makes known. Exod. xviii. 16.

and a half between each new moon, it can never happen on that day four weeks, without which no such division could have been devised.

The first man on the first day of his existence would see the sun, traditionally said to have been in Leo at his creation. He was divinely directed to give names to visible things, and he would name this most glorious object, probably calling it Chres (Hhres), the warm ; for after its setting on his first evening the night would be cool, its return in the morning would bring warmth, and that name seems the most widely diffused among his posterity. Perhaps on that first morning's dawn, wholly engrossed in anticipating the return of the sun, he would not observe the moon, near its change, and lost in his increasing splendour, until the second day, when he might see it in Cancer, pale in the golden glow, and call it Lebana, the white.

It might not be long before he observed the movements of the planets among the fixed stars. If man was created when the sun was quitting Leo for Virgo, Mars if in Aries would be very bright, and its motion soonest perceptible, the first luminary discovered to be a planet. If Mercury were in Virgo, it would be perceptible for a while in the evening twilight, and then disappearing prove itself a planet. Jupiter in Sagittarius would be splendid in the midnight sky ; Venus in Libra, towards the morning ; and Saturn (Sabbatei, the star of rest), perhaps first observed near Jupiter in the midnight on the Sabbath, distinguished as a planet by its pale orb, its movement as yet imperceptible.

These signs are called in astrological tradition the houses of these planets. If they were first observed in them, a reason may be given for that apportionment, for which none other has ever been alleged. The succession of the planetary names in the week, as found in all ages and climates, may also be accounted for by the planets having been first recognized in that order. If by Adam, as here suggested, and from him made known to Noah, the wide diffusion of the traditional succession may be understood, which is otherwise unintelligible, neither according with magnitude, brightness, nor time of revolution.

In the arrangement of these planets so as to be discovered in this order, there might be fore-shown the course of prophecy : the sun in daily return proclaiming that He who was to come, shall come, shall go, and shall return ; the moon, that even in His absence His light shall illuminate the darkness of the earth ; Mars, by all his equivalent names expressing that He should bruise the enemy, but Himself receive the wounds beheld by the prophet, with which He should be wounded in the house of His friends[5] ; in Mercury, the consoling prospect that He should return with intensified lustre ; in Jupiter, the reign of truth and righteousness ; in Venus, the beauty of His sister-spouse[6] the Church ; in Saturn, the rest that shall remain for the people of God.

The two families, the children of Isaac and of Ishmael, immediate descendants of Abraham, to whom the transmission of astronomy is attributed, never gave these names to the seven days of their week, which they distinguished, according to the primitive pattern (in Gen. i.), by numbers; but among the Egyptians and the people of India this usage is of undefined antiquity. From the Egyptians the Romans are said to have adopted these appellations in the third century of our era, when their conquests had brought them into daily intercourse with the nations who divided their time by weeks, of which original institution the Romans had retained but a very faint tradition. The northern nations among whom we find it use the same names for planets and for deities, nearly resembling in mythological attributes those of the southern nations from whom they had early separated, taking their course through western India towards the North. The traditions and the roots of the language of these Semitic nations may be traced in those of the tribes who inundated Europe from the North, from the time of the shepherd kings in Egypt, till the downfall of the Western Empire. Since these nations have begun to cultivate letters, Olaus Rudbeck, one of their early writers, in his patriotic enthusiasm for the glories of his race, claimed for them the invention of astronomy during their sojourn in the frozen North, adapting the emblems of the zodiac to its climate. One specimen of this adaptation may suffice to show on what unsubstantial foundation it stood. Gemini, he says, was to show that now children may safely bathe in the thawing rivers. It is, however, amply proved that none of the descendants of Noah ever so completely forgot the science of their forefathers as to have the opportunity of re-inventing it. The very savages of Polynesia gave a better account of the two bright stars that mark the heads of the figures of Gemini, when they said that they were twin children, who, ill used on earth, had been translated to heaven. The name they gave these stars, Ainana, remarkably coincides with the Semitic אחים, brethren, and ענה, afflicted.

As, however, the Arabs, through whom we receive the names of the stars, and the Hebrews, through whom we receive the prophecies with which they are shown to correspond, did not annex the names of the sun, moon, and five planets to the days of the week, that annexation might seem to be a contrivance of later days than those of the invention of the celestial emblems, of those days when, as in the time of Job, men had begun to pay undue reverence to the orbs of heaven "walking in their brightness." If, however, this application to the days of the week be

---

5 Zech. xii. 6.   6 Cant. iv. 9, 10.

of later origin and inferior authority, still the arrangement of the names in the order here shown to be accordant with prophecy, may have been part of the lesson of divine truth, intended by the early fathers of mankind for their posterity, to be nightly read in the golden characters of the starry heaven: an arrangement commemorating at once the order of their appearing to the eyes of man, and the development of those promises on which hang the hopes of his future destiny, solving the great enigma of the restoration of a ruined world.

NOTES.

"Assyrians, Arabians, Egyptians, Persians had the week." (Dict. Belles Lettr.)

The Brahmins, Singalese, and Siamese have the week, naming the days from the planets in the usual order, but beginning the week on Friday.

"The division of time into weeks extends from the Christian states of Europe to the remote shores of Hindostan, and has equally prevailed among the Hebrews, the Egyptians, Chinese, and northern barbarians—nations some of whom had little or no intercourse with the others." (Horne's Introduction.)

The division into years, months, and days depended on natural causes; but that into weeks is not so dependent, four weeks not being exactly equal to a lunar revolution; a tradition older than the dispersion of mankind can alone account for it, that tradition being of the seven days or periods of creation.

"This division of time was universally observed among the descendants of Noah."

The ancient Jews reckoned the month from the actual appearance of the moon, and continued so to do till their dispersion.

"The seven-days' cycle was not adopted from any thing in nature."

"Some writers, as Acosta and Humboldt, find its origin in the seven planets as known to the ancients, from the planetary names of the days of the week; but these were not used by the Hebrews."

"The division of time into weeks of seven days was not peculiar to the Jews, but was a universal custom, and much older than the time of Moses." "The planetary names of the days of the week were not so ancient or so universal as the week." (D. M'Donald, Creation and Fall.) He controverts the theory of Ideler, that the week was invented as the fourth of the lunar period, as the week is not the exact fourth, and consequently the new moon takes place on continually varying days of the week. This may be shown by any almanack.

"The ancient Persians, the nations of India, and the old German tribes regarded seven as a sacred number[7]."

Hesiod, Homer, and Callimachus apply the epithet *holy* to the seventh day. Eusebius declares that almost all the philosophers and poets acknowledge the seventh day as *holy*; and Porphyry states that the Phœnicians consecrated one day in seven as holy[8]: but these were *after* Moses.

The Egyptians were acquainted with the seven-days' cycle, so were the Assyrians, the Babylonians, the Chinese, and the nations of India. Traces of the same usage have also been detected by Oldendorf among the tribes of the interior of Africa. It has also been met with among those of America.

Josephus affirms that there was scarcely any Greek or barbarian but in some degree acknowledged or conformed to a seventh-day's cessation from labour. Lucian says it was given to school-boys as a holiday.

Its antiquity and universality show beyond all question that the notion was not borrowed from a Jewish source or Mosaic institutions, but had an origin anterior to both.

A recent writer speaks of "the ancient and almost universal belief that the week of creation was in brief the type of the great week of the world; that is, that the six working days of the creation-week correspond to the six thousand working days of the week; and that as the former ended in the Sabbath day of rest, the latter will culminate in the Sabbath of a six thousand years, —what St. Paul calls σαββατισμός, 'the rest that remaineth for the people of God.' " (School of the prophets, *Times*, Nov. 3, 1859.)

This analogy has been thus further carried out. On the first day, and for the first thousand years, light shone upon the earth. On the second day the waters were divided from the waters, as in the second thousand years the servants of God were divided from those who served Him not, as at Babel, and as Abraham from the Canaanites. On the third day the earth brought forth trees and herbs, as in the third thousand years the world was peopled. On the fourth day the luminaries of heaven shone forth, as in the fourth thousand years, first the revelation by Moses, and then that of Christianity came forth, typified by the sun, as the Church by the moon. On the fifth day a higher and more abundant creation took place on the earth, as in the fifth thousand years the world was more widely inhabited and peopled. On the sixth day a still nobler creation took place, completed in man, as in the sixth thousand years more enlightened

[7] Winer, Bib. R. W.   [8] Cox, Bibl. Ant.

Christianity has prevailed, and, it is hoped, will be succeeded by a purer still, on which the rest of the millennial reign will descend, giving peace to the suffering and troubled earth. This glorious prospect may add hope and happiness even to the blessed institution weekly restoring the mind and body of wearied humanity, where its divine wisdom is duly appreciated.

" The week[9] was not in the calendar of the Greeks, who divided the month into three periods of ten days; and it was not adopted by the Romans until the time of Theodosius, in the latter part of the fourth century of our era. There is properly no word in the Latin classics equivalent to the term week. Hebdomada signified seven of any thing." (Lardner.)

" Pope Sylvester tried to change the planetary names of the days of the week to numerals; but even with his own people he could only succeed in calling the first day Dies Dominica, the Lord's day." (Polydore Virgil.)

Some religious persons have had a great objection to speak of the days of the week by the names in common use. Many do not like to call the Lord's Day Sunday, but to those who have been brought up so to speak, it may be useful to remember that the Sun is the Scripture type or emblem of the manifestation of our Lord Jesus Christ, the true light, as making Himself known to mankind, as it were shining on them. That Oriental name of the Sun, Shemish[10], most used in Hebrew and Arabic for the Sun, means ministering, as the Sun ministers light, and as Christ's abode on earth is often called His ministry, giving light to the souls as the Sun to the bodies of men; but in other Eastern dialects names are used signifying who cometh, another attribute of the Sun peculiarly befitting him as the type of the great theme of prophecy, the Sun of righteousness who should arise with healing on His wings, " He who should come[11]."

In calling the next day Monday, or the Moon's day, we may also remember that the Moon is the Scriptural type of the visible Church of Christ. Every day of the week should be in some sort a day for the Lord, and the remaining five days bear traces in their names of those ancient prophecies of Christ, from which the Gentiles formed many of their idols. The third day some of the Northern nations named after their hero-god, Tuisco, who like Mars[12] was called the god of war, but the Oriental root of his name means, who saves; therefore in using our name of this day, Tuesday, He might be remembered to whom the name best applies, and from a traditional prophecy of whom it originated. Wednesday, called the day of Mercury, said by the Romans to be the son of Jupiter and to have power over the souls of the dead, in many other particulars showing that here too we have a tradition of ancient prophecy concerning Christ, by our Northern ancestors was named, as was their demigod or great hero, Woden or Odin, whose name means Judge or Lord, and is nearly the same word as that used in Psalm cx. of the Messiah; here again let us think of Him, rather than of the heathen hero. Thursday was called by the Northern nations the day of their god Thor, the god of heaven, and of thunder and lightning; one meaning of the name Thor is light, but it also means, who bruises or is bruised, as Christ the Seed of the woman in the original prophecy, concerning which they evidently had some tradition, but it was also by some understood as referring to *light*, whence he was considered as the god of the Sun and of lightning[13]; and was not Christ revealed as the true light? John i.

Friday the Northerns named after a goddess whose Roman name Venus means gracious, or beloved, and whose Greek name Aphrodite, and Northern name Freyga or Freya, means, bearing fruit, fruitful, as a branch, and from the Northern name of Freya we call this day Friday, on which Christ died upon the cross for His people, His Church, whose duty to Him and to each other we may remember in so naming the sixth day of the week.

Saturday was called by the Northern nations the day of their god Sater, a name which means to hide, and it may remind us that on this day our Lord's body was hidden in the grave.

Surely those Christians who use these names should be glad to remember, that however corrupted to the service of idolatry, they had a foundation in the ancient prophecies still to be traced among all the children of Adam[14].

---

[9] The explanation attempted by Dion Cassius is a failure, as is the astrological theory on the subject.

[10] Heb. שֶׁמֶשׁ, also Arab., &c.   [11] Matt. xi. 3. Luke vii. 19, 20.   [12] יָשַׁע.

[13] Of Thor, Verstegen says, " On his head he wore a crown of gold, round about and above the same were set twelve bright burnished stars, and in his right hand he held a kingly sceptre." " He caused lightning and thunder." " Of the weekly day that was dedicated to his service we yet retain the name of Thursday, which the Danes and Swedians do yet call Thor-day. In the Netherlands it is called Dundersdag, that is, Thunder's-day; and in some of our old Saxon books I find it to have been written Thunresdeag." Thus the German Donnerstag is accounted for. The hammer, the well-known attribute of Thor, which breaks, bruises, has been derived from the other possible sense of the name; and both interpretations would be borne out by the prophecy, that He who should give light to the world should be Himself the bruised, and should bruise the head of His enemy.

[14] See Bp. Horsley's Essay on the Prophecies of the Messiah, &c.

MEMORIAL LINES FOR THE PLANETARY WEEK, AS CONNECTED WITH PROPHECY.

Sunday, think of Him who rose,
Who comes again even as He goes;
Monday, think how in His light
His faithful Church is calm and bright;
Tuesday, of His pierced side,
Wounded for His sister-bride;
Wednesday, of His sure return,
Soon may we that day discern;
Thursday, of His truth and love
Shining on us from above;
Friday, of His hour of anguish,
Lest our love of Him should languish;
Saturday, His silent grave,
Dying those He loved to save.

NAMES OF THE DAYS OF THE PLANETARY WEEK OF THE BRAHMINS [1]
AS GIVEN BY LE GENTIL.

			Texts.	Hebrew or Noetic roots.
Friday.	Soucra Varam *,	Venus' day, *morning twilight.*	Cant. 6. 10.	שחר
Saturday.	Sani Varam,	Saturn's day, *repose, sleep.*	Ps. 127. 2.	שני
Sunday.	Aditta Varam,	Sun's day, *who cometh, passeth.*	Job 28. 8.	ערה
Monday.	Soma,	Moon's day, *who accompanies.*	Job 19. 13.	אח
Tuesday.	Mangala,	Mars' day, *who wounds and is wounded.* *stricken*	Isa. 53. 4.	נגע
Wednesday.	Bouta [2],	Mercury's day, *who comes and goes.*	Gen. 19. 1.	בא
Thursday.	Brahaspati,	Jupiter's day, *bright* *, { *clear.* clear { *regulated.* ordain	Cant. 6. 10. Isa. 26. 12.	בר שפת
	* Varam, *day*, from בר [3], *clear, bright*, as above.		Cant. 6. 10.	בר

SINGALESE NAMES OF THE DAYS OF THE PLANETARY WEEK,
AS GIVEN BY LE GENTIL.

			Texts.	Hebrew or Noetic roots.
Friday.	Sikoura-da,	day of Venus, *morning dawn.*	Ps. 127. 2.	שחר
Saturday.	Sani-soure-da,	„ Saturn. { rest { governed	Isa. 9. 6.	שני שרה
Sunday.	Iri-da,	„ the Sun, *who sends forth rays.* shoot	1 Sam. 20. 20.	ירה
Monday.	Handou,	„ the Moon, { accompanying. { going forth. passed	Job 19. 13. Job 28. 8.	אח ידה
Tuesday.	Angarharoura,	„ Mars, *striking.* stricken	Isa. 53. 4.	נגע
Wednesday.	Bouda,	„ Mercury, as Bouta.		
Thursday.	Bragoura [4],	„ Jupiter. *glittering*	Deut. 32. 41.	ברק

[1] Which is begun from Friday. Mahomet seems to have adopted his Friday's Sabbath from the Indian week.

[2] From בא, Lat. *vado*, Ital. and French *va*.

[3] From this root בר the Latins would have *veritas*, and the European languages similar words for *truth*, as being clear. The English word *truth* was by H. Tooke explained as what man *troweth*, or knows. Is it not rather what *God* troweth?

[4] In Bragoura may be traced the Scandinavian deity Braga.

Da, like our word day, and the Scandinavian Dag, from יד, to appear, to come forth, to make known.

As the Singalese names differ from the Brahminical, it may be inferred that these were in use before the Hindu conquest of Ceylon. But though differing in the roots from which the names are derived, the similarity of the meaning points to a common origin in the tradition of the names given by the first inventors of astronomy, transmitted by Noah to his descendants, and best preserved by the posterity of Shem, by whose chief dialect they are here interpreted.

SIAMESE NAMES OF THE PLANETARY WEEK,

ACCORDING TO LA LOUBERE[1].

			Texts.	Hebrew or Noetic roots.
Van Athit,	day of the Sun, *who comes.*		Job 3. 25.	אתה
„ Tchan,	„ the Moon, *who accom-* { *companion*		Job 30. 29.	אח
	panies. {		Isa. 53. 4.	נגע
„ Angkoan,	„ Mars, *wounded or wounding.*		Gen. 12. 17.	נכע
„ Pout,	„ Mercury, *who comes and goes.*		Gen. 19. 1.	כא
„ Prahaat,	„ Jupiter, *bright, clear, who comes.* {	Cant. 6. 10.	בר
			Job 3. 25.	אתח
„ Souc,	„ Venus, *twilight.*		Cant. 6. 10.	שתר
„ Saou,	„ Saturn, *reposing.* *restoreth*	Ps. 23. 3.	שב

La Loubere gives Pra as a Siamese name of God. He also says that they apply the epithets Bali, Pra, powerful and bright, to whatever they most honour; as, the sun, Pra Athit, the bright who cometh; the moon, Pra Tchan.

Van, going forth, from בא, as *venit*, Lat., &c.

MEMORIAL LINES FOR THE DAYS OF THE WEEK, IN ANALOGY WITH

THOSE OF CREATION.

Seven days the week for man
Measuring life's narrow span;
Seven were the periods named
In which earth and man were framed;
Number perfect and complete
Wherein earth and heaven meet.
On day One, shone forth the light,
Earth's first millennium saw heaven bright [2].
The Second day gave separation,
With Noah's, Abram's revelation.
Day the Third brought forth on earth
Plants, the type of human birth.
Day the Fourth, Sun, Moon appear,
Christ and His Church proclaiming clear.
Day the Fifth, the swarming floods
Show the Church's multitudes.
Sixth day beasts and man arose,
Man's high lot the Gospel shows.
Seventh day man's rest made known,
Earth's rest in coming times foreshown.

---

[1] "Roy. de Siam."   [2] 2 Pet. iii. 8.

Memorial Lines,

ACCORDING TO THE ORDER OF THE SIGNS.

[These "Lines" are not offered as poetry, but as aids to memory.]

Fulfilment.		Early Prophecies in word or type.	Later Prophecies in the Old Testament.	References in the New Testament.
John 19. 20.	The ram, the Lamb, once slain, but reign-	Gen. 22. 13.	Exod. 12.	John 1. 29.
Mar. 16. 19.	ing now ;	Ibid. 8.	Isa. 53.	Rev. 5. 6.
Mat. 28. 18.	The bull, his ruling, twins united show	Ibid. 17.	Ps. 72. 8.	Rev. 12. 5.
1 Cor. 15. 25.		Ps. 110.	Zech. 6. 13.	Mark 12. 36.
Luke 1. 35.	The Son of God and man ; the crab keeps	Gen. 49. 10.	Isa. 27. 3.	John 17. 12.
John 17. 12.	fast ;			
Mat. 25. 32.	The lion rends apart, prevails at last ;	Ibid. 9.	Ezek. 1. 10.	Rev. 5. 5.
Rev. 5. 5.		Jude, or Enoch.		
Mat. 1. 21.	The virgin bears the seed ; the balance	Gen. 3. 15.	Isa. 9. 6.	Mat. 1. 21.
1 Tim. 2. 6.	buys ;		Ps. 74. 2.	1 Cor. 6. 20.
Mat. 27. 35.	The scorpion wounds ; sent forth, the	Ibid.	Zech. 12. 10.	Luke 24. 26.
John 17. 8.	arrow flies ;	Gen. 49. 10.	Exod. 4. 13.	John 7. 16.
John 19. 34.	The kid is pierced ; the water rises, flows ;	Gen. 4. 4 ;	Zech. 12. 10.	John 19. 34.
Acts 2. 17.		22. 8.		
		Ps. 68. 18.	Isa. 44. 3.	John 4. 14.
Acts 4. 32.	The fishes, multitudes redeemed disclose.	Gen. 15. 5.	Ezek. 47. 9.	Mat. 4. 19.
Rev. 7. 9.		Gen. 22. 17.		

MEMORIAL LINES, ACCORDING TO THE COURSE OF PROPHECY.

By Woman borne, the Branch, the seed ;
The Balance shows redemption's need ;
The Scorpion wounds He must endure ;
The Archer tells His coming sure ;
The Goat, His death in sacrifice ;
The Water, that He shall arise ;

The Fish, His Church in union bound ;
The Lamb, once slain, but now enthroned ;
The Bull the victory shall gain ;
The Twins, Divine and human reign.
The Crab His sure possession tells ;
His foes then Judah's Lion quells.

In lectures on astronomy, the speaker, even if undeceived as to the usual meanings attributed to the signs, may be disinclined to bring before a mixed audience the higher Scriptural bearing of the emblems, thinking it may be right not to hazard any unreverential use of sacred names. The alternatives afforded by parts of Scripture where the emblems are used as types may be usefully adopted. It should be made clear that the figures do not represent the person, but the actions, the coming and the sacrifice of the promised Redeemer.

ARIES,	The ram, or lamb of Abel's offering and of Abraham's sacrifice.	Gen. 4. 4 ; 22. 13.
TAURUS,	The bull of the sin-offering and consecration of Aaron.	Lev. 4. 3, 14. Exod. 29. 14.
GEMINI,	The figures being sometimes twin kids, the two goats of the great day of Atonement.	Lev. 16. 5.
CANCER,	The multitudes of the Jewish and Christian Church, figured in the great nebula, or cloud of stars, visible to the unassisted eye.	Isa. 60. 4. Rev. 21. 24.
LEO,	The lion of the tribe of Judah, their well-known standard.	Gen. 49. 9.
VIRGO,	The woman of prophecy, bearing the promised seed.	Gen. 3. 15.
LIBRA,	The scales of righteousness.	Ps. 62. 9. Job 31. 6.
SCORPIO,	The enemy trodden under foot.	Gen. 3. 15. Ps. 91. 13.
SAGITTARIUS,	The sending forth of the Gospel.	Ps. 45. 5. Rev. 6. 2.
CAPRICORNUS,	The goat of sacrifice, the sin-offering, sinking down as slain.	Lev. 16. 15.
AQUARIUS,	The pouring forth of the water of purification.	Exod. 29. 4. Isa. 44. 3.
PISCES,	The two fishes, the Church before and after the going forth of the Gospel ; the fish being an ancient emblem of the Church.	Ezek. 47. 9. Matt. 4. 19 ; 13. 47.

The pious and learned Dr. Watts has not disdained to put the names of the signs into memorial rhymes, but without annexing any explanation to them.

8

Memorial Lines for the Constellations.

WHO would look upon the sky,
When the stars of night are high,
Glorious in their sun-bright glance,
And deem that they were named by chance?
O who would with incurious eyes
Gaze on the splendour of those skies,
Or look to earth as those may do,
The beasts who perish, to whose view
The midnight stars were never given,
Death doom'd, nor form'd to gaze on heaven?
It was not so in man's first day;
Time-honour'd records all convey
The one tradition; *Man*, the same
To beasts below who gave their name,
Found names instructive for each light
That pours its beauty to the night,
And, Eden lost below, would raise
The soul to heaven, and there would trace
Promise of paradise regain'd,
City of God, by sin unstain'd;
Reclined in peace 'mid Eden's bowers,
Its cedar-shades, its streams and flowers,
But forty days, if 'tis received
As Abraham's offspring long believed,
To God's command His creatures cleaved.
Those days, past o'er, begun when shone
Midsummer's sun with silent Moon [1],
Once man beheld her lovely light
Increase and lessen from his sight;
But ere full orb'd it rose once more,
Eden was lost and bliss was o'er.
All else was changed, without, within,
Earth felt the curse for human sin,
But not the everlasting Stars,
They gleam'd 'mid elemental wars,
The same as when on Eden shone
Each radiant orb from azure throne.
To them look'd up repentant man,
And soon in memory began
To treasure by their changeless orbs
The promise that his soul absorbs,
Of Him, the coming One, to rise
Even as those stars in darkening skies,
Calling the brightest by that name,
"He who shall come," whom all proclaim.
The glorious Sun he deem'd must show
His glory who should come even so.—
The changing Moon fit emblem seem'd
Of fallen man, and man redeem'd,
Enlighten'd by the living Lord,
Dark when unmindful of His word,
And ever in her loved return,
Bidding new hope within us burn.
In heaven the Sun's sure path he traced,
And in its stars twelve emblems placed,
Dividing them to human sight
By the full [2] Moon supreme in light.

---

[1] Hid in her silent interlunar cave.—Milton.
[2] Manzil al *Kamar*, Arab.

Through these twelve emblems should he go,
The Sun that lightens all below.
He the true light on earth to shine,
Is figured in each mystic sign.
And first, the Branch, seed to be born, } VIRGO.
The woman and the spike of corn ;
The ransom next, His loss, our gain ;   LIBRA.
The wound foretold, in conflict ta'en ;   SCORPIO.
The coming forth as arrow sure ;   SAGITTARIUS.
The death the Conqueror must endure ;   CAPRICORNUS.
The rising water pour'd from high ;   AQUARIUS.
And multitudes in unity ;   PISCES.
The Lamb enthroned that had been slain, } ARIES.
But comes again o'er all to reign ;
The Prince and Ruler over Earth ;   TAURUS.
The Son of God, in human birth ;   GEMINI.
The purchased people, countless crowd ;   CANCER.
The overthrow of rebels proud ;   LEO.
When final separation comes
Of good and evil's endless dooms.

DECANS.

Stars above and stars below
Every sign, the heavens do show ;
There are placed with mother mild, } CONSTELLATIONS
Coma, the desired, the child,   WITH
Then beneath, the Centaur, known
As King man shall despise, disown.
Bootes, coming ; rising high, } VIRGO.
Arcturus, diamond of the sky.
The Cross beneath, the Crown above, } LIBRA.
The Victim tells redeeming love.
The serpent in the Conqueror's grasp,
And He who kneels as stung by asp, } SCORPIO.
With Ophiuchus join'd below,
His foot upon the reptile foe.
The Dragon round the pole entwines,
The Victim's altar faintly shines, } SAGITTARIUS.
Above the Eagle rising bright,
Bearing the harp in victor flight.
The Arrow sent to give to death
The falling Eagle seen beneath. } CAPRICORNUS.
The Dolphin swift, fit type to be
Of the sure course of prophecy.
The Swan returning from afar
With hastening wing, unsetting star,
And Pegasus, poetic name,
The flying horse, alike proclaim } AQUARIUS.
In clouds He went, He comes the same.
The Southern Fish, the Church, drinks in
The living stream that heals from sin.
The Band the fishes to unite,
Of old revered, though faint to sight,
Each night, returning shadows bring
Cepheus, the branch, the crowned king, } PISCES.
Andromeda, the chained bride,
Soon to be raised her Lord beside.
What he has promised he will do,
Although the Serpent-foe pursue.
Then Cassiopeia, Queen so fair,
Setting free her braided hair.
Next Medusa's snake-wreath'd head,
Whence Algol's changeful beam is shed, } ARIES.
By Perseus held, who breaks the chain
And frees his bride from grief and pain.

Orion, splendid, comes in light,
The swift, the mighty, and the bright;
Eridanus in winding fold,
The River of the Lord, behold!
Auriga, the good shepherd there,
Makes His following flock His care.
 } TAURUS.

Lepus, the lurking serpent-foe,
Beneath Orion's foot lies low,
Procyon, Branch, Redeemer, see,
Oft second Sirius said to be.
Sirius, the prince of heavenly host,
Brightest of stars, revered the most.
 } GEMINI.

On high the lesser sheepfold dim,
Yet ever centred upon Him.
And next the greater flock and fold
Around the steadfast pole are roll'd.
Argo, the company below
Of travellers to Heaven who go.
 } CANCER.

At the Lion's foot are view'd,
Hydra, enemy subdued,
The cup of wrath, the bird of prey,
Fix'd on the foe, at that great day
When Heaven and Earth shall pass away.
 } LEO.

When contemplated as connected, the constellations form four magnificent groups of significant and consistent meaning. That group which spreads over the darkening skies of autumn may be thus explained as presenting the types of prophecy. Ophiuchus, the serpent-bearer or holder, whose foot is on the enemy, whose head is united to the head of another human figure (sometimes called Hercules) above, represented kneeling on one knee, as from the predicted wound in the heel. The crown which is yet to be worn is before him, the altar of sacrifice beneath his feet; one foot is on the head of the scorpion, the other held up as wounded; the two eagles, the falling and the ascending, follow him; and above is the swan, the bird of passage, who goes away to return again. Here then we behold the conflict with the serpent-enemy, the wound received, the suffering, the wrestling of Him who was to come, at His first coming, who at His second is to return in triumph.

In the clear nights of winter the brilliant group that fills the sky is yet more magnificent, even as it should be, representing the second coming in glory, without sin unto salvation, of Him who had been slain. The group that thus embodies its wordless prophecy has for its centre Orion, the splendid, who cometh swiftly as the light, as his name imports; the enemy being under one foot, the other raised as if from the wounded heel. With him are his attendant stars, Sirius, the coming of the prince, the brightest of the starry host; below, Procyon, the Redeemer; above, the two stars of Gemini called Castor and Pollux, the archer and the judge united, one bearing a dart to signify he shall come forth, and the other a branch, the earliest symbol of Him who should come: the bright star of Taurus, Aldebaran, the ruler or the ruling; the Pleiades, centre of our system, on one side; Cancer, the multitude of the purchased flock, on the other; Argo, the company of Him who cometh, below, each showing the multitudes of His people; and there too are the stars of Aries, the ram, the Lamb as it had been slain, whose foot is on His bounden enemy, shown in the Leviathan or sea-monster, Cetus, towards the west.

The balmy evenings of spring are illuminated by Leo, the victorious Lion of the tribe of Judah, with his foot on the head of the finally subdued serpent-enemy, on whom abides the cup of wrath and the devouring bird of prey. Then also shine the stars of Virgo, the seed-bearing woman, with Spica, the seed, almost rivalling Sirius in brilliancy; the Northern Crown above, the Centaur, the king who cometh, below, under whose feet was visible in the early ages of mankind the splendid Southern Cross, remembered in tradition after it had disappeared from view.

At each and every season, but especially in summer twilight, turn to the north, and it is occupied with another group equally significant and expressive. The crowned King, whose branch or sceptre touches the throned woman, who in one hand also holds a branch, as a token of her union with the king her liberator, and with her other hand sets free the tresses of her hair[1]; the Greater Bear, or sheepfold, with the sheep as coming forth and following their shepherd and their king, he who is their keeper, as expressed in the name of the bright star

---

[1] Shedar, who sets free, or is set free, being the name of her chief star; a word in Arabic specially applied to a woman casting loose her hair.

Arcturus, in Bootes. The javelin in the hand of this figure equally denotes that He who cometh shall be sent forth, and that He shall be pierced. Bootes also holds a branch, denoting that this, as the other branch-bearing figures, is a representation of Him so often called in the prophets "the Branch."

Persons who are learning to distinguish the stars are generally told that those forming the curve, so strangely called the tail of the Bear, always point to and seem to follow Arcturus, and that two in the square or body of the same constellation, called the pointers, in their rotation still always point to the immutable polar star, round which they revolve. The polar star thus seems to belong peculiarly to that group of which the Great Bear, or sheepfold, forms the most remarkable portion. This star is called by the Greeks Cynosure [1], meaning, in the Oriental dialects, the established, the centre of the constellations. This star is still called by the Arabs the kid, the sacrificial emblem of Him "by whom all things consist." The whole constellation is called Kochab, the waiting on Him who cometh, in His sacrificial character, while His kingly dignity is expressed in Bootes, whose hand is extended as to the Northern Crown. The polar constellation Draco again shows forth the serpent-enemy, whose head is under the foot of the kneeling Hercules below. Auriga, the shepherd, holding in his bosom Capella, the she-goat, and followed by the kids typifying His people, touches the foot of Perseus [2], the breaker of the bonds of Andromeda, the chained woman, representing the Church. Perseus holds in his hand a head, called of Medusa, a word signifying the trodden under foot. This head is surrounded by serpents, and was named by the ancient Hebrews the head of Satan, and Al Onè, the subdued [3]: by the Arabs it is called Al Ghoul, the evil spirit. This constellation is remarkable less for its splendour than for its significance: Algol, the chief star in the head of Medusa, being changeable, the most visibly so of any in the heavens, and consequently an expressive emblem of the adversary, the fallen, who kept not his first estate. This group may be seen in summer nights, while the three birds, the exalted [4] and the falling eagles, and the swan, form a large triangle overhead.

It is to be remarked that one foot of the figure of the promised deliverer mostly contains in the foot, as in Hercules, Ophiuchus, Orion, Auriga, Aquarius, Cepheus, a peculiarly bright star, generally with a name meaning bruised; and it is drawn up as if wounded. By the foot also, as has been already shown, the emblems are most frequently connected, so evidently calling to mind the prediction, "Thou shalt bruise his heel." A tradition of this primeval prophecy was preserved by the Greeks in the stories of Hercules and Orion, and in that of the lameness of Vulcan (son of Juno without a father) and of Erichthonius, one name of Auriga; ar other, Heniochus, being wounded in the *heel*. It is also remarkable that those groups of stars which comprise changeable ones have been chosen to represent the enemy, as Medusa's head and Cetus. Those which contain nebulæ, or multitudinous groups of stars visible to the unassisted eye, were also chosen to represent the Church, or congregated multitudes of the redeemed, as Cancer and Andromeda.

Are there not here marks of design as exquisitely complex in execution as sublimely simple in intention? He cometh, to suffer and to reign, is the sole end and aim of all these beautifully arranged coincidences in the emblems attributed to the luminaries vivifying the skies of night with glimpses of a coming day, to whose intensity of splendour those rays will be but darkness—even the great, the final Day of the Messiah, which afar off Abraham saw and was glad, and which was ever present to the minds of those earlier prophets who named and grouped those stars of heaven to which Abraham was divinely directed to look for prophetic consolation.

---

[1] Some later Greek authorities have supposed that this word, which might in their language convey the strange and incongruous idea of a dog's tail, was derived from a hill so called, over which mariners approaching the Athenian Piræus saw the pole star: but no doubt the hill was so named from that circumstance the Cynosure hill, the name being (as a much higher authority, Plato himself, informs us that many foreign words were) perverted by the Greeks into what the sound might suggest in their own language.

[2] The same star being reckoned in both.

[3] Aben Ezra.

[4] This constellation (properly, as anciently figured, an eagle) bears the lyre, a figure added to it apparently by the Greeks.

Memorial Lines for the Names of Stars.

To the brightest stars of heaven
Ever the same names were given :
Still preserved by Ishmael's race [1],
These the desert-dwellers trace,
And from them to us they came,
Self-interpreting each name.
In the dialect they speak,
There the hidden sense we seek ;
Yet a few the Greeks retain [2],
Or from Egypt's lore we gain—
All transmitting, none explain.
To God's glory all were named [3],
Him they rightly have proclaim'd,
Since from Eden newly driven,
Adam look'd in faith to heaven,
And sought the promise to record
Of Him to come, his Son and Lord,
There to read, in starry lines,
Message that their beam outshines,
Consolation to his sorrow
In that splendid coming morrow.
There he traced Messiah's day,
There inscribed Messiah's sway ;
From the guardian Cherubim
Framed appear these signs, by him
Who those mystic forms had seen ;
Faces four, where placed between
The Lion, who the prey will rend,
And Bull in sacrifice to bend,
The second Adam, to be slain,
But eagle-like come down again.
In their names that tongue divine
We trace, as in the patriarch line,
In which Eve named her progeny,
Ere confusion, from on high,
Scattering Babel-builders far,
Yet spared the name of many a star,
And sent abroad, like shiver'd rock,
Splinter'd in convulsive shock,
Fragments with each wandering race,
That all their common source may trace.

Spica, the SEED the woman bears,
Arcturus, *he shall come* declares,
Almurredin, *comes to reign*,
The branch, the seed, we find again
In Al Zimach. Of yore has been
In Coma, star no longer seen,
Once vertical o'er Bethlehem ;

} VIRGO.

Al Phecca too, the crown's bright gem,
Centred o'er Jerusalem.
Al Merga, the bruised, Ramih [4], sent,
As *arrow* forth, the dart so meant.
Zuben Akrabi tells the *gain*
Purchased by the *conflict's* pain.

} LIBRA.

---

[1] See the Arab Astronomy.
[2] Hesiod, Homer, Aratus.
[3] Isa. xl. Ps. xix.; cxlvii.
[4] Or Aramech, see p. 17, in Bootes.

Antares marks the *wounded* heel;
The reptile's head the bruise shall feel.
} SCORPIO.

Vega of *triumph* tells on high,
With eagle rising in the sky.
} SAGITTARIUS.

Ethanim is the *dragon* foe,
Al Tair eagle *slain* doth show,
Al Gedi, victim-*kid* below;
} CAPRICORNUS.

In Fom al *haut* the *fish* is found,
The Church as *moved* by Gospel's sound.
Al Pheras shows the winged *horse*,
Scheat, *returning* from his course.
} AQUARIUS.

Markab, *the comer from afar,*
Al Deramim, arctic star,
Who comes again; Mizar, *the bound;*
Al Maach, the sad, with chain around.
} PISCES.

Al Natik, *pierced, bruised* means,
Showing Calvary's dread scenes:
Passover star when Israel slew
The Lamb of God they little knew.
Mesartim, from *the bound* ones named;
Al Sheratan, *the slain* proclaim'd;
Shedar, *which from bonds is freed;*
And Shalisha [5], Deltoton's head.
} ARIES.

Mira, *the rebel,* changeful star,
At Aries' foot lies bound afar;
Aldebaran, red and bright,
Lawgiver, ruler marks to sight.
Pleiades, the *multitude,*
Where still Alcyone has stood,
Central point of stars that crowd
The milky way, for 'tis allow'd
That gravitation's law is given
To every orb in depths of heaven.
Hyades, *assembled* cluster,
Shining with a fainter lustre.
Capella is the victim *kid*
In the shepherd's bosom hid;
Achernàr, *the river,* where
Its *after-part* is seen, and there
Phäet in the utmost south,
Marks the river's end or *mouth.*
Betelguez, *who cometh fast,*
Saiph, *the bruised,* to *bruise* at last;
Rigol, Bellatrix, shall *tread,*
Coming swift, the serpent's head.
} TAURUS.

Castor, *archer swift to come;*
And Pollux, *wonderful,* the *judge* of doom.
Procyon, the *Redeemer,* then
Sirius, *Prince* of stars and men.
} GEMINI.

The *multitude,* in Præsepe;
Canopus, o'er the southern sea,
Possession of the Prince to come.
Then, above in heaven's high dome,
Dubhè, *flock,* and Mizar, *fold,*
Al Cor, *the Lamb,* and, famed of old,
Benetnash, *assembled daughters* [6]
Of the flock, by quiet waters,
Pastures of rest, for ever led
By the good shepherd at their head.
Kochab, the *mighty coming one,*
The Cynosure which long has shone
The *Central* star, the pole far famed,
The victim-kid by Arabs named.
} CANCER.

---

[5] Shalisha, *triangle.* [6] Job ix. 9; xxxix.

Then Regulus, upon the head
Of serpent-foe who comes *to tread ;*
Al Phard, who lies in *separation ;*
Al Ches, the *cup* of desolation.
Al Goràb, *devouring* bird,
Fulfilling the prophetic word ;
Wrath pour'd out while death shall prey
On rebel foe at judgment-day.

} LEO.

It will be observed that the succession in which the names are given is that of the signs in the primeval year, following the course of prophecy from the first coming of the promised Seed to His final victory. The words in Italics give the meaning of the ancient names that precede them.

There are some among these names which may appear to be Greek or Latin, but which are here explained by their Oriental roots, because other names, evidently either Hebrew or Arabic, are attached to the same figures of similar meaning. The science of astronomy has been preserved and transmitted chiefly by the Arabians. The Greek and Latin authorities, Aratus, Hipparchus, Ptolemy, Macrobius, &c., give no reason for, nor explanation of, the names and figures they record ; while Ulugh Beigh, transmitter of the Arabic names of the stars, sometimes does so ; and Aben Ezra, from whom we chiefly derive the little that is known of the ancient Hebrew nomenclature, gives some explanations that may authorize the corresponding interpretation of the rest ; as Rosh Satan, the head of Satan, and Al Oneh, the evil one, in the head of Medusa Auriga, the shepherd. called by the Romans the charioteer.

It is said on the high authority of Plato, that the Greeks, if they met with a foreign word (as Melech, king) rendered it by the word in their own language corresponding in sound, as Melikos, sweet, and immediately invented some legend about bees and honey. Thus we are led to the solution of many of the dark histories with which Greek and Latin writers abound. Scriptural explanations, instead of the idle tales usually resorted to, will thus be substituted for the legends of ancient mythology, so unworthy of connexion with these sublime objects, and so incongruous in the usage of Christian students of the grandest of human sciences.

NOTE.—"When He who is to come shall come" is a common expression in the Talmud concerning the Messiah ; and "He cometh" is the constant theme of the starry emblems and their names.

NOTE ON THE NAMES OF THE STARS.

Some of these names have been referred to Syriac and Chaldee : they are, however, mostly Arabic, but from the similarity of these dialects with the Hebrew, their meaning is evident to the Hebrew scholar. Changes of vowels are frequent, such as occur in the names of the letters of the alphabet, where Gimel, confessedly a camel, represents the Hebrew Gamal ; and the z is sometimes changed for d, and s or sh for t and th.

The names of things are not mere arbitrary combinations of letters ; in every language they are more or less easily traceable to their root, the noun or verb, whose signification they convey. In derived languages this root is sometimes not to be found without referring to the more ancient ones whence their words were taken : for instance, in Latin the enclitic ve, having the signification of and and but, cannot be accounted for till it is shown to be the Hebrew conjunction vau, meaning and or but. In English, words from a variety of languages are in constant use, conveying to the English ear no meaning : these are, however, easily to be referred to other languages, in which they have a meaning. Persons speak familiarly of panoramas, polytechnics, and photographs : the reasons for which these expressive names were given are not the less certain, for not being always borne in mind by the speaker. By constant use we may cease to think of the original meaning, but it is not the less to be found there. Ox-ford and Cam-bridge are obvious instances. Battle Abbey may still bring to mind the fall of the Saxon rule in England ; but the earlier memorial of Battle Bridge is dimmed by the mist of ages. Who now thinks of Boadicea there ? Magna Charta Island, named in a foreign tongue to record the memory of an event of vital importance to England, and perpetuating to all posterity its salutary remembrance, bears, perhaps, the closest analogy to those traditional names of the stars, whose corroboration of the meanings here claimed for the emblems is so important. In the Holy Scriptures the significations of many names, and the reason why they are so applied, is given ; and in Concordances all, or nearly all, are explained from their Hebrew roots. The names of the stars, Syriac, Chaldee, or Arabic, are all equally explicable from the corresponding Hebrew roots, as Yorkshire and Kentish names of places and persons (Scarbro' and Folkestone, Constable and Oxenden) are equally to be explained from the English or its mother tongue, the Anglo-Saxon. These names of stars, having these ascertainable meanings, could not be given without a reason. No such reason can be assigned from the appearances of the starry heavens. Among those scattered orbs of varying brilliancy, it seems as if any other stars might as well be reckoned to represent the woman, or the serpent; but the reason of their being so reckoned may be sought and found in the correspondence of the names with the emblems to which they are annexed, when explained from the Hebrew roots, and when those emblems are explained by the Scripture prophecies in which their figures occur as types.

This triple coincidence of the name, the emblem, and the prophecy, did it occur but once, might be regarded as a possible chance; but when every emblem is found to be used as a type in corresponding prophecies, and to contain names sometimes more appropriate to the prophecy than to the emblem, and sometimes equally applicable to both, how can we fail to admit the proof of design from the evidence of adaptation?

The names, emblems, and prophecies are known to have existed before the event to which they refer; and fables were even then connected with them so similar in import to those prophecies, as might leave it dubious whether the constellation or the prophecy originated the fable. Those sceptics [7] who would try to account for the prophecy from the constellation, have not attempted to show why certain stars should, from the beginning of the world's history, have been called by the names of objects to which their groups have no sort of resemblance; and why the woman, the seed, and the serpent should thus have been selected for commemoration, unless the prophecy, as all tradition indicates and Scripture declares, had preceded the application of these names and emblems, which so remarkably express it, to those vaguely dispersed and irregularly assembled brilliant points in the heavens, with which they have no sort of analogy, but with which tradition so uniformly connects them.

Those names transmitted to us through the Hebrew appear to have been the most ancient, the original; other nations varying the sounds, but preserving the ideas. Tradition long retained the number seven, which has been supposed to exclude the earth, and include the sun and moon; but among the Assyrian remains, the sun, moon, and seven stars are found together; and the Egyptian divinities of the third order were seven. The planets that can be recognized by the human eye are seven; the seventh having been occasionally seen since its modern discovery, may well have been visible to eyes that were to last 1000 years. The Planetoids and the eighth planet recently discovered being beyond all human sight, and even beyond the probable power of such aids to it as the glass found in the Assyrian remains, or the "tube" spoken of in the Chinese annals, make no part of ancient astronomy.

---

[7] Dupuis, &c.

On the Mansions of the Moon,

OR LUNAR ZODIAC.

THE same unity of purpose which connects the Decans or other constellations with the twelve signs, pervades also the names of the Mansions of the Moon, or lunar zodiac. These names are given to spaces in or between the signs. Emblems are assigned to them in the astronomy of India, but none by the Arabians and those nations who seem to have derived these names from the same source. Those modern writers who mention the mansions of the moon, speak of them as remains of most ancient astronomy, wholly disused by the Greeks and Romans, and apparently by the Egyptians. They have, however, been the continued theme of Arabian and Indian study, and incorporated not only with the mythology of India, but with the habits of domestic life. Children are still named according to the mansion of the moon in which they were born. In India the names have been much changed, and various emblems attached to them. In one of them it is to be observed, that the Pleiades are figured as seven, whilst the fable relating to them makes them but six, thus tending to prove the antiquity of the figure to be greater than that of the fable, as it said that the seventh Pleiad disappeared about the time of the Trojan war, going off like a comet towards the north pole. The Arabic names are intelligible by their Hebrew roots agreeing with the meanings attributed to the signs in which they are found. Thus is afforded another line of evidence that those meanings are the original ones. The interpretations attached to these names in modern Arabic lexicons are generally vague and doubtful, but in a few places corroborate those here given, thus authenticating some and giving a strong presumption in favour of the rest; for if some certainly alluded to the import of the sign in which they are placed, under the aspect here presented, it is probable that *all* should do so. Their great antiquity is ascertained by the record that the Emperor Yn introduced them into the astronomy of China in the twenty-third century before the Christian era. They have been in use there ever since, differing indeed in names, but agreeing in situation with those of the Arabs. In one name, however, Mao, the Pleiades, we trace Maia, the multitude, preserved by the ancient Greeks as that of one of the stars in the cluster. Perhaps from this name we have that connected with the sweet influences of the month of May.

The Chinese series commences in Virgo, thus coinciding with the beginning of the year of the ancient Hebrews, the anniversary of the creation. The Chinese solar year began from the middle of Aquarius, where the winter solstice took place, about the time usually reckoned as that of the Deluge. The selection of spaces [1] where no bright stars occur, as at the foot of Gemini, in Sagittarius, &c., being perfectly arbitrary and found in both the Arabic and the Chinese, points to a common source for the differently named series: the agreement of meaning in the appellations of the Arabian lunar mansions with those of the solar zodiac, authorizes us to consider the intelligible and consistent system of the Arabians as the original, rather than that of the Chinese astronomy, and it also affords an indication of both the solar and lunar having emanated from the same mind.

The Sethites having originally arranged the lunar as well as the solar zodiac, the first lunar mansion was probably placed, as the Arabian, in Aries. The Chinese astronomy must have been transmitted through Noah, whose posterity had far to migrate ere they reached China, while the elder branch, through whom was to come the Messiah, the theme of prophecy, remained in the countries where the Arabian arrangement has been preserved. There also the language is still radically the same with that in which they are named, probably the dialect of Noah and the primitive language of mankind. Commencing in Aries, the intention in so doing must not be sought for in any natural epoch, solstice, or equinox; for of these, in the earliest time assigned to the invention of astronomy, none there occurred.

If we follow the guidance of prophecy, we find that as the sun was the type of the Messiah, so was the moon of His Church, enlightened by His light, bright when looking full upon Him, dark when turning away to gaze as it were upon the earth. Where, then, could be more suitably fixed the first mansion or place of the type of the Church, than over the head of the Lamb as it had been slain, in whose book of life the names of those who belong to it are written? Here, therefore, we find the first mansion of the moon, called by the Arabian astronomers Al Sheratan [2], the wounded or pierced, or slain in sacrifice.

---

[1] The moon passes frequently much above, frequently much below these particular spots.

[2] The name Al Sheratan is also applied to the star β in the head of Aries. A list of the names of 23 Chinese "constellations," apparently the Mansions of the Moon, is given by Duttalda.

The yet extant names, with their meanings given in the Hebrew root of the word, in some places corroborated by the Arabic interpretation, are presented in the foregoing table [3] according to the traditional correspondence with the sign. Scripture texts in which the root is used in this sense are there given.

NOTE.

In some cases, where the roots contained in these names are not commonly used in Arabic, they are in Hebrew; though in a few instances a root used in Arabic is scarcely traceable in Hebrew: however, it seems probable that these names were given when both nations spoke the same dialect, that of Noah. The Sanscrit name Ahiliam, in Gemini, containing the Hebrew roots Ah, אח, brother, and Am, עם, joined, while no figure of twins occurs here in those of the Indian lunar zodiacs, indicates a similar origin for the Brahmin astronomy. The Sanscrit names of the Mansions of the Moon are given by Le Gentil, "Voyage dans les Mers de l'Inde."

In India and Arabia, from time immemorial, the signs of the zodiac and the lunar mansions have been interwoven with all their science and their poetry, with their public worship and their private economy; the figures embodied in the forms of their idols, and the appellations transmitted in the names of their children. In Scandinavia the signs have been claimed by Olaus Rudbeck as having there originated. In Mexico they are still to be traced. The Burmese have preserved them well: the Polynesians have not totally forgotten them. Wherever the posterity of Noah, the children of Seth, are found, there are recognized some vestiges of this their ancestral science. During the dark ages of Europe, when the study of astronomy was merged in that of astrology, it however flourished in the East: Al Fergani at the court of the caliph of Bagdad, Haroun Alraschid, and Albumazer, at that of the Moors in Spain, in the ninth century, whose works were commented on and elucidated by Aben Ezra in the eleventh, restored it in the West. Thus has been transmitted to us some account of the ancient Persian, Indian, and Egyptian spheres. Ulugh Begh, the Tartar prince and astronomer, grandson of Tamerlane, has preserved the ancient Coptic names of the signs, supposed to be used by the ancient Egyptians, and also many names of the fixed stars, which appear to have come through the Arabs. The lunar mansions, and the division into decans, or thirty-six constellations beyond the zodiac, which seem scarcely even remembered by modern European astronomers, were by him enumerated and described. As the Jews have guarded for us in their precious integrity the Hebrew Scriptures, so Mahometan or rather patriarchal Arabs have transmitted to us in wonderful precision the names which so remarkably correspond with the language of those Scriptures, each setting forth the glory of Him not as yet revealed to either of those nations, children of Abraham according to the flesh, who will one day hail their long unrecognized kinsman Redeemer, when the flocks of Kedar and the rams of Nebaioth shall be gathered unto the Lord, and His glory shall have arisen upon Zion.

These are some of the leading ancient astronomers, who have preserved and transmitted to us such important evidence of the antiquity of these emblems, and of the unity of design in the ancient division and nomenclature of the starry heavens. The interpretations here given are assimilated as closely as possible to their concurring testimony: separated by ages of time, by distance of habitation, by language, and by religion, where they agree surely it must be in the truth.

Another chain of evidence has descended to us through the Greeks. Hesiod, about 1000 years B.C., treats of the rising and setting of the constellations, whose names and emblems he transmits as from immemorial antiquity. So speaks Homer of those which he mentions. Aratus, a Greek at the court of Antigonus, king of Macedonia, about 277 B.C., in his poem on astronomy describes much more particularly the constellations, in number, name, and figure nearly as now represented. Hipparchus, the celebrated Greek astronomer, who died 125 B.C., enumerated and is said to have given names to the stars; but Hesiod, Homer, and Aratus having previously recorded them by name, this can only mean that he made them a regular enrolment. Hyginus, a freedman of Augustus, gives the names and figures as his predecessors, and relates of them the various fables in his time vaguely attached to the constellations, of the uncertainty of which he frequently speaks, thus making more remarkable the invariable certainty of the appellations and symbols.

Ptolemy of Alexandria, in the time of Antoninus, made the celebrated catalogue of the fixed stars, describing the constellations as we now have them, particularizing the remarkable union of

---

some with others, by reckoning the same star in each, as the foot of Aries on the band of Pisces, the foot of Auriga with the horn of Taurus, the Cup and Raven with the serpent Hydra. From him we have derived them without variation, till the English astronomer and unlucky adversary of Newton, Flamstead, in the reign of Queen Anne, unfortunately took it into his head, in attempting to give names to the stars not reckoned in the ancient constellations, to mingle with these sacred and significant emblems such senseless figures as the fox and goose, or such unimportant ones as the shield of Sobieski and bull of Poniatowski, which now disfigure the modern sphere. He did not even suspect they had any meaning, therefore it is evident that this great astronomer had not in the course of his studies met with any account of their possible signification which appeared to him worthy of notice. It is in Jewish antiquity alone that we find any vestige of a received meaning being attached to them. But neither among the ancient Hebrews, nor the Greeks or Romans, are any allusions to be traced to the mansions of the moon, so influential in India, and so venerated by the Arabs, in which, as is here shown, a similar development of the course of prophecy is consistently pursued.

MEMORIAL LINES FOR THE MANSIONS OF THE MOON.

ZODIAC tells the path, the way [4],
Which the Sun measures day by day.
The Moon has her own zodiac given,
Traced by stars in midnight heaven,
Those eight and twenty mansions known
To Arabs still, by names here shown [5].
Messiah's reign the signs begun,
Which tell the progress of the Sun ;
The Moon, the Church to glory led,
Begins her course in Christ her Head,
Ordain'd to end in union blest
With Him above in endless rest.
The lunar mansions still began,
The slain, the bruised, Al Sheratan ;
That name too tells the princely reign,
The Lamb shall rule that has been slain.
Not to one purpose do we find
God's word or works alone confined ;
These starry records early made
More than one meaning oft convey'd.   } ARIES.

Botein, *the trodden on,* below,
Thuraiya *multitudes* to show.
The ruler, Aldebaran red [6] ;
Heka, *He comes,* Orion's head.   } TAURUS.

Al Hena, *wounded,* at the feet
Of the bright twins, and placed as meet,
Dirâ, *the seed,* their heads upon,
Al Nithra, *gain,* possession won.   } GEMINI.

Terpha, *the prey,* the separation.
Al Gieba, *highest exaltation,*
Of ancient solstice was the measure.
Al Zubra, *gather'd* as a *treasure.*   } CANCER. LEO.

Serpha, *the branch ;* He, *the desired,*
Awa, the Babe the Wise admired [7].
Simak al Azal, she who *holds*
The Branch, the seed her arm enfolds.   } VIRGO.

Caphir below, *atonement* made.
Al Zubena, *the price* He paid.   } LIBRA.

Iclil, *completion,* Kalb, *the cleaving*
In conflict with the reptile heaving.   } SCORPIO.

---

[4] P. 5, Second Part.   [5] P. 25, Second Part.   [6] Chaucer, Aldeboran.   [7] Matt. ii.

Shaula, the dart *sent forth*, Al Naim,
The *gracious* One, to bless, who came. } SAGITTARIUS.
Beldah, *sent forth with speed;* beneath
Dabih, *the victim*, sinks in death. } CAPRICORNUS.
Bulaa, *the drinking in*, Al Su'ud,
Out-pouring of life-giving flood.
Achbiya, *vase*, in which ascends
The water ere its stream descends. } AQUARIUS.
Al Pherg-Muchaddem, *multitude*
Of former times, in union view'd
With later gain'd, Muacchar named,
Both as His own their Lord has claim'd.
Al Risha, band, wherein to hold
United thus the crowds untold,
The multitudes redeem'd by Him
Whom all these types foreshadow'd dim. } PISCES.

The Mythology of India,

IN CONNEXION WITH ANCIENT ASTRONOMY.

		Texts.	Hebrew or Noetic Roots.
India [1], and Hindu, *the glorious*	{ *India*	Esth. 1. 1.	הדר
	{ *glory*	Jer. 22. 18.	הדה
THE THREE CHIEF GODS, OR POWERS, OF THE HINDOOS.			
Brahma, *the great Creator,*	{ Brah, *he creates*	Gen. 1. 1.	ברא
	{ Ma, Sanscrit, *great, multitude, many*	Gen. 17. 4.	המה
Vishnu, *he who saves*		Job 5. 15.	ישע
Sivah, *he who does justice, avenging, destroying, rewarding* .		Job 33. 27.	שוה
{ *justice,* Arab. sense.			

Above these it is believed that there is a supreme deity, too holy to be invoked. It is said his incommunicable name was Brahm, the great Creator, as Brahma; but by these personified attributes he governed the world and was to be worshipped [2]. To these no allusion is made in any sign, emblem, or constellation.

The close resemblance between the yet extant astronomy of India, corrupted and perverted as it is, with the more perfectly preserved astronomy of the Arabs, needs only to be examined to be recognized.

Some of the constellations are still called by nearly the same names, as, for instance, those of Cepheus and Cassiopea. The correspondence of the Indian Mansions of the Moon with those of the Arabs has been pointed out [3], and the identity of the figures of the twelve signs under names of similar import. The message of all these is "He cometh," the name Budh, or Budhu, containing it, as does the word Avatar, applied to ten incarnations and comings of a divine person, Vishnu, who comes to save, to deliver. Of these, nine are said to be past, the tenth to come.

Krishna—whose name has been derived from Chres, the sun, the type of Him who should come born of a virgin, conqueror of the serpent, and bitten by it in the heel—seems to have followed the sun among the signs in some of the actions attributed to him. He is often represented as painfully wrestling with the serpent. who bites his foot; and again, with kingly crown and royal ornaments, as crushing the serpent's head [4], so personifying the constellations Ophiuchus and Hercules. In the Bhagavad Gita, or divine song, the divine Krishna, in describing his own nature and the relation of man to him, is made to say, "I am the sacrifice," thus connecting himself with the signs Capricorn and Aries. This "divine song," which is very ancient, is a conversation between Krishna and Arjuna on divine things, so resembling that between Odin and Vafthrudni, as to lead to the supposition that they had a common origin.

NOTES.

The Brahminical creed teaches, "That matter has no existence independent of mental perception, that external sensation would vanish into nothing if the Divine energy for a moment subsided. That the soul is a particle from the creative spirit, and will be finally absorbed. That nothing has a pure and separate existence but spirit, and that an exclusive love of God is the only feeling that offers no illusion to the soul, and secures its eternal felicity." And yet on this sublime creed they have overlaid the absurdities of the vulgar belief [5].

---

[1] The insertion of *n* frequently represents the guttural sounds in Hebrew roots.

[2] Dr. Max Muller says that Brahma means originally force, will, wish, and the propulsive force of *creation.*

[3] Pp. 24, &c., Second Part.

[4] As figured in one of the publications of the Religious Tract Society. In the Sanscrit dictionary, compiled two thousand years ago, Krishna is said to be born of a woman. He is said to have slain in his boyhood the serpent Caliya, the destroyer, slaying and slain, חלל, or חלה. Job xxiv. 12; Gen. xxxiv. 27, &c.

[5] See Charles Grant's (Lord Glenelg's) prize poem on the subject, where "Maya" is fully developed. The coincidence of the Brahminical metaphysics, so called, with the system of Bishop Berkeley, is there developed and is otherwise recognized.

About the year A.D. 64 the Chinese Emperor sent messengers into India to inquire if the long predicted Holy One of Confucius was born, Confucius about 550 B.C. having said the Holy One must be sought in the West; it is said they took back Buddhism. Du Halde's China.

"The Divine name in the Hebrew religion is found in a Chinese book written 600 B.C." Finn's Jews in China.

Fohi, or Buddha, like Krishna, was said to be born of a virgin.

The late Abbé Huc in his last work, "Christianity in China, Tartary, and Thibet," comes to the conclusion that "the philosophy of Confucius, the traditions of Buddha, the legends of the Vedas, and the dogmas of Mahomet are all destined shortly to wane before the Gospel of Christ."

This distinguished missionary seems to have given the fullest account yet obtained of the present state of religion in China. In the lapse of four thousand years, the simple truths which the children of Noah carried everywhere with them, have been overlaid by such a multitude of human inventions, as to be difficult to trace out, but two remarkable coincidences with the religion indicated by ancient astronomy are to be recognized. The Jesuits, who first made China known to Europeans, were struck with amazement on seeing in so many temples the figure of a woman with an infant in her arms, called the Queen of Heaven. They tried to connect this worship with their own of the Blessed Virgin and her holy Child, but failed to recognize the connecting link between the two, which may be found in the sign Virgo, the woman and infant of the ancient zodiac. The well-known cognizance of China, the national emblem of the dragon, is again astronomical, and must have been adopted by the first founders of the empire, as that of the enemy to be subdued, when after bruising the heel of the coming Messiah his own head should receive the final bruise; thus recording what may have been the saving faith of those who first adopted that well-known symbol, but too soon corrupted by manifold inventions.

Ting-hae (China). In the principal temple of worship in that city, "the Queen of Heaven" is the most conspicuous object of admiration, robed in silk and rich embroidery. She appears emerging from the sea, the right foot resting on the head of an enormous fish [6], and bearing a child on her left arm. Above and below this towering divinity are attendant angels or demi-gods, *the white dove;* and on the altar beneath, massive candlesticks with burning tapers occupy the foreground. The illusion is startling, and forcibly reminds me of its near resemblance to the Virgin and Child in Roman Catholic Chapels.—Letter from Chusan, July, 1840.

A small temple of Boodha, or Budh, was brought from Ceylon some years ago, and exhibited in London, as here described. The name Boodh, or Budha, referred to primitive roots, signifies "He who cometh," or "He who should come." Matt. xi. 3. Heb. ix. 14—22.

Buddhism holds that at intervals of vast ages a Buddha (באת, who cometh) is developed, who, though born of earthly parents becomes omniscient. This religion teaches, that as pain and instability characterize all existence, the aim of all should be to pass with the next Buddha into the golden region of Nigban [7], or annihilation. This is granted to all that attend to certain moral precepts and acts of worship. By such deep darkness has the light of primitive revelation been overclouded; yet it may be traced in the name Buddha, which in the Semitic dialects would mean He who cometh, and in the blood-stained hands held up, typifying the atonement by sacrifice. By this name, Buddhism is connected again with the sign Virgo, one of whose Decans is Bootes, He who cometh.

The first Buddha, whose *coming* is recorded to have been in the seventh century B.C., appears to have taken to himself the promises of the great One who should come, known to the heathen by the prophecy of Noah, "He shall dwell in the tents of Shem," Job xix., and by that of Balaam, in whose widely circulated prediction of the "Star" this expectation was diffused among all nations.

Ceylon had been earlier conquered by the Hindoos, whose acquaintance with the prophecies has been often recognized, especially the one great prophecy, "He shall come, the Desire of all nations." Hag. ii. 7.—Tennent's Ceylon. The Poli, or sacred dialect of the Boodhists, is said by Dr. Leyden to be a dialect of the Sanscrit.

B.C. 850, Meni says, "God created to give happiness;" yet he speaks of catastrophes and renewals of the surface of the earth and of its creatures. The traditions of patriarchal religion were still in existence, and less obscured by human inventions than they afterwards became. Long after the time of Meni, Zoroaster predicted to the Magi, or chiefs of Persia, the future appearance of a star announcing the birth of a mysterious child, the Almighty Word which created the heavens, whom he commanded them to adore. So affirms Abulfaragius, a well-known Arabian writer.—Hyde de Vet. Rel. Pers.

---

[6] The fish, the emblem of the Church.   [7] Nigban, נבג, dried up, exhausted.

The Mythology of the Scandinavian Nations,

AS CONNECTED WITH THE ANCIENT ASTRONOMY.

	Texts.	Hebrew or Noetic Roots.
Scandinavia, { *the dwelling*	Deut. 12. 5.	שכן
{ *of the lords or rulers*	Gen. 42. 30.	ארן
Odin, *the lord or ruler*	Gen. 45. 8, 9.	ארן
Thor, *who gives* { *light* (Orion)	Isa. 45. 7.	אור
{ *lightning*	Job 37. 3.	אור
{ *or who wounds, bruises,* as Tyr.	Isa. 46. 1. *Bel*	בל
Bel, or Baal, *the lord*	Hos. 2. 16. *Baal* — 1 Kgs. 18. 19.	בעל
Balder, *the lord who dwells, or returns,* Arab. sense	Dan. 4. 9.	דר
Tyr, *who wounds and is wounded, tear, tore,* Arab. sense	*a razor* Num. 6. 5.	תער
Tuisco, *who saves, delivers*	Judg. 2. 18.	ישע
Sater, *who hides, gives shelter*	Deut. 32. 38.	סתר
Lok, *the scorner, the mocker*	Job 34. 7.	לעג

The Scandinavian tribes are considered by Biblical scholars to be descended from Japhet. The three sons of Noah must have spoken the same language, at least till the confusion at Babel; that confusion being of the lip, the pronunciation only, the roots of words, their characteristic letters remained unchanged, and among the recognized descendants of them may be called Semitic, but among those of the other two sons of Noah, *Noetic* seems the preferable designation.

The Scandinavian mythology, like the emblems of the constellations, has no reference to the one great Creator, the All-father of the northern nations, the one God of whom the wise among ancient Greeks and Romans spake, as above the personifications of traditional prophecy by the names of which they called the gods. Inferior to Him, the Supreme Creator, were Odin, the lord, the ruler; Thor, armed with a hammer, like the evil demons of the Etrurian remains, the implement of breaking or bruising, agreeing with one sense of his name Thor, העֹר, the breaker, or he who shall bruise; Tyr, who returns, also called Tuisco, who saves, delivers; Freya, who brings forth; Sater, who shelters, gives rest. These were personifications of the ancestral prophecies of a promised Deliverer, interposed for objects of worship. Those concerning the Messiah are most peculiarly to be traced in the character and history of Balder, the God who shall return, the Beloved of all creation, "the Desire of nations."

The mythology of the Northern nations affords abundant traces of the worship of the host of heaven, the first corruption of the patriarchal faith. Into this corruption the human mind easily declined, from paying undue reverence to the symbols of the objects set before them by divine revelation for the exercise of their faith.

The Sun, the ruler of the visible heaven, typifying the true light of the world, and passing through the twelve signs, denoting the progressive manifestation of his great prototype, the promised "Sun of righteousness," was substituted for Him under the names of Bel and Baal, the lord, and Odin, the ruler, as the object of veneration along with, and at length in the place of, the great Coming One, whom he represented. The virgin mother of the zodiac, Virgo, who bringeth forth, is fruitful, by the equivalent names of *Freya*[1] or *Fregga*, was, as the memory of the prophecy became obscured, called his wife, and the infant in her arms their son. This divine offspring, the mild, the merciful, the beloved of all creation except the evil one, Lok, the enemy of God and man—this god, who was born to die, was called Balder[2], the Lord who comes again. After a while imagination prevailing, as usual in tradition, over memory, the twelve zodiacal emblems of the course of prophecy were interpreted as the twelve companions of the sun. They were called the twelve Aser[3], or princes, who attended on the supreme divinity, called Odin, the ruler, or he who cometh[4]. These mythological personages

---

[1] פרה, to be fruitful.
[3] שר, prince.
[2] בעל, the lord; דר, to return, go round.
[4] עד, or (א)רין.

were objects of veneration, if not of worship, before the appearance of the second Odin, the great human conqueror, whose era and whose acts are alike involved in the mists of remote antiquity. He took, as the Roman emperors and others have since done, the appellation of the god the nation worshipped, an appellation which he might borrow as the human ruler from him who was worshipped as the divine. Following up the analogy, he chose twelve companions from among his adherents, called Aser, the princes. His time has been supposed to be the seventh century before the Christian era, or the sixth, when he is by some authorities said to have fled with a colony of Goths before the victorious arms of Darius Hystaspes. Again, at a much later period, supposed to be the last century before the Christian era, we meet with the third Odin, the conqueror and lawgiver, acknowledged to be a real historical personage. He is considered to have been the leader of a tribe dwelling between the Euxine and the Caspian seas, and driven from thence by the Roman conquests under Pompey, in the Mithridatic war. He also bore the name of office, Odin: whether he took it to ally himself with the god and the worshipped hero, or whether he brought it with him from the East, where it long existed as a title of sovereignty, may be rather matter of conjecture than of certainty.

The Scalds or Bards, as had been done by the poets of Greece with the name and history of Hercules, frequently applied the name and praises, attributes and actions of the Divine One to the hero, and of both to the lawgiver. The well-known poem of the Descent of Odin seems to combine the two first characters; that of the Victory of Odin over the giant Vafthrudni [5] gives the divine alone. The wild and melancholy catastrophe predicted to the hero-race and their warrior deities Odin and Thor, when the scorner Lok let loose, should prevail, and the twilight of the gods obscure the face of earth and sky, is well known in poetry and tradition ; but it is less remembered that above all this terrific creed, dark and storm-boding as their wintry sky, shone a sun of better augury. After that twilight of the gods, in which all these worshipped demons were to perish, Scandinavian Bard and prophetic vaca looked for the final reign of the one true God, "as the light of the morning when the sun ariseth, a morning without clouds," when a new and better race of men should spring up "as the tender grass out of the earth, by clear shining after rain." Then they believed that the unseen All-father should reign over a renewed heaven and a renewed earth, but not without the risen and restored Balder the beloved, then rescued from the power of Hela, to whom below "his head was given [6]."

NOTE ON HELA.

Hela, the dweller in darkness, the Scandinavian goddess of *hell*, so named from her, has had her name from the primitive root *Hel*, חל, to which Æschylus appears to allude in the Agamemnon, where he says of Helen,—

> " Who was it that gave the name
> In all ways truthfully ?
> One whom we see not,
> Foreknowing thus the coming fates,
> Speaking with happy tongue,
> Of that bride of spears and raging,
> Helen, for most fitly she so called,
> Destroying vessels and destroying men,
> Destroying also states."

Helen is here referred to the primitive root חל, *to destroy*, but it is more likely that she had been named from הל, *to shine*, whence Hλιos, the sun.

NOTES.

Scandinavia, שבן דן, the dwelling-place of Odin or the lord, chief, or judge, or of the lords of men, a title still claimed by the Danes.

The celebrated Danish writer Ingeman, in common with many of the leading minds of the present time, has been led to reject the ordinary explanations of the starry emblems, and to look in them for some reference to revelation. He says [7], "As from the oldest time the suns of other worlds have been distributed into groups, is it not allowable to inquire whether there were not a unity of purpose and connected meaning in them, though these grotesque figures are represented as hieroglyphs which we trace to the Chaldeans and Phœnicians?" He con-

---

[5] The Vafthrudnis mal, is a dialogue between one of the giant race and Odin in disguise, concerning the gods and the universe.

[6] Gray's " Descent of Odin."

[7] " Symbolism of the Constellations," a poetical sketch, by Ingeman.

siders the serpent held by Ophiuchus, with Hydra and Draco, as representing "the demoniacal agent in the world."   Again, "the world-snake Midgard" he traces in these figures, "reminding us of the Northern myths."   "These things are divided into three large groups, each of which contains its own principle."   Ophiuchus, herald of light and warmth, fills the north; Orion, magnificent in the winter nights, the south, accompanied by Sirius, the brightest of the starry throng.   "Orion holds the same place among the starry heroes that Odin accompanied by Thor does among the Asers."   Perseus he likens to Braga; "Hercules, in his mediatoriness, takes part in the struggle with the demoniacal principle, setting his mighty foot on Draco, leaning his head on Ophiuchus.   This figure is one of the deepest import in the symbols of the world, the head figure of the grotesque figures of the paintings of the heavens."   "Ophiuchus, the starry hero of summer, as Orion of winter."   He finds Odin and Balder in Ophiuchus and Hercules, and says the raven is Odin's bird, and with the cup belongs to the great destroyer of the serpent [8].

The root Or, Aur, "light," being in both names, Orion and Thor, the Scandinavian deity of light and thunderstorm, the northern tribes connected the constellations with the names of their gods and their heroes; these would be assimilated.   While the Southern nations named their heavens *cœlum*, blue [9], and *ouranos*, light, those of the North spoke of it as sky [1], dark, cloudy; did the cloudy heavens of Scandinavia obscure to their eyes the emblematic constellations, though traditions remained of the planets and the planetary week?

NOTE ON NOETIC.

The roots, radical or characteristic letters, which are to be found in the names of the signs and other constellations, pervade all ancient languages in the senses here attributed to them. They may also be traced in modern dialects derived from the ancient, and even, but more rarely, in modern barbarous tongues.   For instance, the root Kan, in Cancer, appears in ancient Sanscrit and modern Australian, as she who *gains* offspring as Eve, Cain, Kana, being in Sanscrit, a female, and Gin in Australia; G and C or K being well known as interchangeable letters.   In these dialects the roots are Noetic, even when also found in the Semitic languages.

---

[8] "In Egyptian remains Horus is frequently represented as piercing the head of the serpent." (Wilkinson.)   Rather *bruising*.

[9] Cœlum, blue, כלה (ח).   Exod. xxv. 4, as covering, completing the sky.

[1] Skỳ, dark, σκια, overshadowing, סך.   Job xl. 22.

Memorial Lines

FOR THE NAMES OF INDIAN MYTHOLOGY AS CONNECTED WITH ANCIENT ASTRONOMY.

INDIA, glorious land, long shrouded,
In mysterious veil, o'er-clouded
Thy rich realms with mists of error,
Demon-worship, shapes of terror.
Yet these idols dire above
Thou hast own'd a God of love ;
Nameless, formless, yet supreme,
In light o'ershining evil dream
Of blood-stain'd horror's midnight gleam.
Beneath this Great One, Brahma, known
Creating God, thy millions own ;
Vishnu, who comes to save, returning ;
Siva in wrath to sinners burning ;
The mighty Three, who send on earth
Krishna divine, of wondrous birth,
The Virgin-born, by serpent foe
Bruised in the heel for mortal woe ;
Virgin and branch, so shown on high,
Scorpion and dragon of the sky.
Buddha, who comes, goes, comes again,

Leaving his heaven, on earth to reign,
Whose image oft is framed to be
Past, present, future, One in Three.
As Krishna, virgin-born, thus told
Of the same origin, of old,
The starry Virgin, babe divine,
Were view'd as orbs of evening shine.
In furthest China too is seen
The child, and she, of Heaven the Queen,
The Virgin-mother, and the dove
That rested on the Son of love [1] ;
The dragon-foe, as trophy worn,
On temple and on standard borne.
All these the world-wide influence show
Of starry lore on man below ;
In lines of light on heaven's high dome [2]
They told of Him who was to come.
He came, He went, to come once more,
Heaven's piece begun, earth's sorrows o'er.

In the seventh century, before the incarnation of Christ, Buddha was assumed to have been born of a woman without a human father; so, even earlier, was it written of Krishna.

In a Review of Müller's "Ancient Sanscrit Literature, so far as it relates to the primitive religion of the Brahmins," (*Times*, Nov. 8, 1859,) it is said,—

"Who are these Aryans, of whom we now hear so much ? The answer is, we are *all* Aryans. All the nations that have made our world what it is are of the great Aryan stock. The word in Sanscrit is used as well-born, or lord [3]. This term has taken the place of those awkward compounds, Indo-Germanic and Indo-European [4]."

Is not Aries, primarily the head or chief, ראש (א), belonging to the same train of ideas as Aryan ?

"The Brahmin philosophers believed in a real externally existing eternal Divine Being, all else only *seeming* to exist." "Their life was a yearning after eternity." "Their existence on earth a problem, their eternal life a *certainty*."

"The Vedas presuppose and imply a long period of anterior development : to them the idea of God is old and familiar [5]."

442 B.C. there is a record of "the Council of Palibuttra protesting against the corruption of the religion of India."

There is a remarkable analogy between the twelve signs of the zodiac and the Avatars, or successive comings to earth, to save and to deliver, of Vishnu, he who saves, the second person in the Indian Trinity, called Tricourtee in the sacred books of the Brahmins, the syllable tri, three, pervading most languages, as Persian, Greek, Latin and its dialects, as well as English, German, &c., in modern Europe. The word Avatar combines three ancient words for "to come," ab, or av, from ba, to come, at, from atha, to come [6], and ar, or arah, to come. The Avatars are his comings to save, to deliver, interpositions whenever the earth and man were in peculiar danger. Nine are past, the tenth is yet to come.

In the first Avatar he assumed the form of a fish, as the sign Pisces, to destroy an evil giant, to which perhaps the human figure in Aquarius may have given occasion.

In the second Avatar, Vishnu took the form of the boar, in Capricornus, the swine being the natural enemy of the serpent, and as such appears in the Egyptian planisphere and other monuments.

---

[1] Matt. iii. 17.   [2] Ps. xix. 1.

[3] It is used in Heb. and Arab., &c., as a lion-like man, brave, invincible. Isa. xxi., &c. Thence the conquering invaders in every land have been called Aryans.

[4] Noetic, through Abraham, whence the Hebrew roots allowed to exist in the Sanscrit, as well as the idea of but One Triune God, and an offspring virgin-born, partaking of both natures, Divine and human, as Krishna and Buddha. The Reviewer says, "Philology is taking a higher place in the examinations at Oxford and Cambridge." "Roots are examined about."

[5] The Reviewer also says, "the idea of God is no part of natural religion"—revealed to the *first* man. In Africa alone missionaries have found tribes who had no idea of God. *They* were not *Aryan*, of which *noble* is another possible sense, whence derived, the epithet hero, heroic, high, dignified, from the primitive root Her, הר, whence we also trace the German "Herr."

[6] Job iii. 25, 26. אתא בא, א.

In the third, as a man holding the amreeta, the cup of immortality, the urn of Aquarius.
In the others, as Krishna, the divine and human offspring of the great God.

The human nature being traceable,

In Aries[7], as Perseus.
In Taurus, Orion.
In Gemini, the twins, divine and human.
In Cancer, Soheil, the desired.
In Leo, half man, half lion.
In Virgo, Bootes, Arcturus, the guardian, the keeper.
In Libra, where the ancient Persians placed a man as in wrath.

In Scorpio, Ophiuchus bruising the serpent's head, and Hercules wounded in the heel, in both which aspects Krishna may be seen represented.

In Sagittarius, the rider, the archer, where, in the tenth Avatar, he is yet to come, on a white horse, overthrowing his enemies[8], to root out evil from the earth.

In the fifth Avatar, Vishnu, in human form, is said to have measured the earth with one step, the heavens with another. In the ninth he assumed the form of Boodh, or Buddha.

It has been observed that "1000 years B.C. there existed amid the Indian systems of philosophy, so profound and so complex, alternately scaling the sublimest heights of metaphysical speculation and sinking into the lowest depths of folly and degradation, the great doctrine of divine communion."

The Brahmin philosophy teaches that nothing has a pure and separate existence but spirit, and that a deep and exclusive love of the Divine being is the only feeling bringing no illusion to the soul, and securing its eternal felicity. These sublime views shine amid the darkness of idolatry as the stars of heaven are brightest in deepest midnight: doubtless they descended with their astronomy and their appellation from their divinely illuminated ancestor, Abraham.

The wide-spread traditions[9] of the early world have been compared to the aurora borealis of the northern regions; are they not rather like to the long abiding twilight of the polar night, telling of the sun, set indeed to actual vision, but leaving a gleam of glory in the sky, still illuminating the horizon, and foreshowing his return in the brightening east? Mythologies were not inventions, but the traditions of the first revelation, and the ancient prophecies added to and disguised. In the Northern, in the partly human character of Odin, there is the exaltation of man; in the Oriental, as in the Avatars, "the glorious humiliation of the Godhead." Traces of the first revelation, teaching the whole human race to cling to the One man, the second Adam, "He who should come," the seed of the woman, the conqueror of the serpent, survived among all nations, an imperishable tradition, the ivy clinging to "the Rock of ages[1]," having everlasting strength.

That the "seed" should be virgin-born seems to have been revealed to Eve after the birth of Cain, for no such mistake as hers with regard to her first-born is recorded in the whole Jewish history. No Jewish woman ever again presumed to say, "I have gotten a man, the Lord," though so many among the surrounding nations claimed for their offspring a divine father. The prophecies of the Messiah, scattered among the nations, were kept in memory by their connexion with the emblems of the constellations, like the ivy, never so vigorous as when it cleaves to the rock. Tradition might be perverted, but the starry skies changed not, the rock to which it clung.

---

[7] According to Le Gentil, the Brahminical year begins at the sun's entrance into Aries, and their names of the signs are nearly similar to ours, but the constellations differ. Dr. Hyde says that Perseus, Andromeda, and Cepheus, are Indian constellations, thus preserving the traditional prophecies of the Deliverer, the Church in affliction, and the Beloved, He who cometh and cometh again, the King. Part II., pp. 9 and 23.

[8] Campbell's Pleasures of Hope. "The tenth Avatar comes."

[9] "The miraculous conception of the Great Deliverer was widely known long before the Christian Era, as is shown in the Asiatic Researches, Vol. xi., &c." Edinburgh Review on Huc's Travels.

It has long been observed that "the system of Pagan religion being the same in all parts of the world is a strong confirmation of the Mosaic history." Vallancey's Anted. Astron.

[1] Isa. xxvi. 4, margin.

MEMORIAL LINES FOR THE NAMES OF SCANDINAVIAN MYTHOLOGY.

Scandinavia, dwelling high
Of lords of men 'neath arctic sky,
Iron and man, warrior and sword,
Those regions stern, nor gold to hoard,
Nor grape juice to allure, afford.
The great All-father fear'd above,
Too high for worship or for love,
Dwelling beyond the freezing sky,
Revered and thought of silently.
Odin, deem'd ruler of the world,
And Thor, the thunder-bolt who hurl'd;
Bel, lord of all, they own'd, whose name,
To Eastern climes was curse and shame,
These three ancestral worship claim.
Tuisco saving, wounding, Tyr,
Freya[1], who loves, all loving her;

Balder, her son, who shall return,
Beloved of all, yet must he learn
Malice of Lok, the serpent-foe,
And to the realms of Hela go.
Odin shall free, Sater give rest,
Freya in him again be blest.
Yet "twilight of the gods" must fall
On blood-stain'd earth, and perish all
The warrior gods, Lok rage no more,
And Hela's dreary reign be o'er.
So Scald and Vala's prophet-lay
Tell of returning light and day,
When war and slaughter never more
Shall bathe the shrinking earth in gore;
Odin and Thor, names of the past,
Balder beloved, reign at last.

---

[1] As in some parts of the East and in Egypt the Triune Deity was corrupted into a triad of divinities, of which one was a woman, so Thor, Odin, and Freya, wife of Odin, and mother of Balder, were the Scandinavian triad. Freya was identified with, or represented by the moon, and Venus, like those, an emblem of the Church of the faithful under all dispensations, antediluvian, Mosaic, Christian. Lok, the adversary of gods and men, was beautiful (as an angel of light), his wife Angerbode the prophetess of evil* or wrath, according to her name. They had for offspring the wolf Fenris, of evil aspect, the serpent Midgard, and Hela, whose table for those who feared to die in battle was hunger, whose bed was sickness.

Olaus Rudbeck † traces the Asiatic origin of the Scandinavian tribes by the oriental roots he finds in their dialects, chiefly in the words connected with their mythology and astronomy. He thus relates the story of the death of Balder. Balder had evil dreams; Frigga, or Freya, his mother, demanded an oath of all created things that they would do him no harm; but when she saw the musteltein (or mistletoe) she passed it by, as too young, too weak. Lok made an arrow of it, and placing it in the hand of the blind Hoder, bade him shoot; he did so and killed Balder ‡.

The Nornas§, the veiled virgins, whom Odin saw, when he was recognized by the prophetess, were the past, present, and future, invisible to mortal eye, each alike mourning for Balder, the beloved of all creation, the divine son of Odin, doomed to an inevitable death, to be avenged by his brother Veli ||, who shall arise. There, as in so many other similar traditions, may be traced the prophecies of the second coming in glory, as well as of the first coming to suffer and to die of "the Desire of Nations."

---

* See Gray's Descent of Odin. Fenris. פנרש.

† He gives a print of Thor on a throne, with twelve stars round his head. In Danish and Icelandic the Wain (Ursa Major) was anciently called the chariot of Thor. The name of Thor, sometimes sharing the divine honours of Odin, and sometimes even superseding them, may be derived from the same root as that of Orion[1], to come forth, as light, or who wounds, bruises. Both senses appear to have been followed out; that of bruising by his attribute of the hammer, and the names which he has in common with the evil demons of Etruria, thus indicating the same origin to both superstitions, and being an instance of the affinity of all languages, indicating their common origin from that divinely imparted to Adam at his creation, and traceable in all the dialects of his descendants.

‡ Atlantica (Brit. Mus.).

§ (רן) singers, as Runes, &c. The sixteen Runic characters are said to be named after constellations.

|| Veli, עלה, who comes or arises.

---

[1] If as Orion, from אר, the Th are only servile letters; if they are radical, it is from to wound or bruise, תער.

MEMORIAL LINES FOR THE PLANETS, AS CONNECTED WITH ANCIENT ASTRONOMY.

THE Sun, the Moon, have told the praise
Of Him whose glory dims their rays,
And stars along their glittering road
His suffering and His reigning show'd.
But what to those the message given,
Bright wanderers o'er the arch of heaven,
Who, like the Moon in varying lustre,
Pass lonely o'er each far-off cluster?
How named by those who earliest saw,
And lived to ascertain their law?—
By those who named the weekdays seven,
Seen in the order they have given.

SUNDAY . . .⎫	The Sun, the Moon, they reckon'd first,
MONDAY . . .⎭	Whose light on man had earliest burst.

TUESDAY . . . Then saw they Mars, the star so red,   *Adam, red,* אדם
And from the blood that should be shed   *blood,* דם
For man, Ma'adim this they name,
The red, the human, and the same
As, Adam, meaning likeness-bearing,   *likeness,* דמה
And also to be slain declaring.   *to be slain* [1], דים
    דם

WEDNESDAY . . Soon might they view a brilliant light,
Swift darting rays of keenest white,
Coming and going round the Sun,
Circling in haste the course begun.
The strong in light, who comes, Catab,   ⎰*strong,* כח
Called Mercury, by some Cochab.   ⎱*who cometh,* אבא
In Mercury we the meaning see   ⎰*from far,* מרחק
Circling from far, contain'd to be.   ⎱*circling,* ריר

THURSDAY . . Then Jupiter, with stedfast light,
They traced, illumining the night:
Zedek, True, Just, the names deserved,   *just,* צדק
Who from due circuit never swerved.

FRIDAY . . . Next, fairest star of all the host
And brightest, Venus, loved the most.   *beloved,* חינה
Nogah, the splendid, brilliant, named,   ננה
As Hesperus and Vesper famed,   *pleasant,* שפר
Which beautiful and fair proclaimed.

SATURDAY . . At length, slow-moving, seen afar,
Saturn they traced, reposing star,   *repose,* שב
Called Sabbatei in Eastern clime,
And Saturn, type of hidden time.   *to hide,* שתר

DAYS OF THE WEEK⎫ The nations who from Babel turn'd
NAMED FROM THEM.⎭ Retain'd the order they had learn'd
Of observations earliest made
On planets seen in Eden's shade:
And many a tongue and people seek
From them to name the seven-day week.   חר

APPLICATION AS TYPES⎫ In one alone these orbs preserve
OF THE CHURCH. ⎭ The likeness careful eyes observe
To changing moons, in splendour mild.
Venus by all is female styled.
In waxing, waning, wavering light,
Though in the Sun's own radiance bright,
She might not show the Lord of all;
But in the changes that befall,
She, as the Moon, might well pourtray

---

[1] Gen. xxxvii. 26. Josh. xx. 3. 6.

The Church oft darken'd in her way,
And brightening from the fount of day.
Such was the view, it seems, they took,
Who first thus read night's starry book;
For heaven-taught prophecy was theirs,
And such the message that it bears.
When all these orbs were seen and known,
Faint and afar Uranus shone,
Rahini, weak [2], in Eastern lore
'Twas call'd, and soon observed no more.
Even such their view of Eden state—
The Church unfallen, how short its date!
In Saturn, Sabbatei, more bright,
Saw they their own calm faith and light
Restored by that blest promise given
To Adam, when from Eden driven.
In Zedek, just, call'd Jove, they saw
The Patriarchal Church and Law,
When Job and Abraham from the Lord
Received direct the holy word.
In Mars, Ma'adim, might they see,
The Church, pourtraying when should be
The sacrifice mysterious slain,
Of Him to die and yet to reign.
Then came the earth whereon He stood,
And shed for sin His victim blood.
Earth named to tell the bruised, the broken,   *bruised,* ארץ
Of Him it told; of her when spoken
It well describes the state we know,
The shatter'd frame of earth below.
Next, as the Church, now dark, now bright,
And looking up to him for light,
Venus the splendid, like the Moon,
From fullest orb declining soon,
Yet glorious with her Lord to rise,
The star of morn in orient skies.
In Mercury there might be view'd,
Type of the Church when earth renew'd
Shall blessèd habitation give
To those, who privileged to live
Beneath the rule of Zion's King,
For His return shall praises sing,—
The glorious Church, in power to come,
Bright in His rays, their happy home.

ON THE NAMES OF THE PLANETS.

It is remarkable that in the name affixed by modern astronomers to the long-forgotten planet now called Uranus, is contained the root of that given to it in Oriental astronomy, *Uranus* having the chief letters of Rahini, the Burmese name [3] of the traditionary planet.

The name given to that planet which the ancients never knew, contains in it a root applicable to the wonderful process of its discovery: by *faith* in the deductions of science the planet Neptune was found.

The more recently descried planet between Mercury and the Sun has also had a name given to it, belonging to one of the twelve great gods of the Greeks and Romans [4], Vulcan, the beneficent Deity, *lame* in the foot, and acknowledging no father, whose name means He cometh, and whose functions as to fire and heat are here peculiarly applicable.

But is it not a desecration to call these glorious works of the great Creator by the names of pagan idols, suggesting the idle and corrupt fables of heathen mythology? Might they not be appropriately named in our own wide-spreading language by words conveying the ideas expressed in the ancient appellations, and connected with yet more ancient prophecy?

---

[2] Weak, Arab. sense; Isa. xliv. 8, afraid.   [3] Sir W. Drummond.
[4] Part II., p. 83.

Might we not suppose that man had here been unintentionally following up the design of the overruling Providence, in giving names capable of being adapted to those of the already existing series, and like them of conveying instruction in alliance with prophecy.

Names now adopted from the Latin.	Proposed Descriptions of the Planets.	Ancient Names.	Texts.	Hebrew roots.
NEPTUNE.	The star of faith, As found by faith in science.	——	Gen. 9. 27, persuade.	(נ) יפה
URANUS.	The star of memory, As faintly seen, faintly remembered.	Rahini.	Isa. 40. 8, failing.	והה
SATURN.	The star of rest, As moving slowly, reposingly.	Sabbatei.	Gen. 2. 2, resting.	שבת
JUPITER.	The star of truth, As just and true in movement.	Zedek.	Isa. 45. 25, justified.	צרק
MARS.	The star of sacrifice, As red in colour.	Ma'adim.	Exod. 25. 5, dyed red.	מאדם
VENUS.	The star of beauty, As above all others splendid.	Nogah.	Joel 2. 10, shining.	מה
MERCURY.	The star of light, As returning with most powerful ray.	Cocab.	Job 23. 6, he cometh in power.	אז כח
VULCAN [1]	The star of warmth, As nearest to the sun [2].		Lu. 24. 32.	

MEMORIAL LINES FOR THE PLANETS.

Star of faith in things unseen ;	2 Cor. 4. 18.	Heb. 11. 1, &c.
Star of memory, what has been ;	Ps. 135. 15.	Isa. 43. 18.
Star of rest, in Him our peace ;	Lev. 16. 31.	Matt. 11. 28.
Star of truth, with light's increase ;	Ps. 43. 3.	2 Cor. 2. 13.
Star of sacrifice for sin ;	Lev. 17. 11.	Heb. 9. 22.
Star of beauty, grace to win ;	Cant. 6. 6.	Ephes. 5. 27.
Star of light, at His return ;	Isa. 60. 1.	Ephes. 5. 8.
Star of warmth, in love to burn [3],	Ps. 39. 3.	Lu. 24. 32.
From these names such lessons learn.		

	Persian Names of the Planets. From Elem. Ling. Pers.					Texts.	Hebrew roots.
SATURN.	Kivan, firm (Chiun)	.	.	.	.	Deut. 13. 14.	כיון
JUPITER [4].	Bergis, bright-shining	.	.	.	.	Ps. 144. 6.	ברק
MARS.	Beheram, fiery	.	.	.	.	Exod. 3. 2.	בער
SUN.	Afrab, coming, as in a chariot	.	.	.	.	Cant. 3. 9.	אפריון
VENUS.	Bahid, bright-coloured	.	.	.	.	Esth. 1. 6.	בהט
MERCURY.	Ter, going about	.	.	.	.	Num. 15. 39.	תר
MOON.	Mah, accompanying	.	.	.	.	Job 30. 29.	את

These ancient oriental names among others tend to show the antiquity and the universality of meanings here annexed to those of modern usage.

That the names of the planets in ancient and widely dispersed languages and countries are all capable of being explained, and with a similar signification, by extant Hebrew roots, furnishes

---

[1] The Latin name Vulcan, in Hebrew meaning, he cometh, from ילך ; the Greek, Hephæstus, the deliverer, from חפש, and the beloved, from נפץ.

[2] Vulcan, the star of warmth, as nearest to the Sun. Luke xxiv. 32.

[3] Ps. xxxix. 3 ; Luke xxiv. 32.

[4] The Greek name, Pheton, or Phaeton, given Part II., p. 118, for Jupiter, may be derived from יפה, fair, or bright, or יפע, shining. As the Greek φαινω, from whence also φανεροω, to make manifest, as truth ; John ii. 11, &c.

evidence of one common origin of mankind, and of one original language of which the Hebrew is the best exponent. The Arabic, though having the same roots, often disguises them by the addition of many vowels. The names of the planets in use among the Romans, apparently of Etruscan origin, and, like those of other nations, containing coinciding Noetic roots, seem likely to be preserved among those nations formerly under their rule. These names are indeed so interwoven with the literature of Europe and America, that it may seem a vain attempt to change them. It might, however, be well to annex to them meanings which, while consistent with their ancient and original appellations, free them from their connexions with the vain and evil fables of Greek and Roman idolatry [5].

The signification of Saturn is every where rest; in astrology, the rest of death. Jupiter, the ruler, dealing prosperity, as in justice. Mars denotes slaying, or at least wounding. Venus is lovely and beloved. Mercury, going and returning. Uranus, Neptune, and Vulcan being unknown to the Greeks and Romans, any meanings attached to their names can be only as it were adaptations of the Noetic roots the names contain.

These Roman names may be thus explained by their ancient roots, as has been previously shown.

SATURN,	Resting, from the slowness of his motion.
JUPITER [6],	Just and true, as undisturbed by others.
MARS,	Wounding and wounded, from his colour.
VENUS,	Beautiful.
MERCURY,	Going and returning.
VULCAN,	Coming.

This explanation of these names seems unobjectionable for common use; while, in religious education, an equally appropriate and consistent use may be made of applicable texts of Scripture, as thus:—

SATURN,	There remaineth a rest to the people of God	Heb. 4. 9.
JUPITER,	Just and true are thy ways, Thou King of saints	Rev. 15. 3.
MARS,	The blood of Christ cleanseth from all sin	1 John 1. 7.
VENUS,	We love Him, because He first loved us	1 John 4. 19.
MERCURY,	In His light shall we see light	Ps. 36. 9.
VULCAN,	Fervent in spirit, serving the Lord	Rom. 12. 1.

Among the various speculations as to the planets being inhabited, another may be mentioned. Many of those not having a shadow of evidence, might not the meaning of the names throw a twilight gleam, however faint, on the obscurity of the investigation? The foundation for the ancient name of Uranus is indeed slender, but might it not be imagined, that spirits invested with pure and etherialized bodies are there located, while of those who inhabit Saturn a calm and sweet repose is the portion? Of the dwellers in Jupiter, a serene and equable adjustment of their nature to their lot, bright and even as the course of their planet; in Mars a greater similarity to our earth, even to the possibility of blood-shedding; in Venus, what brilliant felicity for sensitive beings adapted to their splendidly illuminated abode? In Mercury, what intensified enjoyment for beings such as the Divine Author of life and light could form to delight in the contemplation of His glorious attributes, and to revel in the splendour that He has created them to inhabit?

Whoever gave names to the fixed stars [7] must also have given names to the planets.

The first man must have been the first astronomer. He would soon perceive that the planets were not suns, shining by their own light, but, like the moon, reflecting that of the sun. By

---

[5] "The Pagan worship has been generally of evil beings." Abp. Whately on Bacon.

[6] Sat, given as an Egyptian name of Jupiter, seems a corrupt abbreviation of Zedek. Zedek is an appellative of Christ, in Isa. xlv. 21; liii. 11; Zech. iv. 9.

Authorities for the Hebrew names of the planets will be found in the Lexicon of Sebastian Munster, from the Rabbinical writers, also in Gaffarell's Cur. Lit.

[7] The few names of stars given in the popular translation of Arago's Lectures on Astronomy are very incorrect, as may be seen by comparison with ancient authorities, such as Ulugh Begh and others. The attempts there made to explain Arabic names connected with the twelve signs are very unfortunate; the Hebrew equally so, as where it is said, "the Hebrew word Fafa signifies *obtenebrescere*, to darken," whereas it means to be bright, beautiful, *fair*, as in Ps. xlv. 2.

Though Arago says "the names of the constellations were mostly capriciously given," yet he says, "astronomy is coeval with the world:" a most valuable admission. He traces it first to Chaldea, afterwards he finds it in Egypt. Thales, he says, brought astronomy to Greece from Phoenicia, whence Pythagoras brought the Copernican system, the belief that the planets were inhabited, and the fixed stars were suns, having planets of their own, and also that the comets evolved round the sun.

their change of place and apparent magnitude he would discern that they were not fixed stars, but were moving round a centre, evidently not the earth, and gradually ascertained to be the sun. That spirit of prophecy which enabled Enoch to predict the final judgment might enable him to see the analogies between these lights placed in heaven to illuminate earth's night and the revelations by which man's mental darkness should be brightened. It is a fact that the planets were so named; it is a fact that such successive revelations were predicted, and were given. The connexion between the two facts is not indeed revealed as intentional, but may it not be inferred as probable? May it not be well to connect the prophetic idea with the familiar name rather than the idle fables with which it is usually associated? These ancient names of the planets, according with their aspects, have also in them analogy with the prophecies afterwards expressed in the emblems of the constellations. He that should come would bring rest and restoration to the believer's soul, but must be bruised for their redemption; should then have a loved and loving Church, which should follow Him in His departure, and return with Him at His coming again.

The silvery rays of the almost moveless Saturn, the reposing, might speak of peace and rest, such as might come to Noah before the dispersion of Babel; as the ancient poets delight to tell of the golden age, the Saturnian age of placid happiness. The vivid brightness of the next planet might declare the glories of unclouded faith, such as enlightened the days of Abraham. The reddened hue of Mars might speak of atonement by sacrifice. The golden lustre of Venus, the beloved, of the Church brilliant in the light of her Lord. The diamond sparkle of Mercury, of the increasing intensity of His splendour at His second coming. And should we not strive to associate these beams of divine truth with those of the much slandered and debased orbs of night common to all the climes of earth, while the prophetically commissioned constellations belong but to one hemisphere [3]? The spirit of prophecy by Enoch had taught the later prophets to regard the sun as emblematizing the revelation of the glory of the promised Messiah as the "Sun of righteousness" to His creation, earth, moon, and planets rejoicing in His light. That revelation shines and is overclouded, is more or less bright, which His person cannot be. So after a while it would be perceived that these planets were not "companions" of the earth, as the moon was soon discerned to be, "going forth" and circling around her. They seem to have been named in exact accordance with their natures, and their places in creation, to which these ancient names, apparently given by these first astronomers, are perfectly suitable. Our sun of this world shines on them, our eclipses do not reach them: if we might hope that neither does our sin and sorrow do so, it would be delightful to look on them, as abodes of obedient, unsinning creatures cheered by the same influence of Him who is "a sun and a shield," as those abodes are, even where they are the farthest off, by the central orb of the system [9]. To every planet of our solar system the constellations present the same aspect. Do they declare to them the same truths? Are their inhabitants saved by faith in a Mediator, who if not their "brother according to the flesh," is their King, by whom and for whom they are and were created [1]. Had they a revelation to faith which cometh by hearing and not by sight? This magnificent creation, even when standing in its first innocence, required a mediator for its imperfections. Behold, O God, our shield, and look upon the face of thine Anointed [2]."

---

[8] "Arctic," that in which He came. תרח, he came, or cometh.

[9] Perhaps in our earth alone, the broken, as its name, ץרר, expresses, shall sin and sorrow be found. Here, alas! we know they are, but may we not hope that here alone do they exist?

[1] Eph. i. and iii. Col. i. 16.

[2] Ps. lxxxiv. 9. "The Messiah," as it is in the Hebrew; "Christi tui," in the Vulgate; Χριστου σου, in the Sept. So said the inspired prophet of old, so may we all say now.

END OF PART III.

MAZZAROTH

PART IV

PREFACE TO PART IV.

The facts on which the explanation of the figures attributed to the Constellations is founded, have been gathered from authorities chiefly ancient, the originals having been examined whenever they could be obtained. The research commenced about 1811, with Hamilton's Ægyptiaca, and books and monuments in the British Museum. Every year has afforded some addition to the materials, and study and meditation have arranged and simplified them, and led to inferences derived from persevering application to the Hebrew and its dialects. Not till after the system had been completely developed did it receive the sanction of any other mind; but great was the satisfaction afforded by finding from Aben Ezra, as quoted by Dr. Hyde, that the ancient Jews had interpreted in the same manner two of the Constellations, and from Albumazer, that the woman had formerly been figured with an infant in her arms; also, that, among the moderns, Humboldt had recognized in Aries the Paschal Lamb of the Hebrews, and that our own great Biblical scholar, Faber, had seen the Messiah to be typified in the human figures of the sphere, with the foot on the serpent's head.

Again, a book that ought to be better known, "Roberts's Letters to Volney," agreed in many of the Oriental derivations, as well as the prophetic references of the figures; but this very interesting contribution to the defence of Christianity, against the French infidelity, is not systematic, nor does it solve all the emblems consistently, therefore perhaps it had so little circulation. The French infidels, however, have done much to establish the explanations that refute their inferences; they show the correspondence between the emblems of ancient astronomy, and the types and prophecies of Revelation; they would derive the prophecies from the emblems, but omit to attempt to account for the existence of those emblems in connexion with the stars. As their leader calls his attack on Christianity "L'Origine des Cultes" (the Origin of Religions), which he considers to be the Constellations of ancient astronomy, the defence, tracing the names and emblems of stellar astronomy to the revelation given to Adam, and transmitted by Noah, may be called "The Origin of the Constellations."

Till every name was solved, every emblem explained and applied, the theory could not be considered complete: those solutions and applications are now brought forward.

The reader is requested to allow for repetitions of the same facts, and even of the same applications, in various places. As in a piece of music the theme with which it begins recurs after each variation, as in the theme itself the melody repeats and closes with the key-note, so with the theme of this inquiry concerning the meaning of the emblems of ancient astronomy: the theme is the correspondence between these emblems and divine revelation as recorded in the Scriptures; the key-note, " The heavens declare the glory of God [1]."

As objects of microscopic examination are presented first on one side and then on another, with various degrees of amplification, in order to attain a knowledge of their aspect and their uses, which one scrutiny would fail to impart, so are existing facts relative to the constellations here brought forward in many points of view, and under many kinds of investigation.

The most important testimonies are also repeatedly adduced as equally essential to the establishment of the different proofs. It has also been intended to make the statement of each subject complete in itself, and therefore including a recapitulation of every circumstance essential to the development of it, so that each might be examined at separate times, and as a separate question.

It was a maxim of the first Napoleon, that repetition was a most important figure of speech. His opinion gives some sanction to that figure as here used.

---

[1] The authority of Holy Scripture is established by the fulfilment of the prophecies it contains. That fulfilment is proved by history.

MAZZAROTH;

OR,

THE CONSTELLATIONS.

"Canst thou bring forth Mazzaroth in his [1] season?"—JOB xxxviii. 32.

FOURTH PART.

ON THE EMBLEMS OF EGYPTIAN MYTHOLOGY,

AS DELINEATED ON THE PLANISPHERE OF DENDERA AND OTHER MONU-MENTS OF EGYPT, AND COMPARED WITH THE HEBREW PROPHECIES AS RECORDED IN THE SACRED SCRIPTURES.

HOWEVER desirable it may be to substitute a Christian and rational account of the meanings of the ancient constellations, whether as figured by the Egyptian or Chaldean astronomers, yet scruples may arise as to adopting it, unless there can be shown cause to believe it the true one. A slight sketch of the principal reasons for thinking it so will therefore now be given.

The ancient Jews and Persians held that Seth, the son of Adam, was the inventor of astronomy, as is asserted by the learned Jew Josephus, who lived in the time of the Apostles, in his book on the Antiquities of the Jews, in which he also says that Abraham carried the knowledge of astronomy to the Egyptians.

The Egyptians held that Thoth, or Soth, or Sothus, was the founder of their astronomy; and they made use of the same emblems as the Chaldees for the signs of the zodiac. These emblems were used by all the ancient nations of which we have any records, as the Egyptians, the Indians, the Chinese, the Burmese, the ancient Persians. The Greeks and Romans had both the emblems and the names [2], but did not understand either. Their poets record fables about them generally founded on the name and the original meaning of the emblem; these stories chiefly relating to a son of the Supreme Deity, who was often said to be born of a woman, to suffer, and to die, and after death to be taken up into heaven, as a god or constellation: he was almost always said to be the conqueror of a terrible serpent, and sometimes to be wounded in the heel. Their learned men paid no regard to these traditions, but considered the names and meanings of the constellations as things of which no explanation remained, even in their days, two thousand years ago; therefore when modern books explain them of the seasons, a notion which arose among the Romans in later times, we see it is without any authority from those who must have known it, if such had been the original intention. Thus the most ancient writers who gave the names and figures exactly as we now have them, do not profess to know any thing about either their origin or their purpose: they give them as they received them from their forefathers.

---

[1] Mazzaroth not being in the masculine gender, "its" would be a better rendering than "his."

[2] The Roman names are those we use, the Greek having a similar meaning.

These names all have a plain and consistent meaning in the Hebrew [3] language; they all in some way relate to the promise given to Adam and Eve, of a deliverer to be born of a woman, to receive the wound in his heel, but finally to bruise the serpent's head: to this they add that the same person is to be a shepherd and a king, to have a peculiar people or flock, to be slain as a sacrifice, to rise again, and to come the second time as a conqueror and a king. Seth must have known this first promise well, and the sacrifice of Abel being said to be offered in faith shows that he also had the knowledge that the seed of the woman should be slain as a sacrifice. Enoch, a descendant of Seth, with whom he lived for many years, was, we know, a prophet, and prophesied of the second coming of "the Lord with ten thousand of His saints;" and from him Seth might learn those other particulars as to this great Deliverer who was to come, alluded to in some of the emblems. These same emblems or figures are used by all the later prophets whose prophecies are preserved in the Bible [4], most frequently containing the same words which we have as the names of stars or constellations [5].

The intention of the inventor of these emblems appears to have been to give a memorial of the promise to Adam, and the other prophecies with which he was acquainted. Those prophecies were the same as were afterwards recorded in the Bible, being that the seed of the woman, who should come, should be the Shepherd and the King of His people, that He should be afflicted, pierced, despised, but afterwards come again in glory and triumph; that He should have a peculiar people, or church, or assembly, who should be united to Him and to each other: the names of the emblems that refer to these prophecies are the very words used by Isaiah, Micah, Malachi, and the other prophets who wrote long after the signs and constellations had been made objects of idolatrous worship by the heathen, and who therefore could not

---

[3] Those who have not studied the Hebrew may be surprised why certain letters are considered as fixing the meaning of the word, and others as of no importance; in that language they are distinguished as radical and servile, a difference which may be traced in all languages. As in English, *m, n, t* (as *th*), and *s*, and all the vowels, are servile, or changeable, modifying, not changing the sense of the word. Thus *meat* is what we *eat*, *oxen* is the plural of *ox*, *they* the plural of *he*, *she* the feminine of he. The verbs exemplify the changes of the vowels, as *sat*, *set*, *sit*, and *sot*, one who has *sat* too long to drink. So of all the Northern dialects. In Arabic, though grammars do not so call them, these letters are used as servile. The Greek affords similar instances; in Latin and all its derived languages, the same usage is obvious. Thus, therefore, in the name Sirius the identity with *Seir* the Arabic, and Oseir or Osir in the ancient Egyptian, has never been questioned; the English and French Sire, and English Sir, are obvious derivatives from the primitive root of Sirius, which means to rule. Again, in the name Orion, the final *n* is according to the Arabic usage intensitive, giving force. The word does not perhaps at present exist in this particular form in Hebrew, but is regularly formed by the Hebrew usage, as he who cometh forth, as also by the Arabic, he who cometh. Both these names, however, we have through the Greeks.

[4] From Graves on the Pentateuch, Introduction xxiii., where it is said,
"I would direct the student particularly to Mr. Maurice's history, where in book iv., he will, I think, find it irrefutably established that immemorial traditions diffused over all the East, and derived from a patriarchal source, concerning the fall of man, the original promise, and a future mediator, had taught the gentile world to expect the appearance of a sacred and illustrious personage about the time of Christ's Advent." Graves here refers to his own vol. ii., from p. 311 to 320. He also, p. 307, quotes from Eusebius, Præp. Ev. 9. 8, that Unmenius, the Pythagorean philosopher, said that Jannes and Jambres (Chald. Paraph.) were inferior to none in magic skill, and for that reason chosen by common consent to oppose Musæus, for so the Egyptians called Moses.

[5] Sir W. Jones says, "I am persuaded that a connexion subsisted between the old idolatrous nations of Egypt, India, Greece, and Italy, long before they emigrated to their respective settlements." These are the "ancients" from whom the Greeks derived their comparatively "modern" notions of astronomy. "The astronomy of the ancients" must be looked for in the Egyptian sculpture and hieroglyphic inscriptions mingled with them, as in the planisphere of Dendera, not in the mangled traditions and idle fables of the imitative Greeks. See Second and Third Parts of this work.

borrow them from those nations. It was said by the ancient Jews that Adam and Seth were both prophets; but as this is uncertain, and as we are told in Scripture that Enoch was such, it is safer to attribute the prophecies figured in the constellations to him. The inventor seems to have chosen to divide the whole circle in which the sun appears to move every year into twelve parts because there are always twelve lunations in that time, and to have made them express twelve important truths about the promised Redeemer, and then to have given three more emblems to each, the constellations above and below the zodiac in that place, which should explain and add to them, and also to have given to them appropriate names, in that language given by the Creator to the first of them. These were called Decans[6].

It was as if these patriarchal prophets had said to their descendants, "When ye behold those stars called the *Virgin*[7], remember that the Seed of the woman, the Desired, is appointed to come, to be despised, to be pierced, but to be the King, the Shepherd, and the Guardian of His people. *[Coma, Centaur, Bootes.]* When ye look upon those called the *Scales*[8], remember that He cometh to purchase His redeemed people, that He will finish His work upon the cross, offering up Himself as the sacrifice for sin. *[Crux, Corona, Victima.]* In looking at the *Scorpion*, call to mind the wound He must endure from the serpent-enemy, that He must receive the bruise in His heel, but that He shall bruise the serpent's head. *[Serpens, Ophiuchus, Hercules.]* In *Sagittarius* behold the memorial of His going forth as the Sent of God, who shall triumph in the end; though He must be sacrificed like a lamb upon the altar, yet shall He be exalted over all. *[Lyra, Ara, Draco.]* In *Capricornus* think of Him as the great atonement slain for us; cut off, but not for Himself, falling, but to rise again, and to raise and save His people from wrath. *[Sagitta. Aquila. Delphinus.]* In *Aquarius* look to His arising and exaltation, remembering that He shall return in glory, that He cometh quickly, and shall pour out blessings on His people. *[Pisces Australis, Pegasus, Cycnus.]* In looking to the stars of *Pisces*, remember the multitudes of His redeemed people, united to Himself and to one another in the bond of love, that He cometh quickly, rejoicing, to reign as the King who shall rule in righteousness, when His Church shall be set free from bondage and from the power of the enemy. *[Al Risha the band, Cepheus, Andromeda.]* In *Aries* see Him that cometh, when all shall look on Him who was pierced that His people might be raised up to His throne, being delivered from the enemy by their Redeemer, who shall break their bonds. *[Cassiopeia, Cetus, Perseus.]* In *Taurus* think of Him as appointed Ruler, the Prince of princes; the Light of the world giving the water of life, and being the Shepherd of His flock. *[Orion, Eridanus, Auriga.]* When you look up to the two bright stars of *Gemini*, remember that He is to be the *Son of God* and the *Son of Man*, that His enemies shall be put under His feet, that He is to be a Prince and a Saviour. *[Lepus, Canis Maj., Canis Min.]* In the multitude of small stars in the next sign, view a figure of the great company of the Lord's people, His possession in all ages and countries, the sheep of His fold, ruled over by Him who is the Mighty One that cometh. *[Ursa Min., Ursa Maj., Argo.]* In the *Lion*, His final victory over the last enemy, *[Hydra, Crater, Corvus.]*

---

[6] Decan, division, from דכא, to break. See p. 18.

[7] It is to be borne in mind, that when the sun was in Aries, the stars of Virgo would be splendid in the evening sky.

[8] The Scales of the zodiac are named as of purchase, not, as sometimes supposed, of justice.

when He shall be manifested to have all things put under His feet, the wrath of God resting on the evil one, the great conflict at an end for ever. Behold, the Lord is at hand! Thousands of years may pass before all is finished, but what are they to Eternity?"

The Egyptian names of the signs and Decans interpreted from the Noetic roots they contain will be found to correspond with the meanings here given, as do the Egyptian figures with the purport of those we have received from the Chaldean astronomy.

From the beginning, their beginning, have these heavens which we now contemplate been declaring the glory of God, not only His power who made them and ruled their motions, but the greatest glory of all His great glories, "He that cometh will come." The sunlight of earth cometh, the starlight cometh, they depart and they return, teaching that the Light from heaven shall come, shall depart, and shall return, in no transitory gleam,—a morning without clouds, without an evening, a sunrise without a sunset. The revolution of the heavens so taught the eternal truth developed in time, to shine to all eternity. The sun day by day teaches that He whose type it is comes, goes, and will surely come again. Those who lived before the first coming, lived in a dawning hope of that coming; those who have lived after it, in an evening faith, that He has come and will come again. The faith of the ancient patriarchs was of the early dawn, under a sky brightened by the beams of prophecy, gorgeous, and full of hope; the faith of those who lived while the Sun of righteousness shone on earth, rejoiced in noonday brightness; we who live after its departure, gaze hopefully on the mingled glories of prophecy fulfilled, and prophecy that is splendid with the promise of its return. Those who adapted the ancient zodiac and its accompanying constellations equally to the configuration of the starry heavens and to the revelation of the future destiny of earth then given to them, proclaim from both "He cometh." So daily spake the setting and re-arising of the sun, so proclaimed Orion and Sirius among the stars. So were they named to express first and foremost that all-important truth, He cometh, by those who framed that ancient delineation of the heavens from what they saw and what they had been taught to hope.

The Egyptians chiefly dwelt on His coming to rule, to conquer, to bruise the serpent's head; the Chaldeans more on the equally important and more amazing truth, He shall be bruised. The constellations[9] transmitted by them show every where the bruised heel, the foot held up as wounded; while in the Egyptian planisphere the foot of the conqueror is on the serpent: thus it is made evident that they were not borrowed from each other, but had some common source, from which both series of emblems were derived, that source being the original prophecy, "He[10] shall bruise thy head, and thou shalt bruise his heel."

---

[9] As described from Hipparchus by Ptolemy. [10] Heb. *He.*

TESTIMONIES TO THE GREAT ANTIQUITY HERE CLAIMED FOR THE EMBLEMS OF THE CONSTELLATIONS, EGYPTIAN AND CHALDEAN.

In the book of Job, by the majority of learned men deemed the most ancient book now extant, and among the first ever written, we find the names of Ash, Chesil, and Chima rendered in the authorized English translation, Arcturus, Orion, and the Pleiades. Near Bootes, sometimes called Arcturus, we still find the name Benet Nash in Ursa Major, the daughters of Ash, or the congregation. Aben Ezra on Job ix. 9, interprets Ash the seven *congregated* stars of the Plough, or Great Bear. Chesil is still found at the foot of Orion; while Chima may be traced in the Pleiades.

Mazzaroth in the 38th chapter, 32nd verse, was held by the ancient Jews to be the circle of the twelve signs, so called from זַרְ, to bind or put together, as the stars to form a constellation, and the signs to form the zodiac. The word zodiac or zodion, awkwardly derived from the Greek verb to live, as a circle of living things, when one of them is Libra the balance, to which life cannot be attributed, if written in Hebrew letters צַעֲדִיוֹן [1], is a way, and precisely that kind of way which is composed of distinct steps, thus exactly describing the Sun's way through the successive signs of the circle.

That the twelve tribes of Israel bore the twelve signs on their banners in accordance with the command of their father Jacob, as transmitted to us in that earliest of poems, the blessing of Jacob, in the 49th chapter of Genesis, we have undeniable testimony. Josephus informs us that they did so, and the Chaldee Paraphrase, supposed to be of an earlier date, adds that the figure of a man (Aquarius) was on the standard of Reuben; a bull, Taurus, on that of Ephraim, who represented his father Joseph; a lion, Leo, on that of Judah; and an eagle on that of Dan, as recorded by Aben Ezra. It is also said that the Targums attribute to Dan a basilisk, or crowned serpent, representing two of the decans of Scorpio, with which the eagle (in Lyra) comes to the meridian. These four cardinal signs where the two solstices and the two equinoxes took place in ancient times, that is, between B.C. 4000 and B.C. 2000, correspond with the four Cherubic faces, and the tribes which bore them were the leaders of the four divisions of the host of Israel, as arranged by divine command in the 2nd chapter of Numbers. Whatever might be done in after times, when the prohibition of the second commandment had been so often disregarded, it seems probable that only the marks representing the chief characteristics of the signs were at first borne on the standards of Israel. Some of the emblems are alluded to in the prophecy of Balaam, Numbers

---

[1] With the Arabic nunation, יּ, a way proceeding by steps, Ps. xxxvii. 23. This dialectic termination occurs elsewhere among the constellations. Many Hebrew nouns also are thus formed.

xxiv., spoken when from the hill-top he saw " Israel abiding according to his tribes, encamped beside his *ensigns*," as the word שבט may be rendered, in obedience to the divine appointment in Numbers ii. The prophet of Midian uses the very words of the blessing of Jacob as to the lion of the tribe of Judah, and that the tribe of Judah always bore a lion on its standard is an admitted fact. It was then full in view, and when the images of the pouring out of water, of the seed, and of the sending forth of arrows are found in his parable immediately connected with that of the lion, it appears that these emblems also were before his eyes. There they might be seen on the banners of Reuben, who bore Aquarius, Zebulon Virgo, and Asher Sagittarius, and the allusion being to water, not to the man, to the seed, not to the woman, and to the arrow, not to the horse and his rider, thus is confirmed the opinion that they were so borne in their respective characteristic marks, rather than in the entire imagery of the signs [2].

" There shall come a star out of Jacob," were the words divinely put into the mouth of the reluctant speaker, thus consecrating to prophecy the image of a star as a type of Him who was to come out of Jacob, under whose sceptre should be gathered to-gether all the children of Seth [3], who should have dominion, and destroy the remnant of strife ; thus transmitting to distant climes and future ages the prediction of the King of Glory, the Prince of Peace, under the symbol of a star, a symbol expressively typical of the glory of Him who was to come to be a light to lighten the nations.

The prophecy of Balaam is supposed to have been known to the wise men, the Magi [4], who saw in the East the star of Him who was born King of the Jews. This knowledge it is thought they derived through the ancient sacred books of Zoroaster [5], which contained a prediction that the birth of the expected great one should be announced by the appearance of a star in the figure of a Virgin ; the Virgin of the zodiac, bearing the promised infant, the branch or ear of corn, occupying the place now indicated by Coma, vertical over Jerusalem, over Bethlehem : thus if this were indeed the place where the new star appeared, it stood over where the young child was. If according to tradition His birth took place about the winter solstice, this new star would rise after midnight, and shining during the hours of sleep, would be little known, except to those who, as the Magi, watched the starry heavens. Science [6] had declined in Egypt, and the shepherd-astronomers of early days had, in Greece, given place to hirelings who knew little of the heavenly bodies. The new star arising in the East might be deemed by many who saw it to be one of the planets in their varying

---

[2] Every Almanack supplies these marks.

[3] The children of Seth included all mankind, none others survived the flood, they could not therefore be all to be destroyed, by the sceptre of the coming Sovereign. The root of קרקר, rendered "destroy," is frequently used as to cause to meet, Gen. xxvii. 20, to gather together as in a city, קיר, Num. xxi. 28.

The word עיר in Num. xxiv. 19, rendered the city, is rendered by the Septuagint, trembling, and " terrors " in Jer. xv. 8; it is used as stirring up wrath and strife, and evidently has the root of our word war. The resemblance in the Sibylline prediction in Pollio is striking.

[4] Magi, from מנאה, to be exalted, chief men.

[5] Zoroaster, called also Zerdusht, may have had his name partly from צר, a stranger, a foreigner: there were at least two great men of the name, the first a king and an astronomer, not long after the deluge, who is said to have originated fire-worship ; the second, cotemporary with the prophet Daniel, and supposed to have been one of his disciples, is said to have restored the ancient religion of the Magi, perhaps that patriarchal faith which had preceded the time of the first Zoroaster, and from which the Magi who hailed the new-born Saviour may have learnt to expect and to adore Him.

[6] Hipparchus had lived long before, Ptolemy lived long after the Christian Era : probably from the want of any great astronomer at that time, the first appearance of this star was not recorded, and even the noonday darkness of the crucifixion but once or twice. See Part II. p. 104.

aspects and courses. Those who were watching their flocks by night, under its rays, needed the Angel's voice to tell them its forgotten embassy ; but though not recognized when it shone forth, except by the Magi, yet in the traditions of the nations we trace the wide diffusion of the promise of its appearance. Thence probably a star was often an attribute of the Divine and Heroic character. Romulus and the first Cæsar among men, the Dioscuri[7], the Twin Deities, among Divinities, were so distinguished.

The new star seen by Tycho Brahe, in Cassiopeia, which blazed for a short time and then disappeared, sufficiently authorizes us to regard this star as no meteor of our earth or sky, but as one of the heavenly bodies, pre-ordained to the glorious office of heralding, by an increase of its own brightness, the coming in splendour of Him, the true Light, by whom and for whom all things were created. (Col. i. 16.)

The principal stories of all ancient mythology, as well as that of Egypt, have been by great authorities[8] asserted to have originated from the prophecies of the Messiah scattered among the nations, but they have not added that the names and figures attributed to the constellations furnished the connecting link[9]. Others have shown the connexion between the fables and the emblems, but have not adverted either to the corresponding names, or to the originating prophecies[1]. Others again, learned and ingenious, but wanting the "one thing needful," without which man's wisdom is but folly, have traced all mythology, all worship, to the figures traditionally attributed to those groups of stars so vague and formless to the eye, the ancient constellations ; but they have not sought any reason for these groups being called by the names of visible objects to which[2] they bear no resemblance. Thus they content themselves with the supposition that causeless effects, motiveless appellations, and meaningless delineations may have produced the mighty consequences of universal delusion, a world-wide veneration of symbols, purposeless and absurd as they receive them, but which nevertheless become important in testimony, and beautiful in adaptation, when derived from, and interpreted by prophecy.

Some theories would refer the fables of Grecian and Oriental mythology to Noah's flood, but do not seem to have carried conviction with them. Noah and the Ark, and the wickedness and destruction of the old world, are indeed to be traced in the traditions of all nations, but they do not afford the pervading theme of mythology ; that theme is ever found to be the Virgin-born, the suffering and dying, the beneficent rejected and finally triumphant Deliverer, Hercules, Prometheus, Krishnu, Balder, or whatever else may be the name under which is designated the subject of all prophecy, the suffering seed of the woman, the King Messiah.

The name of the Ark of Noah and the infant Moses, was Theba. The word ark, used by the Latin translators, misleads those who, not knowing the original name, would connect the ark with the fabulous ship Argo, as to which, whether there be any foundation in fact is very doubtful. The word Argo would mean the company[3]; what company is meant is declared by the name of the chief star, Canopus[4], the possession of Him who cometh ; a very similarly sounding word signifies *long*[5], the frequent epithet of the vessel Argo, which is said to have been the first *long* ship. This word is used in Gen. vi. 15, as to the length of the Ark of Noah. Sephina, the multitude[6] or abundance, is a name yet remaining in Argo ; a similarly sounding word

---

[7] Plutarch informs us that Κυρος (Cyrus) was a Persian name of the Sun, evidently from חרס.
[8] Horsley, Faber, Gladstone on Homer, &c.   [9] Maurice.   [1] Dupuis, Origine des Cultes.
[2] The Crown and the Cross may here be considered exceptions.
[3] ארח, the company.   [4] קן אבא, Him who cometh, a flock.
[5] ארך, long.   [6] שפעה, company or multitude.

being used as ship[7], might assist in the formation of the story, and give rise to the modern appellation [8].

The Mexicans, like the Chinese, appear to have lost their astronomy for a time (probably during their migration from Asia), and like them, attempting to revive it from memory, displaced the signs; they remembered the figure of the Fish, the Goat in Capricornus, and perhaps the name, calling it Cipactli; they had the water for Aquarius, and the tiger for Leo; they had also the woman, the scorpion, the archer, the ram, the twins, giving them, however, wrong relative positions. It is generally admitted that the date of a system of astronomy is to be ascertained from the place among the signs from which the beginning of its year is reckoned. As the Mexicans began theirs from Capricorn, it is to be inferred that the winter solstice had passed into that sign at the time of their emigration, which is supposed to have been from Egypt. The records of the Persian and other Oriental nations indicate a far earlier origin, beginning their year from Taurus, so referring to the time when the vernal equinox was in that sign. Above all in antiquity is to be ranked the Jewish year, which primitively began in Virgo, when the summer solstice took place about the time assigned as the era of the creation of Adam, as deduced from the book of Genesis.

A great similarity has been observed between the Mexican and the Tartar constellations, the solar and lunar zodiacs being traced in both. The Mexicans have a cycle of such wonderful accuracy, as to indicate that they received it from a nation, probably Egypt, more deeply versed in science than themselves. The Toltec tribes, to whom is attributed 500 years' priority to the Astec, are also said to preserve great similarity in their computations of time, and in the signs of the zodiac, with Tartar and Buddhist astronomy, thus indicating a common origin, as from their ancestor Noah. The Mexicans have a tradition of the deluge, and of a patriarchal family, saved in a bark, adding that when the Great Spirit Tescalipoca ordered the waters to withdraw, he sent out first a vulture that did not return, and then a humming-bird, which brought back a sprig of leaves. After the deluge, men were said to be dumb till tongues were distributed among them by a bird, in the shape of leaves: we find here an evident allusion to the confusion at Babel; and in the scarcity of traces of primitive roots, in these far western dialects, it may be noticeable that the similarity of sound in a *leaf*, *ala*, and a *word*, *milla*[9], may be a reason for this metaphor or hieroglyphic. The Mexicans had small temples for the astronomical emblems, the tiger or lion, the serpent, the eagle, and the wolf; although the serpent and its sanguinary rites had

---

[7] ספינה, a ship, Jonah i. 5.

[8] At Thebes, in Egypt, are still found walls covered with the figure of a long ship, which we are told was there worshipped, this corroborating the testimony of the name to the tradition of the Ark of Noah, called Theba [*], that which cometh.

Again, we find Thebes in Bœotia connected with the tradition of a deluge, and the reign of a king named Ogyges, said to have married Thebe, the daughter of Jupiter, whose name, Ogyges[†], is from a word meaning to overflow, to rise as water. Ogygian was used as an epithet expressive of remote and obscure antiquity, so uncertain was all connected with his history.

Traditions on the subject of the deluge exist in the mythology of various nations; in that of China there were stories and pictures of a great inundation, from which eight persons were saved; in that of Mexico [‡] was found the deluge of Cos Cos.

[9] מלה, עלה.

---

[*] בא (רת)   [†] אנה, to overflow, rise, as water.

[‡] In an Italian comment on a Mexican picture, it is said, "these two figures are the first man and woman," and that the knife between them showed that "death came into the world from their transgression." "When the sign of the rabbit, Aries, arrivad, they fasted on account of the fall of the first man."

eventually superseded their former and purer worship, they seem originally, like the Peruvians, to have adored the Sun alone, for in wishing to express or fix an hour, they were accustomed to point to that part of the sky where the Sun would then appear, and say Itzi Teotl, "there will be God[1]."

Champollion read on the zodiac of Dendera the title of Augustus Cæsar, on that of Esneh the name of Antoninus. Such may have been the dates of the buildings, or of their repairs. But the headless horse, the ascending node, being placed beyond where Aquarius joined on Pisces, shows a much earlier era for the invention of the zodiac. Dupuis, who calculated the date of the planisphere from 4000 B.C., appears best to have understood it. The zodiac now used is that of Ptolemy's time, rather later than that of Augustus: but as has been observed, Canterbury Cathedral and other buildings on which our ancestors inscribed it are not therefore of that age; so this temple need not be referred to the era indicated by the solstice in Aquarius. The Egyptians depicted the ancient patriarchal zodiac as it had come down to them, adding emblems that belonged to their own times, as did Ptolemy in one instance (the second, or half-horse), and Flamstead most rashly in many others.

Hieroglyphics are said to be of three kinds:—1. Phonetic, when the hieroglyphic stands for a letter. Champollion says that this letter is the initial of the name in the language of the country. 2. Emblematic or symbolic, of the thing represented. 3. Figurative, of the object itself. "The Chinese," probably of the same origin, "present to the eye the same object or quality." So the Hebrew alphabet, according to many authorities.

Champollion gives it as his matured opinion that the three kinds are often combined in the same phrase. He assimilates them with the Hebrew, Greek, and Latin characters.

The interpretation here given to the names of the constellations, whether of those hieroglyphic names found on the Dendera planisphere or astronomy, as transmitted to us from time immemorial, with very slight variations in the Chaldean, Indian, and Burmese, is founded on the principle that the language given by the Creator to Adam differed but little from the Hebrew of the book of Genesis, that difference where it seems to exist, chiefly consisting in the use of some roots more according to the idiom of the dialectic languages, Chaldee, Syriac, Arabic, than to that of the Biblical Hebrew; as for instance, a root only found in the Scriptures as a verb, may be rendered as a noun on the probability that such a noun was once in use, though not occurring in the sacred books.

A proof that the language given to Adam was radically Hebrew, may be found in the fact that the names Adam, Eve, Cain, Abel, Seth, are pure Hebrew words, explained as such in the account of their origin. Another strong presumption is that the names of living creatures in Hebrew are remarkably significant of their distinguishing qualities, indeed, may be said to offer the best definition of them. Again, the names of places given before the confusion of tongues are equally significant, as Eden, the happy place, the land of Nod, of going forth or wandering; it is well known that the confusion is, in the original, said to be of the *lip*, or pronunciation, which accounts for the existence of Hebrew roots in every language.

The meanings here presented of the twelve signs and the other constellations are conveyed in their yet extant names; the agreement between the Arabic, Coptic, and Latin names, when written in Hebrew letters, is remarkable, the Greek appearing to have been merely translations of the original names.

It seems, at first, very extraordinary that the Latin names should so coincide with the import of the emblems and the oriental names, but it may be thus accounted for: the oldest of the Greek writers report that Zeus, the Jupiter of the Greeks, had expelled from the sovereignty of heaven the more ancient deity called by them Kronos, the powerful, by the Latins, Saturn, the hidden. Italy, from him called Saturnia Tellus, was called also by the equivalent name of Latium, the place of hiding; here then we might well expect to meet with traces of the patriarchal religion, there lingering long, as it has been often supposed to have done, after it was driven from the East by the worship of the new divinities; and here, accordingly, we find the Supreme Deity called Jove, an evident corruption of the sacred name Jehovah, and Jupiter, of Jah-pater[2]. Other names of the gods of the Romans, wholly different from those of the Greeks, are also traceable to Hebrew roots agreeing with their attributes; it is allowed that the Romans derived

---

[1] In this apparently most ancient phrase, the Noetic root, to come or go forth, may be traced in the first word, and in the second, a resemblance to Theos, a Greek name of God, allowed to be from יהוה.

[2] כפר, Arabic sense, Creator.

them, with other words of their language, from the Etruscans, whose high civilization is now attracting the attention of antiquarians. From this ancient people, then, it should seem that they also derived their names for the constellations, so widely differing in sound, though agreeing in meaning with the Greek [3]; therefore as the ancient Coptic are considered to preserve the old Egyptian, so the Latin appears to transmit the Etruscan appellations, if from different Hebrew roots, still equally applicable to the universally recognized symbols to which they are applied.

If each and all are found to correspond with the predictions of the Hebrew prophets, the same figures being employed, mostly clothed in words derived from the same roots, as the yet extant names of these emblems, may it not safely be inferred that they relate to the same subject? And that subject we know to be the Desire of all nations, He who was to come, revealed to the first man under the figurative expression *of the seed of the woman*. In many ancient zodiacs we find the woman with an infant in one hand, and an ear of corn in the other; in the Egyptian, with the ear of corn, the seed only; in the planisphere of Dendera another female figure holds the infant below. A star in the place once occupied by the infant, is still called Al-Mureddin, He who is to descend. In the earnest apostrophe of the prophet Isaiah [4], "O that thou wouldest rend the heavens, that thou wouldest *come down!*" the same root occurs in the same sense, applied to the same person; of that infant it is recorded by Albumazer, the Arabian astronomer, that He had a Hebrew name which was by many nations called Issa or Jesus; by the Greeks Christ. That in every sign similar analogies exist has been previously shown.

"The surest and best characteristic of a well-founded and extensive induction is, when verifications of it spring up, as it were, spontaneously into notice, from quarters where they be least expected, or from among instances of that very kind which were at first considered hostile to them. Evidence of this kind is irresistible, and compels assent with a weight that scarcely any other possesses [5]."

Such evidence seems to abound for the "induction" here advocated, namely, that ancient astronomy affords proof of ancient revelation, and of the purport of it.

Albumazer, in the ninth century, said: "Of the Decans, and their houses, according to the Persians, Babylonians, and Egyptians.

"Here follow the Decans, which the Arabs in their language call *faces*, which we will arrange according to the order used by the Persians, Chaldeans, and Egyptians. They are three to each sign of the way, which are called steps. They begin from Aries."

In c. 13, he speaks of the Decans according to the Indians. (Albumazer, Flores Astrologiæ, c. 12, B. M.)

Aben Ezra, in the thirteenth century, says on Albumazer's enumeration of the constellations, that "according to Albumazer none of these forms from their first invention have varied in coming down to us, nor one of their words (names) changed, not a point added nor diminished [6]."

The Indians have them under different names and various emblems, but assign to them stars which identify them with those of the Arabs. (See Le Gentil.)

Ricciolus says that it appears from Arab astronomy that it was as old as Adam, and the names preserved by them antediluvian.

That in the earliest ages of mankind God had spoken is shown by the ancient emblems of Egyptian astronomy; for the prophetic annunciation recorded in the book of Genesis, that the Seed of the woman should bruise the serpent's head, and receive a bruise in His heel, is reflected in them; but in them was also indicated the time when He should come, and receiving the bruise in the heel, be offered as was the Lamb which typified Him, the great atoning sacrifice. In Aries the Lamb, the Ammon of Egypt, it was foreshown that when the sun, the prophetic and scriptural type of Him who, like the sun, was to come, to go away and to return, should come to the spring equinox, at that place in the starry heavens, then the Lamb of God should literally and visibly shed that blood which taketh away sin. God alone, who seeth the end from the beginning, could so appoint the emblematic sacrifice of the Mosaic passover fifteen hundred years

---

[3] The very name Etruria confirms this supposition; in Hebrew signifying very rich, abundant, fertile.
[4] Isa. lxiv. English, lxiii. Heb. Compare John vi. 33, and xii. 24.
[5] Herschell on Nat. Philos. p. 170.
[6] Astrology. according to Lucian, was the work of the first kings who existed.

beforehand, and gradually and yearly approaching the emblem figured in it, and the star whose ancient and well-known appellation, Al Natik, explained it. In the earliest records of Arab astronomy, before the birth of Christ, that sign was so described, and that star so named. In the darkness of the crucifixion that star would be seen, on the Lamb prefigured by the sign it shone.

Such then was the first sign, the Lamb of sacrifice; when the spring equinox reached that sign, the Lamb of God should be slain, the great atonement completed. The next, also a sacrificial animal, emblematic likewise of dominion, and one of the divinely appointed cherubic forms. The union of the two natures, divine and human, in Him who should come, was figured in the third. The multitudes of His purchased people were represented in the fourth. In the fifth, another of the cherubic forms, His final victory. In the sixth, at the traditional anniversary of the creation of man, the Seed of the woman, the head of the new creation. The work of His redemption in the seventh. In the eighth, the predicted bruising of His heel, above which another of the cherubic forms, the eagle ascending and again descending from heaven. In the ninth, the going forth, conquering and to conquer. In the tenth, giving His life, as a sacrifice for sin. In the eleventh, the man, also a cherubic form, arising, pours forth blessings on His people. In the twelfth, the uniting and supporting the multitudes of His redeemed are shown forth. So was filled up the circle, the chief points of which were distinguished according to the divinely ordained similitudes before the gate of Eden [7].

On the first discovery of the planisphere of Dendera, some of the learned of that day, perceiving the great antiquity indicated by the position of the solstice, claimed that antiquity for the temple wherein it was found. But for this there was no foundation. The zodiac according to Ptolemy as sculptured on the Norman porch of St. Margaret's Church at York, and also in Canterbury Cathedral, does not thus indicate that the buildings were as ancient as that zodiac.

The zodiacs of Dendera and of Esnè contain internal marks of the utmost antiquity in their common origin, apparently referring to a time when the winter solstice, 4000 B.C., was quitting Pisces to enter Aquarius. In the signs, the fish, inhabitants of the deep, are followed by the streams of water in Aquarius, and those by the figure half-fish, half-quadruped, to which the solstice had receded in the time of Ptolemy. The figure in the Dendera zodiac over the junction of the kid and fish in Capricorn, might be inserted to show that at the time of the building of that temple the solstice had arrived there; but the headless horse (as other headless figures, a well-known emblem of the ascending node) marks that the place where the sun began to re-ascend had previously been where Pisces joined with Aquarius. That the summer solstice was then in Leo is indicated by the figure under the lion pouring out water from two vases, as representing the inundation of the Nile, always commencing at the summer solstice, and thus perhaps figuring *two* sources of the Nile.

The Egyptian astronomers have always represented the serpent-enemy in a state of humiliation, except it be in Scorpio. The dragon enveloping the pole, so well known from China to Scandinavia, they superseded by the emblems of Him who was to come, the seed, the enthroned conqueror. In the planisphere of Dendera this will be seen.

In Aries the conqueror is twice typified. In Cetus the head of the enemy is under the foot of " Him who cometh." In Perseus He is named the enemy or conqueror of the serpent.

In Taurus He comes in triumph, and treads under foot His enemy.

In Gemini they have typified the two natures, divine and human, by a youth with divine attributes leading a feminine form, expressing the human nature, including male and female.

In Scorpio, the scorpion is of a most disproportionate size, perhaps to make him a fitting antagonist of the conqueror.

In Cancer the passing of the summer solstice, from Leo in which tradition recorded its earlier position, is denoted by the revered Egyptian emblem of the sun, the sacred Scarabæus, from which figure the Greeks derived that of the crab, both creatures holding fast their young, their " possession."

In Leo, no alteration is seen; in each sphere the victor-lion has his foot on the serpent-enemy.

In Virgo, the woman of prophecy bears the seed, the ear of corn; below, the human mother holds the infant, showing forth " Unto us a child is born, unto us a son is given."

In Libra, a youth with the finger pointing to the lip emblematizes " He shall bruise and be bruised [1]."

---

[7] Richer, a recent French writer, has repeatedly said, that in the constellations might be traced the whole primitive revelation; but beyond the woman, the seed, and the serpent, he did not attempt to explain them. Roberts, an English Clergyman, wrote " Letters to Volney," in which he laid down the same principle, but went much further, tracing the bruising of the serpent's head in Scorpio. G. S. Faber also has said, wherever the figure of a man occurs in the sphere, it represents the Messiah, and recognized the serpent as subdued by Him. Still none of these perceived that the whole sphere was a system of symbolized prophecy, nor had the present writer seen their works till far more than they recognized had been deciphered.

[1] שפה, the lip; שוך, to bruise.

In Sagittarius, the Divine and kingly conqueror rides in triumph. Under the horse's foot there appears to be the serpent.

In Capricornus, the victor is the victim, but is named the conqueror of the serpent.

In Aquarius, He pours forth the water of life on the fish, emblem of His people, and there is said "He returneth from afar."

In Pisces, the two fishes united by a band are held by a female figure, called as in Aries, the appointed. It is remarkable that the hieroglyphic name of Set, the appointed, should thus be given both to the first and to the last of the decans, to the lamb and to the woman.

The authority of Holy Scripture is established by the fulfilment of the prophecies it contains. That fulfilment is proved by history, those prophecies are emblematized in this planisphere.

That the seed of the woman shall bruise the serpent's head, and it should bruise His heel, is the foundation on which is constructed the whole of this delineation of the starry heavens, with those of the Indians, Persians, Arabs, or, as in fact these all are, the Chaldean. Abraham was a Chaldean, and traditional history has said a great astronomer. Chaldean astronomy is continually appealed to as the original of the science. It has been supposed that Melchisedek, the righteous king, was Shem in person, who must have known all that Noah knew on the subject, and Noah must have known what Adam, Seth, and Enoch are traditionally said to have established as to the names and positions of the stars. But with the Chaldean astronomy, which is in fact ours, the Egyptian does not always agree. The Egyptians had derived their science from Noah before Abraham came among them, and in this planisphere we have the record of it. The number and purport of the emblems are the same, and similar meanings are traceable in their names by the aid of the roots preserved in the Hebrew Scriptures. In the subsequent tables, the names that have been obtained are so explained, and references given to the parts of the Hebrew Scriptures where the Noetic roots are used in the sense here given to them.

It has been well observed in an essay on the antiquities of Egypt, that the number of coincidences, separately perhaps of little importance, gives them weight and value in the aggregate. This remark introduces evidence giving much support to the foregoing explanations. A small edifice was attached to every Egyptian temple, the entrance to which was through the sanctuary. It was called "the birth-place:" in it are found reliefs and paintings representing the birth of the third person of the triad of divinities to whom the temple is dedicated. This triad is of father, mother, and son. They are sometimes figured with the countenances of the Pharaoh who erected the temple, his queen, and son, as in the temple at Harmonthis, which is said to represent the birth of the god Harphré (meaning He who cometh, the offspring), and also of Ptolemy Cæsarion, son of Julius Cæsar and Cleopatra. The great hope and end which this superstition held forth to its votaries, as the consummation of their religion, was the birth of a god. When we compare these newly recovered evidences with the assertion of the ancient writers on Egypt, that the Egyptian priests copied the figures of their divinities from the constellations, the proofs of the reference of these emblems to the coming of the Redeemer are much corroborated.

In the same work it is shown that the assertions of Dupuis and others, of the great antiquity of the temples of Dendera and Esnè, are confuted by inscriptions bearing the name and date of Augustus Cæsar. These assertions were founded on marks of antiquity in the place of the equinox in the zodiac. The figures of the zodiacs may be ancient, though that identical carving of them might be recent, as in the almanacks of our own time, the sun, moon, and planets are designated by marks of the greatest antiquity, the sun in particular by the very Egyptian hieroglyphic now so deciphered in the most ancient inscriptions. So no one disputes that the figures of the twelve signs on modern celestial globes are at least as old as Hipparchus and Ptolemy, though that globe is of recent construction. The greater antiquity of the original from which this planisphere must have been taken may be seen from the summer solstice, as has been previously shown, denoted by the inundation of the Nile, being shown as under Leo, in accordance with the ancient tradition that once it was there, and also by the headless figure, the well-known Indian mark of the ascending node, being more immediately over Aquarius, where the winter solstice had been, as in China, previously observed. That antiquity belongs to its first formation, and in no way to the date of the erection of the temple. Some later emblems may have been introduced, as those modern ones of Flamstead among the constellations described by Ptolemy. Or as the representations of the zodiac in the Cathedral of Canterbury, and on the porch at St. Margaret's at York, have no reference to the time of the construction of those buildings (the Saxon or Norman architect was not astronomer enough to decipher the age of those figures, nor did he intend by the use of them to give the date of his building, to which they have never been supposed to have the slightest reference); so the Greek, Roman, or Egyptian architect of the temple used these ancient emblems to give a religious sanction to his erection, but with no purpose of exalting its claim to antiquity by their adoption. Their cotemporaries understood not, but they worshipped. Unhappily these records had become instruments of idolatry, as man has too often perverted well-intended memorials to evil purposes.

ON THE ASTRONOMY OF THE ANCIENTS [2].

All authorities, ancient and modern, agree in attributing the origin of the science of astronomy to Chaldea, to "Chaldean shepherds." When Babylon [3], the chief city of Chaldea, was taken by Alexander, records were there found of observations of astronomical phenomena referring back nineteen hundred years, two thousand years and more before the Christian era, thus remounting nearly to the date of the confusion of tongues, of which Babylon was the scene and centre. At that time, about 2000 B.C., the summer solstice had receded from Leo, its earliest recorded position, into Cancer. This position of the solstice is indicated in this and the other zodiacs, as may be seen by the figure of the Scarabæus, afterwards corrupted into that of the Crab, where Leo terminates and the following sign or division of the zodiac commences. Any earlier position of the solstice would indicate observations in antediluvian times, and possibly transmitted by Noah. But no Egyptian monument yet found is without the Scarabæus in the sign Cancer, though in the planisphere of Dendera the summer solstice, once in Leo, is commemorated by the pouring out of water, as in the inundation of the Nile [4].

A memorial of the position of the summer solstice, consistent with the dates usually assigned to the creation of Adam, will, however, be seen in all three of the zodiacs here figured.

In the circular one, the planisphere of Dendera, under Leo is a female figure with vases, as of the pouring out of water. When the solstice took place in Leo, the inundation of the Nile there commenced, and that annual phenomenon of nature has followed and will follow the recession of the solstice while sun and earth endure in their present relations. An earlier winter solstice than that in Capricorn is indicated by the headless horse, the emblem of the ascending node of the solar circuit, being placed over Aquarius. A hawk-headed figure, considered to symbolize the sun, over Capricorn, has been explained as marking that the sun at the winter solstice was there, as it would be when the summer solstice was in Cancer; but in this zodiac it stands in the centre of the sign, where the body of the fish joins the fore-part of the kid, and may have a different signification.

Representations of the twelve signs of the zodiac, such as here given in the planisphere of Dendera, are found on many other ancient monuments of Egypt, and in the oldest records of the Brahmins. Wherever there is any tradition as to their invention, it is attributed to the first fathers of mankind, and where a name is mentioned it is Seth, Soth, or Thoth; among the ancient Persians, Adam and Enoch being also named. In Egypt the twelve signs had each a temple where they were worshipped. Many of the tribes of Arabia, some earlier, some later than Ishmael, took one of the stars for their distinguishing emblem. One tribe is still called Beni Sohail, the sons of Sohail, or Canopus.

From Noah the earlier tribes, from Abraham the later ones, had heard of the promised Messiah (Soheil, the Desired); to Him therefore the homage was originally paid, which afterwards was corrupted into the first form of idolatry, Sabianism, or the worship of the host of heaven.

Other nations speedily sunk into a coarser kind of idolatrous worship, the living creatures whose figures are to be found in the twelve signs being those every where adopted as idols. The stories told of these false gods may be traced to the forms and the most ancient of the names of the constellations, thus showing that originally they had some reference to religion, the first universal religion of mankind, the revelation to Adam and Enoch. Every where we find among the traditions of the nations, that a Son of God, Himself a God, should come, should be the friend of the human race, should suffer, and should die, and should rise again to heavenly glory.

Such were the stories of Hercules among the Greeks and Romans, of Osiris and Horus among the Egyptians, and Krishna among the Brahmins. Balder, the benign son of Odin, beloved of all, yet doomed to die, among our northern ancestors, and the Mexican deity born of a woman, are again remarkable instances of the same fact [5].

Sir William Jones has pointed out that the most ancient nations, in the earliest periods of their history, were acquainted with astronomy, which he considers they received from Noah

---

[2] The "ancients" referred to are not those treated of in Sir G. C. Lewis's work "On the Astronomy of the Ancients," the early Greeks and Romans, but their remote ancestors the Chaldees, Assyrians, and Egyptians.

[3] Isa. xiii. 19.

[4] In an earlier enumeration of the signs, in Gen. xlix., there is no trace of Scarabæus or Crab; but an allusion to the primitive roots of the word Cancer (Kan, cattle, Kir, gained) exists in the yet extant names, the Asselli, asses or cattle, in this position.

[5] The names of these false gods of the heathens bear testimony to their origin. Hercules means, in the Oriental dialects, He who cometh to labour and to suffer; Osiris, the prince or ruler; Horus, He who cometh forth as light; Krishna, the sun.

and his descendants; but their traditions, though often referring to Noah and the deluge, still attribute the invention of astronomy to one who lived before him, to whom they frequently give the name of Seth, Soth, or Thoth.

The worship of the sun might have begun from his glorious appearance and usefulness to man; but we cannot so account for the worship of the twelve signs, which are none of them such remarkable constellations as Orion and the bear, for in some of them there is not even one bright star. But if all the children of Noah had been taught the names and the meaning of the emblems, this would account for the same early astronomy, and the same early religion being found every where. Wherever they went they saw the same stars, which reminded them of the promise to Adam, and of the other prophecies which were given by Enoch.

Though these wandering tribes had traditions of the deluge, there is not among the starry emblems any reference to it. The water in Aquarius is poured out by a human figure from an urn, and is received into the mouth of a fish; that of Eridanus passes under the figure of the sea-monster, called Cetus, but not like the deluge among and over the creatures of the earth. Argo has been thought to refer to Noah's ark, but as Noah's vessel was called Thebah, the name cannot be so derived; and as the other names in that constellation mean the desired, the seed, the branch, and the possession of Him that cometh, some other meaning must have originally belonged to it. One name, Sephina[6], means a multitude; but a word very like it is applied to a ship, and thus may have originated the interpretation of Argo as a ship. There is no reference in any of the starry emblems to the prophecy of Noah, so wonderfully fulfilled, and still fulfilling, as to the future destiny of his three sons; none to the drowning of the human race, or the rainbow. Consequently it would appear that they were invented before the flood, even if the traditions of the nations had not told us that they were so.

From the first beginning of idolatry, in the foundation of Babylon by Nimrod, horoscopes were drawn. Every one is born when the sun seems to be passing through some one of the twelve signs; and according to the purport of that sign, along with the places of the planets, and other circumstances, was predicted what should happen to that person. All the signs which show the humiliation, the sufferings, and the death of the promised seed of the woman, were said to have an unlucky effect; while those that show His second coming in glory were reckoned fortunate. So taught the science of astrology, still referred to in old-fashioned almanacks.

NOTE ON THE ASTRONOMY OF THE ANCIENTS.

(From Southey's "Doctor.")

"According to the Cabalists, the ancient Hebrews represented the stars severally and collectively by the letters of their Alphabet; to read the stars, therefore, was more than a metaphorical expression with them. And an astral alphabet for genethliacal purposes was published near the close of the fifteenth century, at Cracow, by Rabbi Kapol Ben Samuel, in a work entitled 'The Profundity of Profundities.'

"But as this would rest upon an insecure foundation,—for who could be assured that the alphabet had been accurately made out?—it has been argued that the heavens are repeatedly in the Scriptures called a book, whence it is to be inferred that they contain legible characters; that the first verse of the first chapter of Genesis ought to be translated 'In the beginning God created the letter or character of the heavens,' and that in the nineteenth Psalm we should read 'their line' instead of 'their sound has gone forth into all lands,' this referring to their arrangement in the firmament like letters upon a roll of parchment. Jews, Platonists, and Fathers of the Church, are shown to have believed in this celestial writing. And there can be no question but that both the language and the characters must be Hebrew, that being the original speech, and those the original characters, and both divinely communicated to man, not of human invention. But single stars are not to be read as letters, as in the astral alphabet. This may be a convenient mode of noting them in astronomical observations; the elements of this celestial science are more recondite in proportion as the science itself is more mysterious. An understanding eye may distinguish that the stars in their groups form Hebrew letters, instead of those imaginary shapes which are called the signs of the zodiac. But as the stars appear to us only as dots of light, much skill and sagacity are required for discovering how they combine into the complex forms of the Hebrew alphabet. The astral scholar reads them as antiquaries have made out inscriptions upon Roman buildings, by the marks of the nails, when the letters themselves had been torn away by rapacious hands for the sake of the metal. Indeed it is not unlikely that the Abbé Barthelemi took the hint from the curiously credulous work of his countryman Gaffarel, who has given examples of this celestial writing from the Rabbis Kapol, Chomer, and Abindan. In these examples the stars

---

[6] שׁפע, Heb. and Syr., ‏ספינה‎, Arab., Job i. 5 (once), whence our word ship.

are represented by white spots upon the black lines of the Hebrew letter. The Abbé, when he writes upon this subject to Count Caylus, seems not to have known that Peiresc had restored ancient inscriptions by the same means; if, however, he followed the example of Peiresc without choosing to mention his name, that omni-erudite man himself is likely to have seen the books from whence Gaffarel derived his knowledge." (The Doctor, vol. iii. page 208.)

"In Egypt every month was supposed to be under the care of three Decans[7], or directors, for the import of the word must be found in the neighbouring language of the Hebrews and Syrians. There were thirty-six of these, each superintending ten days; and these decans were believed to exercise the most extensive influence over the human frame. Astrological squares calculated upon this mythology are still in existence. St. Jerome called it the opprobrium of Egypt." (Ibid., page 115.)

"Professor Mitchell in his lectures on astronomy, said that not long since, he had met in the city of St. Louis, in Missouri, a man of great scientific attainments, who for 40 years had been engaged in Egypt deciphering the hieroglyphics of the ancients. This gentleman stated to him that he had lately unravelled the inscriptions on the coffin of a mummy, now in the British Museum, and that by the aid of previous observation, he had discovered the key to all the astronomical knowledge of the Egyptians. The Zodiac, with the exact position of the planets, was delineated on the coffin, and the date to which they pointed was the autumnal equinox in the year B.C. 1722, or nearly 4000 years ago. Professor Mitchell employed his assistants to ascertain the exact position of the heavenly bodies belonging to our solar system on the equinox of that year, 1722 B.C., and sent him a correct diagram of them, without having communicated his object in so doing; the calculations were made, and to his astonishment, on comparing the result with the statements of his scientific friend already referred to, it was found that on the 7th October, 1722 B.C., the moon and planets had occupied the exact positions in the heavens marked upon the coffin in the British Museum[8]." (Times, December 31, 1859.)

Mr. Tudor in his work on Egyptian history refers to an ancient zodiac in which the autumnal equinox is placed so as to refer to 1743 B.C.

NOTE ON "1743."

Names of Chaldee Months, with the Signs under which they occurred about B.C. 1743.

Capricornus,	December,	Tebeth, טבת,	(Chaldee) to swell, as floods, &c.
Pisces,	January,	Schebat, שבט,	(Chaldee or Persic) turning, as the new year.
Aries,	February,	Adar, אדר,	(Chaldee) brightening.
Taurus,	March,	Nisan, נשן,	second or reduplicate, being the thirteenth month in every second year, by which the Jewish passover, &c., were kept right.
Gemini,	April,	Ijar, יאר,	shining.
Cancer,	May,	Sivan, שן,	(Chaldee) heat.
Leo,	June,	Tammuz, תמז,	completion, of the length of the day.
Virgo,	July,	Ab, אב,	going away.
Libra,	August,	Elul, אלול,	turning.
	September,	Tisri, שר (ת),	ruling, the first, or ruling month. Jewish new year, supposed to be the anniversary of the creation of Adam.
Scorpio,	October,	Marchesvan, מרחשון,	by Chaldee change of ש, wet, rainy, into ע.
Sagittarius,	November,	{ Chisleu or Kisleu, כסלו,	cold, or frosty, hard.
Capricornus,	December,	{ Tebeth, (as above) טבת,	floods.

---

[7] Decan, the name there given to the Constellations, referred to a Semitic or Noetic root, from דכה, to break, means divisions.

[8] On such a coffin in the British Museum may be seen the twelve signs, and their resemblance to those on the Dendera zodiac observed.

ASTROLOGY OF THE ANCIENTS.

Astrology is man's corruption of astronomy, as idolatry is man's corruption of religion: both originated from the truths they perverted, and testify to the beauty and reality of that which they distort.

If God had led Abraham forth to look for instruction to the stars of heaven, man knelt and worshipped them. If divine truths were set forth in the forms of the cherubim, man made an imperfect copy in gold of one of them, and cried, "These are your Elohim, O Israel [1]."

If Adam, Seth, and Enoch had desired to impress on the memories of their descendants the promise that had been as life from the dead to themselves, by the names they annexed to the lights placed in heaven for signs as well as for seasons, too many of those descendants would attempt to turn the prophetic emblems in heaven of the sufferings and triumphs of the Messiah into foreshadowings of their own destinies on earth. If the stars foretell of Him, said they, why not of us? And accordingly those signs that figured His future glories they held to promise good to themselves; those that figured His sufferings, calamity. There seemed one link between those far-off luminaries and themselves: each had been born when the sun's place was with some of them. That link they seized, and distributed their predictions accordingly. Thus from those signs foreshowing the triumphant reign of the Messiah they anticipated good to the persons born under them; from those which indicate His sufferings they predicted evil.

Aben Ezra, a learned Jew who wrote much concerning the stars in the thirteenth century, records that the ancient Jews called one of the constellations the Shepherd, and another the head of Satan, or the evil one; and Albumazer, an Arabian astronomer in the ninth century, has said that the Virgin held in her arms an infant, called by a name having a meaning which the Hebrews understood of the Messiah, and the Christians of Christ [2]. On such authority may we not look to the starry heavens as indeed "declaring the glory of God?"

Astrology affords a remarkable evidence of the meanings anciently given to the twelve signs, and of the importance of which those meanings were considered to be to mankind. But in modern times people are said to be born under one sign, while in reality they are born under another, because the sun is now seen among different stars at the equinoxes, and consequently in all the other months, from what he was when the globes and maps that modern astrologers use were first made [3]. Therefore all now said must be wrong, calling a person born under Aries, who really was born when the sun was to be seen among the stars of Pisces,—two signs to which astrologers give very different meanings [4]. This kind of fortune-telling is spoken of in the Bible [5] as false, and to be punished. It was much cultivated among the Egyptians, and it has been said that among the figures of the planisphere of Dendera may be traced the horoscope of Cesarion, the son of Cleopatra. If this were so, it could not affect the high antiquity attributed from the positions of the solstices, to this zodiac.

It must be kept in mind that these emblems only represent actions, the human figure no more representing the person of Christ than the figures of the eagle or lion. By confounding the action with the figure used to express it, the first step to idolatry seems to have been taken. It will be seen that the names of the emblems and of the named stars always express an action, foretold to be performed by the seed of the woman, or His enemy [6]; an action, not a person [7].

---

[1] See Part II. p. 51, &c.   [2] See Part II. p. 16, &c.

[3] The Penny Cyclopædia, on astronomy, says, "Astrologers do not allow for the precession of the equinoxes, their Aries being the first thirty degrees of the ecliptic, not the constellation."

[4] Aries they call a fiery, Pisces a watery sign, and predict accordingly.

[5] Isa. xlvii. 13. Deut. x. 10.

[6] "Aphophis, or Apop, is the name given to the serpent, of which Horus is the destroyer. The destruction of the serpent by the god, who standing in a boat *, pierces its *head* with a spear, forms a frequent subject on the monuments." "So the Scandinavian Thor with his mace bruises the head of the great serpent." "So Apollo, four days after his birth, slew the serpent Python, the enemy of his mother." "In the Persian traditions and in the Zendavesta, there is a God-given conqueror sent to destroy a mighty serpent. The same hero appears in the Vedas as a divine being, and is named Trita." D. M'Donald. Is Trita "one of the Three?" from the Persian it might be.

[7] These actions are expressed in the names in the sense which they bear in Hebrew and Arabic. We have received them through the Arabs, whose language has undergone great changes: still by referring to the most ancient and simplest words in Arabic lexicons the same meaning will be found which is here given by referring to the places in the Hebrew Bible where

---

* Boat, which cometh, באה.

NOTE ON THE DECANS.

" They (the Decans) are personified stellar influences, and classed with κραταιοι ηγεμονες of the Greek authors, who mention them in explaining Egyptian star-lore. As such they answer to δυναστας, i. e. personified powers. They were thirty-six in number and extra-zodiacal so far, that in the Egyptian planisphere they formed an outer circle to the signs of the zodiac, above each of which three were placed, and each again divided into two parts of five degrees, making up the three hundred and sixty. They had a strong astrological element, more so than the planets generally; but though their names are known, on what principle they were combined is not known. Cassiopeia was certainly supposed by the Egyptians to have a remarkable virtue[a]." (C. H. Cottrell.)

Since this was written, most of the names of the Decans have been read, and are explained from the Hebrew, on the accompanying planisphere. When words written in hieroglyphics are rendered into Hebrew characters, they contain Hebrew, or rather Noetic roots, having the consistent meaning and application. This is first traced in the still extant, but ancient Coptic names of the Twelve Signs, and afterwards in those most ancient and only lately ascertained names of the thirty-six Decans, or accompanying constellations. By the planisphere it will be seen that the figures of these constellations, if some at first appear to differ, are all reconcileable with the acknowledged import of those of the Chaldean or Shemite astronomy, and indicated in these recently discovered appellations.

---

the words are so used, and almost always so translated in the English version. The Hebrew has undergone no change, though some extension, from the first chapter of Genesis to the end cf Malachi, consequently the reference to the Hebrew is not only the most feasible, but the most satisfactory. By a reference to Lee's Hebrew Lexicon and many others, it will be seen that the same root exists in both these languages, originally derived from Noah, and probably through Abraham, by his two sons Ishmael and Isaac, from whom descended the Hebrews and many of the Arab tribes. In what is now known of the ancient Egyptian dialect the same Noetic roots are traceable, as will be perceived in the meanings thus attached to the Egyptian names of the decans, which when explained by the cognate Hebrew roots are referable to the same prophetic import which their figures convey.

[a] Coleridge's Wallenstein.

PLANISPHERE OF DENDERA.

MAZZAROTH

PART V

THE ANCIENT EGYPTIAN ZODIAC

AND

PLANISPHERE OF DENDERA [1].

A PAINTING from the original in the Museum of the Louvre at Paris, was exhibited in London in the year 1823, of which lithographed copies were sold at the exhibition room, Spring Gardens. From one of these given by the exhibitor to the late Wm. Hone the annexed lithograph has been made.

In the explanatory paper circulated with the lithograph in 1823 it is said, "The figures carved and painted on the four sides of this chamber could not be seen without the aid of torches, the smoke of which had covered the zodiac, and hid it for ages. The appearance of this valuable monument, as exposed at Paris on the floor of the Museum of the Louvre, is that of a very large antique bronze medallion. This zodiac is the only astronomical monument of the ancient Egyptians yet discovered which has a circular form." "Its centre is occupied by a fox or chacal." "It is thought that two emblems exactly opposite to each other, in a line passing by the signs Scorpio and Taurus, may mark the places of the equinox at the period when this ancient monument was constructed." "This zodiac or planisphere was discovered in the interior of the great temple at Dendera, when the French army was in Egypt." "It was carved on the ceiling of an obscure chamber, about twelve feet square." "The diameter of the circle of the planisphere is four feet nine inches; this is inscribed in a second circle or band of hieroglyphics, comprised in a square, the side of which measures seven feet nine inches, French measure [2]." "It was transported to Europe in 1821." "The price paid for it by the King of France was 150,000 francs, or 6250l. sterling."

The painting from it, executed in Paris, three feet four inches square, exhibiting in London in 1823, was shown to every person who purchased the lithograph taken from it by a tracing, from which the accompanying lithograph was taken. It has been

---

[1] Balbi's Geography says: "Denderah—C'est au plafond d'une des salles supérieures qu'était placé le fameux planisphère, que M. Saulnier a fait transporter en France en 1821, et qui, acheté par le roi, devrait former maintenant un des plus intéressans morceaux du magnifique Musée du Louvre. C'est ce même planisphère qui a fait naître tant d'hypothèses pour expliquer a prodigieuse antiquité qu'on attribuait à ce monument, mais qui a disparu devant les faits positifs, du aux savantes recherches faites par MM. Champollion Jeune, Richardson, et autres archéologues."

[2] This second circle has not been included in the accompanying plate, being supposed not to relate to the figures of the constellations in the planisphere which it encloses. Above this second circle are the two emblems supposed to indicate the position of the equinox at the time of the construction of this planisphere, as being nearly 2000 B.C. That under Taurus appears to be a lighted lamp or candelabrum, of which the flame ascends, as the Sun from the spring equinox in Taurus to the summer solstice, then just quitting Leo and entering the sign now called Cancer, but by the Egyptians figured as the Scarabæus.

compared with the plate in Hamilton's Ægyptiaca, and with one in the great French work on Egypt in the British Museum, and found to agree with them in all particulars, except that the fish representing the constellation of the Dolphin is omitted, as is the serpent under the foot of Orion : both of these are here supplied from these authorities.

Various opinions have been brought forward as to the time of the erection of the temple in which the carving was found. It is now generally considered to have been founded about the time when Egypt passed from Greek to Roman dominion, and to have been repaired under other emperors whose names have been deciphered on it. The date of the building has no connexion with that of the invention of the figures of the planisphere; these ancient and traditionally sacred emblems, no longer understood, were still venerated by the builders, and placed in it as mysterious memorials of the primeval religion of Egypt.

THE ANCIENT COPTIC NAMES OF THE TWELVE SIGNS OF THE ZODIAC,

ACCORDING TO ULUGH BEIGH.

Latin Names.	Coptic Names.	Explanations.	Hebrew Roots.	
ARIES.	Tametouris Ammon,	Reign, *dominion, government.*	משרה	Isa. 9. 6, 7. E. V.
	Regnum Ammonis.	Ammon, *established.*	אמן	Isa. 7. 9. Jer. 42. 5.
TAURUS.	Isis or Apis, Horias, Statio Hori.	Isis, *who saves or delivers.*	ישע	Zech. 9. 9.
		Apis, *the head.* Apes, Egyptian; as Aleph, Heb.; *captain, chief.*	אלף	Jer. 13. 21.
		Horias, { *who cometh, traveller,* *to save.*	ארח ישע	2 Sam. 12. 4.
GEMINI.	Clusus, Claustrum Hori.	*The place of Him who cometh, wayfaring man.*	ארח	Isa. 33. 8.
CANCER.	Klaria, Statio Typhonis.	Klaria, *cattle-folds.*	כלה	Ps. 50. 9.
		Statio Typho- } *who smites, is smitten.* nis,	חפף	Nah. 2. 7.
LEO.	Pi Mentekeon, Cubitus Nili.	Mentekeon, *the pouring out.*	נתך	Ex. 9. 33.
VIRGO.	Aspolia, Statio Amoris.	Aspolia, השבל, *ears of corn, the seed.*	שבל	Gen. 41. 5.
LIBRA.	Lambadia, Statio pro-pitiationis.	{ Lam, Arab. *gracious.* { Badia, *branch.*	להם בד	Ezek. 17. 6.
SCORPIO.	Isias, Statio Isidis.	Isias, *salvation.*	ישע	Ps. 35. 3.
SAGITTA-RIUS.	Pi Maere, Statio Ame-nitatis.	Amenity, *graciousness, beauty of the appearing or coming forth.*	מראה	Gen. 24. 16.
CAPRICOR-NUS.	Hupenius, Brachium sacrificii.	Hupe, *place or chamber* Nius, *of Him having salvation.*	חף נושע	Ps. 19. 5. Zech. 9. 9.
AQUARIUS.	Hupei Tirion.	Hupei, *place or chamber* Tirion, *of Him coming down as rain.*	ירה	Hos. 6. 3.
PISCES.	Pi-cot Orion, Piscis Hori.	Cot, *fish, the congregation,* or *company of.* Orion, *Him who cometh* (Arab. form, or formative of the noun), *wayfaring men.* Hori, *of Horus, Him who cometh,* as above.	חיות ארח	Ps. 104. 25; 68. 30. Jer. 9. 2.

These names, thus given by Montucla, Hist. des Mathématiques, are considered to represent the ancient Egyptian. Their great antiquity may be seen from the Cubitus Nili, referring to the inundation of the Nile as under Leo, where the summer solstice, at which it takes place, only remained till about B.C. 2000: also from there being no allusion to the Scarabæus, where it afterwards was introduced to mark the recession of the solstice to Cancer, which occurred about the time of the Christian era, Cancer being here called Statio Typhonis, station of Typhon, the enemy who smites and is smitten, to whom was consecrated the ass, mentioned in Gen. xlix. 14, and borne afterwards on the standard of the tribe of Issachar. Typhon was anciently figured by the Egyptians as having serpents for legs and girded with a serpent, thus identifying him with the serpent-enemy of Genesis. The name Isis, given to Taurus, is not here referred to the so-called goddess of after times, but to the verb ישע, to save, with the Egyptian pronoun masculine *S* affixed, "this saves." Pi-mahi, the united, is elsewhere given as the name in Gemini. The fish is a well-known emblem of the early Christian Church, or congregation of the Lord, multitudinous in offspring, drawn out of the water, a frequent type in the New Testament, and by them often engraven on their tombs.

The Copts of the present time are believed to be the descendants of the ancient Egyptians. Their language is considered by Scaliger and others to be that of ancient Egypt, with a slight intermixture of Greek. Their letters bear some resemblance to the enchorial or demotic character. Their language has no inflexions, but has letters and particles prefixed. This language exists in a translation of the Scriptures. (Encyclopædia Britannica.)

According to Scaliger and others, the name Copt is derived from Αιγυπτος, Egypt, and Egypt from הפה, to cover, veil. It will be remembered that figures of the Nile were frequently as veiled, and also that of Isis. The Biblical name is always Mizraim (narrow, straitened), and in the dual number, perhaps as Upper and Lower Egypt. (Rees' Cyclopædia.)

When Josephus says Yses or Isis meant in Egyptian "preserved," he evidently refers it to the root ישע, to save.

Montucla says that among the Egyptians almost every thing belonged to Isis, Orus, or Osiris.

Josephus: "In the Egyptian mythology Osiris is said to have been slain by Typhon when the sun was in Scorpio."

"The eight divinities are said to have existed before the twelve," as the planets were known before the naming of the signs.

When Manethon says that Hyc is "king" in the sacred tongue, he identifies the *sacred* with the ancient Hebrew language.

For the first 2000 years of the Hebrew chronology the summer solstice took place in Leo. After perhaps about 1700 years of that time, Egypt was settled and civilized, preserving prophetic and astronomical traditions from the Antediluvians, through Noah and Ham, their more immediate ancestors, to which these names testify. In the first thousand years of that time the inundation of the Nile occurred, while the sun was still in Leo, at the summer solstice; to this time then the origin of these names must be referred, where Pi Mentekeon, the pouring out, is translated Cubitus Nili.

The solstice passing into Cancer 2000 years B.C., the Scarabæus, an emblem of the sun of Egyptian origin, was introduced there; in the long zodiac evidently so. In these names no allusion is made to it, but the original emblem of cattle is there Klaria, and Statio Typhonis, or the ass. Gen. xlix.

The Scarabæus was an emblem of the sun and of the human soul before it was placed in the zodiac to denote the solstice.

In the long zodiac a large figure of the Scarabæus is below the place of the sign Cancer, and a figure of another smaller kind of beetle seems ascending to the line of the signs near to the figure of a beeve, agreeing with the more ancient emblem of cattle, in Ceno-kir, the possession held, and Sartan, held fast, bound; this emblem, cattle, being still in memory, while in the planisphere it is not in the zodiac, but appears below in Argo. The beetle, or Scarabæus, has its head detached from the body (or thorax); that of the crab is not so divided. The name Klaria, the cattle-folds, points to the time before the beetle had been introduced into the zodiac, as it is acknowledged the Scarabæus was by the later Egyptians. The solstice had not receded into the sign Cancer till about B.C. 2000, considered to be about 150 years before the abiding of Abraham in Egypt, whether learning or teaching astronomy.

NOTES ON LIBRA.

"The balance of Amente, or truth, in the Egyptian pictures of the judgment of the human soul, has the figure of a deity, or an ostrich feather (a divine attribute) in one scale, a heart in the other. Horus with a hawk's head, and Anubis with that of a dog, (both names of the sun in the Egyptian triads, both in their primitive roots meaning 'He who cometh,') attend the scales, and sometimes seem to give additional weight to that of the heart." אבר, a wing-feather, strong, mighty, whence used as a divine attribute.

The primary meaning of the Noetic root Zadik is the equal poise of a pair of scales. The scales and the balance are mentioned as divinely employed in Isa. xl. 12, in Dan. v. 27, and used as a prophetic emblem, Rev. vi. 5.

EXPLANATION OF THE PLANISPHERE.

I.

ARIES.

DECANS. Names now in use, and Hiero-glyphic Names.	Egyptian Hieroglyphic Names and Figures[1].	Noetic Roots traced by the Hebrew.		Used in the Hebrew Bible.
1. CASSIOPEIA, the throned woman. SET.	Set, set up. (Bunsen's Vocabulary.) A female figure, under which are the hieroglyphic signs denoting a female, an oval or egg[2], ביצה, and a half-circle or hill, תל, for Beth, *a daughter*. According to Albumazer this decan was anciently called "the daughter of splendour."	Set, set up, appointed.	שת	Gen. 4. 25.
2. CETUS, the sea-monster or serpent-enemy. KNEM.	Knem[3], subdued. Kan-nu, victory. (B.) Here figured as a monstrous head, trodden under foot by the swine, the natural enemy of the serpent, united to which is the wolf[4], whose name זאב signifies *He cometh*. The hawk, also a natural enemy of the serpent, crowned with the mortar, the emblem of *bruising*, is over this figure. It corresponds to the head of Medusa, carried by Perseus.	Triumph. Established. Swine. Who turns. Mortar, to bruise. Medusa, trodden on.	נאה כון חזיר כתש דוש	[21, &c. Exod. 15. 1, Gen. 41. 32. Lev. 11. 7. Ezek. 1. 9, 12, 17. Prov. 27. 22. Job 39. 15.
3. PERSEUS, He who breaks or bruises. KAR KNEM.	Kar Knem. Kar, who fights. (B.) The figure of a man with the tail of a quadruped appended as to a girdle, signifying *This cometh*, by the word *tail*, זנב, *this cometh*, or shall be sent forth. He has a royal diadem or fillet round his head.	Who fights. Who destroys, subdues, Arabic. *this.* Cometh. Or is sent forth.	ער זה בוא נבא	1 Sa. 28. 16. Ps. 139. 20. Dan. 4. 16. Gen. 5. 9. Gen. 2. 22.

[1] The Hieroglyphic names here used are given on the authority of Mr. Birch, of the British Museum, by whom they were furnished to C. H. Cottrell, translator of Bunsen's Egypt, and by him they were given to the present writer.

[2] Egg, Job xxxix. 14; hill or heap, Deut. xiii. 16; hill, Arab.

[3] Bunsen says that the sound of the letter G is mostly rendered by K in hieroglyphics. Probably the guttural sound of ע would also be so expressed. The addition of the servile letters M or N is common in the ancient dialects, whether Shemitic (Hebrew, Arabic, Syriac), or Hamitic (as the Egyptian), as in the name of the country Mizraim, from צר, narrow, straitened, Num. xxii. 26,) as the valley of the Nile.

[4] The wolf is now considered the genus, of which the dog is a species, כלב, which *cleaves* to man.

II.
TAURUS, THE BULL.

DECANS. Names now in use, and Hieroglyphic Names.	Egyptian Hieroglyphic Names and Figures.	Noetic Roots traced by the Hebrew.		Used in the Hebrew Bible.
4. ORION. HA-GA-T.	Ha-ga-t, who triumphs. In the lower circle are hieroglyphic characters that read Oar, Orion having been anciently spelt Oarion. T is the article affix, the or this. (Bunsen.)	Ha, the chief. (B.) גא, ga, triumphs.	נא	Exod. 15. 1, 21.
5. ERIDANUS, the river. PEH-TA-T.	Peh-ta-t, mouth of the river, originating from the urn of Aquarius, figured by water in Pisces.	Mouth, פה; river, א׳(ת); water, Aa. (B.)	מים	Gen. 8. 9.
6. AURIGA, the shepherd. TUM.	Tum, sceptre, power. (B.) Who subdues, tames. He carries the head of an animal (Ba [5], He cometh) on a cross or sceptre. The cross was said to be emblematic of life, divine life, among the Egyptians, whose belief in the immortality of the soul is well known.	Subdued, put to silence, tame. (Heb.)	רמה	Ps. 94. 17.

III.
GEMINI, THE TWINS.

The union of the divine and human nature, in Him who was to come, is expressed by a youth leading by the hand a young woman. The man has the frequent appendage of the tail of a quadruped, signifying "this cometh."

7. LEPUS, (Arnebeth, the enemy of Him that cometh.) BASHTI-BEKI.	The enemy of Him who cometh, trodden under foot, here figured as the hoopoe, an unclean bird, standing over the serpent under the foot of Orion. Bashti-beki, confounded, failing. (B.)	Bashti, confounded Beki, failing.	בש בק	Job 6. 20. Isa. 19. 3.
8. SIRIUS, the prince. APES.	The prince, figured by the hawk [6], enemy of the serpent, the Egyptian substitute for the eagle Nesir; called in the Greek sphere the first or great dog, but anciently the wolf, whose name ואן, *this cometh*, denoted the coming to reign. On his head is the pestle and mortar, denoting who shall bruise the head of the enemy. Apes, the head. (B.)	Swiftly coming down. Victory, or a vulture. (B.) Eagle, coming down. Apes, the face or head, commanding.	נץ נשר פה	Lev. 11. 16. Deut. 32. 11. Gen. 45. 21. Exod. 17. 1. Eccles. 8. 2.
9. PROCYON, the deliverer from evil. SEBAK.	The lesser dog or wolf, representing the first coming to redeem, by a human figure with the hawk's head, and the appendage of the tail. Sebak, conquering, victorious. (B.)	Shebah, making captive, Heb.	שבה	Exod. 22. 10.

[5] Ba, in Egyptian any quadruped, also He cometh, בא, whence the heads of such are placed on a human figure to denote "He cometh."

[6] The hawk, נץ, Naz, caused to come forth, sent forth. Nazir, who preserves, guards, keeps. Isa. xxvi. 3, &c.

IV.
CANCER, THE CRAB, OR SCARABÆUS.

DECANS. Names now in use, and Hieroglyphic Names.	Egyptian Hieroglyphic Names and Figures.	Noetic Roots traced by the Hebrew.		Used in the Hebrew Bible.
10. URSA MINOR. API-FENT.	The chacal, or wolf, standing on the ploughshare, אתא, which comes, tearing or bruising the ground. Api, head; Fent, of the serpent. (B.)	Ploughshare. Coming. Head, פה; Fent, serpent, adder. Siphon, Arab.	את אתא אפעה	Isa. 2. 4. Deut. 33. 2. Job 20. 16.
11. URSA MAJOR. FENT-HAR.	A female swine, enemy of the serpent, holding a ploughshare [7], implement of bruising, emblem of coming. Fent-har, enemy of the serpent. Har, who terrifies. (B.) Kark, to smite, with a scimitar, to strike. (B.) This figure holding a ploughshare will account for that title having been given to Ursa Major.	Swine. Who turns. Enemy, ער, Chaldee. Enraged against. Ploughshare. Coming. Bruising, crushing.	חזיר ער חרד אתה חרש	Lev. 11. 7. Ezek. 1. 9. Ps. 139. 20. Dan. 4. 16. Gen. 18. 30. Job 3. 25. Job 1. 14.
12. ARGO, or Canopus, the possession of Him who cometh. SHES-EN-FENT.	A beeve with the crux ansata, cross with handle, or emblem of life, round its throat. Shes-en-fent, rejoicing over the serpent. (B., worm.)	Ba, who cometh. Rejoicing. Fent, serpent, adder [8].	בוא שיש אפעה	Job 3. 22. Job 20. 16.

V.
LEO, THE LION [9].

13. HYDRA.	The serpent under the lion's foot. The name is not given in Mr. Birch's list; but hieroglyphics that read Knem (He who triumphs, who conquers, or is conquered) are underneath these figures [10].	Knem, from Khan, whence King and Khan, established, fixed.	כון	Ps. 93. 2.
14. CRATER.	A plumed female figure, holding a vase or cup in each hand, while responding to the constellation Crater, may be a memorial that at the arrangement of the emblems, the invention of astronomy, the summer solstice was there, and consequently the pouring forth of the inundation of the Nile.	There are characters below, which may be "sent forth," as water from the vase. Her seat is figured as the thighs of a beast. Thigh.	ירה ירך	Exod. 15. 4. Ps. 45. 3.
15. CORVUS. HER-NA.	The bird perched on the serpent at the heel of the lion. Her-na, great enemy. (B.)	To send forth. Her, as in Cancer. Na, fail, break, enemy failing.	ירה ער נא	Hos. 6. 3. Num. 32. 7.

---

[7] The ploughshare here figured accounts for the name of the plough having been given to this constellation.

[8] Fent, worm, serpent. Shakspeare says of the aspic of Cleopatra, "*worm* of the Nile." Worm, from ערם, subtil, Gen. iii. 1.

[9] אריה, the lion, Ar, Egyptian, to come. (B.)

[10] *Conquer* is probably from the root כון.

VI.

VIRGO, THE WOMAN, WITH THE BRANCH OR SEED.

DECANS. Names now in use, and Hieroglyphic Names.	Egyptian Hieroglyphic Names and Figures.	Noetic Roots traced by the Hebrew.		Used in the Hebrew Bible.
16. COMA, the desired. SHES-NU.	Figured as the infant held by a woman seated beneath. Shes-nu : Shes, son or offspring (B.); Nu, desired, Heb.	Offspring. Desired.	שה אוה	Exod. 12. 5. Isa. 26. 9.
17. CENTAURUS, the appointed offering himself as a sacrifice. KNEMU.	A human figure with the tail, "this cometh," and with the head of a calf or lamb of sacrifice. Knemu : Mu, to die. (B.) The appointed dieth, is bruised.	כנם, appointed, established. To die.	כן מית	1 Kgs. 7. 21. Gen. 2. 17.
18. BOOTES, who cometh. SMAT.	A human figure, as coming, holding the ploughshare, to break or bruise the enemy. Smat, who rules, subdues. (B.) Comes, אתה.	Ploughshare. שם, makes. Ordain, place. Comes.	את שם אתה	Joel 3. 10. Ex. 13. 16. Deut 33. 2.

VII.

LIBRA, THE SCALES.

19. THE SOUTHERN CROSS. SERA.	The figure of a lion, אריה, who cometh to tear, to gain the victory. His tongue is out of his mouth, as in thirst [11]. A female figure offers a cup. He holds the usual hieroglyphic for running waters. Sera, victory. (B.)	Who comes. To draw water, to drink, Arab. sense. Who rules, Heb. Sets free.	(א)בא שאב שר שרה	Gen. 24. 11. Job 37. 3.
20. THE VICTIM, held by the Centaur. SURA.	The emblem called Harpocrates, a child or youth with the finger on the lip. Sura, a sheep or lamb. (B.)	Lip, שפה. Break or bruise. Lamb.	שפה שוף שה	Cant. 4. 3, &c. Job 9. 17. Gen. 3. 15. Exod. 12. 3.
21. THE CROWN[1]. API-AATL.	The enthroned figure above. Api-aatl : Api, head or chief (B.); Aatl, noble (B.), strong, Heb.	Who cometh. The Ruler.	אר אדן אתן	Gen. 42. 30. Num. 24. 21.

[11] Ab, thirst (B.), Heb. who comes. In the swine representing Ursa Major the tongue out of the mouth is thus accounted for.

[1] Corona Borealis, the Northern Crown, is the only constellation whose form corresponds with its name, being a perfect circle. It is vertical over Jerusalem once in every revolution of the earth, and (Isa. lxii. 3) its name comes through the Greeks, as of Ariadne, who comes to reign.

VIII.

SCORPIO, THE CONFLICT[2].

DECANS. Names now in use, and Hieroglyphic Names.	Egyptian Hieroglyphic Names and Figures.	Noetic Roots traced by the Hebrew.		Used in the Hebrew Bible.
22. THE SERPENT, enemy of Him who cometh, held by Ophiuchus. KHU-OR-BAKH.	Figured as the serpent under the foot of the throned figure. Khu, ruled (B.); Or, enemy; Bakh, bows down, ruled. (B.)	Enemy. Caused to fail.	ער בק	Ps. 139. 20. Jer. 19. 7.
23. OPHIUCHUS, the serpent conqueror. API-BAU.	A throned human figure with the hawk's head, as enemy of the serpent. Api-bau, the chief or head who cometh. (B.)	Api, head, face. Bau, who cometh.	פה בוא	Ps. 96. 13.
24. HERCULES, who bruiseth the head, and is bruised in the heel. BAU.	He who bruises, a human figure with the club, as Hercules. Bau, who cometh. (B.)	Who cometh.	בוא	

IX.

SAGITTARIUS, THE ARCHER[3].

25. LYRA, or the harp, held by the eagle, the triumph. FENT-KAR.	Figured as a hawk or eagle, the enemy of the serpent in triumph. Fent-kar, the serpent, worm (B.), ruled.	Fent, worm or serpent, viper.	אפעה	Job 20. 16. Isa. 30. 6; 59. 5.
26. ARA, the altar of the sacrifice. BAU.	A throned human figure holding the flail, the implement of bruising. In the modern sphere this decan is very obscure. There seems here to have been a victim in the Persian sphere. To the throned figure the Egyptian name seems to refer. Bau, He cometh, as in Scorpio.	Bau, he cometh.	בא	Isa. 63. 1.
27. DRACO, the serpent enemy. HER-FENT.	The serpent, or dragon, under the forefoot of Sagittarius. Her-fent, the serpent, or the serpent accursed.	Her, cursed. Fent, as above.	ארא	Gen. 3. 14.

[2] " In ancient zodiacs," apparently Egyptian, "this sign is sometimes represented as a snake, a crocodile, or typhon, with serpents' tails for legs." (Aspin.)

[3] "The Southern Crown is of recent invention, formed from stars formerly belonging to Sagittarius." (Aspin.)

X.
CAPRICORNUS, THE FISH-GOAT[4].

DECANS. Names now in use, and Hieroglyphic Names.	Egyptian Hieroglyphic Names and Figures.	Noetic Roots traced by the Hebrew.		Used in the Hebrew Bible.
28. THE ARROW of slaying. FENT-KAR.	A tailed figure with the hawk's head, standing over the junction of the head of the kid with the body of the fish. Fent-kar, serpent. Kar, enemy. Heb. enemy.	Fent, serpent; suphon, Arab. Kar, enemy.	שפיפן עד	Gen. 49. 17. Ps. 139. 20.
29. AQUILA, the falling eagle. SU-AT.	A bird, goose of the Nile, apparently. Su-at [5], He cometh [6]. Su, He (B.); At, cometh, Heb.	} Cometh.	אתה	Job 3. 25.
30. DELPHINUS, the dolphin. KHAU.	A fish. Khau, multitude, fish; goat ? (B.), or hoped for, Heb.	Khau, longed for.	קוה	Job 7. 2.

XI.
AQUARIUS, THE WATER-BEARER[7].

31. THE SOUTHERN FISH. AAR.	The figure seems to include both the fish and the stream of water on it. Aar, a stream.	Iar, a stream.	יאר	Gen. 41. 1.
32. PEGASUS[8], the winged horse.	The ascending node, of which the headless horse is an enblem [9].	סוס, a horse.	סוס	Job 39. 18.
33. CYCNUS, the swan. TES-ARK.	The swan. Tes-ark, this from afar, ארך, Heb.	Tes, this (B.), afar.	ארך	Gen. 6. 15.

[4] In an Oriental zodiac given by Sir Wm. Jones, this sign is represented as a fish, out of whose mouth is coming forth an antelope surrounded by aquatic birds. In an Egyptian zodiac the sea-goat is held in a band by a figure called Anubis, who shall be sent forth, הנבא; in an Indian one it is said to be "a goat passant, traversed by a fish."

[5] S. the pronoun he, she, or it. (B.)

[6] Bau, according to Bunsen, is the verb "to come," and the noun derived from it, in the hieroglyphic, as in the Hebrew and Greek, and their derivative languages. Ba*, according to Bunsen's vocabulary, is also a beast, cattle, as bos, Latin, βους, Greek, a beeve. In Hebrew, it is "to come," בא, in Latin and in modern languages often taking its sound of v. Hence a beast or beast's head is a hieroglyphic sign for "who comes."

[7] Aru, a river. (B.)

[8] There is another headless figure below Pisces, where the ascending node, or winter solstice, had been B.C. 4000.

[9] No hieroglyphic name was here given in the list from which the others are supplied, but there are two characters immediately below what is here considered as representing Pegasus, a human figure, with a fillet or diadem round the head, whose hand takes hold of the head of a horse. Of these characters, the first is always read as Pe. the second appears to stand for Ka, and Peka, or Pega, is in Hebrew, the chief †; and Sus, the horse, so named as swiftly coming, returning, as the year after the winter solstice, anciently in this sign.

* Baion is a branch, in Greek, of the palm-tree, also in Egyptian (Parkh.).
† As " Pacha."

XII.

PISCES, THE FISHES.

DECANS. Names now in use, and Hieroglyphic Names.	Egyptian Hieroglyphic Name, and Figures.	Noetic Roots traced by the Hebrew.		Used in the Hebrew Bible.
34. THE BAND.	A tailed human figure walking.			
U-OR.	U-or [10] (B.), who cometh, אר, Heb.	To flow forth. Flood.	אר אור	Amos 8. 8.
35. CEPHEUS, the crowned king, the branch. PE-KU-HOR.	The wolf lying on the fore-leg of a beast. Pe-ku-hor, this (B.), to rule (B.), cometh (B. and Heb.).	Wolf, ואב, who cometh ; foreleg, זרע, also the seed.	זרע	Gen. 3. 15.
36. ANDROMEDA, the Church set free.	A female figure, either that in the circle holding a victim, or that holding the band of Pisces, under which are the characters S-r, as of Sirra, one name of Andromeda, which therefore seems most likely.	Lady or Princess.	שרה	Gen. 17. 15.
SET.	Set, set up. Sutn being " a king" (B.), this may be " queen," as the spouse of Perseus the deliverer.	Appointed. Set up as king.	שות	Job 14. 13.

[10] U, to come (B.), Or, to come (B.).
Those creatures who are mentioned by naturalists as the natural enemies of the serpent were peculiarly honoured by the Egyptians, the hawk, the ibis, the ichneumon, the cat, the swine. That they fed on the serpent may be one reason why the Jews were ordered to hold them unclean. Lev. xi. The poisonous serpent, known by the breadth of the head, was the representation of the enemy. The innocuous serpent or snake, whose head is slender and pointed, was the hieroglyphic figure of the progression of time, which its swift and noiseless motion well typifies.

The Twelve Signs and their accompanying thirty-six Decans occupy the central group of the planisphere. In the circle of figures below, and enclosing that group, the five planets may be recognized, each in one of the " houses," or positions, traditionally, and from all antiquity, assigned to them. To the figures thus to be explained, no "tail" is appended; it cannot apply to them, as " this cometh," for they are circling continually, and as it were always present with us.

Marks of reference have been inserted in the lithograph for the proposed explanations. These are, in the twelve signs, Roman numerals, in the thirty-six decans, Arabic cyphers ; for the planets, the five English vowels in capitals, and the four and twenty letters of the English alphabet for other figures. The hieroglyphic names of the decans are said to be found on this planisphere: one at least of the names of the planets is there, Athor, that of the Egyptian Venus, by whose figure it may be read.

ON THE NAMES OF THE TWELVE SIGNS.

(See page 3.)

TAMETOURIS AMMON, the reign of Ammon, dominion, government. The ram's head, crowned as it were with a circle, is below in the planisphere, marked *i*, having two horns, as the beeve, and one of the ram.

ISIS, who saves. Apis and Aleph, chief, as the bull of the herd. A figure with the divine attribute of ostrich feathers on the head, and the tail of the beeve appended, is above, as Auriga, the third Decan of Taurus. Horias, who cometh ; the zodiacal bull being always in the act of coming.

CLUSUS, CLAUSTRUM HORI, place of him who cometh. The figures in Gemini are walking, coming. In the planisphere the second appears to be feminine, and has not the tail; the companion of Him that cometh, the congregation or church of His people.

KLARIA, the cattle-folds or station of Typhon, or the ass, so agreeing with the standard of Issachar, and with the beeve below. These names therefore appear to be of earlier origin than the planisphere, where the Scarabæus, the beetle, marks the position the solstice had attained. In the figure and name of the ass there is no allusion to the solstice.

PI MENTEKEON, the pouring out, the inundation of the Nile, shows the solstice, which was in Leo at the date assigned to the creation of Adam. The inundation is here figured by a woman pouring out of two vases, the solstice remaining in Leo 1000 years; this name and emblem referring to that time—not from observation, but from calculating backwards.

ASPOLIA, the seed, the promised seed of the woman, showing the love of Him who "so loved the world," &c.

LAMBADIA, the branch of graciousness, mercy. Has not the branch been an emblem of peace always and every where? "The olive-branch of peace." Ab, he cometh, may be read here between Libra and Virgo,—the bird, A; the beeve, B. Over the balance the youth touching his lip, he bruises and is bruised; and above, the wolf Zeeb, this shall come; again above him the throned figure with the flail, he shall bruise.

ISIAS, he shall save; the ibis-headed and enthroned figure who treads under foot the serpent.

PI MAERE, the station of graciousness, where the conqueror who shall come, as the arrow from the bow, treads the serpent under foot. The characters under the hind foot read he conquers (Knem).

HUPENIUS, place of the sacrifice, the kid, whose head is united to the body of the fish; the ibis-headed and tailed figure stands over the junction. HE, the head, is joined to His body the Church.

HUPEI TIRION, place of him coming down, poured out. The pourer has not the tail.

PI-COT ORION, PISCIS HORI, the fishes of Him that cometh. Here is the ascending node or winter solstice, where Aquarius and Pisces join, answering to the summer solstice in Leo.

Those who invented the emblems derived them from the prophecies that had been given them in Gen. iii. 15; the seed of the woman shall come, shall be bruised in the heel, and shall bruise the serpent's head. Every name and every figure of this record of ancient astronomy relates to this prophecy, this promise, and to this alone.

The five figures here considered as representing the planets, marked with the five vowels, are,
    A   Jupiter, under his house Gemini.
    E   Mars, hawk-headed, under his house Aries, with hieroglyphics near, which read
"He conquers, bruises, is bruised."
    I   Venus, Athor, under her house Taurus, the Pleiades before her [1].
    O   Mercury, shakal-headed, under his house Pisces.
    U   Saturn, circle-headed, under his house Capricornus.

Egyptian Names of Planets.   (Montucla, Hist. des Math.)

Rephan, Deus temporis, or Pan	.	.	.	Saturn.
Pi-Cheus, Deus vitæ	.	.	.	Jupiter.
Moloch [2], Typhon	.	.	.	Mars.
Pi-Othiris, or Osiris	.	.	.	The Sun.
Thaut, or Pi-Ermes	.	.	.	Mercury.
Surath, or Athor, or Souroi	.	.	.	Venus.
Isis, or Domina Maris et Humidorum	.	.	The Moon.
Pi-Cochos Achtephon, the circle completed.				

The Egyptian week began with Saturday. (Montucla, Hist. des Math.)

In Egypt a branch of the palm, with twelve shoots, was used at the winter solstice, as a symbol of the year completed.

ON THE FIGURES MARKED a, b, &c.

a. A female figure pouring, sending forth, the inundation, when the summer solstice was in Leo [3].

---

[1] These stars, being seven, refer to a time previous to the siege of Troy, when the seventh Pleiad is said to have disappeared, at least 1000 years B.C.

[2] Moloch, Heb. Melech, King, a frequent epithet of Mars.

[3] Near this figure may be seen on the planisphere the representation of the moon, as a female figure sending forth an arrow, as in allusion to the Noetic name Yareah, ירח, going forth, or

b. He who cometh, ibis-headed, coming to destroy the serpent, as does the ibis [4]; pointing to two stars as his, being apparently those of Gemini above, now called Castor and Pollux.

c. The ibis-headed Hermes, Mercury, pointing to the two stars in Gemini as being his " house."

d. Draco, a dragon or serpent, on a pedestal, horned (Cerastes?), not having the poisonous head of the species.

e. Alpha Draconis, the antediluvian pole-star.

f. Three bright stars of Orion, Rigol, Bellatrix, Betelguez. } The tailed figure, He who cometh, points to these stars as his.

g. Aldebaran in Taurus.

h. The seven Pleiades, proving this planisphere to have originated more than 1000 B.C.

i. A cycle beginning in Aries, the ancient zodiac.

j. The later pole-star in Ursa Minor, and the fishes of Pisces.

k. A youth holding a flail, " He shall be bruised," and pointing to the lip, " He shall bruise," or break, שפה, seated on the lotus, " hidden, but to come," as the lotus, beneath the water.

l. He who cometh, ibis-headed, pointing to a star, Al Natik, the wounded, as his.

m. A headless figure, showing the place of the earliest known ascending node, where Aquarius joined Pisces; followed by two heads, of a beeve and a sheep, where the ascending node might have been before the time of Adam.

n. A cycle beginning in Taurus, twelve stars above the twelve signs from equinox to equinox.

o. Eight captives *bound*, as Misam, in Pisces, the nebula in Andromeda.

p. He who cometh, ibis-headed, lotus-crowned, pointing to the two stars Vega in Lyra, and Deneb, the Judge or Lord who cometh, in Cycnus.

q. A cycle beginning in Capricornus, pointed to by a female figure, the moon, ibis-headed, who cometh.

r. Three figures. 1, He who cometh, ibis-headed; 2, Lotus-crowned, hidden; 3, Shakal-headed, who cometh, pointing to a star as his, Antares in Scorpio.

s. The female swine Ursa Major, with three stars, probably the tail-stars. A cycle beginning in Aries. A lotus-crowned figure holding a flail, He shall bruise, having the horns of Aries.

t. He who cometh, ibis-headed, with a cycle on the head.

u. He who cometh with human visage, lotus-crowned.

v.   „   „   pointing to a star, the present polar star, Kochab.

w.   „   „   ibis-headed, pointing to six stars in Ursa Major.

x.   „   „   human-headed, horned, pointing to three stars, in Ursa Minor.

y.   „   „   crowned with the mitre, pointing to three stars in Virgo, Spica being alone above, ibis-headed, followed by a female figure, Virgo, pointing also to three stars, Coma, Zavijavah, and Al Mureddin.

z.   „   „   ibis-headed, crowned with the pestle and mortar of bruising, with characters which read " He who shall conquer," pointing to three stars, Regulus, Denebola, and Al Giebha, in Leo [5].

---

sent forth, intensive from Yarah, to send forth, Ps. lxiv. 4, ירה, an Arabic sense of which is to send forth sparks or rays.

In Hebrew and Egyptian the moon has names of the two genders; in Hebrew Jareah, masculine, and Lebana, feminine.

In Egyptian Aah, a companion, appears to be of either gender. This name is also Persian, as Aah, and is to be traced in Sanscrit, in Hima and Soma.

The Scandinavian Mone and Monath, by some considered to be derived from Mene, מנה, to number, as months the year, but may rather be from Aah, with the frequently added letters *m, n,* and *th.*

Bunsen gives a very similar word, Maha, as an archer; also *Ar,* as a gazelle or antelope, which perhaps, suggested by the name Yareah, gave rise to the usual Greek attribute of the huntress Diana, and perhaps to her being called a huntress, which does not seem a suitable personification of the moon.

Champollion gives *Har* as to go out; also a near approach to Yareah.

[4] The Egyptians punished with death any one who killed a hawk or an ibis. Among them no animal was so sacred as the ibis and the hawk. In the British Museum are many mummies of the ibis.

[5] It has been thought that the animal-headed figures are only masked. See Hamilton's Ægyptiaca.

Ibis-headed figures are frequent. The Ibis religiosa, most sacred among the Egyptian

In this planisphere the stars and emblems are appropriately connected; as in Sirius one star of the first magnitude; in Gemini two stars, one most brilliant in the lion's foot on the serpent, one clear and bright in the head of the bull; in Scorpio one, red as if for wrath and blood, where the enemy bruises the heel, while his own head is bruised by the victor.

It will be seen that the signs of the zodiac are the same in this ancient Egyptian planisphere as those now in use, but that in the figures representing the other constellations there is small resemblance, except perhaps in that of Orion, walking, coming.

The antiquity indicated by the place of the solstice in this planisphere would at once over-throw the already almost exploded idea of the signs having any reference to the seasons.

In the design sometimes called the title-page to the cave at Ipsamboul, a hero-figure with divine attributes, especially the common Egyptian emblem, the vulture over the head, whose Oriental name Ayit, conveys "he that cometh," has been called Sesostris; but the inscription above, like the figure, seems to refer to one greater than Sesostris, to the conqueror who should come : both may have thus been originally intended, and in adulation applied to a human sovereign. It is thus read, "The living good God, the glorious guardian smiting the south country, treading down the north country, the victorious King cometh, smiting with the sword the boundaries of all the nations of the world." The prophecy of Balaam is here recalled to remembrance, of the sceptre that should smite the corners of Moab and destroy (properly subjugate) all the children of Seth.

The figure of the conqueror of colossal stature attended by the lion, and having the reins of his fiery coursers attached to his waist, appears also more divine than human; surely no mere mortal could so guide them: the lion may typify the triumphs of the Lion of the tribe of Judah, predicted in the last blessing of his father, Jacob.

If the inventors, the first framers of the hieroglyphs, understood and intended to express the first prophecies, those who followed would probably add to or change them in some degree. Much, however, has been preserved : the twelve signs marvellously so, in so many, so far distant nations, distant in time and place.

It will be seen that the pervading import of the names and emblems is "He that cometh will come, and will not tarry." Four thousand years before His first coming it was thus announced. He came in the fulness of time, beyond which He would not tarry. The types of His incarnation and sufferings were then fulfilled : they now remain monuments of accomplished prophecy. Those of His second coming in glory point onward, in faith and hope, to that futurity of which the past is a pledge and a foretaste. Of that second coming it has been even more urgently proclaimed, "Behold, He cometh quickly." Near two thousand years have gone by in "the earnest expectation of the creature,"—an interval, long in comparison with man's transitory existence, but short if compared with the ages of earth's duration from that "beginning" to which refer the first words of earth's history. If compared with the infinitudes of eternity to come, it will be short indeed !—a narrow interval of immeasurable results, commencing with the purchase of that glorious realm from which it will be surveyed, and terminating with the return of that King whose expecting subjects have still sighed forth, "Even so, come, Lord Jesus; come quickly."

This explanation is founded on the principle that the prophetic promise recorded in Genesis iii. 15, was known to all the children of Adam, and from Noah [6] to all his descendants, among whom is mentioned Mizraim, son of Ham [7], considered the founder of Egyptian colonization after the flood. Manetho speaks of records preserved in the "sacred language" from before the flood, and translated after that event.

---

symbols, was the well-known enemy of serpents; killing, even if it did not devour. Its reliques were preserved with the care of human ones. With its long sharp beak it slew them, therefore the band denoted the character, the enemy of the serpent.

[6] It is observed in the Chronology of Sir Isaac Newton, that the Egyptians attributed their astronomy to a person, one of whose names was Oannes, who came from the Red Sea, a tradition which points to Noah, especially when it is remembered that the name of Noah's vessel was Thebah, and that on the walls of the Egyptian Thebes were represented figures of a ship.

Modern Egyptologers remark that there is no trace of imperfect civilization in Egypt. That country appears to have been colonized by those possessing all the knowledge in science and in art of the land they came from; and the Egyptians did not improve on either, but they per-petuated both.

[7] The Egyptians called their land Chem, from their forefather, Ham; in Genesis called Mizraim, from his son, derived from the root צור, pressed together, bound up, Isa. i. 6, Syriac, &c. Being in the dual, it is supposed to be Upper and Lower Egypt, or the two sides of the Nile.

Of all the mythology of the children of Adam, the leading, the governing idea is the prophetic declaration, " He shall bruise thy head, and thou shalt bruise His heel." The word שׁוּף peculiarly denotes bruising by biting, or bruising, as the reptile the heel of the man. A human figure (frequently with divine attributes) repeatedly occurs in the hieroglyphics of Egypt, as in those of India, with the foot on the serpent's head. In those of Egypt the victory is generally so represented, the victory of Him who cometh, over the serpent foe, by the action of bruising. The implement of bruising, the flail, is frequently held by this figure (Isa. xxviii. 28), who has also on his head what has been called a pestle and mortar: these also are implements of bruising (Prov. xxvii. 22). " He shall bruise" is the import of these figures. Such also is that of a ploughshare, which breaks or bruises the ground, את, from אתא, he cometh.

Those figures here explained to signify *he cometh*, have the hitherto inexplicable appendage of a tail, the tail of an animal of the beeve kind, whose Egyptian name, Ba, signifies, as in the cognate dialects, Hebrew, &c., Greek, also the verb to come; while the tail, זנב, would signify " this cometh, or is caused to come." זה, this, נאב, caused to come, sent forth; the tail is bound on with a girdle, אזר, round the waist of the walking, or coming human figure: אזר, a girdle or girded, signifying power, strong.

That the Seed of the woman should bruise the serpent's head, and the serpent should bruise His heel, was the prediction. The Seed of the woman, a divine person with no human father, born to die, was also to conquer the enemy of man, the evil one, emblematized by the serpent. This prophetic promise is the foundation of all mythology, from Egypt to Polynesia; while in the astronomy of every ancient nation the signs of the zodiac are preserved nearly the same as they are here delineated in that of Egypt. The woman bearing the seed, the ear of corn, or branch, is most remarkable in all, as the sign Virgo. A human figure, whose foot is on a serpent, is figured in the Chaldean sphere [8], in the sign Scorpio; in the Egyptian and Indian there is only the Scorpion. Still in the decans or accompanying constellations, the conqueror, as in the hieroglyphic names, is seen. In the Egyptian sphere, here delineated, He always appears as the conqueror, the triumphant, sometimes enthroned, but mostly as walking, coming. In the first sign, Aries, called in Egyptian, Tametouris Ammon, the reign of Ammon, or the Lamb, He is seated, dwelling, and as one meaning of the name may be, established; in all the others He is *coming*. The Scarabæus, which has taken the place of the sign between Gemini and Leo, has in the long zodiac [9] the wings extended as flying. That in the original sign was the " strong ass " of Issachar, the animal held by the Egyptians to be dedicated to Typhon, their personification of evil, is to be inferred from the Coptic name of the sign, Statio Typhonis: Typhon being who smites or is smitten.

In the planisphere of Dendera, as in other delineations of the starry heavens, the twelve signs of the zodiac are evidently the chief objects, to which the other figures are in subordination. Their forms are so little different from those on modern globes as to be easily recognized. The ancient Coptic names, supposed to be the ancient Egyptian, are given from Ulugh Beigh.

The same emblems in the same order are given in the catalogue of Hipparchus, drawn up about 130 years B.C. Ptolemy, who transmits that catalogue, added the figure of the half-horse above Pegasus. Perhaps he did this to keep up the number of forty-eight, after the disappearance below the horizon of the north temperate zone, of the Southern Cross, no longer seen there in his time. This precedent seems to have suggested the additions that embarrass our modern globes with air-pumps, easels, and other incongruities. Some of the names of the fixed stars were transmitted through the early Greeks, but many more by the Arabs. These were first communicated to the western nations by the Arab astronomers invited by Alphonsus, king of Castile, to assist in drawing up the Alphonsine tables. The Tartar prince and astronomer Ulugh Beigh about the year 1420 drew up his celebrated tables, which give Arabian astronomy as it had come down to his time, also transmitting the ancient Coptic or Egyptian names as here given. A much earlier authority, however, is found in Albumazer, the great Arab astronomer of the caliphs of Granada, early in the ninth century, and in Aben Ezra, his commentator, in the thirteenth [1].

In the long zodiac the decans appear between the twelve signs that they accompany; the three decans attributed to each sign come to the meridian with it, though a slight allowance must be made for the changed position of the pole, which, at the first arrangement of these emblems, would be in Alpha Draconis, the bright star in the head of the dragon, surrounding the pole. The absence of closer similarity between the forms of these Egyptian figures representing the thirty-six ancient constellations, and those by which the Arabian and Greek sphere denoted them, is, however, supplied by the coincidence in the names. For instance, the hieroglyphic name of Bootes is Bau: Bau, in the ancient Egyptian, having the meaning of " He cometh," and

---

[8] The sphere now in use among ourselves is here referred to as the Chaldean.
[9] For this zodiac, see Hamilton's Ægyptiaca.
[1] This Commentary is in the British Museum, and has been much made use of in " Mazzaroth."

also of cattle, beasts, so coinciding with the purport of the emblem "He cometh," and the office attributed to Him of a herdsman, a keeper of cattle [2]. The common origin of mankind, their descent from the one ancestor, Noah, will fully account for similarity, and the confusion of the lip at Babel for differences. Those who hold that remains of human beings are found in positions indicating a far superior antiquity, should be reminded that the book of Genesis only records the history of the children of Adam, and neither asserts nor denies that a race of beings of similar bodily proportions might have previously existed. If such did exist, all we know of them is that they died. "He who was to come," the great theme of ancient prophecy and ancient astronomy, did not come through them; He was to come, and did come of the race of Adam; the Seed of the woman, bone of his bone, and flesh of his flesh.

This ancient zodiac, or map of the stars of heaven, has, however, been considered to refer to dates perfectly consistent with that usually assigned to the creation of Adam. 1730 B.C. has repeatedly been given as deducible from its figures.

In a recent periodical it is supposed an essential of the Christian faith to believe that "the serpent was Satan." Is it not rather that the enemy took possession of the natural body of the serpent, through which to communicate with the woman [3]?

Kircher says, "A serpent [4] with the tail in the mouth was the hieroglyphic for the year" (and probably for other cycles).

"A serpent was the hieroglyphic by which the course of the stars was explained." (Sir W. Drummond.)

In some Egyptian monument it is said that the figures [5] in Gemini had one, the moon, the other, the sun, on their heads: thus perhaps accounting for one of them being feminine in the planisphere. This might imply that one was of earth, the other of heaven, as Castor and Pollux.

"The leg and hoof of a goat was a Punic emblem" as well as an Egyptian. צרע, a hawk, an emblem of God, according to Clemens Alex.

"A plough which bruises, occurs frequently on the breasts of mummies." (Dr. Clarke.)

Ammonius says, "The Egyptians had a custom of naming the Moon in the feminine."

Manetho, as cited by Dio. Laert., says that the Egyptians taught that the moon was eclipsed by falling into the earth's shadow.

The Arabian geographer Abdraschid, A.D. 1403, calls Saturn, Rephan, Mars, Melockh, and Jupiter, Pi-Cheus. To him were doubtless well known the learning of the astronomers Al Makrisi and Al Fargani, patronized in the ninth century by the Caliph of Bagdad, Al Mamon, the son of Al Raschid, who caused to be made from Greek into Arabic, those translations of Hebrew, Greek, and Latin writers, by which they are in some instances preserved for Europe. (French Institute.)

It has been supposed that the Dendera zodiac contained a horoscope, but inserted upon an ancient planisphere, as is the case with modern horoscopes. There is a human figure near Cancer, without divine or mystic attributes, who might be what is called "the native," the person for whom the horoscope is drawn.

The date of this or any other zodiac may be calculated from the place of the solstices. The sun's place at the solstice recedes from west to east about one sign in two thousand years. According to the usually received chronology, when Noah left the ark it was about the middle of Aquarius, where it is recorded to have been observed in China. In antediluvian times it had just quitted Pisces. The headless horse, type of the ascending node or winter solstice, in the Dendera planisphere appears to be over the figure of Aquarius, perhaps at its middle or fifteenth

---

[2] Zech. xiii. The Egyptian figure having the head of a beeve.

[3] Sharon Turner, Sac. Hist., vol. ii. p. 265.—"It is a curious fact, that the Mexicans had a tradition of the history of Eve, and a representation of it, in their symbolical paintings. Humboldt thus mentions the circumstance. In describing the hieroglyphical paintings of the Mexicans in the Borghian Museum at Veletri, he says, 'that No. 1, Cod. Borg. fol. ii. represents the mother of mankind, the serpent-woman, the Eve of the Mexicans.'—Humb. Researches, vol. ii. p. 834. Of the Codex Vaticanus he mentions, 'the group No. 2 represents the celebrated serpent-woman, Cihux-cohuatl, called also Quilatzi, or Tonacacihua, woman of our flesh. She is the companion of Tonacateuctli. The Mexicans considered her as the mother of the human race. After the god of the celestial paradise, Ometeuctli, she held the first rank among the divinities of Aushuac. We see her always represented with a great serpent.'—Humb. ib. vol. i. p. 195. 'Their Adam is called Tonacateuctli, or Lord of our flesh; he is represented in the Cod. Borg. fol. 9.'—Humb. ib. 226."

[4] These figures of serpents or snakes connected with time, have a narrow-pointed head, as the innoxious species always have; the enemy has the broad obtuse head of the venomous ones, as the cobra, &c.

[5] It is possible the long-robed figure may have been intended as priestly, the Egyptian priests being robed in a long linen garment called Calasiris, Heb. the clothing of the Prince.

degree. This indicates the origin of this zodiac to have been in times when its position was in Aquarius: but the position of the summer solstice had been since altered to suit the precession of the equinoxes, by inserting a scarabæus, beetle, or crab, in the position where the summer solstice began to take place about 2000 B.C. 4000 B.C. it had been where the signs of Leo [6] and Virgo join, being according to tradition, at the time of the creation of Adam, the first observer of the heavens. Such, common sense tells that he must have been, even if tradition had not so called him. The insertion of the crab or scarabæus, to mark the recession of the solstice, indicates a date *less* than 2000 B.C., consequently later than that indicated by the position of the headless figure over Aquarius. In the smaller zodiac the summer solstice is in many ways marked as in Cancer, in that part nearest to Gemini. Therefore it is of a later date than the circular. The Scarabæus, passing its early existence as a worm in the earth, and issuing thence a winged denizen of heaven, was held sacred by the Egyptians as an emblem of the resurrection of the body, in which they firmly believed, and from which they derived their custom of preserving it as a mummy [7].

The figures of this planisphere tend to show, that the primeval religion of Egypt was that revealed to Adam, and transmitted by Noah. That the Seed or offspring of the woman should bruise the head of the serpent, the enemy, and that it should bruise His heel, is the earliest manifestation of that religion on record, and the most universal—still to be traced in the traditions of all nations, but most evidently in the wide-spread monuments of astronomy, the emblems of the twelve signs of the zodiac marking out the way of Him who should come, depart, and come again, as the sun, His recognized type in the heavens.

On this planisphere the twelve signs are represented nearly as described by the Greek astronomer Hipparchus (B.C. 125), long before the supposed erection of the temple on which the planisphere is carved. The Greeks allowed that their astronomy came to them from Egypt; the Egyptians attributed theirs to Chaldea. Abraham, to whom his descendants referred the origin of their astronomy, being a Chaldean and a temporary resident in Egypt, through him they might derive the astronomy transmitted from the antediluvian patriarchs, to whom tradition refers the invention of the science. This would make part of the wisdom of Egypt of which Moses was in possession. The ram or lamb, the bull, the goat or kid, were from the beginning sacrificial animals, typifying the one great sacrifice. Cattle, flocks, and herds, the earliest possession of mankind, represented His people, His purchased possession; while the human figure showed the nature in which He should come for their redemption, the lion showing His coming to victory over His enemies—He who was bruised in the heel coming to bruise the head. Even in lands where the lion was unknown, that figure was pre-eminent as in this zodiac; for the lion was a Chaldean, not an Egyptian animal. The figure of the sheep was in the far East supplied by the goat or antelope. The serpent was every where as universal as the wiles of him whom it represents, or as the stars to which these emblems were annexed.

If, as has been urged, God has spoken, the records of what He has said ought to be searched out. The message of the Book and of the symbols may be shown clearly to agree. The traditions [8] of the nations, like sunbeams on a rapid stream, however broken and confused, yet reflect the primeval light.

Ancient writers have said that the religion of Egypt was derived from the constellations, but not that the constellations were derived from that religion.

Those who invented the emblems of the constellations of course gave names to them, and probably also to their principal stars. Arabian tradition asserted that these names were transmitted unchanged in Arab astronomy. Names are not, as is sometimes supposed, mere arbitrary combinations of letters. All names have meanings explicable by the roots which they contain. The Holy Scriptures occasionally explain the names there recorded from their roots in the Hebrew language, also to be found in the other cognate dialects. All the ancient names of the stars that have reached us have meanings in those dialects suitable to the import of the emblems connected with which they are found. These correspondences furnish strong evidence that the design of the inventors was to transmit to their descendants immortal and life-giving truths.

Evidence of the antiquity of these emblems may be found by those internal traces in the

---

[6] The Egyptian astronomers taught that at the Creation the sun rose in Leo, the moon in Cancer; these signs have always been called their houses. The very ancient science of astrology also gave each of the planets their houses or signs, Aries being called the house of Mars, Virgo of Mercury, Sagittarius of Jupiter, Libra of Venus, Capricorn of Saturn. If at, or soon after, Adam's creation, these planets were in these signs, such might be the origin of this appropriation.

[7] The male Scarabæi are smaller than the female; the male typifying the sun setting to rise again, also, the resurrection of man; the female, the renewed year.

[8] Maimonides says, that according to Jewish tradition the first man who introduced the worship of the stars asserted that it was derived from prophecy.

D

records of the science of astronomy, by which some modern astronomers are led to refer its origin to about 4000 years ago, but those here pointed out refer rather to 6000, the age of Seth and Enoch, whom ancient traditions name as the first astronomers.

The testimony of the ancient Egyptians to this antiquity is preserved by the Greek writers, in the ancient books of the Persians, and by Josephus, the historian of the Jews.

The coincidence of Arab astronomy with the Chaldean and Egyptian traditions and monuments is well known.

The suitability of the names preserved by the Arabs and other ancients, when explained by the Noetic roots found in all languages, to the emblems of the Egyptian zodiacs, indicates a common origin. The name of Seth or Thoth, given by all tradition as that of the inventor of astronomy and the Sothaic period, the wonderful perfection of which is acknowledged by modern astronomers, and attributed to the earliest race of mankind, testifies to this assertion.

Of "the great year" of Josephus, the Sothaic period of six hundred years, Cassini says, " This period, of which we find no intimation in any monument of any other nation, is the finest that ever was invented; for it brings out the solar year more exactly than that of Hipparchus and Ptolemy, and the lunar months within about one minute of what is determined by modern astronomers."

The figures of the constellations only including the stars visible in the latitudes between the sources of the Euphrates and the Nile, indicate their origin or early adoption in those districts.

It is said that "the Egyptians learnt from Hermes[9] the canicular cycle of 1461 years, at the end of which their solar year of 365 years (the deficiency of which they were not allowed to make up by intercalation) had receded through every season, and returned to the same sidereal point of commencement, namely, the rising of the dogstar on the 1st of Thoth. This cycle they called the great year. But there was another great year in more general use, which was the *Neros*, or cycle of 600 years, to which Josephus refers, Ant. i. 3, and which was that most employed at Babylon; this being one of the cycles on the great stone in the India House. The Saros was another cycle, of, according to Suidas, eighteen years and six months, nearly corresponding with the Metonic lunar cycle of nineteen years. This also being inscribed on the stone at the India House, will come under consideration at a future opportunity." (Cullimore on the Origin of the Primitive Sphere of the Greeks, in the Morning Watch, vol. vi. p. 389.)

The sphere described by Eudoxus, Aratus, and Hipparchus, is said by Cullimore to be proved to have been from Egypt; and that Sir Isaac Newton and all others who refer its emblems to the Argonautic voyage, are obliged to reject either historical or astronomical evidence, but agrees with Sir Isaac Newton's placing of the colures.

" Psammeticus, with whom the catalogue of the great Paite family, preserved by Herodotus, commences, began to reign B.C. 672, the first year of the Græco-Egyptian intercourse, and was, according to the Egyptian annals of Manetho, preceded by Stephinathes, Nicepsos, and Nechao I., the father of Psammeticus, according to Herodotus, who reigned respectively seven, six, and eight years. To King Nicepsos, and his contemporary, the philosopher Petosiris, are ascribed the latest innovations or improvements in the Hermaic astronomy of Egypt. They were celebrated astronomers and astrologers, and constructed a sphere into which the decani or decennary divisions of the zodiac were first introduced. Julius Firmicus calls them ' divini viri atque omni admiratione digni.' Nicepsos reigned from B.C. 686 to B.C. 672." The Greek sphere then originated with Thales, whose disciple, Anaximander, first constructed it.

"The zodiacal signs are undeniably of the highest antiquity before the times to which heathen history ascends. Some of them are alluded to in the book of Job, which, if by Moses, was the earliest of his writings, and even in the East these signs remain unchanged, unencumbered by their elephants and monsters." " On the testimony of Berosus, corroborated by internal evidence in the zodiac itself, *we* believe these signs to have been invented by the first Hermes, about 2400 B.C., and when at the vernal equinox the sun was in, or near the Pleiades. The second Hermes perfected what the first had only designed, having ascertained the true length of the year, and fixed the seasons by the solstices and equinoxes. This took place about 1500 B.C., when the sun at the vernal equinox stood in the cloud whence Taurus emerges; and it was near the time of the Exodus, Hermes being contemporary with Moses. The signs so fixed by the second Hermes have passed into all countries where astronomy is known, with no other variation than that occasioned by remoteness of latitude, where the Chaldean animal of some of the signs was supplied by an animal better known in the remote regions of the earth, or by some grotesque form, unlike any thing in nature. Aries passes into the goat or deer in India, and Gemini and Virgo take the Oriental costume; Leo also, though retaining its name and place in the Indian zodiac, has assumed a form as rude as in the heraldic paintings of the middle ages. These facts demonstrate

---

[9] Much has been said of the first and second Hermes, and more of Hermes Trismegistus; Hermes being taken as a proper name, not considering it, as it is, an epithet, חרם, the great, with the common Egyptian affix of *s*. It may refer to Seth or Enoch as the great astronomers.

that the zodiac was not invented in India, but in a country where the lion and other animals were commonly known, such as Egypt or Assyria, and the transport of astronomy to India is further evidenced by Virgo being seated in a ship or chariot in the Cingalese and some other Oriental zodiacs. The forms in the Greek and Roman zodiacs were become wholly arbitrary, and bore no reference to the positions of the stars. But we generally find Aries and Taurus turned from each other, indicating the division to be between Aries and Taurus, as stated above. The fixed zodiac, commencing with Aries, seems not to have been generally adopted till the time of Hipparchus, when the vernal equinox stood near the head of Aries, and the autumnal near Spica Virginis. Ptolemy himself declares that he altered the forms of some of the constellations to give the figures a better proportion, and stars which the older astronomers had placed in the shoulders were thus brought down to the sides of Virgo. He says:—'Multis ergo in locis accommodatiora ipsis figuris attribuentes vocabula, priscorum usum immutavimus, sicut, verbi gratia, figuras quas Hipparchus in humeris Virginis locat, nos in costis ejus sitas esse dicimus, quoniam distantia earum ad stellas quæ in capite sunt major apparet, quam ad eas quæ in extremitatibus manuum collocantur, hoc autem sicut et costis accommodatur.' Bayer turned the backs of the figures to the spectator instead of the faces, and Albert Durer, or some German, put them all into Gothic costume, in which they remained till the time of Flamstead. He revised, or rather re-constructed the forms of the constellations, and first laying down the stars themselves correctly, drew the figures according to that part of the body in which the several stars were said to be placed by Hipparchus and Ptolemy."

While in ancient Egypt the signs of the zodiac were thus engraven on their temples, in India and Arabia from time immemorial the signs and the Lunar Mansions have been interwoven with science and poetry, with public worship and private economy, the figures being embodied in the forms of idols, and the appellations transmitted in the names of children. In Scandinavia they have been claimed by Olaus Rudbeck, as having there originated. In Mexico they are still to be traced. The Burmese have preserved them well: the Polynesians have not totally forgotten them. Wherever the posterity of Noah, the children of Seth, are found, there are recognized some vestiges of this their ancestral science. When the study of astronomy was merged in that of astrology, during the dark ages of Europe, it flourished in the East, cultivated by Al Fergani at the court of the Caliph of Bagdad, Haroun Alraschid, in the ninth century, and at that of the Moors in Spain by Albumazer about the same time, whose works were commented on by Aben Ezra in the twelfth. He has transmitted to us accounts of the ancient Persian, Indian, and Egyptian spheres. Ulugh Beigh, the Tartar prince and astronomer, grandson of Tamerlane, has preserved the ancient Coptic names of the signs, supposed to have been those of the ancient Egyptians, and also many names of the fixed stars, which appear to have come through the Arabs[1]. The Lunar Mansions, and the divisions into Decans of the thirty-six constellations beyond the zodiac, which appear on the planisphere and long zodiac of Dendera, were by them enumerated and described.

These are some of the leading ancient astronomers who have preserved and transmitted to us such important evidence of the antiquity of these emblems, and of the unity of design in the ancient division and nomenclature of the starry heavens. The interpretations here given are assimilated as closely as possible to their concurring testimony separated by ages of time, by distance of habitation, by language, and by religion: where they agree, surely it must be in the truth.

As the Jews have guarded for us in their precious integrity the Hebrew Scriptures, so Mahometan, or rather patriarchal Arabs have transmitted to us the names which so remarkably correspond with the language of those Scriptures, when setting forth the glory of Him not then revealed to either of those nations—children of Abraham according to the flesh, who will one day hail their long unrecognized kinsman-Redeemer, when the flocks of Kedar and the rams of Nebaioth shall be gathered unto the Lord, and His glory shall have arisen upon them.

Another chain of evidence has descended to us through the Greeks. Hesiod, about 1000 years B.C., treats of the rising and setting of the constellations, whose names and emblems he transmits as from immemorial antiquity. So speaks Homer of those which he mentions. Aratus, a Greek at the court of Antigonus, king of Macedonia, about 277 B.C., in his poem on astronomy, describes much more particularly the constellations, in number, name, and figure nearly as now represented. Hipparchus, the celebrated Greek astronomer, who died 125 years B.C., enumerated and is said to have given names to the stars; but Hesiod, Homer, and Aratus having previously recorded them by name, this can therefore only mean that he made of them a regular enrolment. Hyginus, a freedman of Augustus, gives the names and figures as his predecessors, and relates of them the various fables in his time vaguely attached to the constellations, of the uncertainty of

---

[1] Montucla, &c.

which he frequently speaks,—thus making more remarkable the invariable certainty of the appellations and symbols. Ptolemy of Alexandria, in the time of Antoninus, made the celebrated catalogue of the fixed stars, describing the constellations as we now have them, particularly the remarkable union of some with others, by reckoning the same star in each; as the foot of Aries with the band of Pisces and head of Cetus; the foot of Auriga with the horn of Taurus; the cup and raven with the serpent Hydra. From him we have derived them without variation, till the English astronomer, and adversary of Newton, Flamstead, in the time of Queen Anne, unfortunately took it into his head, in attempting to give names to the stars not reckoned in the ancient constellations, to mingle with these mystic and significant emblems such senseless figures as the fox and goose, or such unimportant ones as the shield of Sobieski and bull of Poniatowski, which now disfigure the modern sphere. He did not even suspect they had any meaning: therefore it is evident that this great astronomer had not in the course of his studies met with any account of their possible signification which appeared to him worthy of notice. It is in Jewish antiquity alone that we find any vestige of a received meaning being attached to them.

Ancient as these zodiacs are, and particularly the circular one, we have a record of much more ancient astronomy in the blessing of Jacob, in which he describes the signs as borne on the banners of Israel, about 1700 B.C.

Great modern authorities in geological science seem now to have agreed, that in every new creation traced in the fossilized chronicles of by-gone ages, the first were the grandest of the formation. The physical constitution of the antediluvian, the first race of man, framed to last near a thousand years, must have been in every respect superior to that now existing, or any of which we can form an idea. If the intellectual, the purely spiritual, were not so too, yet the instruments by which that intellect worked being so far superior, would give an incalculable advantage to its exercise.

The perfection to which these fathers, these kings [2] of men, carried their astronomy, as testified by the famous period of 600 years, affords sufficient proof of the superiority of their organs of sight. Those eyes were to them what the last and greatest telescope has been to their less naturally gifted descendants. The most ancient names of the nebulæ prove that to them was known, what is at last recently acknowledged, that these clouds of light are indeed starry assemblages [3], multitudes.

The Egyptian zodiac as represented in the annexed planisphere of Dendera, though in the main agreeing with that apparently known to Jacob and his family, differs from it in two of the signs. On Issachar's standard was borne the strong ass, still to be recognized in the stars of Cancer, where two stars are called the northern and southern ass, and in the name Statio Typhonis, the ass having been an emblem of Typhon. Also the Egyptian zodiac has in Libra the scales, surmounted by a figure whose finger is on his lips, over whom are two others, a fox or wolf, and a man holding a flail; and it is well known that Libra, the scales or balance, was not borne on any standard of Israel, the place of Levi, to whom it would have fallen, being with Simeon in the blessing of Jacob, and with the tabernacle in the encampment of Israel and the blessing of Moses; the emblem of the scales not being used by Jacob, but the place where it might be looked for, after the serpent or basilisk of Dan, being devoted by the dying prophet to the memorial of that salvation for which he had waited, and which was typified in the balance of redemption, the cross, the victim, and the crown. These were no human attributes, and to none did he appoint them. The figure enclosed in a circle has been called Harpocrates, a name which may be referred to the primitive roots אר, He who cometh, פ the Egyptian article masculine before כרה or כרה, cut in pieces as a sacrifice (Jer. xxxiv. 18, &c.): He who cometh to be a sacrifice. He has a finger on the lip (שפה being the lip, and שף to bruise), referring to one first great and universal prophecy as to Him who should come, that He should bruise the head of the enemy and be Himself bruised in the heel; the fox or wolf, Shual or Zeeb, expressing "He who cometh;" the figure with the flail expressing "He shall bruise," also "He shall return," as the flail on the corn. The decans of this sign are the cross, being represented by the lion, who rends a figure with the face and horns of a lamb, the victim; and the enthroned figure with the flail and the crown.

---

[2] "The ten kings before the flood" have been spoken of in very ancient writers. Josephus gives as a reason for the long life of the antediluvians, that they might complete their discoveries in astronomy.

[3] See the Tables in Part II., for the Pleiades, Cancer, Orion, and Andromeda. Sephina in Argo is also probably the nebula in that place, visible to antediluvian eyes, if not to ours.

That the Seed of the woman shall bruise the serpent's head, and it should bruise His heel, is the foundation on which is constructed the whole of this planisphere, with those of the Indians, Persians, Arabs, or, as in fact these all are, the Chaldean. Abraham was a Chaldean, and traditional history has said a great astronomer, and Chaldean astronomy is continually appealed to as the original of the science. It has been supposed that Melchisedek, the righteous king, was Shem in person; if so, he must have known all that Noah knew on the subject, and Noah must have known what Adam, Seth, and Enoch are traditionally said to have transmitted as to the names and positions of the stars of heaven. But with the Chaldean astronomy, which is in fact ours, the Egyptian does not always agree. The Egyptians had derived their science from Noah before Abraham came among them, and in this planisphere we have the records of it, for the headless figure, where Aquarius joins on Pisces, refers to a time long before Abraham; another headless figure with the horns of Aries, more immediately under Pisces, may have originally been intended to refer to the winter solstice having receded from Aries into Pisces before the earliest era in tradition. This might be the figure which led some French astronomers to attribute an antiquity far beyond Scripture chronology, a time when the winter solstice would be in Aries, if the heavenly bodies then existed. In the Egyptian and Chaldean spheres, and those of Persia and India as described by Albumazer, the twelve signs are exactly alike; and in the other constellations, the thirty-six decans [4], there is sufficient resemblance to show that all had one origin; the astronomy of which all tradition, and particularly the Egyptian, calls Seth the originator. The traditional names Hermes, and Hermes Trismegistus, seem to refer to Seth, as Hermes, the great one, and Adam, Seth, and Enoch, as the three great ones who originated the science.

In the different ancient spheres the number and purport of the emblems are the same, and similar meanings are traceable in their names by the aid of the Noetic roots preserved in the Hebrew Scriptures.

In the annexed tables, the names said to have been obtained from the planisphere are so explained, and references given to the parts of the Hebrew Scriptures where the Noetic roots are used in the sense here given to them.

Authorities have been asked for the inference that the twelve signs and other constellations of Egyptian astronomy symbolize the prophecies concerning Him who was to come, the Messiah, frequently personified as Osiris and Horus, the Prince and the Divine Infant. It is answered that the inference is made on the authority of the ancient traditions connected with the emblems, and the meanings conveyed by the ancient but yet extant names,—as Osiris, the Prince; " Sir," in Isa. ix., born of no human father, born to die, and revive again; Isis, or Isha, wife of Osiris, mother of Orus or Horus, He who cometh, who shall come; Typhon, the evil one, the smitten or wounded, or the smiting or wounding. The great authority here is the meaning of the names and similarity of the traditionary characters. Osiris reigns, but dies and lives again; Horus comes to rule and live; Typhon smites, and is smitten.

In the figures of Egyptian astronomy one foot of the conqueror is on the head of the serpent, the other held up as wounded, bruised. The astronomy of the Egyptians is not corrupted like their mythology.

NOTE ON THE SCARABÆUS.

The metamorphosis of insects has often been considered to typify the resurrection of the human body. "We see therein the resurrection painted before our eyes, and exemplified so as to be examined by our hands," was said by the celebrated naturalist Swämmerdam.

The larva, caterpillar, or grub, was thought to represent the state of man in life, the pupa or chrysalis the dead body, the perfect insect the resurrection. The Egyptians held the immortality of the soul, and the future resurrection of the body, to be reunited to the soul, and enjoy with it a more glorious and heavenly existence. This patriarchal truth they afterwards encumbered with the notion that the preservation of the body was necessary to this future reunion; and hence the national practice of forming it into a mummy. There is a *likeness* between the chrysalis and the mummy which might suggest the shape of the mummy: the Scarabæus often on its breast; let us hope, a token of patriarchal faith yet surviving the darkness of heathenism.

The Scarabæus seems to have been introduced into the later zodiacs, not being among the more ancient Coptic names, as emblematizing the sun in his re-ascending state, completed when he reached the summer solstice in Cancer about 1500 years before the Christian era. Such seems to have been the popular interpretation of the emblem; but that there was a higher meaning, even that of resurrection, is evidenced by the figure of the Scarabæus on the breast of mummies, and by the representation of it as ascending on high with figures below in attitudes

---

[4] Note " on Decans."

of wonder and adoration ; a remarkable instance of this may be seen on the sarcophagus, called that of Alexander, in the British Museum.

The Scarabæus does not occur among the thirty-six decans, either in their figures or their hieroglyphic names, but the figure in the planisphere called the Crab is a beetle, having no tail, and attennæ not pincers, though somewhat more resembling a crab than the figure in the smaller zodiac, which is evidently a beetle, and on the long zodiac there is a Scarabæus with its wings extended, with the smaller and less definite figure of a beetle, not however a crab.

One of the hieroglyphic names in Cancer being Fent-har, the·serpent's enemy, may have led to the introduction of the Scarabæus, as typifying a conqueror, and also the sun victorious over darkness.

NOTE ON MANETHO.

Manetho, or Manethos, was High Priest of Heliopolis, under Ptolemy Philadelphus, 304 B.C. His history, written in Greek, is lost, but his dynasties are preserved by Eusebius, and fragments of his history in Josephus' work against Apion. The subject-matter he asserts to have been extracted from the sacred pillars of the first Hermes Trismegistus, from inscriptions made in the sacred language of Thoth, translated after the Flood, written in the sacred character, and deposited in the sacred recesses of Egypt. His first book was history of heroes and demi-gods, his second of eight dynasties, and his third of twelve.

It should be borne in mind, that Manetho, though beginning his record of the traditional history of Egypt in a remote and shadowy antiquity, lived only three hundred years before Christ, when not only inspired but uninspired records were in existence, and familiarly appealed to by the Jews, who in addition to their own holy books had brought with them from Babylon much of the wisdom of the Chaldeans, among which the Rabbins lament to reckon that "Astrology," which they say obscured the light of the ancient Jewish Astronomy. Still they appealed to the blessing of Jacob and standards of the tribes as of undoubted authority, and with unshaken veneration.

(Josephus against Apion [5], Book I.)

" What is set down by the Greeks is now but of yesterday. But among the Egyptians, Chaldees, and Phœnicians, the memory of their writings is ancient and infallible."

" Manethon, an Egyptian born, skilful in the Greek tongue (for he writ in Greek), compiling a history of the customs and religion of his forefathers, collected (as himself reporteth) out of the Egyptian holy writings, often reprehendeth Herodotus, who being indeed ignorant, did much help the Egyptians." " This Manethon," he goes on to say, " among other things, speaks of a nation called Hycsos, which signifies kings, shepherds, for Hyc, in the sacred tongue, signifies a king, and Sos, a shepherd or shepherds." But Josephus adds that Hic, or Hac, in the Egyptian tongue, signifies a captive [6].

" Manethon reporteth those kings and shepherds to have ruled Egypt 511 years, after which they were expelled." " Further, in another book of Egyptian affairs, Manethon saith that in the holy writings he findeth these shepherds called captives."

Manethon gives the descent of kings after the expulsion of the Shepherds, down to Egyptus and Danaus. " Thus far Manethon."

" Berosus, a Chaldean born, in the Grecian tongue, did write astronomy and the Chaldees' philosophy. He writeth of the Deluge."

" Manethon confesseth himself to have gathered the Egyptian history out of their holy writings."

" Manethon, while he followed the ancient writers, did not much err."

" I have opposed myself against Manetho, Chæremon, and others." Manetho saith that the Jews departed out of Egypt about the time of Tethmosis, 396 years before Danaus fled out of Greece. The name Manetho is used by some translators, Manethon by others.

" In my opinion profound minds are the most likely to think lightly of the resources of human reason ; and it is the pert, superficial thinker who is generally strongest in all kinds of unbelief. The deep philosopher sees chains of causes and effects·so wonderfully and strangely linked together, that he is usually the last person to decide upon the impossibility of any two series of events being independent of each other ; and in science so many natural miracles, as it were, have been brought to light, that the physical inquirer is seldom disposed to assert confidently on any abstruse subjects belonging to natural things, and still less so on those relating

---

[5] Apion accused the Jews of worshipping an ass in the temple. Did they confound Athon, an ass, with אתון, " Him who cometh ? "

[6] חיך, bound.

ZODIAC OF ESNÈ.

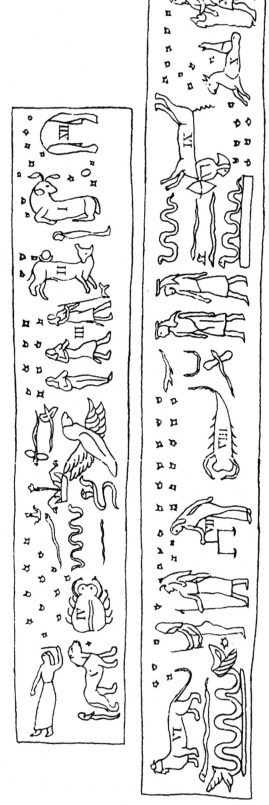

[To face p. 23.

:o the more mysterious relations of moral events and intellectual natures." (Sir H. Davy, Salmonia, p. 150.)

Socrates says that he learnt from a book by Anaxagoras, that "it is Intelligence that sets in order all things:" to which he himself added, "in such a way as shall be best." He also says, ' The soul is imperishable and immortal."

Jamblicus states that the Egyptians acknowledged a Spirit superior to nature, and an Intelligence superior to that soul by whom the world was created.

ZODIAC OF ESNÉ [7].

[The only explanation of this zodiac furnished by the Writer of "Mazzaroth," consists of the numbers (evidently marking the Twelve Signs) annexed to some of the figures, the word ' Sphinx" written over No. 6, and the subjoined note.—C. D.]

In this zodiac the winter solstice appears to have been placed in Pisces B.C. 4000 years, the summer in Leo, where joining Virgo, giving the same date; the serpent under Virgo appears to be of the venomous species, by the broad head; all the others, having pointed and narrow heads, are snakes not venomous, typifying time in their swift motion. The Scarabæus, denoting the sun's place at the solstice, shows that this zodiac, though recording an earlier era, had been altered to the time of the building of the temple, after the Christian era.

[Explanations of the remaining figures were probably in the Writer's mind, but not having been committed to paper are irrevocably lost. The following elucidations have, however, been kindly offered by a Clerical Friend of the Writer, residing in Norfolk, who had been much in correspondence on the subject of "Mizraim," and whose sympathy and aid had been very valuable during the closing period of the Writer's literary labours.]

" In Aries is an hieroglyphic emblem, an oval or egg, denoting a female, as in the same sign in the Dendera Planisphere. This emblem denotes the constellation Cassiopeia, the throned woman or church, which is marked by the nine stars in this Planisphere. Aries seems to be looking the reverse way towards this constellation. Does this represent the Lamb seeing of the travail of His soul and satisfied?

* * * * * * * * *

" The mistake seems to me (and it is an important one) in numbering the Sphinx VI. instead of Virgo, the female figure standing above the prostrate serpent or dragon, and holding in her two hands the Spicum or ear of corn, the ' Seed,' in whom is finally and completely bruised the serpent's head."

[Possibly the Egyptians, having made the Sphinx represent Virgo, and being yet aware that the ear of corn was an essential part of the sign, added the female figure holding the ear as supplemental to their own invention of the Sphinx.—C. D.]

---

[7] See M. L'Abbé Halme, " Examen et Explication des Zodiaques d'Esné," 8vo., Paris, 1821, Pl. II.

Addenda.

[A Chapter on the INDIAN ASTRONOMY, showing its correspondence with the system of "Mazzaroth," was contemplated by the Writer, and would have been appended to this work had life been prolonged.   In a letter dated January 9, 1864, is the following passage.—C.D.]

"Have I told you I have lately got *seven* Indian Zodiacs in a Bengali Almanack, *none older* than Abraham, none Egyptian, but ancient Chaldean Astronomy?   They came when I was very ill, and I have not written yet what I see in them, fixing the origin of *these* and probably all Sanscrit Astronomy to about the time of Abraham.   Cancer is there, no Scarabæus, no cattle in that sign.   In the more modern, Taurus is the little humpy Hindoo Bull; in the others, a grand, but scarcely made out, fine Eastern Bull."

[Amongst Miscellaneous papers has been found the following, endorsed " For India."]

Perseus and Andromeda and Cepheus are Indian constellations.

Nipla, modern Chaldaic for Orion (Maurice).   Name of the Pleiades in Sanscrit, Carteek, this constellation was called in India, " The general of the celestial armies."

Maurice thinks that the Indian mythology was formed " when the year opened in Taurus, and the Pleiades rose heliacally" (as at the antediluvian vernal equinox, F. R.).   He also thinks that when the Grecian sphere was first formed, the seventh Pleiad was becoming fainter; it is said to have vanished at the siege of Troy.   Hyginus says it retired as a comet to the arctic circle.

Vallancy, Oriental Collections, says that " the plan of Pagan Religion is the same every where," from antediluvian astronomy transmitted through Noah.

Saturn, from the Oriental root, sater, to hide.   Satyavarmon, the Indian *Urah,* as hidden in the ark.

De Grunès says an Egyptian hieroglyphic for science is dew falling from heaven.

De la Loubère.   The Siamese week.   Planetary names nearly the same as the other Indian ones, beginning however apparently with the *Sun,* the *first* day.

[The following also appears partly to bear on the subject.]

The " Primitive Astronomer," observing the sun rise and set, who could this be but the first man?

The Greeks, by the mouth of Plato, say they learnt the little they knew of Astronomy from the Egyptians.   The Egyptians [attribute] theirs to Oannes, Thoth, and Soth.   The Chaldeans, whose records went back nineteen centuries in the days of Alexander, attribute the origin of theirs to Seth and Enoch.   Astronomy has ever been by modern astronomers attributed to " Chaldean Shepherds;" and was not Abraham a Chaldean Shepherd, only a few generations from Noah? did he not preserve and transmit the records of those eclipses of nineteen centuries pleaded by the Babylonians to Alexander?   Antediluvian records would be preserved by Noah, as was the astronomy of Seth, Soth, or Thoth, and transmitted by the sons of Noah to Egypt and Chaldea, and why not to India and China?   Was it not one invention, emanating from one inventor, known to posterity by varying names?

THE PLANETS.

[A few very short notes on the names of the planets, in a fragmentary state, have been found since the decease of the Writer. They were evidently intended as rough notes of matter to be incorporated with this work. Such very slight arrangement as was practicable, has been adopted in giving the substance as below in the words of the writer, without interpolation, excepting where marked by brackets. A part of the page entitled "The Planet Venus" was already in the press, as was also a part of that headed "The Pole."—C. D.]

To Seth is attributed the origin of the names of astronomy, and in his time it is said it was begun to call by the name of the Lord (Gen. iv. 26). This may imply the naming of the stars by names to the glory of the Lord, as is maintained in the previous pages of Mazzaroth. It may also include the having given names to the planets; from their brightness and varying position it seems likely that they were the earliest noticed and named. The names of the five that would be early noticed as bright, large moveable stars have come down to us as given in Mazzaroth, Part III., page 5, in the East, and as still in use in Europe in the West, different in sound, but in some degree corresponding in meaning.

The name Planets is derived from moveableness, so distinguishing them from the fixed stars. Seth would early perceive they derived their brightness from the light of the sun, and that they appeared to attend on him their common centre. The sun, the minister (Chald.) of light [1].

The heavens declare the glory of God, by His name El, Al, the Allah of the Oriental languages, frequently applied in the sacred writings to the Second Person of the Triune God. To this purpose the yet extant and unchanged names of the fixed stars are shown to turn; the names of the Planets were not intended to speak [directly] of the glory of the Creator or the Redeemer, but [as seen] in His work, the Lord's people, the congregation of the Lord, so called before His first coming, the Church of Christ since that coming, dark in themselves, enlightened and light-giving in the light of Christ.

When the Arabian astronomers brought to Europe, under the patronage of Alphonso, king of Castile, the ancient names of the fixed stars now in use among us, the planets were found familiarly and universally known by names in use among the Romans. These names the Romans appear to have found in use in that early Italy, of which they preserved other fragmentary traces in their language, referable, like all other ancient words, to the first language of mankind. These names so originating and so transmitted to us, are still in use, and are to be explained by the Noetic or Hebrew roots they contain.

Saturn, resting.
Jupiter [2], the Lord hath set free. 1 Chron. ix. 34; 2 Chron. xxiii. 10.
Mars [3], the wounded.
Earth, the broken.
Venus [4], the beloved.
Mercury [5], going and returning again.

---

[1] That *Shemish*, usually masculine, is sometimes feminine, accounts for the varying gender of the sun in different languages, as in German.

[2] Jah, corrupted into Ja, offers no difficulty to the Bible student. "Praise Him in His name Jah," will occur to every one such. Pether, or Piter, to open as a gate, as a line of descent, whence Pater and Father in modern languages, to set free. "Setting free" *originates* a stream of water and a course of events; and the line of a pedigree is originated by the father, man by Adam, the Jews by Abraham. So Pater may be referred to the Hebrew root Patar, whence "Pater," Latin, &c. One meaning of Zedek, the Oriental name of Jupiter, is to set free by justifying.

[3] Mars, the wounded, as Christ for His Church, His Church in Him.

[4] Venus, in all countries and languages feminine, the Church from Adam downwards.

[5] Mercury, whose old Italian name Mercurius has the Hebrew roots, from afar returning; whose Greek name means coming.

The first three planets and the fifth in the Heb. and Arab. are not feminine, but masculine; the fourth in all languages feminine, as the "congregation of the Lord" in the Old Testament, and the Christian Church always feminine; "reposing," "set free," "by blood," applying to both genders, as "returning," the masculine always including the feminine when needful. In the ancient names, however, the gender of the fourth is doubtful, like the Church, including both. Zedek, "set free," applies to both genders; the Ja, masculine, is a post-Noetic addition.

The inventors of Astronomy could not omit the Planets in the nomenclature of the stars, by which they desired to make the heavens declare the glory of God. The evidence of that design is in the names themselves.

The Coptic names of the Planets, given by Montucla from Ulugh Beigh, are Rephan, Saturn; Picheus, Jupiter; Melochk, Mars; Surath or Athor, Venus; Thauth, Mercury.

The Rabbinical names, as given by Sebastian Munster, are "Sabbater, rest; Zedek, just; Ma'adim, red; Nogah, splendid; Mercurium, Cochab, or Catab, as it is written."

Kronos, the Greek name of Saturn, resting. קר Arab. quievit, Prov. xvii. 27, Marg. cool.

Latin, Saturn from סתר, hid (as Latium).

HOUSES OF THE PLANETS.

♂	♈ ♏	Mars,	Aries, Scorpio.
♀	♎ ♉	Venus,	Libra, Taurus.
♃	♐ ♓	Jupiter,	Sagittarius, Pisces.
♄	♑ ♒	Saturn,	Capricornus, Aquarius.
☿	♍ ♊	Mercury,	Virgo, Gemini.
☾	♋	Moon,	Cancer.
☉	♌	Sun,	Leo.

From remote antiquity such have been called "the houses," or appropriate stations of the five planets, the sun, and the moon. Belonging to Mars, who bruises and is bruised, are Aries, the Lamb bruised, wounded in sacrifice, and Scorpio, where He who should come is shown as bruised.

Venus: Libra, redemption; Taurus, deliverance.

Jupiter: Sagittarius, deliverance by Him coming forth; Pisces, whose are the congregation.

Saturn: Capricornus, the sacrifice slain; Aquarius, the water of purification.

Mercury: Virgo, the branch; Gemini, the two comings.

It seems probable that these agreements must have been arranged by the discoverers of the planets, the inventors of the emblems of the signs.

ON THE PLANET VENUS.

In the Egyptian Planisphere this planet is delineated as a woman, under her name Athor, she who cometh; the Christian Church, or the Church of God, in all ages. She is in a kneeling position under her house Taurus, seven stars, the Pleiades, before her. As after the time of the siege of Troy tradition says one vanished, this figure refers to a date previous to that time, 1000 B.C. The swine, enemy of the Serpent, is after; the Ram, of the sign Aries, with the circle of a complete era on his head, before.

From the little respect paid by the Egyptians to the planets, compared with that paid to the more brilliant of the fixed stars, it may be inferred that they knew them to be but earths, while the stars were suns, probably by tradition from the great founder of the science, the Hermes Trismegistus of Egypt and Greece, the great, thrice great, who did not share the destiny of other men, the Prophet Enoch, of whom is recorded, "God took him."

The Egyptians knew, what the Greeks did not for a long time, that the morning and the evening star were the same planet: Pythagoras is said to have been the first who pointed out this fact to the Greeks; he is also said to have acquired his astronomy with other knowledge in Phœnicia. What the Phœnicians then knew must have been known to the Hebrews, at that time a highly civilized nation, and having had the instruction of Solomon. They therefore must have recognized the planet under both its aspects. As an evening star it is not mentioned in Scripture, and it is doubtful whether it is alluded to as a morning star, except in the Apocalypse. In Isaiah xiv. 12, Lucifer is in the original Hillel, the shining, the brilliant, a name which has no affinity with any extant of the planet Venus, though much with many names of the Sun, as Heli, Sanscrit, and Helios, Greek. If, however, from the mythology of the ancients, we may infer the original symbolization of the planet Venus, as a type of the Church of Him who was to come, the Sun of Righteousness[1], both these aspects will be found expressive and suitable. Before the first coming, the Church as the morning star, heralded the Sun by prophecy; and in the evening star typified the declension of the Jewish dispensation, still however transmitting some rays of the splendour of the promised Messiah. After the Sun of the first coming was set, the twilight of the great apostasy began to close around; when the Church, as the planet Venus, receding from the source of light, became less bright, even while increasing in apparent magnitude, it might well be typified by the evening star; again approximating to the Sun, disappearing from our sight, to rise in renewed splendour as the morning star announcing His return.

Venus, the beloved, the bright, the star of evening, descending and declining in brilliancy after the departure of the sun, but to return as the morning star with increased splendour at his reappearance,—by all tradition spoken of as the bride of a divine person, of Mars or of Odin,—is an expressive and suitable type of the Church, falling away and to be restored at the second coming of her Lord, as the bride of Christ, the Lamb's wife of the Apocalyptic vision. The invariableness of this tradition is the more remarkable, as the Germans and other northern nations made the moon masculine, as in the well-known legend of Anningait and Ajut among the Laplanders.

This planet was considered sacred to the Assyrian goddess Baltis, בעלת, who is represented with a star on her head, and standing on a lion. "A female divinity called by Diodorus Siculus, Hera (who bears, חר), held in her right hand a serpent by the head, and in the other a sceptre," probably originally a branch. Layard identifies her with Astarte[2], starry, צהר, and Mylitta, bringing forth, ילדה.

"You ought, if possible, to get a sight of Lepsius's Introduction. Only one volume is out, and not translated. I hold him to be a great charlatan in many things, but as regards scholarship he is unrivalled; and in this volume every thing that can be said on Greek and Egyptian astronomy is to be found. It is a quarto of magnificent print, and I can lend it you if you like. If you look to Pliny, Hist. Nat. ii. 6, you will see what he says about Pythagoras and the evening star. The Greeks strictly called Hesperus the evening star, Phosphorus the morning star; the Latins, Lucifer and Vesperugo.

"What Lepsius says is briefly this, 'Authorities are then given.' The fifth planet, the star of Aphrodite, is called by the Greeks Heosphoros, called by Aristotle Hera. The morning

---

[1] Mal. iv. 2.   [2] Zohara is the Arabic name for the planet Venus.

star is Sion or Toone, Toone being *morning*.   Kircher said the Coptic for Venus was Souroh [3]."
(C. H. Cottrell.)

NOTES.

A Spanish missionary wrote in Mexican (1529) the traditions of their religion, &c., which he had gathered from the Mexicans themselves. This is published in vol. vi. of Lord Kings-borough's great work. (B. M.)

At Palenque is found a vulture slaying a serpent, and the cross among sacred emblems; also, a woman and child, holding a branch, receiving offerings; also, seven stars on a blue ground, probably the Pleiades (?); and a man and woman with a sword between them.

Many Hebrew words may be found in the dialects of the Indians, as Abba, father.

The name of the sun was Naolin, נעלה, who arises, comes. (Lord Kingsborough, B. M.)

When the sign Aries (the white rabbit) arrived, they fasted for the fall of the first man.

Much has been written on the Cabiri of Samothracia, the three potent divinities. Cabir appears to have been the Gentile equivalent of Cherub, "like the mighty," Cabiri being "like the strong" or "mighty," also, though from a different root. The triad of the Greeks and Romans was, of the god of the heavens, the god of the sea, and the god of the infernal regions, or separate state; but the Egyptians and Oriental heathen made theirs of father, son, and mother. (This mother was however not like the Freya of the Scandinavians, but represented the planet Venus; she was Isis, Isha, the woman of Gen. iii. 15, and of the sign Virgo.) Such, too, we find it in Mexico; while in Polynesia we find it of father, son, and bird, as may be seen in the London Missionary Museum.

[The following is an extract from a letter of the clergyman referred to on p. 23. It was received by the Writer of Mazzaroth a few days before the close of life, and accepted as a correct and beautiful application of the figures to which it relates. A friend, who was in daily intercourse with the lamented Writer of this work at the time, testifies of the pleasure with which the idea contained in the letter was dwelt upon by the spirit so soon about to pass from amid symbols to realities.]

"The figures of the five planets in the Dendera Planisphere are all of them distinctly charac-teristic. One of them is unclothed, Venus, and in a kneeling attitude, with four dolphins erect on her head. Does this figure symbolize the Church of Christ (Nogah), His 'beloved,' here in her state by nature, to be clothed only in His righteousness, and made 'to sit with Him in heavenly places?' If so, such raising up may be indicated by the four dolphins erect on the head of this kneeling figure—a dolphin being the ancient symbol of raising or lifting up. The Church's future elevation in glory seems indicated likewise by a youth sitting on a lotus on the right of the four dolphins, the meaning of which is, 'hidden but to come.' 'When Christ who is our life shall appear, then shall we also appear with Him in glory.'

"If my rendering of the Planet Venus in the Dendera Planisphere is correct, it might account for the Greek fable of Venus rising from *the sea*."

---

[3] Heb. שחרה, star of twilight.

THE POLE.

In the time of Seth and Enoch the Pole was among the stars of Draco, the emblem of the enemy; the constellation of the lesser sheepfold had no relation to it, but by degrees the Pole drew nearer to the brightest star in that constellation; the sheep, represented by three of its other stars as quitting their earthly fold (the believing Church), seemed going forth to the cynosure faintly typifying Him who was and is the object of their faith. In the brilliant intensification of this emblem of the fold and sheep going forth, the greater fold (called the Great Bear), it is strikingly represented that their course is to the great Shepherd and guardian of the flocks, typified in Arcturus, He who cometh and returneth. The three stars, daughters of the flock, seem following, seeking Him; but two, representing the boundaries of the fold, point above to the star typifying Him in the earlier dispensation, the lesser and as it were further removed fold. There *He*, the great Shepherd of the sheep, is figured above, gone before; and below in Arcturus, as about to return in greater glory. The foot of the other figure, the *suffering* mighty One, is on the head of the Dragon below. There is no distinguishing mark of the position of the Pole at any time in the Egyptian planisphere. Those who first named the stars seemed to have been aware that this position was not permanent. In the time of Seth and Enoch it was near the bright star Alpha Draconis, belonging both to the head of the Dragon and to the foot of Hercules, placed as bruising it.

Sir J. Herschel—"The Pole is nothing more than the vanishing point of the earth's axis."

"The bright star of the Lesser Bear, which we call the Pole-star, has not always been, nor will it always continue to be, our cynosure. At the time of the construction of the earliest catalogues of the stars it was 12° from the Pole, it is now only 1° 24′, and will approach still nearer, to within half a degree, after which it will again recede." "After about 12,000 years, the star Alpha Lyræ, the brightest in the northern hemisphere, will occupy the remarkable situation of a Pole-star, approaching within about 5° of the Pole." "At the date of the erection of the great pyramid of Gizeh, which preceded by 3970 years (some say 4000) the present epoch . . . the place of the pole of the heavens was near A Draconis, the Pole-star at that time." "It is a remarkable fact that of the nine pyramids, six, including all the largest, have the narrow passages by which alone they can be entered, inclined downwards." "At the bottom of every one of the passages, therefore, the *then* Pole-star must have been visible," "doubtless connected," "with the astronomical observation of that star." Thus therefore we find a mark of the date of the erection of those pyramids, "that is, while A Draconis was the Pole-star" 4000 years ago.

Those who called the remarkable constellation, now miscalled the Great Bear, the fold and flock proceeding from it, and following their great Shepherd, emblematized in Arcturus, Him who should come, and come again, seem also to have seen a fainter emblem of their own Church, fold and sheep, in what is called the Lesser Bear, an irregular square, from which seem to proceed, as in the larger emblem, three faint stars towards the larger and brighter one now called the Pole-star, but with which then the Pole of the earth's axis had no connexion. They saw, as we see, that the Church on earth go forth towards Him their precursor, gone before, and but faintly seen by the most gifted sight of faith. Not such they found in the greater fold, whose sheep, or daughters, go forth and follow their Shepherd and their King, Arcturus of Bootes.

These emblems made part of the ancient astronomy, but the guiding star was not the Pole-star then, nor will it always be. Still while to us it seems to be so, it is well to connect it with Him to whom the hearts of His people turn "as the needle to the Pole."

These leading or guiding stars, Arcturus in Bootes, and Kochab or Cynosura in the lesser sheepfold, have both symbolized the Great Shepherd of the sheep,—Him whom they follow in life, and trust in, to attain to His side in departing to be with Him, "which is far better."

THE END.

GILBERT AND RIVINGTON, PRINTERS, ST. JOHN'S SQUARE, LONDON.

COSIMO

COSIMO is a specialty publisher of books and publications that inspire, inform, and engage readers. Our mission is to offer unique books to niche audiences around the world.

COSIMO BOOKS publishes books and publications for innovative authors, nonprofit organizations, and businesses. **COSIMO BOOKS** specializes in bringing books back into print, publishing new books quickly and effectively, and making these publications available to readers around the world.

COSIMO CLASSICS offers a collection of distinctive titles by the great authors and thinkers throughout the ages. At **COSIMO CLASSICS** timeless works find new life as affordable books, covering a variety of subjects including: Business, Economics, History, Personal Development, Philosophy, Religion & Spirituality, and much more!

COSIMO REPORTS publishes public reports that affect your world, from global trends to the economy, and from health to geopolitics.

FOR MORE INFORMATION CONTACT US AT
INFO@COSIMOBOOKS.COM

❋ if you are a book lover interested in our
   current catalog of books

❋ if you represent a bookstore, book club, or
   anyone else interested in special discounts
   for bulk purchases

❋ if you are an author who wants to get published

❋ if you represent an organization or business
   seeking to publish books and other publications
   for your members, donors, or customers.

**COSIMO BOOKS ARE ALWAYS
AVAILABLE AT ONLINE BOOKSTORES**

**VISIT COSIMOBOOKS.COM
BE INSPIRED, BE INFORMED**

Lightning Source UK Ltd.
Milton Keynes UK
UKOW05f2103130817
307195UK00005B/95/P